American Realism
NEW ESSAYS

American Realism
NEW ESSAYS

Edited by Eric J. Sundquist

The Johns Hopkins University Press
Baltimore and London

The Johns Hopkins University Press, Baltimore, Maryland 21218
The Johns Hopkins Press Ltd., London

American realism.

Includes bibliographical references.
1. American fiction—History and criticism—
Addresses, essays, lectures.   2. Realism in literature—
Addresses, essays, lectures.   I. Sundquist, Eric J.
PS374.R37A47   813'.009'12   82-3010
ISBN 0-8018-2796-5   AACR2
ISBN 0-8018-2795-7 (pbk.)

CONTENTS

PREFACE

Any assessment, theory, or description of American realism should keep in mind at the outset a few relevant entries in Ambrose Bierce's *The Devil's Dictionary* (1881-1906):

> *REALISM, n.* The art of depicting nature as it is seen by toads. The charm suffusing a landscape painted by a mole, or a story written by a measuring-worm.

> *REALITY, n.* The dream of a mad philosopher. That which would remain in the cupel if one should assay a phantom. The nucleus of a vacuum.

> *REALLY, adv.* Apparently.

Bierce's definitions typify the ironic and often perverse directions American literature had taken by the last decade of the century—that fierce, gas-lit period when so many nineteenth-century theories and ideals came to final collapse and so many twentieth-century preoccupations and dislocations of belief appeared more inevitable. But the 1890s, in many respects *the* decade of literary realism in America, reflects as well the ironies to which imaginative attempts to capture the complex realities of American society had already been exposed in preceding decades; for even though it is a period of intense experimentation with literary form and narrative point of view, that experimentation quite often betrays a supreme resistance to realism, to literal and orderly structures of containment, and an explicit refusal to disavow those complexities of vision that characterize the American "romance" of pre-Civil War fiction.

No genre—if it can be called a genre—is more difficult to define than realism, and this is particularly true of American realism. In material it includes the sensational, the sentimental, the vulgar, the scientific, the outrageously comic, the desperately philosophical; in style it ranges from the exquisitely fine craft of James to the resonant colloquial idioms of Twain to the blocklike profusions of Dreiser; in purpose it approaches the cultural essay, aspires to the utility of propaganda, seeks to dramatize the theater of social manners, cuts its own throat in deliberate parody. It is and does all these things—often at the same time. But while the literature of the period between the Civil War and the first decades of the twentieth century is of peculiar and extraordinary interest, it has attracted comparatively little satisfying commentary. Some of the best general studies of American fiction, for instance, make strange detours around the age of realism, moving from Poe, Hawthorne, and Melville—with obligatory glances at Twain and James—to Hemingway, Fitzgerald, and Faulkner in defining the "classic" tradition of the American novel. The best studies of the period, in fact, have been either wide-ranging literary and social histories like Warner Berthoff's *The Ferment of Realism,* Larzer Ziff's *The American 1890s,* and Jay Martin's *Harvests of Change,* or books devoted to single authors like Laurence Holland's *The Expense of Vision: Essays on the Craft of Henry James,* James M. Cox's *Mark Twain: The Fate of Humor,* Ellen Moers's *Two Dreisers,* and Kenneth Lynn's *William Dean Howells: An American Life.*

The problem lies in part in the central difficulty of describing the program of a group of writers who virtually had no program but rather responded eclectically, and with increasing imaginative urgency, to the startling acceleration into being of a complex industrial society following the Civil War. Those responses became as varied and complex as the society itself; and if we in turn only see the dimensions of that complexity more clearly, it is because we live in the century that the nineteenth-century explosion of industrial capitalism made possible. More particularly, we live in a critical age that has grown remarkably attentive to (some might say obsessed with) the ways in which literary texts restructure or subvert the "real" social structures they claim to represent, and in doing so call attention to the fictions that the fabric of reality contains and depends on for its apparent order. It would be a mistake, however, to suppose that our techniques of inspection, and the problems they seek to uncover, were not largely anticipated by the writers themselves; for the age of American realism—or rather, its originating age, since it can hardly be said to have ended—was one in which the literal itself was under severe and often disabling pressure.

The essays collected here propose, as a group, no specific ideological or theoretical program on behalf of realism. They represent, instead, the complexity of response that defines the period itself; and while they certainly incorporate and extend recent developments in critical thinking, they do so in order to reveal both our renewed interest in the subtle interpenetrations of the fictional and the ideological, and the express power of the original texts to embody and predict concerns more visibly realized in the literature of American modernism. Though the 1890s is, conveniently enough, the decade that now appears to have made modernism inevitable, the essays that follow are unified as well in their diverse arguments that the end of the nineteenth century began much earlier and lasted much longer than we have yet adequately recognized.

ACKNOWLEDGMENTS

This collection originated in a panel on American realism that I chaired at the annual convention of the Modern Language Association in 1979. I thank the MLA for that opportunity, and more particularly I thank three of the participants—Richard Brodhead, Evan Carton, and Eric Cheyfitz—for their contributions then and now.

For suggestions concerning my introduction and the collection in general, I thank William Cain, Catherine Gallagher, Gerald Graff, and Walter Michaels. For his generous patience and assistance, I especially thank William Sisler, of The Johns Hopkins University Press.

American Realism
NEW ESSAYS

Introduction
THE COUNTRY OF THE BLUE

In a short story entitled "The Next Time," which appeared in 1895—the same year in which *The Red Badge of Courage* appeared as a book, in which Norris gave up his first attempts to publish *McTeague* and took off for South Africa, in which Howells recoiled from the previous year's publication of his utopian romance, *A Traveler from Altruria,* and in which Twain wandered aimlessly between *Tom Sawyer Abroad* (1894) and *Tom Sawyer, Detective* (1896)—Henry James's novelist-hero, after failing yet again to become commercially successful because he is too good a writer, simply floats away "into a grand indifference, into a reckless consciousness of art." What happens to Ray Limbert, says James of his admitted fictional double, is that "he had merely waked up one morning again in the country of the blue and had stayed there with a good conscience and a great idea." He dies shortly thereafter.

The country of the blue is, of course, an exceptionally Jamesian territory; and while one can define the dilemma of American realism by the example of James only through rather calculated effort, I want to suggest that Ray Limbert's career, by a variety of analogies the following essays unfold, is representative of that dilemma. James's story, as R. P. Blackmur points out, is a fable of the writer "who struggles desperately to make society his prey, but fails because he cannot help remaining the harmless, the isolated monarch of his extreme imaginative ardent self."[1] This is not to say that all American authors of the period necessarily had either the fine talents or the crass motives of Ray Limbert, but rather that the gulf between the "real world" and their own isolated, imaginative selves often remained a conspicuous one or, on the contrary, collapsed altogether and left them in the bluest of countries, the country of American romance.

Though few readers completely agree on definitions or examples, the perennial distinction between the "romance" and the realistic "novel" in American fiction remains a useful one. The most familiar and influential argument for this distinction is made by Richard Chase, who emphasizes that the romance rejects verisimilitude, continuity of plot, and the reconciliation of character to society, and embodies instead "the aesthetic possibilities of radical forms of alienation, contradiction, and disorder."[2] While it is not my intention to extend this view in detail—or to promote it as the greatest distinguishing feature of American fiction—I do want to suggest that it is within the framework of these widely accepted terms that the significance of American realism must initially be considered. To cite briefly two examples: what possible relationship is there between Crane's frantically stylized war novel and the Civil War itself? And what outrageous claims must be made about Twain's *Pudd'nhead Wilson* (1894) in order to include it in more classical or traditional definitions of realism? No matter that we know *The Red Badge of Courage* derived factually from a *Century Magazine* series on "Battles and Leaders of the Civil War" and that its action can therefore be anchored rather precisely in the battle of Chancellorsville: to point to this evidence, interesting though it is, may only make its final relevance more disquieting; just as pointing to Twain's interest in a famous case of Siamese twins or in racist evolutionary theories and laws (*Plessy* v. *Ferguson*, 1896, was just around the corner) or in the development of fingerprinting does not prevent the novel from seeming a bizarre instance of naturalistic farce but guarantees it.

Like James, Crane and Twain also inhabit the country of the blue, not in their case because they failed of popular success (in this respect they were more properly his opposite) but because their reckless, imaginative selves refused to yield to the literalizing demands of a strict realism. One might object that Crane and Twain, for example, are no more representative of the school of realism than James himself is. The point, though, is that American realism virtually has no school; its most dominating and influential advocate, William Dean Howells, often seems to ride along in a strange vacuum, nearly unheeded in his continual insistence on the proprieties of the everyday, stable characterization, and moral certainty, while almost every other important author of the period simply refused, in these terms, to become a realist.

If it has had a definable life at all in America, realism has surely had a life that stretches beyond the boundaries proposed by this collection. To establish a definition by beginning with the writers who made their professional appearances after the Civil War, however, is not particularly difficult to justify, for such a definition can with some freedom even claim the participation of Whitman, the consummate spokesman in both poetry and prose for democratic realism; but to conclude with Dreiser is an act nearly impossible to defend. One might rather say that American realism begins with Dreiser's *Sister Carrie* (1900) and reaches maturity some twenty to thirty years later in the works of Lewis, Dos Passos, Farrell, and Hemingway. But if Dreiser stands at the beginning of such a tradition, the age that made him possible is of particular interest. And it is precisely because the period between the Civil War and the first decades of the twentieth century resists convenient generic classification and satisfactory theoretical containment that it displays most openly the intense struggle of realism in America.

What Alfred Kazin noted of nineteenth-century American realism in 1942—that it "had no true battleground, as it had no intellectual history, few models, virtually no theory, and no unity"—was by implication also true of the twentieth-century literature he proceeded to examine and (by further implication) true as well of the critical thought that sought to characterize those periods. This remains partially true today not at all because of critical disinterest or ineptitude but, rather, because of the utter diversity even among writers who claimed in their own right, or were so acclaimed by their readers, to have certain alliances or affinities with each other. One origin of the problem, as Kazin remarked, lay in the fact that, while various European traditions of realism could more clearly be seen to have grown out of identifiable and logically successive climates of political and philosophical thought, realism in America "grew out of the bewilderment, and thrived on the simple grimness, of a generation suddenly brought face to face with the pervasive materialism of industrial capitalism."[3] To say that American realism had no philosophical or political program, no reliable public spokesmen, and thus no literary "heroes" is to pose a problem requiring further attention, but one that reminds us that the heroes of this age were certainly not novelists and were seldom—with the possible exceptions of Grant and Roosevelt— political leaders. Rather, they were inventors and entrepreneurs, or financial wizards such as Rockefeller and Gould, Carnegie and Yerkes; and their careers, particularly as they verged on and incorporated the mythical, help to reveal the importance of Kazin's claim.

Both the ideals and the public idealizations of the founding fathers seemed at best badly shaken, and at worst impossibly irrelevant, following the Civil War, and a corresponding pressure may be discerned in the literature that at once incorporated that loss in the tribute of muted nostalgia and in part gave way to its consequences. Not Captain Ahab but the Captains of Industry were the new cultural embodiments of heroism. If we only see this clearly in retrospect (just as Ahab has only been seen clearly from the perspective of the twentieth century), it is because we live in the society that they—as forefathers do—made possible and necessary, and therefore feel more fully the psychological implications of the transfiguration of "father" and "family" into "boss" and "corporation." One has only to cite in abbreviated form a modern analyst's description of this transfiguration to sense a concomitant evolution and relocation of one of the prominent concerns of American romance, the validity of patriarchal authority, in the more socially complicated textures of realism:

> The development of a hierarchical system of social labor not only rationalizes domination but also "contains" the rebellion against domination. . . . The guilt of rebellion is thereby intensified. The revolt against the primal father eliminated an individual person who could be (and was) replaced by other persons; but when the dominion of the father has expanded into the dominion of society, no such replacement seems possible, and the guilt becomes fatal. . . . With the rationalization of the productive apparatus, with the multiplication of functions, all domination assumes the form of administration. At its peak, the concentration of economic power seems to turn into anonymity: everyone, even at the top, appears to be powerless before the movements and laws of the apparatus itself. . . . Corporealization of the superego is accompanied by corporealization of the ego, manifest in the frozen traits and gestures, at the appropriate occasions and hours.[4]

Marcuse's argument, so suggestive of Dreiser's position at the climax of one century and the outset of another, also suggests incidentally a secondary subversion of the self's "natural" relationship to the figure of fatherly authority; for the public incorporation of that authority is matched from below and within, as it were, by the location of inherited models of behavior in the physiology of the organism itself. By something of a paradox, it is the interiorization of authority manifest in Darwinian social theories (and later in the rise of psychoanalysis and the professional social sciences) that makes possible, even inevitable, the corporate externalization of authority. While Marcuse's assessment is not by any means the whole story, it is nonetheless an indication of the complex contours of realism in America and of the fact that, as Kazin reminds us, the social and psychological effects of industrial capitalism constitute the place at which one must begin.

The seemingly sudden and demonstrably swift acceleration into being of finance capitalism based on industrial technology following the Civil War underlies the many forms of intellectual reaction that, by twists and turns, by adventurous challenge and imaginative endorsement, followed from it, reaching backward to include strains of motivation prevalent in earlier American thought and writing, and extending forward in ways that render any single definition inadequate. Which is to say again that the life of American realism exists, perhaps, either everywhere or nowhere; like "the real" itself, it resists containment, and for the very good reason that "the real" in America, like the country itself, has always had a notoriously short life. Why then, should the period it entitles be particularly subject to this pressure? I want to suggest, returning to James's parable of the writer, that one conspicuous reason is that the period between the Civil War and World War I is one in which American writers felt most compelled, and tried hardest, to become "realists"—and failed. With imperial relentlessness they sought to master a bewildering society that seemed always, in turn, to be mastering them; under such pressure, they returned ever more feverishly to the imagination—to its shaping and distorting powers—and as a consequence kept waking up in the country of the blue, which of necessity was America itself.

They did not, quite obviously, fail to write important and sometimes great fiction; neither did they fail to explore through documented fact and extrapolated theory the pervasive influence of social Darwinism on the structure and values of the American community, nor did they back away from probing the very real, and therefore enchanting, relationship between the calculations of business and the imaginations of literature. Quite the reverse: precisely because the consequent entanglements of these investigations were so thoroughly felt and so actively represented, American realistic fiction—like the literature of romance that preceded it, and like the ostensibly nonliterary documents of religious and political thought that were the country's first works of the imagination—kept spilling out into the "neutral territory" of romance that Hawthorne had made emblematic of American fiction, "appropriating a lot of land which had no visible owner, and building a house, of materials long in use for constructing castles in the air." Like its preface, *The House of the Seven Gables* (1851) reaches into the past in order to propel itself forward, tying together in a complex network of fully realized symbolic action the dreams of a nation on the brink of portentous social revolution. In this respect and others it contains a wealth of American themes—the simultaneous exhilaration and anxiety felt, and expressed, in the disavowal of tradition; the intense probing of literature's necessary connection to social and commercial realities; the risks of mimetic fidelity; and the constant pressures brought to bear upon the domain of the self by the material world. The actions of Hawthorne's characters, and the action of Hawthorne himself as narrator, constitute the point of transition that the "neutral territory" itself is; and by doing so they anticipate a central activity (to bring the imagination to bear upon reality) and a continuing difficulty (to resist capitulation to that reality) of American realism.

Hawthorne's novel is one example of an earlier work to which predominant themes running through American realism can be traced.

The list is long and would surely, for example, have to include Brown's
Arthur Mervyn (1799–1800), Poe's "The Man of the Crowd" (1840),
Lippard's *The Quaker City* (1844), Cooper's *The Crater* (1847), and
Davis's *Life in the Iron Mills* (1861). But let us simply add that, by dwelling excessively on the material and technological details of American life,
and by measuring the distance between the sovereign territory of the
individual self and the powers of social or political community that surround and create individual destiny, *Moby-Dick* (1851) and Whitman's
poetry and prose at once define an American tradition that is beyond
generic classification and emphatically point toward prominent concerns
in the age of realism. If it also seems that Hawthorne, Whitman, and Melville resist the intrusion of the real into the territory of the romance,
however, one can bound the age of realism in exactly those terms by
noting that, like America itself, the struggle had simply moved west by the
end of the century. For the poet-hero of Norris's *The Octopus* (1901), his
imaginative vision of the "huge romantic West" is urgently troubled by
the imposed mapping of telegraph wires and ranch fences, and is stopped
cold by the leviathan railroad, a "note of harsh colour that refused to
enter into the great scheme of harmony. It was material, sordid, deadly
commonplace." In Presley's vision, as in Norris's own, "the romance
seemed complete up to that point. There it broke, there it failed, there it
became realism, grim, unlovely, unyielding."

Such a view is certainly not sustained by the end of the novel, where
Presley's romance expands dramatically to include the harsh, unyielding
forces of technology; and because he insisted that naturalism was indeed
a form of romance, and therefore utterly opposed to realism, Norris's
case is perhaps a singular one. But his initial insistence on this opposition
helps define the remarkable intrusion of romance into the work of nearly
every writer of the period. Even Howells, writing from his editorial throne,
felt compelled to imagine a way around this difficulty when he ventured
in an essay collected in the classic statement on American realism, *Criticism and Fiction* (1891), that there was little significant difference between romanticism and realism, because each sought, in its own day, "to
widen the bounds of sympathy, to level every barrier against aesthetic
freedom, to escape from the paralysis of tradition." When the romance
had "exhausted itself in this impulse," Howells declared, "it remained for
realism to assert that fidelity to experience and probability of motive are
essential conditions of great imaginative literature." When realism in turn
becomes "false to itself" and fails to accomplish this, Howells predicted, it
too will perish. There is no room here to do justice to the complexity of
Howells's full argument, but one is tempted to note that, for some of the
very reasons Howells points to, American realism (including much of his
own work) did not achieve a certain and stable force, exhaust that force,

and perish; rather, it failed case by case by refusing to renounce romance and by levelling the barriers of aesthetic freedom too completely.

To escape the "paralysis of tradition" is, of course, the typifying American gesture—in religion, in politics, in business, in literature, in life. This is one reason *The House of the Seven Gables* is so instructive a turning point, one whose revolutionary fervor recapitulates earlier American projects in religious and political rebellion (which, like the Pyncheon curse, have a power that can neither die nor be fully implemented) and predicts the threatened paralysis of the commercial or material "real" in the age of capitalism. Like several of Melville's works, Hawthorne's novel precedes the Civil War but in retrospect seems to have comprehended in advance its effects and aftermath. The other side of the coin is Twain, whose whole career exemplifies the agony of retrospect. By merging his own involvement in the paralysis of social (and literary) traditions with the real, bewildering presence of social and economic revolution, Twain demonstrated with considerable power that the Civil War, morally and culturally iconoclastic as it may have been, was not a clean break; instead, it represented a translation of materials and a transfiguration of figures of authority themselves—from the tyranny of the family to the tyranny of the corporation, say—one in which what Whitman in his 1872 preface to *Leaves of Grass* called America's "vast seething mass of materials" became more visibly and vexingly the dominant force in the construction of social reality, but also one in which fiction, as Howells remarked, would make "Reality its Romance."

Let us say, though, that the Civil War is followed by extraordinary progress in the development of communication and transportation, in the spread of education, and in the suddenly increased mobility of people and ideas; that it produces, therefore, a kind of "temporal concentration" that unifies the nation but also

> abrogates or renders powerless the entire social structure of orders and categories previously held valid; the tempo of the changes demands a perpetual and extremely difficult effort toward inner adaptation and produces intense concomitant crises. He who would account to himself for his real life and his place in human society is obliged to do so upon a far wider practical foundation and in a far larger context than before, and to be continually conscious that the social base upon which he lives is not constant for a moment but is perpetually changing through convulsions of the most various kinds.

This apt description of America following the Civil War comes, however, from Erich Auerbach's description of the social aftermath of the French Revolution.[5] It is appropriate not simply because Auerbach is accounting here for the great age of French realism, which America lags slightly behind, but also because it clarifies the way in which the social and economic results of the Civil War can be seen, both figuratively and actually, to extend and recapitulate America's own democratic revolution in 1776, while at the same time threatening to subvert its opulent possibilities of freedom by turning wilderness into mines, ranches, and oil wells; theology into science; men into machines; and founding fathers into executives of the State. Though the frontier, as an imaginative territory, was not closed by the time Frederick Jackson Turner claimed the physical frontier was in 1893, it is nevertheless true that the mapping, filling, containing, and controlling of both territories—the one in theory, the other in practice— that took place between the war and the end of the century was awesome. That romance remained a persistent force in American realism must be ascribed in part to the extraordinary force of the idea of the boundlessness of the country, a wilderness of fancied space that Whitman and Norris, for example, could celebrate even as they saw it cut, calculated, sold, and turned into cities.

The threat to physical space during the period is matched and, at times, fully accommodated by concurrent threats to ideal space—that is, the space of God, the space of beauty, the space of the self—of the kind elaborated in Dreiser's late essay "The Myth of Individuality" (1934), which depicts man as something "lived" by an incomprehensible cosmic force struggling "to express itself." Again, though, one must be careful to note, as Richard Poirier has, that this notion of individuality is not a sudden development in the American tradition, but might be said to "adapt Emerson's idea of the Over-Soul to the metropolis," so that from a social point of view (and the point of view of the novelist) the self becomes "anonymous" and individuality is achieved precisely "by the surrender of those features which define the individual as a social or psychological entity."[6] The transfiguration of Nature into City—or more simply into the one idea of FORCE at once acclaimed and lamented in *The Octopus* and *The Education of Henry Adams* (1907), for example—is an abstract emblem of those pervasive extenuations of the self that may be traced in the intrusion of technology, not simply into the lives of the novel's characters, but more particularly into the dominion of the novel's own enterprise: police surveillance in *The Princess Casamassima* (1886); fingerprinting in *Pudd'nhead Wilson;* dentistry and mining in *McTeague* (1899); the magazine and the elevated railway in *A Hazard of New Fortunes* (1890); the cash register in "The Blue Hotel" (1898); the newspaper and the camera in *An American Tragedy* (1925); the bicycle, baseball, and telephones in *A Connecticut Yankee in King Arthur's Court* (1889).

As it is an age of inventions, so it is an age of ideas—"ideas so passionately held," Jay Martin points out, "that they even seemed adequate substitutes for ideals."[7] In effect, ideas and inventions at times come so nearly to approximate one another that their very production becomes conspicuous; and becoming conspicuous becomes frightening, to the extent that Adams in the *Education* could inaugurate the century of paranoia by declaring that the universe is no longer an absolute but a "medium of exchange" in which personality itself is differentiated into "complex groups, like telephonic centers and systems." The evolutionary theories promoted by and derived from Herbert Spencer and Thomas Henry Huxley could—and did—justify almost any social, economic, or religious program, just as surely as they could—and did—undermine or invalidate any program that failed to "produce." In this atmosphere, the market becomes the measure of man himself; for as the Protestant ethic divides and conquers, the gap between inherent values and their external representations widens until it dissolves altogether: inner values of the spirit are drawn outward until they appear at last to merge with the things from which one cannot be distinguished and without which one cannot constitute, build, or fabricate a self. The self becomes an *image* of the real, and the real becomes an advertisement of and for the self.

The influence of Spencer, Huxley, and their disciples was immense; but an overemphasis on the infiltration of science into philosophy and theology alone might lead us to miss the equally important proliferation of systems of classification in other, more particular fields. William James's *Principles of Psychology* (1890), which stressed an acute connection between the mind and the nervous system and defined them together as an organized habit of adjustment to environment, and Oliver Wendell Holmes's *The Common Law* (1881), one of the first treatises to see laws themselves as evolutionary and adaptive rather than as static ideals, are dignified works of scholarship. But how distinguish them in importance for the world in which we live from Frederick W. Taylor's *The Principles of Scientific Management* (1911), which promoted increased industrial production through minute, systematic improvements of worker efficiency, or Daniel Edward Ryan's influential *Human Proportions in Growth* (1880), which made possible the standardization of measurement in men's and boy's clothing? Cash registers, adding machines, electric lighting, factory mechanization, quality control, mail-order firms and their catalogues, all manner of transportation and communication improvements—machines everywhere reminded man of the mechanism his body was in fact and the machine it threatened to become in action. In an age in love with competing systems and transfixed by the inevitable importance of exact detail, the problems of the novelist and the man in the street alike are dispiriting: How can life be organized, governed, made plausible? in the romance of man among the beasts, what remains of the mystic, the invisible? who, as Dreiser asks in *Sister Carrie*, "shall translate for us the language of the stones?"

The pressure of these disruptive questions may be felt throughout the literature of the period—in such diverse but equally intense investigations of guilt and sanity as *The Damnation of Theron Ware* (1896), *The Turn of the Screw* (1898), *The Red Badge of Courage*, and "The Yellow Wallpaper" (1892); or in the more exact probings of the "fictions of law and custom" that control and define society in *Pudd'nhead Wilson*, *Billy Budd* (1924), and *The Financier* (1912), where Dreiser's miniature essay on "verdicts" assumes a frantically large compass:

> Men in a jury-room, like those scientifically demonstrated atoms of crystal which scientists and philosophers love to speculate upon, like finally to arrange themselves into an orderly and artistic whole, to present a compact, intellectual front, to be whatever they have set out to be, properly and rightly—a compact, sensible jury. One sees this same instinct magnificently displayed in every other phase of nature—in the drifting sea-wood to the Sargasso Sea, in the geometric interrelation of air-bubbles on the surface of still water, in the marvelous unreasoned architecture of so many insects and atomic forms which make up the substance and the texture of this world. It would seem as though the physical substance of life—this apparition of form which the eye detects and calls real—were shot through with some subtlety that loves order, that is order.

In this passage, which centers on the trial of a character (Frank Cowperwood) modelled on one of the financial geniuses of the nineteenth century (Charles T. Yerkes), we find a peculiar convergence of the "forms, measured forms" that haunted Melville's Captain Vere and the quasimystical "phase of the Real, lurking behind the Real" that Whitman adumbrated in the 1876 preface to *Leaves of Grass*. What could be more real than the romance of system?

The realistic novel oftend depends upon translating a sufficiency, even a superfluity, of detail into determined hierarchical but mutually dependent orders—not only in order to correspond to the complicated fabric of contemporary life but also to make of such staggering detail its own ordering technique, one in which the value and scope of the self (and of value itself) is measureable and in which, as a result, the distinction between aspects of the self and its implemented devices becomes increasingly obscure. Such a problem is, again, not entirely new to the age; and the concomitant exhilaration and fear it promotes may be seen to reanimate the unconscious eruption of the gothic into an earlier age of reason. Twain's *Connecticut Yankee*, for example, appears quite literally to comprise a nightmare of contemporary industrial technology;

its madman hero is the corporate "Boss" of his own "Republic," and its apocalyptic annihilation of thousands by electric fences seems inarguably modern—until we recall that Benjamin Franklin, in 1773, advocated the convenient and efficacious mass slaughter of animals and fowl by electricity. A more precise index of the reactivation of eighteenth-century concerns can be found in the manifold resemblances between the gothic and naturalism, which in its most extraordinary (and therefore representative) forms envisions a kind of biological sublime. The gothic is the grandfather of naturalism as surely as Erasmus Darwin is the grandfather of Charles Darwin. When Charles Brockden Brown appealed to the elder Darwin's *Zoonomia* in order to validate his theory of "Mania Mutabilis" in *Wieland* (1798), he anticipated by about a century the scientific characterization of abnormal behavior indulged in by Dreiser and Norris—with this difference: in naturalism, the abnormal becomes the barely submerged norm.

In this respect and others B̶e̶n̶j̶a̶m̶i̶n̶ ̶F̶r̶a̶n̶k̶lin Norris quite rightly differentiates the dull, commonplace realism of Howells—"the drama of a broken teacup, the tragedy of a walk down the block"—from the "romance" of naturalism, which takes its theoretical method from Zola's influential essay "The Experimental Novel" (1880) and works, Norris maintains in *Responsibilities of the Novelist* (1903), as a finely tempered, flawless "instrument with which we may go straight through the clothes and tissues and wrappings of flesh down into the red, living heart of things." Revelling in the extraordinary, the excessive, and the grotesque in order to reveal the immutable bestiality of Man in Nature, naturalism dramatizes the loss of individuality at a physiological level by making a Calvinism without God its determining order and violent death its utopia.[8] The ease with which naturalism verges upon parody, especially in Crane and Norris, thus results in part from a gothic *intensification of detail* that approaches the allegorical without finding release into or through it; the characters inhabit alien landscapes filled with inflated symbols, and they die not in bed, at home, of old age and natural causes, but in open boats, in Death Valley, in the electric chair, in silos of WHEAT, in the nowhere of the Yukon—in blinding fields of force, sudden traps of mysterious making. And they do so at the level of technique by becoming bloated figures in which the human constantly threatens to detach and deform itself into the bestial (as in Norris) or, at extremity, in which the human disappears completely into the beast (as in London). It is no simple coincidence, therefore, that *The Call of the Wild* (1903) depicts the seemingly inevitable union of naturalism and aestheticism, and vividly endorses—in a Paterian moment of pure *symbol*—the extinction of the social, civilized self in a frenzy of sensation:

There is an ecstasy that marks the summit of life, and beyond which
life cannot rise. And such is the paradox of living, this ecstasy comes
when one is most alive, and it comes as a complete forgetfulness that
one is alive. This ecstasy, this forgetfulness of living, comes to the
artist, caught up and out of himself in a sheet of flame; it comes to
the soldier, war-mad on a stricken field and refusing quarter; and it
came to Buck, leading the pack, sounding the old wolf-cry. . . . He
was sounding the deeps of his nature, and of the parts of nature that
were deeper than he, going back into the womb of Time.

Romance, as Norris quite correctly saw, remained the visceral, spiritual
essence of the real.

In theoretical terms, Norris's case (and certainly London's) is a peculiar
one; but it is worth remembering that, in terms of social dramatization,
his definitions distinguish him only from Howells but not necessarily from
Twain, Dreiser, and Crane or even, perhaps, from James and Wharton. For
them as well, survival in the social world, as in the physical world that
may be its model and origin, depends upon the kind of adaption and
manipulation Dreiser makes emblematic of both the "constructive genius
of nature" and the "creative power" of man's achieved mastery of nature
(or the city, or society, or Wall Street) in his fable of the Black Grouper
at the conclusion of *The Financier:* "Its great superiority lies in an almost
unbelievable power of simulation. . . . An implement of illusion one might
readily suspect it to be, a living lie, a creature whose business it is to appear what it is not, to simulate that with which it has nothing in common,
to get its living by great subtlety." The obsession with lying as a gesture
that at once defines the environment in which one lives and expresses the
necessity of masks and disguises in mastering that environment equally
illuminates Wharton's and James's dramatizations of a self that is at constant risk of surrendering its powers of will and is therefore willing to perform the many roles necessary to survival in the theater of social manners.
And the most elaborate American representations of the lies of which
society is constructed—*Adventures of Huckleberry Finn* (1885) and *The
Confidence-Man* (1857)—remind us here how Twain and Melville, always
enthusiasts of the masquerade, serve to define an age that may be various-
ly limited by *Moby-Dick* and *The Gilded Age* (1873) on one side and
Billy Budd and *The Mysterious Stranger* (1908) on the other.

As these works and others press toward and anticipate modernism, both
the absorption of the self in the façade of the material world and the increasingly visible "construction" of social reality become by necessity
part of the technical apparatus of the novel, which, like the self and like
the landscape, gets filled up and, in the end, used up. "We are no longer a
raw-material reservoir, the marvel and despair of less fortunate cultures,"

remarks Wright Morris of the dilemma of American modernism anticipated by Crane and Dreiser, for "our only inexhaustible resource at the
moment is the cliché. An endless flow of clichés, tirelessly processed for
mass-media consumption, now give a sheen of vitality to what is either
stillborn or secondhand."[9] To qualify this assessment properly, one would
have to note the obvious ways in which the production of clichés continues, quite unavoidably, to express the amplitude of American raw
material by transforming what is scarce or unattainable into what is
evidently abundant. But Morris, for the moment, takes us farther than
we can arguably go.

Although the freedoms of action, belief, and imagination that are under
pressure in the age of American realism threaten at times to dissolve into
marketable clichés, they are nonetheless fully involved with very real
political and industrial forces; and the same forces that appear to render
the imagination suspect or marginal, or to leave it in unnerving postures of
acquiescence and accommodation, also bring literary art more conspicuously into the world of business by making it resemble or become a business
itself. This in itself is not a particularly new development: for Emerson,
for Hawthorne, for Poe, for Melville, the burdens of having to "stammer
out something by way of getting a living" (as Melville put it in *Moby-
Dick*) were a subdued but continual theme. But it is in the work of Twain,
Howells, James, and Dreiser that the survival of literature in the community of the marketplace becomes more than a minor obsession. That so
many writers of the period made a living—both initially and along the
way—as magazine and newspaper journalists is a rather accurate measure
of stylistic and thematic developments as well as an indication of the
changing configurations of literature as a profession.[10]

One should notice in this connection that the professional (and symbolic) role of the central character in *A Hazard of New Fortunes* is that
of "editor," a professional position that Howells brilliantly exploits in
order to scrutinize, more than slightly autobiographically, the moral
hazards of literature's tentative encounter with both the world of business
and the world of social oppression for which it may be responsible. As
"the missing link between the Arts and the Dollars," the magazine *Every
Other Week* occupies the mediating position that the editor himself does;
the editor in turn bears the burden, as Basil March does, of balancing
aesthetic and social responsibilities, of putting money in service of art
without capitulating to it, and therefore of maintaining an integrity that
continually risks becoming immobilized in neutrality. When Crane ap-
provingly reported in the *New York Tribune,* 1891, that Hamlin Garland
had called *A Hazard of New Fortunes* "the greatest, sanest, truest study

of a city in fiction," he paid a deserved compliment (which Howells returned when *Maggie* appeared, first in 1893 and again in 1896) but at the same time, perhaps, began to mark off the glib, ironic stance that his own roles of aesthete and journalist would make possible in his fiction. Howells's novel dramatizes these potentially compromising dangers most vividly in its depiction of the social voyeurism that March and his wife engage in while traveling on New York's elevated railway, where

> the fleeting intimacy you formed with people in second and third-floor interiors, while all the usual street life went on underneath, had a domestic intensity mixed with a perfect repose that was the last effect of good society with all its security and exclusiveness. March said it was better than the theater, of which it reminded him, to see those people through their windows: a family party of workfolk at a late tea, some of the men in their shirt-sleeves; a woman sewing by a lamp; a mother laying her child in its cradle; a man with his head fallen on his hands upon a table; a girl and her lover leaning over the windowsill together. What suggestion! What drama! What infinite interest!

While it is the purpose of the novel to develop the ironies implicit in this scene and in Basil's exultation, this is the Howellsian aesthetic of realism in miniature. And it is also the position of the editor, who is manifestly carried along and above society by the mechanisms of mass transit and quick transition that propel society itself, and who is resolutely caught in the position of an enthused but ineffectual spectator.

As *A Hazard of New Fortunes* makes apparent, the professionalization of literature reflects, both by challenge and by endorsement, the escalating professionalization of thought and life in later nineteenth-century America, which in turns reflects and extends the proliferation of the various modes of mechanization that have made it possible. It is an age in which money, machines, and men become, not exactly interchangeable, but analogous to the extent that distinctions among the values each might seem inherently to possess are broken down on a large scale. The realistic novel, then, depicts not so much the disappearance of value as the transfiguration of value itself into something whose power is a function of the many pressures of the economic and social market. The obsession with material reality that characterizes some definitions of American realism must therefore be understood to encompass the particular powers—of moral commitment, of adaptive roles, of the staging of action—that material reality can make manifest but cannot always fully define or control. In his important essay on "Reality in America," for example, Lionel Trilling complains that "in the American metaphysic, reality is always material reality, hard, resistant, unformed, impenetrable, and unpleasant. And that mind is alone felt to be trustworthy which most resembles this reality by most nearly reproducing the sensations it affords."[11] The crucial shift in emphasis that Trilling's statement contains is likely to go unnoticed unless we recognize the implications of moving from the "material" to "sensations" through the mediating terms "reproducing" and "affords." It is precisely the purpose of industrial capitalism to translate the material into the sensational (and then back again into the material, and so on) both by making it appear to afford something we need and to be itself affordable.

It is worth noting once again that the basis of this translation lies in "reproduction," an idea of virtually limitless importance for the period since, in a psychological sense as well, reproduction is itself entwined in the technology of capitalism with the very possibility of boundless opportunity and possession. A complete appreciation of the figurative centrality of reproduction in the age of realism would clearly have to take account of the ramifying problems of sexuality—the sacrifice of intimacy to public life, the increasing divorce of domestic and business concerns, the endless appetite for sentimental plays and novels—examined with equal apprehension by Howells, Norris, Adams, James, Gilman, and Wharton, but perhaps most melodramatically characterized by Dreiser (ever the armchair Freudian) when he wrote in "Neurotic America and the Sex Impulse" (1920) that out of the "defeated pursuit" of sexual gratification "comes most of all that is most distinguished in art, letters, and our social economy." Though we may judge that Dreiser has the cart before the horse, and though we may certainly object to his maintaining that beneath every "displacement" or "transferal" of sexual impulse into "desires for wealth, preferment, distinction and what not" there lies "a deep and abiding craving for women," there is little gainsaying his characterization of one of the primary psychological effects of capitalistic reproduction, in which the biological becomes mechanized and exteriorized, and the self is turned into a virtual product of its eminently desirable and reproducible products. The "incorporation" of fathers by business (or, on the other hand, the biological internalizing of them by theories of evolution) may in this respect be the most troubling sign of the concomitant suppression and sentimental idealization of women that female authors struggled against and the feminization of the self that many male authors both courted and feared.

The agitation over the breakdown of traditional sexual roles that marks much realistic fiction, as well as the portrayal of domestic spheres of action in forms of imprisonment or landscapes of utopian isolation, may thus be understood to derive from a more pervasive recasting of organic laws; and the systemization of manners and beliefs as evolving forms of habitual response may be seen both to resemble and to produce the models of capitalistic reproduction: everything evolves upward and outward, constantly positing the *desirable* and the *valuable* as something to be strived for. The fact that literature, in its representational capacity, is always implicated in a special mode of reproduction makes it particularly susceptible to the cumulative pressures of such power. As a way of sketching an approach to this problem, we might keep in mind the transfiguration of inherent value that Walter Benjamin has observed to take place in "the work of art" when it is brought to inhabit—and particularly when it is produced in—"the age of mechanical reproduction." What is in jeopardy in this age, Benjamin notes, is the "authority" or "aura" of the object: "the technique of reproduction detaches the reproduced object from the domain of tradition," and by making it eminently reproducible undermines its very claim to authenticity.[12] Benjamin speaks here rather strictly about the extreme consequences for the visual arts brought about by the development of photography; and with respect to any narrow understanding of the authority and reproduction of the work itself, the case of literary art is surely a somewhat different one. But with respect to the authenticity of the experience it seeks to describe by its own representation or reproduction, the realistic novel necessarily includes (as many of its theorists claim) a further documentation of that threat to the aura of tradition depicted in photography's mechanized reproduction of reality and more recently characterized by Daniel Boorstin as the new industrial age's obsession with "making experience repeatable."[13] The camera, the kinetoscope, and the gramophone make leisure a work of mechanical reproduction that is wholly continuous with industrial capitalism; and they quite certainly must be understood to usher in an age of special anxiety for the book—an anxiety, as Wright Morris reminds us, that the twentieth century verifies day by day but that Hawthorne, of course, anticipated: the photograph is evidence of ironic necromancy in *The House of the Seven Gables,* but in *An American Tragedy* it is evidence of cold-blooded murder.

This particular liberation from the paralysis of tradition, while it makes possible the maintenance and further secularization of tradition, also threatens to subvert or trivialize it by making it "like" the techniques of reproduction that bring it into being, and moreover by making those who utilize it "like" the techniques themselves. At extremity, in our century, the media versions of reality upon which we so heavily depend offer a particular danger: overwhelmed by mirror images of itself and unable to distinguish between the authentic and the façade of the copy, the self may ultimately reject the external altogether—and exactly to the degree that it has become its mediated victim. An "overexposure to manufactured illusions," Christopher Lasch warns, "soon destroys their representational power. The illusion of reality dissolves, not in a heightened sense of reality as we might expect, but in a remarkable indifference to reality."[14] This too is the dilemma of modernism—and more obviously of post-modernism—but it is important to see its origins in the late nineteenth century. For to the relatively influential extent that realistic literature began to take a photographic reproduction of life as its model, the novel must be seen as an assault on the "aura" of tradition exemplified, in America at least, by the romance—an economic extenuation of that secularization of Puritan experience which the romance itself embodied.

One way to gauge this extenuation in its manifold results is to note, as George Becker has, that the "slice-of-life approach" taken by many realistic novelists "spells the death of the hero as he has been traditionally presented." Because the hero by definition is "heightened" or "distorted" for effect, and personifies "a center of good or evil force" that demands "our identification to an intense degree," he has no place in the realistic novel, whose exemplary quality is "its typicality."[15] To insist on the singularity of this feature would be a mistake (and in the case of American realism would be patently absurd), but it raises important questions about the character of the hero in realistic fiction with respect to the role he performs, the space he can dominate, and the value or authority he is meant to have as the representative embodiment of certain cultural and social values. To the extent that he has these capacities at all, we might want to say that he is exterior to the novel's realistic scheme. That this is only provisionally true in the case of American realism, and in some respects divorces it from European traditions of the same period, does help to define the continued accommodation—indeed, the embracing—of romance in the age of capitalistic reproduction.

That accommodation can occur precisely because the preponderant and tangible materialism of life is always, in terms of utility, set in motion and mediated by money, a thing at once thoroughly abstract and (as Trina McTeague's ecstatic passion in a bedful of gold demonstrates) potently physical. The age of realism in America is the age of the *romance of money*—money not in any simple sense but in the complex alterations of human value that it brings into being by its own capacities for reproduction. As it defines, by changing, our notions of a self, so too it may define a change in our notions of a novelistic hero. For in the anatomy of American realism, the possible distortions of character that might lead the hero out of a society whose debased values and hypocritical entanglements of virtue he appears to reject are countered by those distortions of character that can make the hero the exemplary figure of power within that society. Such a hero does not reject society but masters it, and though the novelist may present in his hero's career a critique of society, he does so by representing the hero not as different from us but rather very much, too much, like us. The hero is democratized not by being swallowed up by the fierce oblivion of materiality (as in the case of Dreiser's Hurstwood or Crane's Maggie) or by being levelled to insignificance (as is often the case in Howells, who adamantly proclaimed that he did "not believe in heroes") but rather by being permitted to incorporate the age's own dream of success, its own special romance.

In this respect, one may very well need to distinguish the American novel of realism from the European, which Leo Bersani has demonstrated in the case of the French novel to be largely ordered by the need of society to provide itself "with strategies for containing (and repressing) its disorder within significantly structured stories about itself." The realistic novel, Bersani argues, permits "psychological complexity" only so long as it does not "threaten an ideology of the self as a fundamentally intelligible structure," and it thus "admits heroes of desire [only] in order to submit them to ceremonies of expulsion. This literary form depends, for its very existence, on the annihilation or, at the very least, the immobilizing containment of anarchic impulses."[16] As it distinguishes the realistic novel from the modernist, and as it defines important dimensions of French realism in particular, this is a very compelling argument. But one must recognize that it is true of the American novel of the period only to a limited extent.

To the greater extent that the novelistic self becomes lost in a seemingly random or tyrannically calculating system of values in the age of industrial capitalism, the most forceful threat to an ideology of the self may appear not in the anarchic impulses of radical characterization but in the psychological complexity produced by society's own manufacture of desire. Though the "hero of desire" who reflects, incorporates, and virtually becomes those values may be expelled, he is expelled not so much because he threatens society as because he is unable to master its intricacies of survival. In an important essay that in part responds to Bersani's theory by noting a crucial difference between the cases of Howells and Dreiser, Walter Michaels has demonstrated a strong alliance between those excesses of sentimentality that Howells abhorred and Dreiser encouraged, and the very production of surplus desire in capitalistic society—an alliance so pervasive that, granting *Sister Carrie* the exemplary status in American realism it seems to merit, we must say "the capitalism of the late nineteenth and early twentieth centuries acted more to subvert the ideology of the autonomous self than to enforce it."[17] To accept this is to accept as well the possibility that "the real" of realism—stable character, coherently static society, the minimizing of excess or surplus in desire— is extraordinarily unstable and constantly veers toward romance through its unavoidable encounter with, and participation in, a system whose ideological essence is the resistance of such qualities.

In an age in which Andrew Carnegie and P. T. Barnum could offer equally popular lectures on "The Gospel of Wealth" and "The Art of Money-Getting," and in which the best of best sellers were Horatio Alger stories and Russell Conwell's *Acres of Diamonds* (1888; originally a sermon and lecture), we must be wary of minimizing society's own desire for more objects of desire. Carrie Meeber's emulation of the desirable—before the looking-glass of store windows, in her bedroom, in the audience and on the stage—depicts a state of desire for possessions in which interior and exterior, stimulus and response, have become thoroughly merged. Unlike Crane's Maggie, whose story would seem an underhanded satire of *Sister Carrie* had it not appeared first, Carrie is able in her acting to "reproduce" what she secs until she has and harbors it herself; like money, like the theater, like the journalistic accounts and advertisements of reality the book contains, Carrie herself becomes a *medium* that pathetically, melodramatically reproduces and multiplies a form of desire that is at once sexual and hauntingly dispassionate. In the end (as Carrie Madenda) she embodies the world around her by offering, as Ames tells her, "a natural expression of its longing." As the "representative of all desire," she takes on an earlier role of the now declining and finally insignificant Hurstwood, in whose seductive voice she once heard "instead of his words, the voices of the things which he represented." Carrie is a classic example of the "conspicuous consumption" that Veblen's *The Theory of the Leisure Class* (1899) portrays as the habitual, emulative goal of American society; and she thoroughly dramatizes the mechanism of that desire, which, as René Girard points out, is one of triangulation where "the value of the article consumed is based solely on how it is regarded by the Other."[18] Carrie's easy transformation from consumer to consumed is thus a concise illustration of the character of success in the age of capitalism: the "possession of self" becomes indistinguishable from the "self of possessions," and the hero of desire, rather than diverging from society, totalizes that society by containing and expressing it in an erotic materialism of the self.

Carrie's case may be as melodramatic as she is, but I want to suggest again that it represents, in particular terms, Dreiser's understanding of the resistance of American realism to literal or actualized structures of social containment by demonstrating American society's own resistance of the literal and its continued incorporation of romance as a prevalence of desire, of "the possible," of fantasy, of the Other. The most thorough incorporation, from the standpoint of fictional technique itself, is of course James, whose whole career—particularly after his eccentric but revealing 1886 excursion into more explicit social realism in *The Bostonians* and *The Princess Casamassima,* and even more emphatically after his failure as a dramatist in the early 1890s—is a sustained augmentation of novelistic powers of inspection in order to locate infinitely richer, more luxurious surpluses of character that in the end are out of all proportion to the action in which character is engaged. The "luxury" that James identifies in "The Lesson of Balzac" (1905), "the extraordinary number and length of his radiating and ramifying corridors—the labyrinth in which he finally lost himself, " describes rather exactly the endless play of speculation and desire to which so many of James's scenes are subject. And by exaggerating strains one may find throughout the fiction of the period, James's courting of this "hallucination" of value reminds us of Tocqueville's prophetic assertion in *Democracy in America* (1835) that the characteristic and paradoxical "restlessness" of Americans in the midst of their obvious prosperity produces a very "strange melancholy" and often a simple "madness."

At the level of action, Tocqueville's remarks predict most accurately the bestialities of Norris and the urban psychodramas of Dreiser, who remarks in *Jennie Gerhardt* (1911) that "the multiplicity and variety of our social forms, the depth, subtlety, and sophistry of our imaginative impressions, gathered, remultiplied, and disseminated by such agencies as the railroad, the express and the post office, the telephone, the telegraph, and the newspaper," produce by their "dazzling and confusing phantasmagoria of life" a stultification of mental and moral nature, and an "intellectual fatigue through which we see the ranks of the victims of insomnia, melancholia, and insanity constantly recruited." But at the level of technique, Tocqueville's observations bear most upon the case of James, whose impressionistic method, working from within various interiors or "centers" of consciousness, makes a virtue of surplus desire to the point that the self disappears not merely into material possessions (for in James possessions are more conspicuously assumed, rather than consumed) but into the further moral and psychological reverberations that the express resemblance between people and possessions can produce. One may speak of Jamesian "realism," then, only by recognizing how urgently the concentration on the *within* presumes the prior incorporation of magnified and ever-accelerating values derived from *without,* and by noting how completely the moral assessment of character is embodied by the narrative imagination that can reproduce and relocate those values without end, a virtue that James rightly designates in *The Wings of the Dove* (1902) as "the imagination of expenditure."

Such a brief sketch can do James's achievements in the novel no justice, but it is worthwhile remembering that the most impressionistic of the nineteenth-century realists—James and Crane—are also the ones who ultimately seem most modern, in part because their concentration on technique anticipates modernist preoccupations, and in part because they demonstrate an increasing discrepancy between the figurative life of the mind and the literal life of the material. In the case of Crane, such experiments in technique are certainly of variable inspiration, ranging from instances of clear motivation (the pressure of combat in *The Red Badge of Courage*) to inexplicable but explosive moral puzzles ("The Blue Hotel") to Brechtian derangements of the literal landscape *(Maggie)*. But the effects very much resemble those James produces, with infinitely richer texture, in his late novels and in *The American Scene* (1907); as technique becomes more clearly a mediating form, mind and material shrink away from one another even as they become wholly dependent and come more explicitly to inhabit the constructed world of language—the world that Crane, with manifold irony, implied in *Maggie* was one of "transcendental realism."

In this respect, however, it is worth remembering also that the psychological realism of James and Crane represents most evidently and most tellingly the continued presence of romance. The writer who assumes such a stance must—as Hawthorne put it in his preface to *The House of the Seven Gables*—"claim a certain latitude" in the management of his "atmospheric medium," and in mingling "the Marvellous" with the "actual substance of the dish offered to the Public" be wary of "bringing his fancy-pictures almost into positive contact with the realities of the moment." The writer insufficiently aware of these risks, or even the one who willingly takes them, may wake up in the country of the blue.

NOTES

Bibliographical note: the critical literature on American realism is diverse, and the following list of books can only be suggestive. Among studies devoted primarily to the period, the most important include: Vernon L. Parrington, *The Beginnings of Critical Realism in America*, vol. 3, *Main Currents in American Thought* (New York: Harcourt, Brace, 1930); Maxwell Geismar, *Rebels and Ancestors: The American Novel, 1890–1915* (Boston: Houghton Mifflin, 1953); Kenneth S. Lynn, *The Dream of Success: A Study of the Modern American Imagination* (Boston: Little, Brown, 1955); Charles C. Walcutt, *American Literary Naturalism: A Divided Stream* (Minneapolis: University of Minnesota Press, 1956); Warner Berthoff, *The Ferment of Realism: American Literature, 1884-1919* (New York: The Free Press, 1965); Donald Pizer, *Realism and Naturalism in Nineteenth-Century American Literature* (Carbondale: Southern Illinois University Press, 1966); Larzer Ziff, *The American 1890s: Life and Times of a Lost Generation* (New York: Viking Press, 1966); Jay Martin, *Harvests of Change: American Literature, 1865-1914* (Englewood Cliffs, N.J.: Prentice-Hall, 1967); Harold H. Kolb, Jr., *The Illusion of Life: American Realism as a Literary Form* (Charlottesville: University Press of Virginia, 1969); Gordon O. Taylor, *The Passages of Thought: Psychological Representation in the American Novel, 1870-1900* (New York: Oxford University Press, 1969); Edwin H. Cady, *The Light of Common Day: Realism in American Fiction* (Bloomington: Indiana University Press, 1971); Harold Kaplan,

Power and Order: Henry Adams and the Naturalist Tradition in American Fiction (Chicago: University of Chicago Press, 1981); and Alan Trachtenberg, *The Incorporation of America: Culture and Society in the Gilded Age* (New York: Hill & Wang, 1982).

   Important studies devoted in part to the period include: Alfred Kazin, *On Native Grounds* (1942; reprint ed., New York: Anchor-Doubleday, 1956); James D. Hart, *The Popular Book: A History of America's Literary Taste* (1950; reprint ed., Berkeley and Los Angeles: University of California Press, 1963); Richard Chase, *The American Novel and Its Tradition* (1957; reprint ed., Baltimore: Johns Hopkins University Press, 1980); Wright Morris, *The Territory Ahead* (1957; reprint ed., Lincoln: University of Nebraska Press, 1978); Marius Bewley, *The Eccentric Design: Form in the Classic American Novel* (New York: Columbia University Press, 1958); Leslie Fiedler, *Love and Death in the American Novel* (1960; rev. ed., New York: Dell, 1966); Leo Marx, *The Machine in the Garden: Technology and the Pastoral Ideal in America* (New York: Oxford University Press, 1964); John Cawelti, *Apostles of the Self-Made Man* (Chicago: University of Chicago Press, 1965); Richard Bridgman, *The Colloquial Style in America* (New York: Oxford University Press, 1966); Richard Poirier, *A World Elsewhere: The Place of Style in American Literature* (New York: Oxford University Press, 1966); David Weimar, *The City as Metaphor* (New York: Random House, 1966); Daniel Aaron, *The Unwritten War: American Writers and the Civil War* (New York: Alfred A. Knopf, 1973); Harry B. Henderson III, *Versions of the Past: The Historical Imagination in American Fiction* (New York: Oxford Univesity Press, 1974); Warwick Wadlington, *The Confidence Game in American Literature* (Princeton: Princeton University Press, 1975); and Henry Nash Smith, *Democracy and the Novel: Popular Resistance to Classic Writers* (New York: Oxford University Press, 1978).

1. R. P. Blackmur, "In the Country of the Blue," *A Primer of Ignorance* (New York: Harcourt, Brace, 1967), p. 196.

2. Chase, *The American Novel and Its Tradition*, p. 2. See also pp. vii–28. A similar account may be found in Perry Miller, "The Romance and the Novel," in *Nature's Nation* (Cambridge: Harvard University Press, 1967), pp. 241–78.

3. Kazin, *On Native Ground*, pp. 10, 12.

4. Herbert Marcuse, *Eros and Civilization: A Philosophical Inquiry into Freud* (1955; reprint ed., New York: Vintage-Random, 1962), pp. 82–94.

5. Erich Auerbach, *Mimesis: The Representation of Reality in Western Literature*, trans. Willard R. Trask (Princeton: Princeton University Press, 1953), p. 459.

6. Poirier, *A World Elsewhere*, pp. 214, 248.

7. Martin, *Harvests of Change*, p. 202.

8. See Chase, *The American Novel and Its Tradition*, pp. 198–204.

9. Morris, *The Territory Ahead*, p. 12.

10. See Ziff, *The American 1890s*, pp. 120–65.

11. Lionel Trilling, *The Liberal Imagination: Essays on Literature and Society* (New York: Viking Press, 1950), pp. 10–11.

12. Walter Benjamin, "The Work of Art in the Age of Mechanical Reproduction," in *Illuminations*, trans. Hannah Arendt (New York: Schocken Books, 1969) p. 221.

13. Daniel Boorstin, *The Americans: The National Experience* (New York: Random House, 1973), pp. 370–90.

14. Christopher Lasch, *The Culture of Narcissism: American Life in an Age of Diminishing Expectations* (New York: W. W. Norton, 1979), p. 160.

15. George Becker, ed., *Documents of Modern Literary Realism* (Princeton: Princeton University Press, 1963), p. 29.

16. Leo Bersani, "Realism and the Fear of Desire," in *A Future for Astyanax: Character and Desire in Literature* (New York: Little, Brown, 1976), pp. 51–88.

17. Walter Benn Michaels, "*Sister Carrie's* Popular Economy," *Critical Inquiry* 7, no. 2 (Winter 1980): 373–90.

18. René Girard, *Deceit, Desire, and the Novel*, trans. Yvonne Freccero (Baltimore: Johns Hopkins Press, 1965), p. 223.

Hawthorne
among the Realists
THE CASE OF HOWELLS

To better your instruction is the highest achievement of which you are capable.—William Dean Howells, *Harper's Monthly*, 1907

I begin with a fact of literary history that is not, I think, widely recognized. This is that although Hawthorne, alone among great American authors, has never been undervalued by later readers, in the two decades after the Civil War he occupied an even more exalted position in American literature than he has since enjoyed. When the canon of classic American literature was formed in the mid nineteenth century, the writers we group with him were either (like Poe) given lesser places, or (like Melville) given no place at all; but Hawthorne was elevated to the highest reaches of the literary pantheon, singled out as the one American writer of classic prose fiction. Well into the 1880s his was the name inevitably chosen to signify the greatest American fiction-maker. And it was so used not just by those who accepted the mid-century canon, but by those bent on reforming it as well. In the revolutions of taste that deflated the reputations of his original literary peers—Longfellow, Lowell, Holmes, and so on—Hawthorne was not deposed but recanonized on new grounds. The literary insurgents of the late nineteenth century consistently treated him as a previously misunderstood practitioner of their own "advanced" art—as the modernists of the 1870s coupled Hawthorne with Turgenev as a model for the new novel shorn of moral commentary; as the modernists of the early 1880s linked him with George Eliot as a patron of the new novel of psychological analysis and moral irresolution. To a remarkable extent, during a period of major shifts in literary preference and practice, Hawthorne held his place, continued to stand for prose fiction at its most subtly considered and perfectly achieved.[1]

As a result of this, the men and women who took up careers as writers

in America in the decades after 1860 moved into a field rather massive-
ly dominated by the figure of Hawthorne. He was inevitably present
to the minds of beginning writers of the next generation, and present to
them not as a master among others but as something like their originator,
the founder of the profession they aspired to practice. Henry James's
experience is typical. As he recollects in *Notes of a Son and Brother,*
he read Hawthorne with new responsiveness on the verge of his own
"positive consecration to letters," and looked to him as proof that the
literary vocation was indeed open to an American:

> His work was all charged with a *tone,* a full and rare tone of prose,
> and . . . this made for it an extraordinary value in an air in which
> absolutely nobody else's was or has shown since any aptitude for
> being. And the tone had been, in its beauty—for me at least—ever
> so appreciably American; which proved to what a use American
> matter could be put by an American hand: a consummation involv-
> ing, it appeared, the happiest moral. For the moral was that an
> American could be an artist, one of the finest, without "going out-
> side" about it, as I liked to say; quite in fact as Hawthorne had be-
> come one just by being American *enough,* by the felicity of how the
> artist in him missed nothing, suspected nothing, that the ambient
> air didn't affect him as containing.[2]

James and his contemporaries are more than familiar with Hawthorne's
writing. They are possessed of it; it has incorporated itself into the deepest
levels of their artistic consciousness. As such it forms one of their imaginative burdens. All of the new American authors of the post–Civil War
generation have to struggle to keep from simply repeating Hawthorne's
authoritative moves, and all of them occasionally lose the struggle, dully
recopying Hawthornesque designs in their own writing. But Hawthorne's
fiction also operates as one of this generation's greatest literary resources.
Its writers regularly return to Hawthorne to find the direction to their
own best work—as George Washington Cable finds his way to *The Gran-
dissimes* by consulting *The House of the Seven Gables;* as Harold Frederic
finds his way to *The Damnation of Theron Ware* by following the lead of
The Scarlet Letter; as James himself organizes phase after phase of his
ficiton by returning to and re-creating Hawthornesque prototypes.

   The processes of cultural selection that erected Hawthorne as exem-
plum gave a generation of writers largely under the sway of realist literary
theories and aspirations as their chief American ancestor an author whose
relation to those aspirations was interestingly ambiguous. They found in
Hawthorne a writer who had in certain important ways anticipated their
new projects—the project of describing politicized behavior, for instance,
or of writing regional history in fiction. But they also encountered in

Hawthorne a writer whose method was conspicuously unrealistic, and more, a writer whose method constituted a vigorous critique of literary realism's operative ideas. The result is that Hawthorne's influence on his heirs in the realist generation takes two quite different forms. He can be very helpful to the followers who engage him at the level of his subject matter. Authors who resort to him for aid in representing this or that regional character type, or this or that kind of social situation, have little difficulty taking over his conceptions and adapting them to their own uses. (Witness the Hepzibahs and Dimmesdales who parade through American local color fiction without making it in any interesting sense Hawthornesque.) But his effect on the followers who to any extent reactivate the imaginative procedures of his fiction tends to be highly disruptive. The realist authors who re-create the deep logic of his fiction find that they have revived, within their work, a voice that calls the validity of their own procedures strenuously into question.

Let me illustrate the kind of importance Hawthorne has to American writers of the later nineteenth century, and also the double influence he exerts on their writing, by concentrating on a representative case—the case of William Dean Howells.

Howells is an author with an overdeveloped organ of reverence. Probably no other American writer has spent so much of his life lavishing so much respect upon so many other writers. Not surprisingly, his respectfulness is especially acute in the years just before his own literary debut. The young Howells regularly invests those who have succeeded in literature with the strength of his own unacted literary aspirations. As his urge to the literary career gathers force in his late teens and early twenties, he loads previous writers with so much projected power that they come to embody, for him, "the sum of greatness."[3] In *My Literary Passions*, the book in which he chronicles his imaginary relations with authors during his young manhood, Howells images the great writers as so many beloveds whose ravishing caresses the young writer courts—the objects of "a passion passing the love of women . . . whom I could offer my intimacy in many an impassioned revery." Or they figure as so many "divinities" for Howells to "bow the knee" to, so many gods at whose "shrines" he learns to worship. Or—an image that becomes increasingly dominant as Howells reaches his early twenties—the great author appears as a "mighty magician," the wielder of an occult power that enables him to "possess himself of what was best worth having in me," a "potent spirit" exercising something like a telepathist's "control" over his youthful writings: "My poems might as well have been communications from him so far as any authority of my own was concerned."[4]

Hawthorne became the object of a particularly virulent strain of the reverential passion that was Howells's normal response to established authors. Howells first read Hawthorne in 1860, the year of his own full accession to the role of author, and the time in his career when he was most responsive to the superior authority of others. (This was also, he recalls, "the supreme hour of [Hawthorne's] fame": the year of *The Marble Faun,* the book that caused Hawthorne's promotion from critical beatification to critical canonization.[5]) Howells met Hawthorne, for the first and only time, in this same year, calling on him in Concord during his 1860 literary pilgrimage to New England.[6] As Howells later describes these encounters, even to his divinity-seeking youthful mind Hawthorne was a god apart. In "My First Visit to New England" he singles Hawthorne out as the only great man of New England letters who did not act the great man before him, who did not set himself apart from his admirer and secretly coax his admiration.[7] Here Hawthorne is distinguished for his superior humanity. But in Howells's recollection of his first reading of Hawthorne in *My Literary Passions,* his distinction is exactly the reverse: he is the only literary divinity whom Howells the reader can in no measure humanize. He responds to the author of Hawthorne's romances not as any possible person but as sheer power—a figure of such potency that he knows he cannot be its friend or familiar, but only its subject. In a passage that brings the imaging of authorship as power and readership as submission in *My Literary Passions* to its climactic expression, Howells writes:

> I read the *Marble Faun* first, then the *Scarlet Letter,* and then the *House of Seven Gables,* and then the *Blithedale Romance....* They all moved me with a sort of effect such as I had not felt before. They were so far from time and place that, although most of them related to our country and epoch, I could not imagine anything approximate from them; and Hawthorne himself seemed a remote and impalpable agency, rather than a person whom one might actually meet, as not long afterward happened to me. I did not hold the sort of fancied converse with him that I held with other authors, and I cannot pretend that I had the affection for him that attracted me to them. But he held me by his potent spell, and for a time he dominated me as completely as any author I have read. More truly than any other American author he has been a passion with me.[8]

In spite of the abject submissiveness that Howells recalls having felt toward Hawthorne at the inception of his career, Hawthorne does not exert any very obvious or important influence on Howells's early writing. This is partly the result of Howells's early authorial strategies. He appears to have recognized that with a faculty of reverence like his, and with his consequent liability to imaginative domination by the authors he revered, he would need to keep well clear of his masters' fields of force in order to be able to do work of his own. In adopting the genres of the travel sketch and the travel novel in the 1860s and 1870s Howells is clearly moving to stake out a territory not already claimed and worked over by his literary forebears. The same desire to avoid contact and competition with the work of the great ones lies behind his choice of scale. It would not be derogatory, but only just, to say that the ambition that governs the production of *Their Wedding Journey* (1871), *A Chance Acquaintance* (1873), *A Foregone Conclusion* (1875), and *The Lady of the Aroostook* (1879) is to write good minor novels—to do work of high quality, but in a different league from that of the masters.[9]

Howells first admits Hawthorne into his writing in *The Undiscovered Country* (1880), a novel in which he reworks the central situation of his favorite Hawthorne volume, *The Blithedale Romance.* Like Hawthorne's Veiled Lady, Howells's heroine Egeira Boynton is a phenomenon in the mesmeric line: a possibly clairvoyant maiden coerced into a career of exhibitionism by her spiritual master (in Howells's case, her father). Howells clearly understands what makes this situation so interesting to Hawthorne. His version, like Hawthorne's, uses the pair composed of a medium and her control to image a relation in which one party is the other's subject—the "passive instrument" of another's resolute "will" (53),[10] the extension of another's mental process. ("It is you who do it," Egeira tells her father; "I see, or seem to see, whatever you tell me" [68].) And his version, like Hawthorne's, suggests that this subjection of one self to another is not a rare aberration but is rather an element latent within the most familiar forms of emotional bonding. Doctor Boynton's power is that he is Egeira's father; she submits to his control because she loves him as a daughter. With her, then, as with her Hawthornesque predecessors, to love is exactly to *be* in someone's power: to deliver oneself over to one whose object is to make you his possession, to subject you to the laws of his desires.

Given that he recognizes the interest of this Hawthornesque situation, it must be admitted that Howells handles it rather tamely. Or, more accurately: Howells returns to this situation in order to *make* it tame. For all of his revisions in *The Undiscovered Country* move to render benign what is in Hawthorne a frightening exercise of power. To begin with, Howells adopts what is already the mildest version of domination to be found in Hawthorne's fiction. His Mr. Phillips explicates Egeira's moral status as follows:

If she has been her father's "subject" ever since childhood, of course none of the ordinary young girl interests have entered into her life.

She has n't known the delight of dress and of dancing; she has n't
had "attentions"; upon my word, that's very suggestive! It means
that she's kept a child-like simplicity, and that she could go on and
help out her father's purposes, no matter how tricky they were, with
no more sense of guilt than a child who makes believe talk with
imaginary visitors. Yes, the Pythoness could be innocent in the midst
of fraud. (109)

"I'm proud of that conjecture," he adds; "it was worthy of Hawthorne"
(110). Worthy indeed: especially because his thought has already occurred
in Hawthorne—in the "Village Hall" chapter of *Blithedale,* where Coverdale attests that "throughout" Westervelt's crass reign over her Priscilla
"had kept . . . her virgin reserve and sanctity of soul." But Hawthorne
does not customarily believe that the self can subsist unchanged in the
power of another. In the tale "Alice Pyncheon," in *The House of the
Seven Gables,* he envisions mediumistic possession as necessarily costing
the virgin spirit its integrity and sanctity. Even Miles Coverdale has thought,
elsewhere in *The Blithedale Romance,* that to become a telepathic subject
is to have one's "individual soul . . . virtually annihilated."

Having adopted the Hawthornesque model of domination that shows
the self least altered by the subjections it endures, Howells then goes on
to imagine domination itself as easily dispelled. As if by magic, Doctor
Boynton is dispossessed of his demon of possessiveness. He falls asleep
and wakes up cured of his coercive designs on his daughter, and as soon
as he is cured, Howells hastens to proclaim his coercions innocent—
because Boynton did Egeira no lasting harm, the book twice repeats, he
is not to blame for his treatment of her. At the same time Egeira herself
is exorcised of her demon of subjection, and exorcised without a struggle.
Her clairvoyant powers are simply "termina[ted] by the lapse of time"
(291); they expire by the process of nature's law. In Howells's kindly
version of family relations, the dominating parent gets tired of dominating
and lets go, while the submissive child gets tired of submitting and grows
up. Father and daughter can now enjoy a new relation, one not poisoned
by the element of power and subjection.

Howells's domestication of Hawthornesque power can be seen even
more tellingly in the love plot of *The Undiscovered Country.* In *The
Blithedale Romance,* Priscilla is rescued from spiritualism into love,
but only after Hollingsworth uses the stronger magic of his love to overpower the weaker spiritualistic magic of Westervelt. *The Undiscovered
Country* plots the same rescue for Egeira, but effaces the struggle that
brings Priscilla's rescue about. It covertly suggests that the displacement of
filial by adult heterosexual passion involves the overpowering of one
form of love by another: Egeira loses the power to perform her father's

stunts when Ford is nearby because his magnetism interferes with and neutralizes Doctor Boynton's; Ford's reappearance at the Shaker community where the Boyntons have sought refuge causes Doctor Boynton to suffer a disabling blow. But overtly this novel is at great pains to deny that Ford is in any sense Doctor Boynton's successor as Egeira's control. When Ford inadvertently slips into the idiom of enchantment—"Come, Miss Boynton . . . confess that I am some malignant enchanter, and that I have the power of casting an ugly spell over you, that deprives you of the wholesome satisfaction of telling me that I'm detestable" (332)— Egeira recoils, dreading the possibility that Ford as lover will renew the psychic enthrallment her father subjected her to. But in the novel's clarification scene Ford convinces her both that his love is respectful and considerate, not domineering, and that in yielding to him she is swayed not by his love for her but by her own love for him—that she submits to a coercion that is in the deepest sense voluntary, the expression of her own will. A potentially malignant enchantment is converted, in *The Undiscovered Country,* into that form of white or garden magic that *The House of the Seven Gables* calls love's sorcery. The book then ends with a conclusion that out-*Seven Gables Seven Gables* in depicting the charms of normalized existence. Ford patents a lucrative household device, Egeira becomes an Episcopalian, and they live happily ever after, in a house in the suburbs.

In one sense Howells's project in *The Undiscovered Country* is to imagine the domestication of love's more coercive forms of power. But in another sense his project is to convert influence itself into an innocent process. Throughout this novel he expresses exorbitant parental power in exactly the same imagery through which he figures the power of literary masters in *My Literary Passions*—the imagery of spells, possession, subjection, and mediumistic control. And Doctor Boynton clearly embodies the same threat to Egeira that his masters embody to the young Howells: he is a figure loved too intensely, in a way that gives him the power to replace her words and thoughts with his.[11] Read in terms of literary instead of family relationships, the fantasy of *The Undiscovered Country* could be restated in this way. The potent influences the young author inevitably submits to do him no harm. They do not scar him, or make him something other than himself—like Egeira, he keeps his integrity in the midst of domination. In the ripeness of time, through a gradual, natural process that does not involve violence or struggle, those influences lose their power over him. He outgrows dependency and becomes immune to external intrusions on his mental world. At this point early relationships can be reestablished, on grounds that are elective, not coercive. The former dependent can freely turn back to the figures that previously enthralled him, embracing them now because he loves them, and doing so at the risk of no new loss of self.

Read in these terms, the action of *The Undiscovered Country* exactly describes the sort of relationship that Howells is seeking to establish with Hawthorne through the writing of this novel. Through his allusions to *The Blithedale Romance* Howells would look back to an early master and acknowledge the relation between them, while at the same time making it clear that he is really no longer under his power. And he is right that, as the author of *The Undiscovered Country,* he has passed out of Hawthorne's potent spell. This book's indebtedness is quite superficial. As Howells hopes, it incorporates Hawthorne materials without becoming in any deep sense Hawthornesque, and without disrupting or displacing the urbane fluencies of Howells's own style. But as a description of the whole of their relation, *The Undiscovered Country* contains a good deal of wishful thinking. *A Modern Instance,* written and published two years after *The Undiscovered Country,* makes it clear that Howells has by no means outgrown Hawthorne's spell. A novel much more deeply and directly influenced by Hawthorne's fiction, *A Modern Instance* demonstrates Hawthorne's continuing power to wrest control of the patterns of Howells's imaginings—and in so doing to give surprising turns to Howells's intended designs.

A Modern Instance is a work in which Howells significantly raises the level of his artistic aspirations. This is the book through which he seeks to launch a new career for himself as a full-time novelist (he resigned the editorship of *The Atlantic* in February 1881).[12] It is also the first of his novels in which he consciously aims to take on major subjects. "I believe that I have got a *great* motive," he writes in a letter of the same month outlining the book to the editor of *Scribner's;* "I feel that I have a theme only less intense and pathetic than slavery."[13] *A Modern Instance* represents the moment in Howell's career when he wills to bring his self-appointed minority to an end, and to appear as the author of major creations of his own. The change in the level of his aspiration brings with it a change in his relation to his masters. Instead of avoiding competition with them, he now seeks to reclaim for himself significant portions of their powers—a situation that both gives his work new sources of strength and makes him newly vulnerable to the incursions of their influence.

Both aspects of this new relation are clear if we compare *A Modern Instance* with *The Undiscovered Country.* In *The Undiscovered Country* Howells elaborates on a Hawthorne theme; in *A Modern Instance* he lays claim to Hawthorne's artistic project. He takes up the Hawthornesque task, thus, of disclosing through fiction the dynamics of the social and spiritual history of New England. He takes up too Hawthorne's analytical function—the task (in the words of "Roger Malvin's Burial") of "penetrat[ing] to the secret place of [the] soul where motives lay hidden." But Hawthorne's inspiration, felt in a general way throughout *A Modern*

Instance, suddenly becomes much more insistent in its later chapters. Ben Halleck, a minor figure heretofore, becomes the principal character of *A Modern Instance* after chapter 32; and as he does so he changes in nature from a Jamesian observer to a Hawthornesque hoarder of guilt. Halleck particularly resembles Dimmesdale in that he harbors an adulterous passion within a nature that is morbidly conscientious, such that the experience of his desire makes him feel ever more abominably loathsome and sinful. Like Dimmesdale he becomes a "remorseful hypocrite," the prisoner of a reputation for virtue that makes his efforts at oblique confession unavailing. "I wish I could convince somebody of my wickedness," he tells the lawyer Atherton in chapter 33, "but it seems to be useless to try. I say things that ought to raise the roof, both to you here and to Olive at home, and you tell me you don't believe me, and she tells me that Mrs. Hubbard thinks me a saint" (287).[14] Like Hawthorne's guilt-hoarders—Reverend Hooper, for example—Halleck's obsession with his own secret sin enables him to intuit the secret sins of others. In a reversal of aggression with close precedents in "The Minister's Black Veil" and "Egotism; or the Bosom Serpent," Halleck now leaves off torturing himself and begins denouncing the collective hypocrisy by which others keep their similar inward conditions from showing: "Such is the effect of character! And yet out of the fulness of the heart, the mouth speaketh. Out of the heart proceed all those unpleasant things enumerated in Scripture; but if you bottle them up there, and keep your label fresh, it's all that's required of you, by your fellow-beings, at least. What an amusing thing morality would be if it were not—otherwise" (287).

Next Halleck falls into a Dimmesdalean fit of eschatological longing, a fantasy of the pleasures attendant on the final exposure of earthly secrets. Now paraphrasing the tenth chapter of *The Scarlet Letter,* he continues: "Christ being imagined, can't you see what a comfort, what a rapture, it must have been to all these poor souls to come into such a presence and be looked through and through? The relief, the rest, the complete exposure of Judgment Day—" (287–88). Then in another reversal Halleck turns from fantasies of divine exposure to fantasies of communal exposure, of a ritual uncovering of the mass of foul sin that hides itself behind the community's virtuous exteriors (his source now is "Young Goodman Brown"):

> "Every day is Judgment Day," said Atherton.
> "Yes, I know your doctrine. But I mean the Last Day. We ought to have something in anticipation of it, here, in our social system. Character is a superstition, a wretched fetish. Once a year wouldn't be too often to seize upon sinners whose blameless life has placed them above suspicion, and turn them inside out before the community,

so as to show people how the smoke of the Pit has been quietly
blackening their interior. That would destroy character as a cult."
(288).

Halleck's address in chapter 33 of *A Modern Instance* shows Hawthorne seizing much tighter control of Howells's writing than he did,
for instance, in *The Undiscovered Country*. And once Howells moves
into Hawthorne's field of force, other elements in his novel begin to
behave in Hawthornesque fashions. The whole career of Halleck in the
rest of the novel is perfectly Dimmesdalean, especially his move from
guilty desire through draining self-torment to a renewal of the desire
he still experiences as guilty. (Halleck's abrupt conversion into an or-
thodox minister in the last chapter might be said to complete his transformation into Dimmesdale.) Marcia Gaylord's daughter, Flavia, previously a dormant character, now begins to play the part of Hester's
little Pearl, asking preternaturally intelligent questions about her ambiguous family structure ("What *is* Mr. Halleck, mamma? . . . Is he my
uncle, or my cousin, or what?" [341]) between bouts of impish merri-
ment.

The Hawthorne aspect in *A Modern Instance* is most intensely associated with Halleck; and to say what Hawthorne's vigorous intrusions
do to Howells's designs in *A Modern Instance* it is necessary to describe
the role of Halleck in the novel's final section. The most salient fact
about Halleck is that he travels through this novel in partnership with
Atherton, appearing principally in debating scenes with him, and functioning principally as a counter to his voice. Atherton, the portfolio
manager and all-purpose sage, is himself newly prominent after chapter
32, and like Halleck at this point he changes his role. Previously Atherton has functioned as the voice that called Halleck's neurotically moral-
istic judgments into question. In his principal prior appearance he has
tried to argue Ben out of his melodramatic vision of Marcia's marriage
—to convince him that Marcia does not see herself (as Ben does) as the
innocent victim of her husband's base nature; that even if she does feel
victimized, she will know how to convert her injury into marital revenges
in the future; in other words, that marriage is a state of mutual forbear-
ances and mutual victimizations, such that a moral judgment of either
of its partners in isolation is impossible. But from chapter 33 on,
Atherton functions exactly as what he was not before: the agent of
judgment, the voice of the law. From now on his job in the novel is
to determine and name the moral status of others' wishes and acts—
"I tell you that you are suffering guiltily" (292), he tells Halleck—and
then to repeat his verdict over and over, in case anyone missed it the
first time: "You know he wasn't right, Clara" (332); "Don't you see

that his being in love with her when she was another man's wife is what he feels it to be,—an indelible stain?" (362).

Atherton's new office is to compel those human situations he had previously found enigmatic to range themselves under the headings right or wrong, innocent or guilty. This form of determination is not only new for him; it has also been conspicuously missing from the novel as a whole in its first thirty-one chapters.[15] The goods and evils Atherton now sees as polarized Howells had earlier shown as inseparably mixed: before he becomes (in the book's eyes) simply a scoundrel, Bartley Hubbard had been both shifty and oddly winning, both self-indulgent and occasionally thoughtful; before it becomes (in the book's eyes) a sacred institution to be maintained at any cost, marriage had been recognized as a scene of shared help and shared cruelty, a structure of support that also breeds within it the energies of its own destruction.

Above all, however, judgment has been rendered difficult in this novel by the very movements of its prose. The narrative voice of *A Modern Instance,* for all that it withholds overt comment, is by no means morally neutral. This voice registers intense moral anxiety about the forms of conduct and relationship it has to speak of. It cannot allude to an attribute of Bartley Hubbard without becoming disturbed, without enshrouding it in an atmosphere of suspicion—Bartley's carriage, out for a ride on the Sabbath, is already on the second page of the novel an "ill-timed vehicle" (2); that Bartley does not consider the editorship of the Equity *Free Press* a lifelong commitment raises grave questions about his sincerity and stedfastness of purpose. But typically, once the narrative has evoked an attitude of judgment, it then renders questionable the position from which judgment was arrived at. It notes the apparently telling fact that Bartley's college letters of recommendation praise his intelligence but fail to comment on his "moral characteristics" (16)—but then goes on to reflect that moral characteristics may not, after all, be pertinent qualifications for the job in question. It mentions the flirtatious correspondences Bartley has kept up with a number of young women—surely, further proof of the egotism by which he arranges to enjoy the affection he inspires in others without committing himself to reciprocate it; but the narrative then reflects that such correspondences are perfectly commonplace in America, a custom permitted and encouraged by "the laxness of our social life" (19). It dwells on Bartley's shopping around at various houses of worship—confirming, again, his essential opportunism, the casualness with which he invests himself in relationships that require deep commitment; but then it notes that the code from which this judgment would proceed is itself in abeyance—that Equity has reached the stage of religious liberalization where attendance at a single church is not only not required, but not even preferred.

A Modern Instance describes a culture moving into a phase of "relaxation and uncertainty" (18). It describes a culture whose previously rigid communal codes—domestic, ethical, religious, professional—have recently lost the force of their social authority. Howells analyzes this cultural moment quite brilliantly; but the interesting thing about *A Modern Instance* is that the novel itself more or less consciously participates in the process it describes. In Howell's narrative, as in his Equity or Boston, the moral instincts associated with an older, stricter social order survive—the "modern" consistently strikes this novel as lax, degenerate, demoralized. But every time Howells tries to implement old-fashioned principles, he ends up exposing their lack of authority at the modern moment. *A Modern Instance* is morally open-ended not because its author knows that experience is complex and hard to judge, and not because its author is too good an artist to render judgment overtly. It is morally open-ended because it lacks the means by which to make itself closed: because it knows that the cultural standards it would invoke to render judgments are in abeyance, deprived of cultural force. It moves forward in a rhythm of invoked and suspended judgment, recoiling from ethical "relaxation" into a posture of renewed rigidity, then lapsing from rigidity into renewed uncertainty.

It is well known that somewhere around chapter 31 the writing of *A Modern Instance* became too much for Howells. He suffered a nervous collapse that left him bedridden for nearly two months, and he completed the novel while still in a state of convalescence.[16] Kenneth Lynn has plausibly argued that Howells collapsed under the strain of dealing so intimately with the unruly impulses in himself and his own marriage.[17] But surely the major strain Howells was under in the first thirty-one chapters of *A Modern Instance* was that of persisting in the state of moral anxiety I have been describing—in the anxiety generated by his repeated exposure that judgments he deeply wished to make were without real foundation. When, resuming the novel after his collapse, Howells moves Atherton to the fore and recasts him as the arbiter of morals, he is attempting a fictional solution to the crisis of authority that has led him and his novel to break down. Using the privileges of fictive invention, he constructs a character who still has that clarity and certainty of vision that Howells has not been able to locate within the contemporary social world. And exploiting the rhetorical power of authorial eloquence, he lets that figure voice his vision in such accents that it once again sounds authoritative and unassailable. Atherton might be described as the means by which a lapsing social code rhetorically reconstitutes itself as a binding moral law, objectively sanctioned and universally enforceable. This is the action performed by all his major speeches:

Have you really come back here to give your father's honest name, and the example of a man of your own blameless life, in support of conditions that tempt people to marry with a mental reservation, and that weaken every marriage bond with the guilty hope of escape whenever a fickle mind, or secret lust, or wicked will may dictate? Have you come to join yourself to those miserable specters who go shrinking through the world, afraid of their own past, and anxious to hide it from those they hold dear; or do you propose to defy the world, and to help form within it the community of outcasts with whom shame is not shame, nor dishonor, dishonor? (317–18)

No one sins or suffers to himself in a civilized state—or religious state; it's the same thing. Every link in the chain feels the effect of the violence, more or less intimately. We rise or fall together in Christian society. It's strange that it should be so hard to realize a thing that every experience of life teaches. We keep thinking of offenses against the common good as if they were abstractions! (334)

What Ben Halleck embodies in *A Modern Instance* is resistance to the thrust of this coercive moralisation. Halleck's office is to hold out against the dominations of Atherton's rhetorical process, both by opposing it with another kind of voice, and by exposing the factitious nature of its authority. This is where Hawthorne comes in: for the Hawthornisms of *A Modern Instance* are exactly the means by which Halleck (and the novel) unmask Atherton's neoorthodoxy. The ironic vision of Hawthorne's secret sinners gives Halleck and Howells the means to reveal that Atherton's apparently objective codes of value are really only conventional labelling systems, systems that bear no relation to the true nature of inward experience: "Out of the heart proceed all those unpleasant things enumerated in Scripture; but if you bottle them up there, and keep your label fresh, it's all that's required of you, by your fellow-beings, at least" (287). The same Hawthornesque vision gives Halleck and Howells the terms to say that Atherton's apparently objective moral scheme is really only a communal fabrication, a fabrication that bears no relation to that community's own real nature: "Character is a superstition, a wretched fetish. Once a year wouldn't be too often to seize upon sinners whose blameless life has placed them above suspicion, and turn them inside out before the community, so as to show people how the smoke of the Pit had been quietly blackening their interior. That would destroy character as a cult" (287–88).

When Hawthorne rematerializes within Howells's consciousness in *A Modern Instance,* he is evoked there by an imaginative crisis, a crisis in the determination of ethical significance. And the part he plays in this crisis is to fend off another force it has evoked—the narrow-minded and ill-grounded moralism with which Howells responds to the uncertainties of modern instances. This crisis and Hawthorne's role in it become the more important when we recognize that the conflict between Athertonian moralism and its Hawthornesque counterforce in *A Modern Instance* plays out a conflict within the conception of literary realism that Howells is evolving in the early 1880s. Fiction, Howells now begins to emphasize, informs its audience—both in the sense of bringing it information about the world, and in the sense of effecting the shape of its understanding of the world. Realism's nobility, for Howells, is that it does not abuse fiction's power of reality-making. It rightly informs its audience's sense of human reality; it does not ensnare real minds and hearts in fictive delusions. But how exactly the realist performs this function is the subject of some debate. On the one hand, Howells believes that the right-informing of his contemporaries requires the disrupting and correction of their conventional understandings. From this flows the strain of his fiction that seeks to mortify our preconceptions—to make us acknowledge, ruefully and with some discomfort, that our own familiar experience does not warrant the judgments we habitually make. On the other hand, Howells just as deeply believes that the right-informing of his contemporaries requires the reinforcement of their enfeebled mechanisms of moral judgment. The novelist would be no better than "the attendant who fills [the] pipe" of "the *habitué* of an opium-joint," he writes in an important essay, if he did not "distinguish so clearly that no reader of his may be misled, between what is right and what is wrong, what is noble and what is base, what is health and what is perdition, in the actions and characters he portrays."[18] From this flows another strain of Howells's fiction (Atherton is an egregious early example of it), one that seeks to shore up and reclarify those structures of moral perception that he fears contemporary experience is blurring and eroding.

The latent contradiction between these two conceptions of realism's moral office is what *A Modern Instance* exposes. Howells sets his heart on honesty in this novel. No other of his works, not even *A Hazard of New Fortunes,* delivers so strong a dose of painful candor as this book does in its early chapters. But Howells's embrace of the doubt-inducing half of his office touches off a kind of ethical backlash in him,[19] and he flees into the other half of his office, loudly instructing his readers in the rightness of the right, and the wrongness of the wrong. Halleck emerges in the final section as a new embodiment of that vision which makes not for judgment but for the suspension of judgment. Through his Hawthornesque speeches he disputes the validity of realism itself, conceived as the right-naming of ethical values. He asks whether this kind of realist's operative values are not themselves so many consensual opinions, as much in need of candor's corrections as any other set of conventions. And he asks whether this kind of realist's social function does not really consist in the enforcement of repressive communal codes—in the reattaching of the ethical labels used by those of blameless life, whatever in fact lies behind them.

Hawthorne has no univocal or easily predictable effect on his heirs in the realist generation. His influence on them depends on who invokes him, and under what circumstances. His effect on Howells, at that moment in Howells's career when his effect on him is the greatest, is to become the friend of his doubt—his doubt about social and moral questions, and his doubt about his own literary program. The Hawthorne who moves Howells most deeply is Hawthorne the master of uncertainty. His final word on him in *My Literary Passions* is that

> none of Hawthorne's fables are without a profound and distant reach into the recesses of nature and of being. He came back from his researches with no solution of the question, with no message, indeed, but the awful warning, "Be true, be true," which is the burden of the *Scarlet Letter;* yet in all his books there is the hue of thoughts that we think only in the presence of the mysteries of life and death. It is not his fault that this is not intelligence, that it knots the brow in sorer doubt rather than shapes the lips to utterance of the things that can never be said.[20]

The abiding presence of this great doubt-bearer keeps Howells, in the writing of *A Modern Instance,* from caving in to his own desires for premature ethical certainties. But what Howells derives from their encounter here is perhaps best looked for not within *A Modern Instance* but in the writing that follows it. Howells carries on, in the novels of the next decade, with the task of trying to formulate a contemporary social ethic and to enforce its reign within his culture. But even while he does so he always retains a certain suspicion of the fabrications he may be engaging in, and of the coercions he may be performing on his audience. That this is so is due in part to his meeting with Hawthorne in *A Modern Instance.* For what Hawthorne helps him to understand there is that the literary ethicist is never in such danger of perpetrating a new communal fiction as when he is most assured that he is saying what is really right.

NOTES

1. On the history of Hawthorne's reputation in the Gilded Age, see Edwin H. Cady, "'The Wizard Hand': Hawthorne, 1864–1900," in *Hawthorne Centenary Essays,* ed. Roy Harvey Pearce (Columbus: Ohio State University Press, 1964), pp. 317–34.

Hawthorne is grouped with Turgenev, for instance, by Richard Watson Gilder, who recommends the two of them as models in his editorial correspondence with Cable. Arlin Turner, *George W. Cable* (Durham, N.C.: Duke University Press, 1956), pp. 70–71. He is grouped with Eliot as the model for a "new school" practicing a "finer art" of the novel by Howells in his 1882 essay "Henry James, Jr.," reprinted in *Howells as Critic*, ed. Edwin H. Cady (London: Routledge & Kegan Paul, 1973), pp. 70–71.

2. F. W. Dupee, ed., *Henry James: Autobiography* (New York: Criterion Books, 1956), pp. 477, 480.

3. William Dean Howells, *Literary Friends and Acquaintance* (Bloomington: Indiana University Press, 1968), p. 38.

4. William Dean Howells, *My Literary Passions* (New York: Harper & Bros., 1895), pp. 16, 88; 116, 64; 71, 115, 130.

5. Howells, *Literary Friends and Acquaintance*, p. 52. On the reception of *The Marble Faun*, see Bertha Faust, *Hawthorne's Contemporaneous Reputation* (Philadelphia, 1939), pp. 118–30 and especially pp. 141–42.

6. For Howells's account of his meeting with Hawthorne, see *Literary Friends and Acquaintance*, pp. 47–53.

7. See ibid., p. 51: "In my heart I paid [Hawthorne] the same glad homage I paid Lowell and Holmes, and he did nothing to make me think I had overpaid him. This seems perhaps very little to say in his praise, but to my mind it is saying everything, for I have known but few great men, especially of those I met in early life, when I wished to lavish my admiration upon them, whom I have not the impression of having left in my debt."

8. Howells, *My Literary Passions*, p. 139.

9. Howells associates the genres of his own work with those unpracticed by the New England luminaries in *Literary Friends and Acquaintance*, pp. 101–2. His letters show his self-consciousness of the restriction of his early work's scope: "I understand that you want me to try a large canvas with many people in it. Perhaps, some time. But isn't the really dramatic encounter always between two persons only?" "Perhaps I'm really without desire for the sort of success you believe in for me. Very likely I don't want much world, or effect of it, in my fictions." Howells to Charles Dudley Warner, 4 September 1875 and 1 April 1877, *Life in Letters of William Dean Howells*, ed. Mildred Howells, 2 vols. (1928; reprint ed., New York: Russell & Russell, 1968), 1:210, 233. Howells's reverential avoidance of the paths of his precursors puts him in strong contrast to Henry James, who aggressively appropriates and revises the work of fiction's great masters even in his very early writings. The difference is clear again in Howells's 1880 review of James's *Hawthorne*: James's briskly revisionary moves in that book elicit from Howells the censures of a custodian of Hawthorne's official reputation. See Cady, ed., *Howells as Critic*, pp. 50–55.

10. William Dean Howells, *The Undiscovered Country* (Boston: Houghton Mifflin, 1880). Robert Emmet Long has noticed and briefly described the resemblances of *The Undiscovered Country* to *The Blithedale Romance* in "Transformations: *The Blithedale Romance* to Howells and James," *American Literature* 47 (January 1976): 552–71. Long usefully suggests *The Undiscovered Country* as the missing link in the line of descent from *Blithedale* to James's *The Bostonians*.

11. Kenneth Lynn notes how much Boynton also resembles Howells's own father, William Cooper Howells; clearly he is a composite figure of all Howells's parents, real and literary. Kenneth S. Lynn, *William Dean Howells: An American Life* (New York: Harcourt Brace Jovanovich, 1971), pp. 246–47.

12. "Many a time in the past four years I have been minded to jump out [of the editorship] and take the consequences—to throw myself upon the market," Howells writes, in a letter of this month to Horace Scudder. *Life in Letters*, 1:294.

13. Howells to J. G. Holland, 18 February 1881, cited by William M. Gibson in his introduction to the Riverside edition of *A Modern Instance* (Boston: Houghton Mifflin, 1957), pp. vii–viii.

14. I quote from the Riverside edition of *A Modern Instance,* cited above.

15. Not that the difference between the novel's halves is total: Henry Nash Smith has pointed out the presence of overdetermined moral structures even in early chapters of *A Modern Instance.* See his important chapter "William Dean Howells: The Theology of Realism" in *Democracy and the Novel* (New York: Oxford University Press, 1978), pp. 75-103. But as Smith notes, these structures are recessive through most of the novel, then heavily dominant in its last ten chapters.

16. On Howells's collapse, see *Life in Letters,* 1:303-7. Edwin H. Cady establishes that the collapse took place near the end of chapter 31 of *A Modern Instance* in *The Road to Realism* (Syracuse, N.Y.: Syracuse University Press, 1956), p. 210.

17. See Lynn, *Howells,* pp. 237, 253-54. Kermit Vanderbilt links Howells's collapse to his distress at the fatalistic logic that governs the breakdown of the Hubbards' marriage, and notes Howells's revival in the novel's final phase of a rhetoric of responsibility and free moral agency. *The Achievement of William Dean Howells* (Princeton: Princeton University Press, 1968), especially pp. 80-82.

18. Cady, ed., *Howells as Critic,* pp. 101, 100.

19. Howells has diagnosed exactly this process at work in the literature of his New England forebears. He reads their "intense ethicism" as a compensatory device, a response to the guilt they feel for having broken faith with the certainties of an earlier cultural moment: "They or their fathers had broken away from orthodoxy in the great schism at the beginning of the century, but, as if their heterodoxy were conscience-stricken, they still helplessly pointed the moral in all they did." *Literary Friends and Acquaintance,* p. 101.

20. Howells, *My Literary Passions,* p. 140.

ERIC CHEYFITZ

A Hazard of New Fortunes
THE ROMANCE OF SELF–REALIZATION

> No man, unless he puts on the mask of fiction, can show his
> his real face or the will behind it. For this reason the only real
> biographies are the novels, and every novel if it is honest will
> be the autobiography of the author and biography of the
> reader.—William Dean Howells, *Years of My Youth*

The above citation, taken from William Dean Howells's autobiographical
fragment *Years of My Youth,* can suggest for us the realist's investment in
his fiction. It is only in this form, the form of a "mask," that the author
can realize himself, and this self-realization intimately involves the author
with the members of his reading public; for if this mask "is honest [it]
will be [both] the autobiography of the author and biography of the
reader." A good fiction, Howells suggests, realizes the common life of
its author and readers; and this common, or fictional, identity is also,
perhaps paradoxically, the individual, or real, identity of each of the
members of the community. Indeed, for Howells, in another passage
from *Years of My Youth* that describes the process of growing up, the
life of the individual and the lives of the members of the community he
inhabits are always mixed in a "self-portrait" where it seems "impossible"
to distinguish the figure of the individual from the community figures
that surround it:

> Through the whole time when a boy is becoming a man his auto-
> biography can scarcely be kept from becoming the record of his
> family and his world. He finds himself so constantly reflected in
> the personality of those about him, so blent with it, that any at-
> tempt to study himself as a separate personality is impossible. His
> environment has become his life, and his hope of a recognizable
> self-portrait must lie in his frank acceptance of the condition that
> he can make himself truly seen chiefly in what he remembers to
> have seen of his environment.[1]

Although Howells suggests in this passage that the only self-portrait is a portrait of many "blent" selves—a situation that makes it "impossible" for the individual "to study himself as a separate personality"—he still seems to retain a "hope" that "a recognizable self-portrait" of the individual personality might emerge from or through the community composite that seems to constitute the self. This hope of self-recognition, Howells tells us, lies in the power of memory, which, the preceding passage suggests, retains a distinct, or clearly individual, component even in the face of the communal portrait that Howells paints for us. But if memory here seems to retain a hope of self-recognition in which the individual, truly seeing himself, can paint his self-portrait, Howells, at the beginning of *Years of My Youth,* complicates this hope and the individuality it envisions by suggesting that the memory of the individual is itself a composite, a confluence of stories told to the "individual" by the members of the community he inhabits:

> It is hard to know the child's own earliest recollections from the things it has been told of itself by those with whom its life began. They remember for it the past which it afterward seems to remember for itself; the wavering outline of its nature is shadowed against the background of family, and from this it imagines an individual existence which has not yet begun. The events then have the quality of things dreamt, not lived, and they remain of that impalpable and elusive quality in all the after years.[2]

Although Howells here begins by telling us that it is "hard" to distinguish the individual memory from the process of community storytelling that informs it, he does not tell us that it is impossible. Perhaps, he seems to suggest, there is a hope for a truly individual self-portrait, if the memory will only work hard enough to distinguish itself from the varied stories that articulate it. But as the passage progresses, this hope seems to dissolve in Howells's portrait of the emerging individual whose own memory is only a semblance of individuality, masking the community stories that compose it. And from these stories that make it up, the self, seen now as a "wavering outline . . . shadowed against the background" of its community, "imagines for itself an individual existence which has not yet begun," which, indeed, never begins except as a shadowy story emerging from the shadows of stories that "have the quality of things dreamt, not lived, and remain of that . . . quality in all the after years."

In the passages from *Years of My Youth* that I have been considering, Howells's portrayal of self-realization, involved as it is with the shadowy, "impalpable" processes of dream, imagination, and storytelling, suggests the metaphors of moonlight that Hawthorne uses to characterize Romance and to distinguish it, though not without touches of irony, from the broad daylight of the Novel, or realistic tale, which "aim[s] at a very minute fidelity, not merely to the possible, but to the probable and ordinary course of man's experience." Whereas Hawthorne's description of the Novel, taken from his preface to *The House of the Seven Gables,* suggests that this mode of storytelling bears a representational relationship to something that is both distinct from and prior to it called "man's experience," Howells's description of self-realization suggests that this experience or reality is the process of storytelling itself, a process that, if less formal or self-conscious than literary art, comes no less under the heading of what we traditionally call "fiction," that category which implies the act of fabrication, or narration. And, indeed, if reality is nothing but a process of community storytelling, then reality, conceived of as a substantial realm prior to this process, is a romance, a figure in a story, a figure believed in with such force of conviction that it seems to take on that substantial priority that can tell each member of the community who he or she is.

Indeed, in his long essay "Criticism and Fiction," Howells, paraphrasing Carlyle, tells us that fiction "has, in the highest and widest sense, . . . made Reality its Romance" and that it is realism's job, as the highest form of fiction, to realize this Romance. Ironically and paradoxically, the form of this realization, as Howells describes it in his essay, takes the form of what is, perhaps, the most powerful American romance, a story of liberation told to us continually in the works of both our literary and political founding fathers, a story, as Howells phrases it, that speaks of an "escape from the paralysis of tradition" (an escape in Emersonian fashion from the oppressive stories imposed on us by the geniuses, or great men, of the past) and in place of this tradition articulates a self-reliance on "the simple, the natural, and the honest." This "simple honesty and instinctive truth . . . [would be] as unphilosophized as the light of common day"; it would be, Howells tells us, echoing Tom Paine, a real "common sense" through which "the mass of common men" "hitherto" "browbeat[en by the literary authorities, the critics] . . . into the self-distrust that ends in sophistication" could "apply their own simplicity, naturalness, and honesty to the appreciation of the beautiful."[3]

In "Criticism and Fiction," Howells's romance of realism—his desire to escape from the shadows of tradition into the light of a community without memory where authentic self-trust is possible—is interwoven with another story of escape, that of a liberation from the "personal." In this story, putting on the mask of fiction, in its form as realism, allows the individual author to lose one self while he realizes another, a new self that is not isolated, like his former, from the community of common men it wants to speak to, but is a part of this community so that the sense this self speaks is the common sense of the members of this community. In a paradoxical way—a paradox that is part and parcel of the American dream—the self that the mask of fiction realizes finds its individuality by losing it in the mass of common men. For Howells, this journey toward the frontier of realism—this migration from the personal to the personality of the "impersonal" (a personality he labels "scientific" and "objective") —entails a process of growing up in which the realist must leave behind him vestiges of his former self, vestiges that, in "Criticism and Fiction," Howells figures in terms of the childish, the primitive (or savage), and the feminine. The country of realism, Howells suggests, will be a land purged of infants, Indians, and women (at least those women who have not shed that savagely personal skin, the "feminine"); it will be a land populated entirely by grown men.

For Howells, at certain moments in his work, the type of these grown men, the hero of his romance of realism, is the businessman, one of the great, if not the greatest of, heroes in the romance that nineteenth- and twentieth-century America tells itself for both its edification and enjoyment. But for Howells, the literary artist, who, he tells us in "Criticism and Fiction," "has always something feminine in him, which tempts him to coquet with the reader,"[4] the businessman is an equivocal figure, looked up to and down at simultaneously. This double vision comes into play in Howells' essay "The Man of Letters as a Man of Business," where the literary artist finds himself neither truly a businessman nor a working-man, but "in a transition state"[5] between the two, without a distinct social identity to inhabit. And this vision also structures Howells's novel *A Hazard of New Fortunes,* a novel concerning the venture of a new literary magazine, *Every Other Week,* a magazine run by men—businessmen and artists (both graphic and literary)—but whose goal is to articulate the "*ewig Weibliche*" (the eternally feminine) for a largely female audience. It is to this novel, one in which art and business, the feminine and the masculine, and romance and realism are intimately involved with each other in the political life of late-nineteenth-century America, that I want to turn now; for it is in this particular mask of Howells that the problem of self-portraiture that I have been discussing appears.

The trouble with all these talented girls is that they're *all* woman. If they weren't, there wouldn't be much chance for the men, Beaton. But we've got Providence on our own side from the start. I'm able to watch all their inspirations with perfect composure. I know just how soon it's going to end in nervous break-down. Somebody ought to marry them all and put them out of their misery.—William Dean Howells, *A Hazard of New Fortunes*

The scene in *A Hazard of New Fortunes*[6] that I use as a frame for the following discussion takes place early in the action of the novel in the Leighton's New York apartment. Alma and her mother are alone, waiting for prospective boarders, whom they need in order to survive economically in the city, where they have recently arrived, after the death of Alma's father, from their home in the village of St. Barnaby. Mrs. Leighton is sewing; her daughter is sketching (the two have come to New York so that Alma can pursue her art), and "the room [is] pinned about with other sketches, which show . . . with fantastic indistinctness in the shaded gas-light" (107). In terms of furthering the action of the novel, Howells employs this scene to introduce us to and give us the history of, in addition to Alma, who will be the illustrator of the first cover of *Every Other Week,* another of the novel's main characters, Angus Beaton, who will be the magazine's art editor. Like Alma, he is an artist (he is a writer as well); in fact, the two of them are the only working artists (graphic or literary) that appear among the major characters in the novel. Basil March, the editor of *Every Other Week* and the character who would appear to be the logical choice for the figure of Howells in the text, never gets around to writing at all but can only formulate projects that he continually postpones to pursue his editorial work. And, indeed, in Alma's father, who is dead at the time of the novel and whose character we learn about from the narrator, we find some correspondences with Howells's own father as he portrays him in *Years of My Youth:* a man of excessive cheerfulness with a poor business sense, "one of those men [Alma's father] of whom the country people say when he is gone that the woman gets along better without him" (104). And so although at the beginning of the scene that I am narrating we find Mrs. Leighton worrying, in what may appear to be a stereotypically feminine way, about the absence of a man in the house, we find shortly that she was and is more capable of managing things than her husband was or would have been.

If Alma and Howells share a father, their creative talents do not come from the male. In Alma's case, although we are told of her father that "it was not from him that his daughter got her talent" (104), we do not know the origin of her art. But in *Years of My Youth* Howells remarks on the origin of his: "My great-grandfather was apparently an excellent business man, but I am afraid I must own (reluctantly, with my Celtic prejudice) that literature, or the love of it, came into our family with the English girl whom he married in London."[7] The tone of the preceding passage is light enough, almost too light to comment on. There seems to be no particular masculine bias (or corresponding fear of femininity), only a casual "Celtic prejudice," as if Howells's concern in tracing his talent had to do with race (and even then only in a light-hearted way), not sex. But in a different context, narrated by Kenneth Lynn, who quotes in part Howells himself, both the tone of voice and the focus of the concern change:

> For years, Howells had lived in the shadow of the knowledge that the writer in post-Civil War America was no longer considered "a type of greatness" . . . but instead was derided as "a kind of mental and moral woman, to whom a real man, a business man, could have nothing to say after the primary politenesses." Tolstoy, however, now awakened in the soul of a writer who had been ashamed of the womanish role in which American society had cast its artists "the will to be a man."[8]

At the end of *A Hazard of New Fortunes,* it is Alma who will express this "will to be a man": "I shall pick and choose, as a man does; I won't merely be picked and chosen" (477), she says. Her decision is a wish to pursue her own art "at first hand" (476)—not to live vicariously through Beaton's—to articulate herself rather than merely be articulated by someone else. And, certainly, it is a wish that we can appreciate, without irony, within the social, or political, context that Howells's novel both incorporates and suggests, a context within which to be a man is to be empowered, relative to woman, with much greater means of self-realization. But it is also a decision, a wish, that comes, with some irony, at the end of a novel where no one has been able to articulate simply himself or herself—to control the terms of his or her ongoing story—and where we notice that the men, who, as a sex, figure Alma's ideal of activity, are particularly dependent on the women to tell them stories in which they appear capable of independent action.

As a way to beginning to understand these relationships of dependency within the context of community storytelling and its relation to self-realization, I want to focus on a comment of Howells's narrator, made late in *A Hazard of New Fortunes,* which, though it applies immediately to the relationship of Madison Woodburn (who, along with her father, the very type of the old Southern Colonel, rooms and boards with the Leightons) and Fulkerson (the inventor and promotional genius of *Every Other Week*), I want to explore (before returning to its specific context) as a statement that can tell us something central about the larger community of relationships that make up Howells's novel. "She did not idealize him," the narrator tells us, "but in the highest effect she realized him" (381). The preceding citation raises a question that concerns my interest in a romance of self-realization: What are the meanings of the terms *idealize* and *realize* within the context of Howells's novel? And as an elaboration of this question, are the two terms opposed, as the syntax of the citation suggests, or do they have a more intimate relationship?

The larger context of the citation within the novel is a dispute between Basil March and Jacob Dryfoos, a self-made millionaire and the financial backer of *Every Other Week.* The dispute (the specific details of which we will return to) is over Berthold Lindau, Civil War hero, socialist revolutionary, and March's boyhood intellectual mentor, whom March meets unexpectedly in New York after years of separation. Lindau is poor and living with the poor (a choice dictated by his political principles); and, at Fulkerson's suggestion, March offers him work as a translator for *Every Other Week,* which he accepts, unconscious that the source of his pay is one of the "aristocracy of railroad wreckers and stock gamblers and mine-slave drivers and mill-serf owners" (the words are Lindau's [193]), against whom his whole life is an investment. At a "man's dinner" (325) held to celebrate the initial success of *Every Other Week,* Lindau and Dryfoos finally come face to face and not even Fulkerson—who has been so successful at mediating the possible conflicts between the socially and intellectually heterogeneous members of the magazine and organizing what March calls a "perfect menagerie" (149) and thinks of as "a fantastic fiction of sleep" (195) into the semblance of a community, however tenuous—can prevent the violence that this confrontation compels: "The dinner went on from course to course with barbaric profusion, and from time to time Fulkerson tried to bring the talk back to *Every Other Week.* But perhaps because that was only the ostensible and not the real object of the dinner, which was to bring a number of men together under Dryfoos' roof, and make them the witnesses of his splendor, make them feel the power of his wealth, Fulkerson's attempts failed" (337).

What Fulkerson fails to do is to control the terms of the discourse at the dinner, planned so carefully by him to celebrate his invention, *Every Other Week.* And, we should note (before I take up the specific confrontation between Dryfoos and Lindau, and Dryfoos and March) that if this celebration, as the narrator suggests, is only the "ostensible" "object" of the dinner, then its "real" object, the celebration of "the power of [Dryfoos's] wealth," is not simply opposed to its apparent one, not only because it is Dryfoos's wealth that realizes *Every Other Week,* but also because Fulkerson identifies himself and his project so closely with Dryfoos. As March perceives, Dryfoos is "Fulkerson's fetich [sic]" (214); and throughout the novel we see Fulkerson's obsessive delight in verbally "painting the character" (214) of his "angel," a portrait, a biography, that is also a self-portrait, an autobiography, inasmuch as the portrait that Fulkerson paints of an individual named Jacob Dryfoos is representative, "proof of the versatility of the American mind, and of the grandeur of institutions and opportunities that let every man grow to his full size, so that any man in America could run the concern if necessary" (215).

If Fulkerson's portrait of Dryfoos as Everyman (and thereby a portrait of Fulkerson, among others, as well) seems idealized—a businessman's "Song of Myself" (and Fulkerson himself is "aware of painting the character too vividly" [214])—we should note that the language of the painting is couched not in terms of the ideal, but of the real. In Fulkerson's obsessed imagination, Dryfoos, far from being the representative of messianic possibility, is pictured in a term that suggests the empirical and practical: he is "proof," not of a potential America but of an apparently actual one, populated by men who, nurtured by "the grandeur of institutions and opportunities," have realized their "full size" and "could run the concern if necessary." The only suggestion of the virtual in Fulkerson's portrait is the conditional "could," and it is a condition grounded in the present indicative mood of the rest of the passage and in the metaphors of business ("run the concern") and science ("proof") that forge Fulkerson's fetish into a certain shape for him, the shape of an idolized, wealth-producing technology. "I believe in Moffitt" ([86], Dryfoos's midwest hometown and the site of his initial rise to wealth as a natural gas magnate), Fulkerson exclaims to March early in the novel, when he is indirectly introducing his friend and the reader to Dryfoos by narrating the millionaire's history. And, as the notions of belief and fetishism suggest, this representative history has, for Fulkerson, a strong component of the sacred in it.

As I have been suggesting, one of the ways in which we can understand the relationship of Fulkerson to Dryfoos, a way the novel emphasizes in its introduction of the millionaire *through* the narrative of the advertising man, is that of author, or painter, to subject.[9] Fulkerson is the author of a story we could title "The Biography of Jacob Dryfoos, Portrait of the Self-Made Man." And this biography, through its representative status, is also the autobiography, the self-portrait, not only of Fulkerson, but of all of the figures that, directly or indirectly composing the community of *Every Other Week,* have hazarded their fortunes, their money, and/or their fates, in an attempt to realize themselves (although, as we will see shortly, in the case of Lindau, it is not a story that all of them accept as representative). Further, this history and the selves it articulates, a history we have seen Basil March conceive of as "a fantastic fiction of sleep," cannot be separated from a particular romance: the romance "of the grandeur of institutions and opportunites that let *every man* grow to his full size so that *any man* in America could run the concern if necessary." This romance, we recognize, is the sacred American romance of equal opportunity

(at least for white men, and here we should note the narrator's repetitive
and exclusive use of the term *man*) in which it is revealed that all men are
equal, for "every man" is "any man" and any man is capable of running
the concern. "There seems to be some solvent in New York life," Howells's
narrator tells us, "that reduces all men to a common level, that touches
everybody with its potent magic and brings to the surface the deeply underlying nobody" (243). This romance of democratic self-realization, then,
figured in this case by the movement of the characters from their original
homes to the melting pot of New York, this rising of the solvent self "to
the surface," which is at once a fall, a reduction of the self "to a common
level," is a story of the dissolution of the self "in the deeply underlying
nobody" that the fluid self becomes as it enters the mainstream of American life. In articulating this movement of democratic self-realization, the
term *solvent* is particularly useful, for in its punning capacity it suggests at
once the independence of financial integrity and the dissolution of the
metaphysical integrity of identity, as if the rise to the former in American
life automatically sets in motion the effects of the latter.

As the preceding citation suggests, self-solvency in America is marked
by a movement from the personal to the impersonal, from the appearance
of being somebody (on the surface) to the realization that, deep down,
one is "nobody." When formulating his "scheme of a banquet to celebrate
the intitial success of *Every Other Week*," Fulkerson (through the narrator), in words that mix the "prophetic and historic" (without apparently distinguishing between the two), describes the magazine as a "new
departure," "something in literature as radical as the American Revolution
in politics: it was the idea of self-government in the Arts; and it was this
idea that had never yet been fully developed in regard to it" (213). Fulkerson's revolutionary idea of self-government (which is at once an
actuality *for him*) is also structured by the movement of the personal to
the impersonal, of the somebody to "the deeply underlying nobody";
and we can see this structure operating in a scene where Fulkerson is
explaining its mechanism to Beaton:

> I don't want you to work the old established racket—the reputa-
> tions. . . . But my idea is to deal with the volunteer material. Look
> at the way the periodicals are carried on now! Names! names!
> names! In a country that's just boiling over with literary and artistic
> ability of every kind the new fellows have no chance. The editors all
> engage their material. I don't believe there are fifty volunteer contri-
> butions printed in a year in all the New York magazines. It's all
> wrong; it's suicidal. *Every Other Week* is going back to the good old
> anonymous system, the only fair system. It's worked well in litera-
> ture, and it will work well in art. (123)

In language that, without batting an eye, mixes the rhetoric of revolutionary idealism with that of shrewd business practice[10] the preceding passage suggests that Fulkerson's conception of self-government is one in which the traditional self, an individual, a somebody distinguished by a name, will be obliterated and replaced by "the good old anonymous system, the only fair system," in which individual names will be suppressed and replaced by a collective, quite matter-of-fact one, *Every Other Week.* If the establishment system of representing the individual through the publication of names is "suicidal," we can also see "the good old anonymous system, the only fair system," as "suicidal" in its own way; for if it allows the "new fellows" a "chance" at self-expression, it simultaneously complicates the self expressed by rendering it individually nameless in a collective name, that "fantastic fiction of sleep" entitled *Every Other Week.* Like its namesake, the American Revolution, Fulkerson's "good old anonymous system, the only fair system," is not without its paradoxes and ironies. It is the new that, as it proclaims its radical break from the old, curiously repeats its ancestry, if in mutated form; it is the fair that, while proclaiming the equality of everybody, suggests that some, in this case the system's owner, Dryfoos, are more equal than others (that "we the people," the putative communal author of the text that generates the historic and prophetic form of "our" existence, does not include all the people in the uniform way its articulation suggests); and it is a self whose moment of self-expression is both constituted by and wrested from an enduring moment of self-dissolution in communal forms, a self that, in his journals of 1834, Emerson, in a tone that both delights in and despairs over his own violently heterogeneous constitution, calls a "Congress of nations."[11]

The term *congress,* within the context of Fulkerson's evocation of the American Revolution to characterize his magazine, is a useful one for helping us understand the community of *Every Other Week,* because the term does not simply suggest a unity, but, through one of its "obsolete" definitions—"an encounter in opposition or combat" (OED)—a precarious unity that is constituted as a conflict of heterogeneous elements, a conflict hopefully contained, as the U.S. Constitution hopes to contain the conflicting forces in American life, institutionalizing the boundaries of the conflict in a system of "checks" and "balances," and as Fulkerson hopes to contain the conflict of his own congress, *Every Other Week,* by limiting the boundaries of the talk at dinner. But, as already noted, Fulkerson fails to control the terms of his "fantastic fiction of sleep," finding that he is not the sole author of this fiction, but that he must share its authorship with the figures of the fiction (thereby becoming a figure in the fiction himself).

Immediately, the disruption of Fulkerson's authority comes when the table talk turns to politics, triggering Dryfoos's and Lindau's mutually exclusive visions of the world. Although there is no official break between the two at the table, the dinner to celebrate Fulkerson's "American Revolution" ends in an alienated state; and the following day, Dryfoos, attempting to assert his singular authority as owner of the magazine, orders March to fire Lindau, apparently for his political views.[12] March refuses Dryfoos's authority in the matter, refuses, that is, to become "an agent to punish [Lindau] for his opinions" (357). "I don't know you, in such a matter as this," March tells the owner. "My arrangements as editor of *Every Other Week* were made with Mr. Fulkerson. I have always listened to any suggestion he has had to make" (348).

With these words, March promulgates his own declaration of independence from Dryfoos's authority; but it is a declaration that, rather than clearly conferring the authority on March, seems ambiguously to divide it between March and Fulkerson, whom March nominates in the last lines of his declaration as his advisor, without declaring whether he will take the advice or not (as these lines tell us, he will only listen to Fulkerson's suggestions). But when Fulkerson enters the offices of *Every Other Week,* the ambiguous division of authority inherent in March's declaration becomes momentarily clarified: "I leave this matter with you," March tells Fulkerson. "What do you wish done about Lindau?" Finding himself the figure of authority in March's drama, Fulkerson decides to fire Lindau. But March immediately qualifies the authority of this decision with a question: "If I decline to let him drop . . . what will you do?" (351).

Confronted with the force of this question, which insists that he decide between his loyalties to March and Dryfoos, Fulkerson is helpless to take a position, weakly oscillating between the opposing sides. This ambivalence angers March, who, momentarily assuming full authority for himself, tells Fulkerson: "When you bring me [Dryfoos's] apologies or come to say that, having failed to make him understand they were necessary, you are prepared to stand by me, I will come back to this desk" (352).

Their interview ended, with March's final words suggesting that he and Fulkerson may never understand each other (352), March returns home, hoping that the sympathy of his wife, Isabel, will support the authority he has declared. But this sympathy is not immediately forthcoming. Rather, Mrs. March is appalled at her husband's action because it threatens the livelihood of the family. Assuming March's consciousness, the narrator tells us that Isabel's mind, for the moment, is solely on the domestic situation, a situation from which March momentarily finds himself excluded: "He had allowed for trouble, but trouble on *his* account: a sympathy that might burden and embarrass him; but he had not dreamt of this merely domestic, this petty, this sordid view of their potential calamity, which left him wholly out of the question, and embraced only what was most crushing and desolating in the prospect. He could not bear it. He caught up his hat again, and with some hope that his wife would try to keep him, rushed out of the house" (355).

As the preceding citation suggests, March's sense of himself as an independent actor is dependent on his wife's sympathetic "view" of him; when this sympathetic prospect is absent, March seems almost not to exist. Without his wife's sympathetic vision, March's authoritative sense of himself as a *man* of independent, moral action seems gone. After leaving the house, he "wander[s] aimlessly" through the morning, has lunch, and returning home feels "quite willing to talk [the matter of Lindau] over" with Fulkerson, to compromise the authority he had at first given to and then taken back from his friend (355). When he enters the house, however, he is not met by the woman he "left weeping in the morning" but by that woman transformed into "another":

"I told the children," she said, in smiling explanation of his absence from lunch, "that perhaps you were detained by business. I didn't know but you had gone back to the office."

"Did you think I would go back there, Isabel?" asked March, with a haggard look. "Well, if you say so, I will go back, and do what Dryfoos ordered me to do. I'm sufficiently cowed between him and you, I can assure you."

"Nonsense," she said, "I approve of everything you did. But sit down, now, and don't keep walking that way, and let me see if I understand it perfectly. Of course I had to have my say out." (356)

What we witness in this brief conversation are two acts, each of which is dependent on the other. First there is a declaration of defeat by March—a defeat marked by his declared dependence on his wife and the owner of *Every Other Week* (both of whom for a moment constitute an authority that is united against March through being in league with his failed independence). Second, there is the immediate restoration of March's independence, as his wife shifts her allegiance from owner to employee, granting her husband a new-found authority in the approval of her sympathetic gaze, an authority that allows them both to dream of their own independence day:

They began to consider their ways and means, and how and where they should live, in view of March's severance of his relations with *Every Other Week*. They had not saved anything from the first year's salary; they had only prepared to save; and they had nothing solid but their two thousand to count upon. But they built a future in

which they easily lived on that and on what March earned with his
pen. He became a free lance, and fought in whatever cause he
thought just; he had no ties, no chains. They went back to Boston
with the heroic will to do what was most distasteful; they would
have returned to their own house if they had not rented it again; but
at any rate Mrs. March helped out by taking boarders, or perhaps
only letting rooms to lodgers. They had some hard struggles, but
they succeeded. (358-59)

Before turning to its apparent sentimental idealism, what we might
note first about this dream, which in relation to the March's actual
situation, we could indeed call "a fantastic fiction of sleep," coauthored
by the Marches, is its traditional drift, in relation to the social roles of
husband and wife it creates; for in it March, with his heroic and independent will, appears as the model of nineteenth-century manliness,
while his wife appears as a model of the century's womanliness, or self-
effacement, helping out in the shadow of the background. That Howells
places this dream in ironic juxtaposition to the March's actual situation
seems apparent. But if the dream seems simply a sentimental fiction,
what we should note is that it compels action; for while the Marches are
basking in the aura of the dream, which seems to have a really rejuvenat-
ing effect on them, Fulkerson enters the scene, conveying Dryfoos's
apologies and relieving March of the responsibility of firing Lindau, a
responsibility Fulkerson now assumes. Now, however, March, committed
to his dream of independence, dismisses the apology as a "minor matter"
and says he "can't consent to Lindau's dismissal" (360).

March's dream of independence, then, leads to action, which in turn
threatens to compel Fulkerson to choose between March and Dryfoos.
And trying again to avoid such a choice, Fulkerson finally seeks aid
from Madison Woodburn, hoping her father can intervene with Dryfoos
and stop his firing of Lindau. Before seeking out the Colonel, however,
the two of them have a conversation that ultimately compels Fulkerson
to choose March over Dryfoos; and although this choice is finally ironic
—because during the time that Fulkerson is seeking Colonel Woodburn's
help, Lindau visits March, returns the money he earned from his trans-
lations, and withdraws from *Every Other Week*—it is a choice, a realization that, as we will see now, is structured by a particular idealization:

"I'm so glad to get a chance to speak to you alone," he said at
once; and while she waited for the next word he made a pause, and
then said, desperately, "I want you to help me; and if you can't
help me, there's no help for me."

"Mah goodness," she said, "is the case so bad as that? What in the woald is the trouble?"

"Yes, it's a bad case," said Fulkerson. "I want your father to help me."

"Oh, Ah thoat you said *me*!"

"Yes; I want you to help me with your father. I suppose I ought to go to him at once, but I'm a little afraid of him."

"And you awe not afraid of *me*? Ah don't think that's very flattering, Mr. Fulkerson. You ought to think Ah'm twahce as awful as Papa."

"Oh, I do! You see, I'm quite paralyzed before you, and so I don't feel anything."

"Well, it's a pretty lahvely kyand of paralysis. But—go on."

"I will—I will. If I can only begin."

"Pohaps Ah maght begin fo' you."

"No, you can't. Lord knows, I'd like to let you. Well, it's like this."

Fulkerson made a clutch at his hair, and then, after another hesitation, he abruptly laid the whole affair before her. He did not think it necessary to state the exact nature of the offence [*sic*] Lindau had given Dryfoos, for he doubted if she could grasp it, and he was profuse of his excuses for troubling her with the matter, and of wonder at himself for having done so. In the rapture of his concern at having made a fool of himself, he forgot why he had told her; but she seemed to like having been confided in, and she said, "Well, Ah don't see what you can do with you' ahdeals of friendship, except stand bah Mr. Mawch."

"My ideals of friendship? What do you mean?"

"Oh, don't you suppose we know? Mr. Beaton said you we' a pofect Bahyard in friendship, and you would sacrifice anything to it."

"Is that so?" said Fulkerson, thinking how easily he could sacrifice Lindau in this case. He had never supposed before that he was so chivalrous in such matters, but he now began to see it in that light, and he wondered that he could ever have entertained for a moment the idea of throwing March over. (368–69)

After leaving the Marches' and before arriving at the Leightons' to carry on the preceding conversation with Miss Woodburn, Fulkerson went to Maroni's, a restaurant frequented by himself, Beaton, and Lindau, "not without the hope, vague and indefinite as it might be" (364) of finding Lindau there and convincing him either to apologize to Dryfoos or to withdraw from *Every Other Week* for March's sake. Instead, he found Beaton, who, after listening to his predicament of choice, suggested his letting March go as a solution to it:

"Ah, I couldn't," said Fulkerson. "I got him to break-up in Boston and come here; I like him; nobody else could get the hang of the thing like he has; he's—a friend." Fulkerson said this with the nearest approach he could make to seriousness, which was a kind of unhappiness.

Beaton shrugged. "Oh, if you can afford to have ideals, I congratulate you. They're too expensive for *me*. Then, suppose you get rid of Dryfoos?" (366)

Fulkerson, of course, does not want to let go of either his "friend" or his "angel," and it is then that Beaton suggests Colonel Woodburn as an intermediary between the advertising man and the millionaire, which leads to the conversation between Fulkerson and Madison Woodburn cited previously. What I want to note now is that while Beaton, no doubt with a good deal of irony, suggests to Fulkerson that he (Fulkerson) has "ideals of friendship," Fulkerson does not appear to consider this suggestion seriously until it is made by Miss Woodburn (who seems to translate Beaton's suggestion without any intentional irony), to whom he is strongly attracted and whom he will marry at the novel's end. As soon as she begins to conceive Fulkerson in such "chivalrous" terms, he begins "to see [himself] in that light, and he wonder[s] that he could ever have entertained for a moment the idea of throwing March over." Listening to Madison Woodburn's description of him as a man with "ideals of friendship," Fulkerson envisions a portrait of himself as the chivalrous hero of a romance of friendship, a romance, however, that appears quite real to him; for thinking of himself in the light of Miss Woodburn's terms, Fulkerson sees that other self that thought "of throwing March over" for Dryfoos as an object of "wonder," almost as if the other Fulkerson is too fantastic a figure to entertain.

Directly following the conversation in which Fulkerson realizes that he has "ideals of friendship," he and Madison Woodburn approach the Colonel to sound him out on the possibility of his acting as an intermediary between Fulkerson and Dryfoos. The Colonel agrees to take the part; but before performing it, he insists on his "right . . . to ask [Fulkerson] what [his] course will be in the event of [a] failure" (372) to convince Dryfoos not to fire Lindau. Fulkerson is taken aback by the question, for he has hoped he would never have to answer it. But after a brief dialogue with the Colonel, in which the advertising man tries to evade the question without revealing his attempted evasion, he is compelled finally to answer it, immediately because of the persistence of Colonel Woodburn:

Fulkerson drew a long breath, and took his courage in both hands. "There can't be any choice for me in such a case. I'm for March, every time."

The Colonel seized his hand, and Miss Woodburn said, "If there had been any choice fo' you in such a case, I should never have let Papa sti' a step with you." (373)

It is the scene I have been narrating, in which Fulkerson first realizes that he has "ideals of friendship" and then, as the preceding citation demonstrates, realizes these "ideals," that provides the context for the previously cited narrator's remark: "She did not idealize him, but in the highest effect she realized him" The remark appears to confer on Madison Woodburn the authority that we traditionally associate with authorship; for it envisions her as the creator of the Fulkerson that we have just witnessed actualizing his ideals. Indeed, within her family circle, which now includes, in addition to her father, a prospective husband, Howells's narrator seems to give her absolute authority; for not only does she realize Fulkerson, but she performs this function in a significant way for the Colonel as well, who, we are told, "lea[ves] action of all kinds of his daughter" (381), thus allowing her to fulfill him in an arena where identity is always at stake. If, however, Miss Woodburn appears as the author of the family drama that is now taking our attention, the authority that the narrator confers on her must be seen as severely compromised; for it is an authority that is dependent on her giving up authority to the male figures she seems to create; that is, it is an authority based on her appearing to them as the figure of what they imagine a woman should be. If Madison Woodburn realizes Fulkerson *through idealizing him* (for that is indeed the process that their interaction suggests), then this ideally realized (realized, that is, "in the highest effect"), or really idealized, Fulkerson is also the author of a corresponding version of Miss Woodburn. Indeed, he cannot become such an author until he has given up his authority—a hypothesized male independence—to her: " 'Well, men *awe* splendid,' sigh[s] " Miss Woodburn (375), in an apparently unironic and awe-filled response to March's "decision" to stand by Lindau and Fulkerson's "decision" to stand by March, a response that, hopefully, the reader can only take as an ironic abdication, a repression, of Madison Woodburn's authorship of Fulkerson's decision, and, indirectly, of Isabel's of her husband's. This abdication is followed by an exchange, a declaration of dependence, where man and woman put each other in his and her place:

"Oh, they're not so much better than women," said Fulkerson, with a nervous jocosity. "I guess March would have backed down if it hadn't been for his wife. She was as hot as pepper about it, and you could see that she would have sacrificed all her husband's relations sooner than let him back down an inch from the stand he had taken. It's pretty easy for a man to stick to a principle if

he has a woman to stand by him. But when you come to play it
alone—"

"Mr. Fulkerson," said the girl, solemnly, "*Ah* will stand bah you
in this, if all the woald tones against you." The tears came into her
eyes, and she put out her hand to him. (375)

Miss Woodburn, as the preceding exchange shows, also has her ideals
of friendship: she "will stand bah" Mr. Fulkerson. And, as a sign of
these ideals, she offers him her hand, which he takes, catching it "to his
breast . . . grappling it tight there, and drawing her to him" (375). Fulkerson, then, turns a moment of apparently supportive friendship into one
of sexual conquest. His sudden gesture puts Miss Woodburn off: "'You
don't *believe,*' she said hoarsely, 'that I meant *that?*'" (375). But after
this denial of intent by way of what appears as a kind of rhetorical question, which Fulkerson, of course, playing the gentleman now, answers
negatively, Madison Woodburn submits to the conquest. Their engagement
is implicit; and in the course of what follows, it is formalized and the
couple marries.

What begins, then, as a scene in which Fulkerson first realizes he has
ideals of friendship and subsequently realizes these ideals, ends as a scene
in which Madison Woodburn first realizes she has ideals of friendship and
next realizes these ideals in the form of marriage. What the reader may
realize is that the scene of Fulkerson's decision to stand by March is a
romance (a scene of courtship, or seduction). Further, it is a romance of
self-realization in which, to use Hawthorne's definition of romance, the
Real and the Ideal "meet . . . and each imbue[s] itself with the nature of
the other."[13] For in this scene, under the compulsion of an authority that
both Madison Woodburn and Fulkerson represent (not singly, but rather
as a couple, a communal unit), but that neither controls, the two lovers
find their places in an "ideal" nineteenth-century story, the story of the
"good" marriage that we have seen Basil and Isabel March both imagining
and living, in which the wife, in order to stand by the husband, must stand
behind him, a dim figure blending with the shadowy background of his
self-portrait, a portrait she paints only by painting herself into the background. "Well, men *awe* splendid," sighs Miss Woodburn, striking (from a
particular male perspective) what might appear as an ideal feminine pose,
a pose, however, that within the structure of Howells's novel (his communal portrait) can be seen as a parody both of itself and the men it appears to idealize. "Oh, they're not so much better than women," replies
Fulkerson, "with a nervous jocosity." Nervous, perhaps, because while
this figure of the advertising man retains an ironic modicum of superiority
for his sex (ironic from the reader's perspective, at least), he may realize,
however dim and distant the realization, the parody that Madison Wood-

burn's words implicate this sex in and the sexual politics that are implicit in the parody. Whereas Hawthorne's definition of romance might suggest that the real and the ideal (Hawthorne terms them the "Actual" and the "Imaginary") are distinct essences, Howells's novel suggests that they are figures in a story, a story about the sexual politics of the real and the ideal in nineteenth-century America, which for as long as the community believes the story, tells it, that is, in its very actions, is nineteenth-century America as well.

The only way to break out of this story of the good marriage (neither into a reality nor an ideality but into another story, I would say), Fulkerson inadvertently suggests, is "to play it alone." Near the end of the novel, in a scene where Beaton is posing for a sketch of Alma's, he says to her: "Well, if there were something you wished me to be, I could be it" (385). The moment, for Beaton, is one of desperate courting (desperate because he is realizing that Alma does not want to "play it" with him). Indeed, Alma is not only deciding not to play it with Beaton, but to "play it [entirely] alone." To put this decision in terms of figures that I have been suggesting are crucial to Howells's text, Alma is realizing, as she sketches Beaton, that she would rather paint her own portrait; that she does not see her role as wishing Beaton, or any man for that matter, into realization. At the end of the novel, Basil March defends Alma's decision "to play it alone" against his wife's championing of marriage over career for women, and in his defense he envisions a romance of self-realization based not on marriage but on a kind of divorce: "Why shouldn't we rejoice as much at a non-marriage as a marriage? . . . I believe that this popular demand for the matrimony of others comes from our novel-reading. . . . By-and-by some fellow will wake up and see that a first-class story can be written from the anti-marriage point of view; and he'll begin with an engaged couple, and devote his novel to *dis*engaging them, and rendering them separately happy ever after in the dénoûement" (479). In the preceding citation, Basil March suggests for us that stories compel the forms of a community, rather than arising as the representations of prior, actual forms, and thus that if the community wants to change its forms this change can only come about through a process of storytelling. Whereas Basil March sees the storytelling authority that generates the forms of the community (in this case in the particular forms of marriage or "anti-marriage") in the form of the novel, authored by a single individual, what I have been trying to suggest is that *A Hazard of New Fortunes,* a story told from both the "antimarriage" and the marriage point of view, suggests this storytelling authority, not as a single individual, but as a process, a complex of forces operating *between* what the conscious community terms "individuals" but what might be termed, if an unconscious perspective were possible, "effects" of the process.

What I want to do now, in the terms of Howells's novel, is to suggest one name for this storytelling process, the *"ewig Weibliche,"* or "eternally feminine," a name that is itself a story (and one that we should be careful not to identify with a single sex[14]); for it is the *"ewig Weibliche"* that, as I have mentioned, gives dramatic shape to that male-dominated magazine *Every Other Week.* In a conversation among March, Beaton, and Fulkerson concerning the relationship between text and illustrations for the magazine, Fulkerson explains what he means by the *"ewig Weibliche"*:

> What we want to do is to work the *ewig Weibliche* in this concern. We want to make a magazine that will go for the women's fancy every time. I don't mean with recipes for cooking and fashions and personal gossip about authors and society, but real high-tone literature, that will show women triumphing in all the stories, or else suffering tremendously. We've got to recognize that women form three-fourths of the reading public in this country, and go for their tastes and their sensibilities and their sex-piety along the whole line. They do like to think that women can do things better than men; and if we can let it leak out and get around in the papers that the managers of *Every Other Week* couldn't stir a peg in the line of the illustration they wanted till they got a lot of God-gifted girls to help them, it'll make the fortune of the thing. See? (141)

The *"ewig Weibliche,"* which "will go for the woman's fancy every time," seems a repetition of the Marches' sentimental dream of independence or of Fulkerson's triumph over Miss Woodburn ("men *awe* splendid"), with the difference that in Fulkerson's advertising dream it is woman who is placed in the heroic role. And whether this role is one of "triumphing" or "suffering tremendously," it will enable women "to think that [they] can do things better than men." Immediately, Fulkerson is promulgating the dream for business purposes (catering to what he believes are the dreams of his female audience) and seems to consider it no more than a fiction of "high-tone literature." But if it is a fiction, it is also a fact within the context of Howells's novel, where the *"ewig Weibliche"* is continually triumphing over the men—and over the women. For their momentary triumph, as I have been suggesting, is always the moment of their self-effacement, of their acting "eternally feminine" (except in the crucial case of Alma), of their telling stories to the men in which the men appear as splendidly independent and the women return to a quietly supportive domesticity, waiting for their heroes to come home.

In Howells's novel and his life, figures of home and independence are intimately linked both to each other and to the problem of man and woman that we have been discussing. Except for Fulkerson, who, although we learn that he comes from somewhere in the West, seems to have no original home, all of the principal figures on whom I have focused in the novel have, quite self-consciously, left a home for New York in order to seek a form of independence. And having left home, some of them exhibit strong signs of homesickness. Jacob Dryfoos and his wife, Elizabeth, suffering repeated social and personal reversals in New York, long for Moffitt, where they remember having a recognizable place (ironically, the novel ends with their leaving for Europe). Colonel Woodburn dreams continually of an ante-bellum South, an ideal patriarchal society he remembers as being free of the commercialism he detests (although for his daughter "no such South . . . had ever existed" and, in a way like Fulkerson, "she took the world as she found it, and made the best of it" [381]). Lindau is homesick for an America of human promise, which he seems to remember, but no longer finds. "Dere *iss* no Ameriga anymore!" (318), he tells March and Fulkerson. Basil and Isabel March, at the very moment of their dream of independence, imagine a return to Boston (her original and his adopted home—he, like Fulkerson, has come from the West); and their search, at the beginning of the novel, for what Isabel conceives of as the "ideal flat," can represent an attempt to realize an ideal home-away-from-home. Even Beaton exhibits a kind of homesickness, in his constant "shame" (however spurious this shame may seem) over his neglect of his father. Only Alma seems purposefully glad to be away from home, where she could never realize her artistic ambitions, her will to be a man.

In *Years of My Youth* Howells says of his mother: "She was not only the centre [sic] of home to me; she was home itself, and in the years before I made a home of my own, absence from her was the homesickness, or the fear of it, which was always haunting me." Homesickness here is figured as a longing for the mother—a longing, we could say, to "inhabit," or "live in," her—and homelessness is an exteriority to her, a being outside her. Howells's mother, we learn, also had had this homesickness as a child (she appears as the only source of the disease in the book) and was unable to cure it by establishing her own home as an adult. So, for what seemed like numerous times to her son, the mother was compelled to take "her homesick visits Up-the-River" to her childhood home. This homesickness, then, becomes a figure of a self shared by mother and son; but the son who wants "achievement and advancement," Howells tells us in *Years of My Youth,* must distance himself from this mixed figure and seek a kind of ideal independence, or manliness: "Throughout his later boyhood and into his earlier manhood the youth is always striving away from his home and the things of it. With whatever pain he suffers through the longing for them, he must deny them; he must cleave to the world and the things of it; that is his fate, that is the condition of all achievement and advancement for him."[15]

Another woman whom Howells left at home was his eldest sister, Victoria; and when we return to the fiugre of Alma in the scene I have been describing, we will also want to think of her. In *Years of My Youth* Howells tells us of their "intellectual companionship." He shared his earliest writings with her, and she helped him "dream a literary future." It was not until "twenty years later" that he discovered, when she sent him a play that she had written about "village realities," that she had a "like ambition." Although she had shared with her brother, twenty years before, a "discontent with the village limit of our lives,"[16] what appears as an almost grotesque portrait of a particular ideal feminine role kept her within these limits: "For thirty years, she . . . stayed home and cared for her helplessly idiotic younger brother."[17] She died in 1886, two years before Howells began *A Hazard of New Fortunes*. In his biography of Howells, Kenneth Lynn narrates Victoria's decision to stay within "the village limit" and be a substitute mother for her brother:

> Vic was caught in a trap from which there would be no escape; someone in the family had to stay home and take care of Henry Howells . . . and Vic volunteered. In the face of her unselfish sacrifice, the ambitious Will wrote her from Columbus that he felt "quite ashamed of myself, and want to do something better than achieve reputation, and be admired of young ladies who read the *Atlantic*."[18]

Like Beaton, Howells wears what might be seen as a mask of shame (at abandoning his family to the hardships of their village life); like Alma, he decides to be a man, and leaves his feminine counterpart behind in the same village to strike an ideally feminine pose, to wear a feminine mask, while he searches for an ideal man's mask in the world of art and commerce. At the same time, we might read in Alma's decision not to live through Beaton a reversal of Victoria's own decision: the undoing of the sacrifice of a female member of the family, a sacrifice that only served the male members.

Alma and Beaton, the narrator tells us, met in Alma's hometown, the village of St. Barnaby. Alma was already painting, and while the ladies who boarded with her and her mother recognized that she had "genius," a professional painter, Harrington, who came to St. Barnaby every summer "contended that she needed to be a man in order to amount to anything; but in this theory he was opposed by an authority of his own sex [Beaton], whom the lady sketchers believed to speak with more impartiality." We are told Beaton treated Alma's work with a "difference" and that she "felt that his abrupt, impersonal comment recognized her as a real sister in art. He told her she ought to come to New York" to study; "and it was the sense of duty thus appealed to which finally resulted in the hazardous experiment she and her mother were now making" (105, 106).

So Alma leaves home to become a man, but her home, her mother—her feminine identity—also come with her. For the moment, the two of them are alone together: the mother doing a woman's work, sewing; the daughter sketching, work whose gender is ambiguous in Howells's world, because it combines both masculine and feminine aspects. At first it appears that Alma is doing a self-portrait: "Alma got up and took a pose before the mirror, which she then transferred to her sketch" (106-7). But by the end of the brief scene between Alma and her mother, we find that there are two figures in the sketch, a "man" and "a young lady." When Alma shows the sketch to her mother, what we first see through Mrs. Leighton's eyes is a "man's face rather weak." Alma concurs with her "critic's" judgment about this "weakness":

> Yes, that's so. Either I see all the hidden weakness that's in men's natures, and bring it to the surface in their figures, or else I put my own weakness into them. And, anyway, it's a drawback to their presenting a truly manly appearance. As long as I have one of the miserable objects before me, I can draw him; but as soon as his back's turned I get to putting ladies into men's clothes. I should think you'd be scandalized, mamma, if you were really a feminine person. It must be your despair that helps you to bear up. But what's the matter with the young lady in young lady's clothes? (107)

Alma's criticism of her male figure has an immediate context. Beaton, whom she is definitely attracted to, has not bothered to call on her since she and her mother arrived in New York. She feels spurned by this "miserable object," who for the moment has "turned his back" on her. He has not acted in this matter like a man, either like a gentleman or a man who is attracted to a woman; and so the male figure receives ambiguous treatment in the sketch. Is he really a man? At the same time this treatment is done behind the man's back. In the context of the novel, as I have noted, the women are very tactful, whether consciously or unconsciously, about how they portray the men to themselves, for the men need manly images to continue in their social roles; and the women also appear to need these images of their men. It is only Alma, at the very end of her relationship with Beaton, who, as I have also noted, will refuse this tact, facing Beaton to "turn her back on him," and that only after she has decided not to realize herself through him, or allow him to realize himself, in the way he wishes, through her. When this moment arrives, her survival will no longer be dependent on any system of articulation shared with Beaton. It is, of course, not simply a man who is becoming a woman in this sketch but also a woman who, while the man's back is turned, is becoming a man. The sketch looks forward to Alma's metamorphosis at the end of the novel and asks us to take a second look at all the apparent men and women in the novel: at the stories they tell to and about one another, which compose their selves, rather than at their all too obvious biological differences.

The other figure in Alma's sketch—"the young lady in young lady's clothes" whom Mrs. Leighton finds "perfectly insipid"—is, in its own way, just as ambiguous as the first figure, for Mrs. Leighton asks: "What's she doing?" To which Alma responds: "Oh, just being made love to, I suppose." For Alma, it appears, the sketch of her two figures represents a kind of romance. What I want to suggest is that the sketch does not simply represent the literal romance of Alma and Beaton; rather; it represents the romance of self-realization, which constitutes both the lives of Howells's figures and the figure of Howells as he appears in the stories he tells us, whether these stories are called autobiography or fiction. What we might note first about the sketch is that there is no distinct male figure in it—as if such an idealistic figure of independence has no place in a portrait that apparently represents Alma's/Howells's world to her/himself—that the male can only appear as androgynous, a man becoming a woman or a woman becoming a man or, better, both at once, realizing a figure whose origin in what we call either "man" or "woman" is ambiguous. A distinct female figure, however, does appear in the sketch, no matter how "perfectly insipid" she is or how ambiguous her actions may seem (an ambiguity that Alma ends with her half-hearted commentary). How are we to interpret this figure, then? Perhaps she is a figure of Fulkerson's "*ewig Weibliche*," being courted here by an ambiguously androgynous figure that, believing in the story of nineteenth-century manliness, even while its androgyny contradicts this story and tells another, believes as well in the century's story of womanliness and so projects this distinct female figure. Perhaps, however, the female figure's insipidness, like the male's androgyny, articulates that this story is failing.

Having used the term *representation* in relation to Alma's sketch and the forces it realizes, I finally want to qualify the term; for in the sense that the sketch *constitutes* both the lives of Howells's figures and the figure of Howells in these lives, it does not *represent* them (in the sense that we might traditionally understand that term as the mirror of a prior reality); rather, it is the context of these lives; it is the constitution that generates what I would call their congressional activity, congressional not only in the political sense of the term, but in the sexual sense as well, with its suggestions of that conflictive unity, the state of marriage, always threatening to become the state of "antimarriage." And this congressional activity, as Basil March reminds us, is a "fantastic fiction of sleep." In this context it is worth noting that when Alma is finished with her sketch, she pins it up with the others where it too must show, not in the broad daylight of a common sense realism, but "with fantastic indistinctness in the shaded gas-light."

NOTES

1. William Dean Howells, *Years of My Youth and Three Essays*, ed. David J. Nordloh et al. (Bloomington: Indiana University Press, 1975), p. 57.

2. Ibid., p. 3.

3. William Dean Howells, "Criticism and Fiction," in *Criticism and Fiction and Other Essays*, ed. Clara Marbury Kirk and Rudolf Kirk (New York: New York University Press, 1959), pp. 51, 15, 14, 39, 12.

4. Ibid., p. 35.

5. William Dean Howells, "The Man of Letters as a Man of Business," in *Criticism and Fiction*, p. 308.

6. William Dean Howells, *A Hazard of New Fortunes*, ed. David J. Nordloh et al. (Bloomington: Indiana University Press, 1976).

7. Howells, *Years of My Youth*, p. 5.

8. Kenneth S. Lynn, *William Dean Howells: An American Life* (New York: Harcourt, Brace, 1970), p. 283.

9. For the notion of Fulkerson as author, I am indebted to an unpublished essay by Amy Kaplan on *A Hazard of New Fortunes*.

10. Fulkerson conceives of the magazine as a profit-sharing operation, where, if the venture makes money, the contributors will reap the benefits. Of course, this allows Fulkerson to cut costs initially, and not to lose money in paying contributors, should the magazine fail.

11. *The Journals and Miscellaneous Notebooks of Ralph Waldo Emerson*, ed. William H. Gilman et al., 14 vols. (Cambridge: Harvard University Press, Belknap Press, 1960), 4:351-52.

12. At the end of the novel, Dryfoos—after the violent deaths of Lindau and his (Dryfoos's) son, Conrad (the latter is shot while trying to help the former, who is beaten by a policeman, during labor strife)—will tell March: "I wasn't tryin' to punish [Lindau] for his opinions" (447). Rather, Dryfoos insists, he was punishing Lindau for comments of a personal nature, attacking Dryfoos, that the socialist had made in German to March at the dinner, not realizing that the millionaire could understand the language. In his insistence Dryfoos seems to be trying to separate the personal and the impersonal (the individual and his political views). This is a separation that March as well tries to make in relation to Lindau, whom he admires personally but whose political opinions disturb him. The force of Howells's novel is to suggest that such separations are impossible.

13. Nathaniel Hawthorne, *The Scarlet Letter*, ed. Sculley Bradley et al., 2nd ed. (New York: W. W. Norton, 1978), p. 31.

14. The *"ewig Weibliche"* might be seen as a story in which the powerless triumph over the powerful. In this sense, men, as well as women, can be the heroes of this romance, as Howells's novel well illustrates.

15. Howells, *Years of My Youth*, pp. 20, 110.

16. Ibid., pp. 106, 108, 109, 107.

17. Lynn, *William Dean Howells*, p. 289.

18. Ibid., p. 105.

LAURENCE B. HOLLAND

A "Raft of Trouble"

WORD AND DEED IN *HUCKLEBERRY FINN*

Criticism of *Huckleberry Finn* has defined a consensus that the book's closing section is seriously flawed, for even those who find the last twelve chapters to be coherent in conception agree that the incidents relating Tom's "evasion" scheme for rescuing Jim are indulgently overwritten and in execution are as embarrassing as Hemingway claimed they were in *The Green Hills of Africa*. After chapter 31, he declared, "the rest is just cheating," and he advised people to stop reading the book at this point, apparently at the end of chapter 31, where "Jim is stolen from the boys" and sold by the fraudulent King.[1] The chapters are nevertheless well enough executed to bear rereading, and the scenes that terminate Tom's evasion scheme are so well done and so vivid that they demand more attention than Hemingway's injunction tempts us to give. In themselves they provide a significant context for the disclosure that Miss Watson has freed Jim in her will, and they illuminate the connections between the final section and earlier parts of the book and the profound folly on which Twain's novel rests. Moreover, the incidents help reveal how Twain's idiom and narrative form create the moving if somberly comic and ironic vision that lies at the heart of Twain's masterpiece.

What *Huckleberry Finn* is about is the process, with its attendant absurdities, of setting a free man free. This is the issue from the moment Huck, born free but staging and feigning his own death, seeks refuge on Jackson's Island, though the book seldom speaks explicitly about this matter in terms such as "freedom" and "liberation." It speaks more often instead of "rescuing" and "saving" important characters. The theme is figured chiefly, however, in the central case of Jim, without being confined exclusively to him, and it is first phrased definitively in the closing section (in chapter 42), when Jim's legal emancipation is divulged: "Tom Sawyer had gone to all that trouble and bother to set a free nigger free!"

Reprinted from *Glyph 5: Johns Hopkins Textual Studies* (Baltimore, 1979).

The process of setting a free man free is left unfinished at the end, but the closing section does not wrench the book from its course; it reveals in sharper light the profound irony that governs the book and that we should avoid simplifying. The central importance of this irony to the coherence of the book is obscured, I think, by a genetic approach to Twain's narrative even in such incisive analyses as those of Henry Nash Smith and Leo Marx, which emphasize Huck's vernacular speech, Huck's role as narrator, and Twain's difficulties in finishing his manuscript, to the comparative neglect of Jim's role and the scapegoating that is entailed by Twain's comic strategies.[2] The irony is shaped by Twain's desperately felt need for liberation and by a mixture of scorn for, and acquiescence in, the impulses, habits, and institutions that leave the quest for freedom still unsatisfied and all but paralyzed. The irony is deepened by Twain's tacit acknowledgment of his own, Huck's, and Jim's involvement with Tom Sawyer's world, and by Twain's recognition of the moral implications of his stance toward his subject and of the fictive form that generates his vision.

At the risk of reading the book backward, let us begin with the incidents in chapter 40, which tells of Huck's and Jim's decision to risk Jim's exposure in order to seek a doctor for Tom. Tom's fantastic escape plans (inspired by the tales and historical accounts he takes for models) have called for enemies, and his insane "nonnamous letter," warning the Phelpses of the impending escape, has brought to the cabin a posse of fifteen farmers equipped with dogs and armed with guns. They shoot at the fleeing threesome and wound Tom in the leg before the three can make it to safety on the raft. Before the fact of Tom's wound is divulged, Jim is allowed to lavish praise on the beauty of the plan and its execution, and Huck is allowed a sigh of relief at precisely the moment when he steps onto the raft and proclaims his joy at Jim's liberation. But in view of the frequency with which Jim has had to be rescued before (to say nothing of what is shortly forthcoming), Huck's exclamation is as comic as it is genuine: "*Now,* old Jim, you're free *again,* and I bet you won't ever be a slave no more." It is somberly comic not only because it is overconfident but also because the recurring necessity of freeing Jim, underscored by Twain's italics of "*now*" and "*again,*" has become by this time at once a moral imperative and an ineffectual routine. Both that moral pressure and that sense of futility lie deep within *Huckleberry Finn.*

The incident continues as Tom's excitement mounts, doubled by his discovery that he has been shot and leading him to disregard his wound in surrender to his fancies. With the cockiness of a young executive and the lunacy of Tom-foolishness he is still superintending the affair at the end of the chapter. His comparison of Jim's rescue to that of King Louis XVI, however, embedded though it is in Tom's indulgent fantasies, has ominous implications. It is disturbing because Jim's royal French counterpart was

not saved from the guillotine and also because Tom's first aid—he is ban-
daging himself with a shirt left behind by the Duke—recalls the fraudulent
King and Duke, who in chapter 19 called out from shore, begged Huck
to "save their lives," and instantly were rescued from the "trouble" on
shore and admitted to the raft.

The insecurity of the raft as a refuge for Huck and Jim, and the inseparable mixture of comic antics (foolish in both word and deed) with
desperately urgent matters, are of central importance throughout *Huckleberry Finn.* In this late incident Tom's foolishness is significantly related
to the matching folly of Huck and Jim, who decide, despite Tom's strenuous objections and attempts to block their efforts, that Huck should venture to shore to bring a doctor to Tom. Saving Tom, freeing him from
danger, is taking precedence over setting Jim free. This decision—the deed
that results in Jim's capture and shortly threatens him first with hanging
and then with being sold at auction—is one of the most important events
in the book and it is made by Huck and Jim in a moment of deliberation
that Twain renders in telling details. These details underscore the fact
that the decision is mutual and that Jim is given the crucial task of putting
it into words.

After "consulting—and thinking" together for a solemn moment in
silence, Huck is certain what Jim will say but insists: "Say it, Jim." And
Jim, revealing to Huck that he is admirably "white inside," reveals their
mutual folly, speaking without a trace of pretense or hollowness in the
dialect that Twain renders so painstakingly. Taking Tom as a model of
unselfish conduct, Jim asks whether Tom, were he the runaway slave,
would urge friends to "save me" instead of helping a wounded comrade.
Jim concludes that role-model Tom would not say that and then concludes: "Well, den, is *Jim* gwyne to say it? No, sah—I doan' budge a step
out'n dis place, 'dout a *doctor;* not if it's forty year!"

Even before the reader learns (or remembers) that their decision has
dire consequences for Jim, their folly is transparent in taking Tom as a
model of selflessness, since Tom's antics consistently assign to himself the
role of heroic superintendent of his adventures. Yet his wound is a fact
and in the days before penicillin it is serious; the Doctor later wants medi-
cal assistance but does not dare abandon Tom to get it. What makes Tom
ludicrous in this scene—his willingness to disregard his own danger—also
lends some support to Jim's feeling that Tom would not put his own safety ahead of a friend's, but does not justify the full measure of heroism
that Jim and Huck credit to him. Both the folly of Huck's and Jim's decision and its moral rightness are sanctioned by the episode, which nowhere suggests that Huck and Jim should follow Tom's fantasy-ridden
advice by neglecting his wound and continuing their flight. And in reaching this decision Huck and Jim are as close in rapport as they have ever

been. The bond between them has been close before—when promising not to disclose each other's whereabouts, when relaxing on the raft, when Huck humbles himself before Jim or listens to that black King Lear's penitent confession of cruelty to a daughter whose mute silence he misunderstood. The bond between them is close again when Jim hugs Huck in joy after their separation, and when they decide finally to cut loose from the King and Duke. But now they actually make a deliberate decision in utter reciprocity and do so in words that Huck asks Jim to speak.

The serious consequences of their decision come to light in chapter 42 when the Doctor returns with Tom feverish on a stretcher and with Jim tied and guarded by the posse of men who recaptured him on the raft. Twain's denouement, the disclosure that Miss Watson legally freed Jim two months earlier, casts the entire narrative in a sharper light, and certain details in which he describes the capture of Jim serve as echoes both of Tom's evasion and of the trip down the river—an earlier "evasion" as it is now made to appear—on the raft.

Before divulging the fact that Jim is already legally free, Twain does nothing to relax the danger that Jim faces. Though in peril frequently before, Jim is now threatened with hanging by some of the posse who wish to make him an object lesson to other Negroes. Moreover, they blame Jim alone for the "raft of trouble," as Huck calls it, which has overwhelmed the Phelpses and the neighborhood, in their ignorance making Jim the scapegoat for the project that Tom, with Huck's grudging assistance, has launched. Jim is saved only by the reasoning that Twain was to treat in its full nightmarish absurdity at the end of *Pudd'nhead Wilson:* Jim's legal owners would demand payment if their property were destroyed by hanging; therefore Jim must be spared and held for a proper period of time before being sold, if unclaimed, at auction. Huck is at once pained and helpless in recounting Jim's reimprisonment. The cruelty is condemned implicitly, and challenged by Huck's intention to tell Aunt Sally about Jim's service to Tom, but it is not challenged in act. One of Huck's longest sentences in the book renders at once the cruelties inflicted on Jim (the cursing and cuffing) and also Huck's anguished paralysis at witnessing Jim's confinement, which seems ominously unbreachable and final. And his account persistently recalls Jim's treatment earlier in the cabin by the Phelpses and by Tom and Huck, making clear that Jim's treatment now, though far worse, is precisely similar to what it was then. This time he is tied with heavier chains to the cabin itself instead of to the bedstead, he is now given only bread and water to eat, the escape hole is filled up, and now a bulldog and armed white guards, instead of approachable Negroes, are posted. But he is put in the "same" cabin; he is chained "again."

What Huck's long and apprehensive sentence prepares for is the Doctor's

recollection of his discovery of Jim aboard the raft—a "yarn," as Huck
calls it, that is intended to arouse admiration and kinder treatment for
Jim, but whose effect on the posse is minimal; it persuades them merely
to stop cussing Jim. Huck's highest hope is merely that they would add
meat and greens to Jim's diet, and lighten the load of chains, and even
this proves sanguine. Huck thinks it best not to "mix in," though he
hopes that when he tells the Doctor's "yarn" to Aunt Sally it will move
her to make Jim more comfortable.

One reason why the Doctor's account is significant is that it is one of
the most moving and genuine tributes to Jim in the book, and one of the
most vivid glimpses of Jim's service to a friend while "resking his freedom
to do it." Rendered in colloquial speech as authentic as Huck's, it functions to strengthen the reader's admiration of Jim's heroism. A second
reason, however, is that the Doctor's sympathy is wholly contained within
the confines of loyalty to the slavery system. His statement returns at the
end to the reductive and negative statement with which he opens his recollection: "He ain't no bad nigger, gentlemen; that's what I think about
him." Yet it includes a strangely tender, nakedly simple description of
Jim's betrayal. The glimpse of Jim's betrayal that the Doctor gives serves
more vividly than the news of his sale by the King to reveal and condemn
implicitly the earlier betrayals that have occurred in the course of the
book. When some men unexpectedly row by the raft at dawn, Jim "as
good luck would have it" is sitting beside Tom in a familiar posture "with
his head propped on his knees, sound asleep," and the Doctor recalls that
"I motioned them in, quiet, and they slipped up on him and tied him
before he knew what he was about, and we never had no trouble."

The facts that the Doctor's tribute to Jim is notably ex post facto, and
that the events of the summer have culminated in Jim's recapture, reinforce the irony of Twain's masterpiece. The raft that is now vulnerable
to incursions by the Doctor and the posse has before been vulnerable to
the King and the Duke, who along with Jim and Huck turn the raft into
an image of the civilization with its discontents on shore. Efforts to protect Jim have had to be repeated repeatedly before. Indeed Huck's dream
of freedom—escape from civilization, liberation from the burdensome six
thousand dollars that was the reward he had won in *Tom Sawyer,* and
escape from Pap and surrogate or adoptive parents—is countered by
another dream of freedom projected in Jim: his longing to escape from
slavery and enter *into* the civilization that chafes Huck; Jim's clinging to
the sacred five-cent piece he wears around his neck and his desire *for* the
money, the eight hundred dollars, that would buy freedom for his family;
Jim's longing to be reunited with his wife and daughter and to *assume* the
role of husband and father. These antithetical dreams of freedom are sustained in an uneasy ambiance through to the end of the novel.

In this context, Tom's evasion scheme, in its very extremes of indulgent excess, is appropriate indeed. Tom's antics confer the burden of heroism on Jim but make a cruel and diseased mockery of it. Jim's is the burden of Orpheus to charm (with a "jews-harp") the rats and serpents that flock around him, but in Tom's fantasies Jim winds up with the head of a rattlesnake in his mouth. Tom's antics are in effect the rehearsal for the ominous enslavement that ensues when Jim is enchained "again" in the "same" cabin. Jim's enslavement, and the process of liberation offered in the book—Jim in chains in the cabin, Jim disguised as King Lear or a sick Arab aboard the raft, Jim chained on the raft pretending to be a recaptured runaway—both make a scapegoat of Jim and are virtual mirror images of each other. Liberation dissolves into enslavement and they come close, without actually doing so, to cancelling each other out. Jim stands at the end, legally free but without the substance of freedom envisioned for him by William Blake in "America: A Prophecy": "Let the enchained soul, shut up in darkness and in sighing . . ./Rise and look out; his chains are loose, his dungeon doors are open;/And let his wife and children return from the oppressor's scourge." Jim stands free but severed from his wife and daughter, all but forgotten by Huck, with nothing like Lear's one hundred knights or Orpheus's lyre, with little but the forty bucks given him by Tom to insure the promise of William Blake and others who have helped invent the American dream. The tortured irony that defines Jim's predicament encompasses also Huck, who at the end stands immobile, the possessor still as Jim informs him of his six grand, fantasizing about an escape to the Territory which seems increasingly impossible of attainment. Huck would go to "the territory ahead of the rest." But that Territory is not a green continent accessible in space but a fleeting moment receding into a past now "Forty or Fifty Years Ago." By the time Huck got there, "the rest"—the Kings and Dukes, the Tom Sawyers, probably the Aunt Sallies—would soon be there in numbers to hail him and seek accommodation on the raft.

In such a world of balked hopes and tortured expectations, Miss Watson's deathbed decision to free Jim is singularly fitting. Even the suddenness, indeed the sportiveness, of its introduction in the text is appropriate to the pre–Civil War era when such emancipations were often afterthoughts, so to speak, all too infrequent, always tardy, and no doubt, like the Emanicipation of 1862, prompted in part by mixed motives. There is nothing careless, nor self-indulgent, about Twain's treatment of the incident in chapter 42. Good-natured Tom, returning to consciousness and (all hope) sanity, divulges the information instantly when he hears that Jim is in danger of being sold: Miss Watson was "ashamed" of her intent to sell Jim and "said so"; just before she died she "set him free in her will." However questionable her motives (they are usually questioned, though there is little evidence about them), these details are telling in a narration where declaring things in spoken speech, willed intentions, and the activity of writing are crucial matters, as they have become long before "yours truly," Huck Finn, stops the story that has become his epistle to the world for the simple reason that "there is nothing more to write about." The reality Huck summons up in the book includes the prose styles and other styles to which Huck, and "The Author" of the opening notice about dialects used in the book, so often draw attention: Pap's way of speaking; Tom's style of behavior, which Huck usually admires; fashions in poetry and painting at the Grangerfords' house, the "ignorantest kind of words and pictures"; charcoal graffiti, in the room where Pap's corpse is recognized by Jim in chapter 9. It includes the Doctor's "yarn," as Huck calls it, and the countless tales Huck tells during his trip down the river, to say nothing of the crucial incident to which I have already attached importance when Jim's saying, and the silent decision jointly made with Huck that it articulates, define at once Jim's moral heroism and his folly. The *virtu* if not the virtue of Tom's evasion scheme is, as Huck grudgingly says in chapter 34, that it will "make . . . talk," and making *talk,* or the illusion of it as Professor Richard Bridgman cautions us to say,[3] is important to Huck's and Twain's colloquial idiom.

More importantly the narrative proper opens with a bibliographical ploy that locates Huck as the figure in a book named *Tom Sawyer,* and in chapter 31 Huck's dramatic decisions—to turn Jim over to the authorities, then to tear up the letter in which he had articulated that first decision and to give over reforming—these decisions are made in a counterpoint of written and spoken speech. Whether genuine and durable or not, Huck's moral commitments are made not in severance from his civilization but in an entanglement, more properly an engagement, with its very foundation, namely language. He makes his first decision in an experiment with written language, then undoes it in an action that redeems, for brief moments, the Widow Douglas's injunction in chapter 3 to "help other people, and do everything I could for other people, and look out for them all the time, and never think about myself." His famous declaration about going to hell, presumably spoken but like everything in the book inscribed in the print that issued from type fonts and presses, is made in the only moral vocabulary Huck has, which folds both the Sunday School or Revival Sermon vocabulary, and Huck's colloquial idiom, into the phrase "go to hell."

This conjunction of spoken speech, decision-making, and writing relates to Miss Watson's will in ways I shall return to presently. But another strikingly controlled notation about Miss Watson's deed—namely, that she did this "two months ago"—illuminates a peculiar resiliency in the prose style of *Huckleberry Finn* and intricacies in the temporal dimension of the narration that I should dwell on briefly. As for the matter of style, what I wish to insist on is that the ostensible "now" of the present tense in the book, and the ostensible "then" of the past tenses, enforce each other insofar as they can be distinguished in the prose, but that they virtually dissolve into each other without actually doing so, and that what Huck presents to us, perhaps obviously, is an act of memory that is sometimes identified explicitly as such in the phrasing.

The stance of *Huckleberry Finn* is that of direct address, careful and conscious, to both the subject and the reader. It places Huck in a continuous present, as we usually call it, before the reader. He talks to us at the opening, telling us in the "here and now" to look him up in the index to *Tom Sawyer,* and addresses us at the end, talking to us about what Tom is doing now and what he plans to do now, signing off as "yours truly" (his narration impulsively becomes epistolary) even after noting "the end." But Huck at times tells us that he is remembering things in a style that sustains the illusion of the "there and then": "I can't ever get it out of my memory, the sight of them poor miserable girls and niggers" (chapter 27). The very illusion of remembering is rendered by the style, even when nothing is said explicitly about remembering. The rightfully famous description of Huck's father, Pap, in chapter 5 is not a sudden response, not the "first jolt" or shock in the so-called immediate present of Pap's ominous return, but a deliberate recapitulation, mounting in intensity, of Pap's appearance, composed on the basis of frequent confrontations and thoroughly digested, considered details: "He was most fifty, and he looked it. His hair was long and tangled and greasy, and hung down, and you could see his eyes shining through like he was behind vines. It was all black, no gray; so was his long, mixed-up whiskers. There warn't no color in his face, where his face showed; it was white, not like another man's white, but a white to make a body sick, a white to make a body's flesh crawl—a tree-toad white, a fish-belly white."

Huck's remembering includes repressed memories of things he refuses to enlarge upon and anticipations of the future: "It made me so sick I nearly fell out of the tree. I ain't agoing to tell all that happened—it would make me sick again, if I was to do that. I wished I hadn't ever come ashore that night to see such things. I ain't ever going to get shut of them—lots of times I dream about them" (chapter 18). Often the vividness of the present inheres in the act of telling or talking to us whereas the incidents spoken of take place in the past: "The way I lit out and shinned for the road in the dark there ain't nobody can tell"—there ain't nobody can tell "now" about the way he lit out back "then." To combine the effect of the vivid present and the remembered past Twain often uses one of the easiest displacements known in colloquial speech: "Well, when they was all gone the King he asks. . . . " (chapter 26) in which past and present tenses are interchangeable. In the famous and beautiful passage at the opening of chapter 19, where Huck in orderly fashion describes the combination of pleasure and apprehensiveness in life aboard the raft, what Huck "could" hypothetically see, what he "would" recurringly see each day, what he "maybe" detected in the sign-language of the river's surfaces, and what he does sense apprehensively as threats to his safety on this far from idyllic raft—these modes and tenses dissolve into each other: "We would watch the lonesomeness of the river, and kind of lazy along, and by-and-by lazy off to sleep. Wake up, by-and-by, and look to see what done it, and maybe see a steamboat, coughing along upstream. . . ." A few paragraphs later, just after invoking a sky "speckled with stars" and the darkness brightened by a "world of sparks" from a steamboat's chimneys: "Just as I was passing a place where a kind of cow-path crossed the crick, here comes a couple of men tearing up the path as tight as they could foot it." The King and Duke are about to ask for and be offered instant refuge on the raft.

The resilience of this style, which makes possible a vivid presentness in narration fueling a process of remembering, and which translates imperceptibly the counterpoint of telling and listening in a fictive present into shared recognition and reenactment of Huck's remembered past, heightens the significance of a feature we too often neglect in considering Twain's masterpiece, namely that it is a historical novel that early draws attention to that fact. Huck's insistence that we refer for his provenance to the earlier book *Tom Sawyer* is in keeping with the cast back into the past that is launched on the title page: "Scene: The Mississippi Valley. Time: Forty to Fifty Years Ago." The future imperatives in the "Notice" to the reader posted by Twain's delegate the "Chief of Ordinance" ("persons attempting to find a plot in it will be shot"), and the note "Explanatory" about its dialects in the present tense signed by "The Author," are already governed by this extension of temporal perspective to encompass the movement back from 1885 to the decade straddling 1840. Whether or not Twain was indulging in the nostalgia that the novelist Wright Morris has found a threat to all American fiction,[4] in *Huckleberry Finn* the past of, say, 1840 stands in a troubled, strained relation with the writing of the book or its publication in 1885. "Forty to Fifty Years Ago" in effect defines a dilemma that is dramatized, in the narration, by the quite exact, seemingly gratuitous specification that Miss Watson's declaration of repentance and her liberation of Jim in her will took place "two months" ago. This fact does not belatedly skew the written structure of the book but buttresses the principles that constitute it. It brings 1885, in its relation to 1840, to the verge of discontinuity but sustains a perilous continuum in which "now" and "then," "now" and "again," both challenge and engage each other.[5]

Once Twain can be presumed to have stumbled or decided upon this

feature of his denouement, he did not arrange a recent demise for Miss
Watson, though her dying as recently as four or five weeks before the concluding episode would have provided Tom with the safety of legality he
enjoys when perpetrating his evasion scheme, while making her death virtually simultaneous with Huck's tearing up his letter to her, his decision
not to inform on Jim. Instead, Twain's timing of her death assigns a priority in time to her words and deeds, her spoken declaration and her written
will, which haunt the resolution of the novel, stir and agitate its rhythms.
The priority of Miss Watson's will underscores the fact that Huck's bold
and solemn decision was not to free Jim, in any tangible and full sense,
but vaguely to protect him, that it was not as crucial as Huck had thought
at the time or not crucial in ways he thought, that his decision was not as
dangerous and courageous as it has seemed. Miss Watson's will gives the
status of a ritual gesture to Huck's momentous decision, places at a distance the drama and urgency of Jim's legal fate, relegates to the past any
opportunity to give Jim the freedom he deserves. Insofar as Miss Watson's
written will is moved further back from the closing episodes of Twain's
denouement, it is removed too from the years in the 1870s and 1880s when
Twain, who never freed a slave in his life, was ensconced in Hartford writing *Huckleberry Finn.* By seeming sportive and unexpected, and distant,
Miss Watson's act enforces the sense of futility that deepens toward the
end of *Huckleberry Finn.* The option to write out or inscribe Jim's legal
freedom was Miss Watson's in 1840. Moreover the chance of setting a
freed Negro free seems dim in chapters 42 and 43, with Jim in chains
again, then freed suddenly to stand jobless and alone, with nothing but a
meal, Tom's forty-dollar payment, and the prospect of a camping trip in
the Territory with the boys to satisfy his dream of freedom in a promised
land. Yet the task of redeeming Jim's legal freedom, fulfilling the promise
that legal freedom makes possible, that unfinished business haunts and
troubles the denouement of Twain's novel. The sequence of incidents that
have come so near to nought in 1840 and stand so far back in time from
1885 in the temporal perspective of the book bring this historical fiction
to the brink of irrelevance for the post–Civil War world. Yet precisely be
cause it verges on irrelevance it speaks with all the more pointed relevance
across the span of forty or fifty years in 1885 to define the task and impose the charge of setting a nation of freedmen free. The flukish fact of
Jim's legal freedom, and the failure of his world to flesh it out with the
family, the opportunities, and the community that would give it meaning,
define with haunting and painful relevance, and with absurd precision, the
problem of setting a free Negro free, which is the pressing problem, in all
its extensions, in post–Civil War America and more recent decades.

In forging this timeliness from the receding past, accommodating the
tensions between Tom's sportive fantasies and the somber realities they

mirror in American society, or accommodating the tensions between the diverging dreams of freedom that are suspended in the comradeship of Jim and Huck, *Huckleberry Finn* becomes not so much a novel as a romance. In saying that I resort to a binary terminology I do not like, and particularly I would not want to imply that the book is any less novelistic in its textures and strategies for being a romance. What I have in mind are basic features of imaginative fiction that Henry James insisted were possible in either the so-called novel or the so-called romance but that are usually denominated by the latter term: the evocation of the "possible" and visionary rather than the "actual"; fiction's status as fiction, its daring, as Hawthorne defined the task of the romancer, to locate itself "on the utmost verge of a precipitous absurdity."[6] *Huckleberry Finn* generates and yields a vision, a possibility made real in language though not yet actualized in the behavior of Huck and Tom or Mark Twain on Asylum Hill in Hartford, nor in the relations generally of white, black, or brown people since. It creates a vision that would redeem the promise of Jim's legal freedom, would redeem the failed and failing effort to set a Negro free, and it sanctions the promise of that vision, makes it the moral imperative, the willed inscription, that governs this fiction. It does this by pushing all the fictive conventions it uses, including what we usually recognize as novelistic ones, to the limit, where they become a fully imaginative act. The very plausibility of its illusionistic representation—the fullness with which this plausibility is achieved in the river landscapes, the spruced-up domestic interiors or the dingy rooms aboard floating abandoned houses, the untidy yards of marginal farms, and above all the colloquial idiom of Huck and the other characters as well—the fully representational illusion that this book prints to us is a kind of fictive magic, a lie, which yields the *Adventures of Huckleberry Finn* and the vision burgeoning within it. It is all the more magical for seeming not to be, for seeming to concede priority to a reality independent of the imagination. And the text is haunted by the recognition of its status as fiction and of the moral hazards entailed in the enterprise of fiction. Indeed it is haunted by the implications of the particular narrative structure that Twain devised for his masterpiece.

Twain begins to play with the matter of lying fantasy on the first page when Huck wryly alludes to the intrusion of lies, or more cautiously "stretchers," in *The Adventures of Tom Sawyer*. Even earlier, faking it in the guise of a deputy "Chief of Ordinance," Twain has taken the preposterous stance of one who will banish and shoot misguided readers, the stance taken in chapter 2 by fancy-ridden Tom Sawyer, who declares that intruders on his gang "must be sued" and second offenders "must be killed." One paradigm for Twain's narration in the book is the episode where Huck and Jim make a decision in silence while Huck delegates to Jim the task of speaking it in words, and then Jim for them both engages in a flight of fancy that is an act at once of folly and of heroism, imagining for Tom a freedom from self that exceeds the facts. Twain, like Huck in this instance, remains ostensibly and actually silent throughout the narration—"Say it, Huck"—creating the lie that Huck speaks or writes the book that unfolds, word by printed word, in the silence of fiction before us.

Twain's narration, and the complicity in the world he projects that is revealed in his narrative form, are illuminated by a hilarious and profoundly revealing essay he wrote in 1882, "The Decay in the Art of Lying." There, addressing Hartford historians whom he said were masters of the art, he defined the lie as a "Virtue. . . , the fourth Grace, the Tenth Muse," and, declaring with guilty abandon that lying is an unavoidable "necessity of our circumstances," he called on all to "train ourselves to lie thoughtfully. . . , to lie for others' advantage, and not our own; to lie gracefully and graciously, not . . . clumsily. . . ," to lie not "with pusillanimous mien" but "firmly" without "being ashamed of our high calling." He defined one particular category of lie that has a particular bearing on *Huckleberry Finn:* the "silent lie," the "deception which one conveys by keeping still and concealing the truth," or what he called in another essay ("My First Lie and How I Got Out of It") the "lie of silent assertion."[7]

On such a "lie of silent assertion" depends the closing section of Twain's book which so disturbs us, when Tom Sawyer starts to blurt out the fact of Jim's emancipation but then smothers it in silence.[8] By his "lie of silent assertion" Tom is able to stage the rescue of Jim, which is so cruel and intended to be so entertaining: the "evasion" with its pretentions to righteousness, it tawdry melodrama, which produces the "raft of trouble" at the end; the fakery and sport that debase Jim and then endanger Jim and Tom both; the "fun" that "makes talk" and that Huck, disguised as Tom, helps perpetrate; the folly that Twain exposes to the shame of our condemnation, Tom-foolishness indeed. Aunt Sally as well as Huck detects the absurdity of "setting a free nigger free." Twain could hardly have overlooked the fact that his own *Adventures* and their suspense are founded on the same silent lie. However much his art depended on improvisation, his improvisations were those of an expert performer who by the 1880s could anticipate the dubieties of fiction and the risks of his own methods. When revising his narrative and giving it the endorsement of his pseudonym, he knew the final shape it had taken. Miss Watson, around 1840, had legally freed Jim but neither Tom nor Twain had told readers so until the last minute.

Moreover it was Twain who stopped Tom in midsentence—"Say it, Tom"—and Twain it was, though with more complex motives than Tom's, who thought up the crude sport that is condemned in Tom, the "adventure" as Tom calls it to which Twain devoted so much of the *Adventures of Huckleberry Finn.* Twain's conscience is therefore stirred not only by the guilt he feels as a Tom Sawyerish, fish-belly white citizen who never freed a slave in his life, but by the lie he perpetrated in the very act of forming his fiction, holding to the logic of its suspense, founding its entertainment and its moral drama on Tom's crude sport and his "lie of silent assertion." As it approaches its completion, the fiction becomes fully confessional. *Mea culpa* (1840): Miss Watson's writing, not Tom Sawyer, not Mark Twain, freed the Negro Jim.

Huck Finn likewise, when he looks back and remembers the incident on the raft when he tore up the letter to Miss Watson, now knows that Jim has been freed. But to reenact the drama that constitutes his heroism, to re-create it in its vividness and moral urgency, Huck must in memory keep to the lie of silence. The very elemental form of the narration inescapably involves its narrator and its author in a fraud or lie and can be made a worthy or redeeming act only if the lie generates in language a vision, with its moral pressure, which extends beyond the facts of incident and warm companionship which the language presents. And the lie can be made to have that effect because the silence is not only a deception but an expressive form that yields concerns, recognitions, and aspirations beyond anything made explicit. The same willed silence that enables Tom and Twain to hide facts is an enabling form. The result is that chapter 31, rendering Huck's crucial decisions, burgeons with a pressure of moral urgency and commitment which most of us have felt but which exceeds anything actually true of Huck's behavior before or since. The actuality of Huck's feelings and behavior since leaving the river, as occasionally on it, have fallen short of the vision presented in this chapter. Indeed the very chapter dramatizes also Huck's lapse into passivity, vague protestations and improvisations, and neglect of Jim that are so conspicuous later. All Huck literally does is to perform an essentially negative act, deciding not to disclose Jim's whereabouts. One of the most terrifying moments in the book, coming directly after Huck tears up his letter to Miss Watson, occurs when Huck's grief-stricken tribute to Jim takes the form of claiming that he, rather than the King or Duke, *owns* Jim. Buried in the lie of silent assertion, hidden or muted but expressed in the silence, is the recognition that Huck has not the power to free Jim, that his act at best postpones the question of how to help Jim gain his dream of freedom. Yet when Huck recalls the incident of writing and tearing up his letter and the experience of making his decision, the deeds become something more, owing to the pressure of Twain's silent guilt, which is all the stronger for remaining tacit, repressed or compressed within the lie of silence. That pressure enforces the pressure of commitment afterward in memory, which commemorates the decision made earlier on the river and strains to make Huck's tribute to Jim the governing vision of Huck's adventure. It becomes the willed commitment to a liberation never made explicit, a fulfillment enacted only in the voiced cadences of Huck's spoken, Twain's written, speech. Created in the lie is the will to make the action convincingly seem, and in the language to be, a commitment of the moral imagination beyond what Twain knows it was then in fact. *Mea culpa* (1885): Jim and all fellow creatures should be, but are not yet, free. Huck's lie like Tom's will be a lie but it must be a better lie than his. Huck's lie must not only hide a fact but generate a vision. The lie must be suspenseful and dramatic like Tom's, and, just as Tom's will dramatize his petty ingenuity and show of valor, Huck's must dramatize his own flawed heroism. But Huck's drama must survive, in the durable rhythm of human speech, Huck's own later betrayals of Jim on the Phelps farm. Huck's lying words must be better prose than Tom's. In sum, Huck's idiom and drama must have better style. And they do, notably in chapter 31, where Huck makes his famous decision. The section opens with words whose recurring "I" sounds identify the protagonist of the drama and the high pitch of intensity to which his colloquial instrument is tuned:

So I was full of trouble, full as I could be; and didn't know what to do. At last I had an idea; and I says, I'll go and write the letter—and *then* see if I can pray. Why, it was astonishing, the way I felt as light as a feather, right straight off, and my troubles all gone. So I got a piece of paper and a pencil, all glad and excited, and set down and wrote:

That paragraph is followed by one of the most efficient letters in English. Huck says that he tore it up, but it appears, usually without so much as a crease or a hyphen, in every copy of the book, defining now and again, then and still, the imminence of Jim's betrayals:

Miss Watson your runaway nigger Jim is down here two mile below Pikesville and Mr. Phelps has got him and he will give him up for the reward if you send.—Huck Finn.

The letter is followed by a long paragraph in which the conjunction "and," the word "time," and the floating "ing's" of present participles recapture what Huck has before betrayed and will betray again but commemorates in the "now" of memory:

I felt good and all washed clean of sin for the first time I had ever felt so in my life, and I knowed I could pray now. But I didn't do it straight off, but laid the paper down and set there thinking— thinking how good it was all this happened so, and how near I came to being lost and going to hell. And went on thinking. And got to

thinking over our trip down the river; and I see Jim before me, all
the time, in the day, and in the nighttime, sometimes moonlight,
sometimes storms, and we a floating along, talking, and singing, and
laughing. But somehow I couldn't seem to strike no places to harden
me against him, but only the other kind. I'd see him standing my
watch on top of his'n, instead of calling me, so I could go on sleeping; and see him how glad he was when I come back out of the fog;
and when I come to him again in the swamp, up there where the feud
was; and such like times; and would always call me honey, and pet
me, and do everything he could think of for me, and how good he
always was; and at last I struck the time I saved him by telling the
men we had small-pox aboard, and he was so grateful, and said I
was the best friend old Jim ever had in the world, and the *only* one
he's got now; and then I happened to look around, and see that paper.

Taut, brief sentences, with clipped "t" sounds and "x's," then define
the final crisis:

It was a close place. I took it up and held it in my hand. I was a
trembling, because I'd got to decide, forever, betwixt two things, and
I knowed it. I studied a minute, sort of holding my breath, and then
says to myself:
"All right, then, I'll *go* to hell"—and tore it up.
It was awful thoughts, and awful words, but they was said. And
I let them stay said; and never thought no more about reforming.

And so *Huckleberry Finn* got banned by fish-belly whites in Concord,
Massachusetts, where there are or were people skinned in white who do
not want their children to know about young Huck Finn, his forged integrity, his charged language and grammatical errors, and the vision burgeoning in his ripe adolescence. And the book more recently has been
forced off the required reading lists in New York City, at the University of
Massachusetts, and in Deland, Florida, at the insistence of collegians
skinned in black who do not see, created in the antics of the Negro Jim,
the aspirations of a people and the stature of a man. And we, with our
fool imaginations, carry the burden of this lying fiction still as we translate it in our rereadings of it, moved in imaginings if not in undoubted
deeds, to set these freedoms free.

NOTES

1. Hemingway's memory was somewhat blurred; the two "boys" were not together when Jim was sold in chapter 31, nor when Jim was recaptured as recounted in
chapter 42. Hemingway's linking of Huck and Tom, however, the implication that
they owned the Negro "stolen" from them, and his incorporation of the term *nigger*

in Jim's name ("Nigger Jim") displays ways in which readers are implicated in the actions of *Huckleberry Finn*. See *The Green Hills of Africa* (1935; reprint ed., New York: Charles Scribner's Sons, 1963), p. 22.

2. See Henry Nash Smith, *Mark Twain: The Development of a Writer* (Cambridge: Harvard University Press, 1962), pp. 113–37, and his recent *Democracy and the Novel: Popular Resistance to Classical American Writers* (New York: Oxford University Press, 1978), pp. 104–27; and Leo Marx, "The Pilot and the Passenger: Landscape Conventions and the Style of *Huckleberry Finn*," *American Literature* 28 (1956): 129–46, and his *The Machine in the Garden: Technology and the Pastoral Ideal in America* (New York: Oxford University Press, 1964), pp. 319–41.

3. Richard Bridgman, *The Colloquial Style in America* (New York: Oxford University Press, 1966), pp. 11, 20.

4. Morris argues the dangers of nostalgia in *The Territory Ahead* (New York: Harcourt, Brace, 1958), passim, but finds that what Huck lost "in the wilderness of his nostalgia" was recaptured by Twain "in this lucid moment of reminiscence and craft," p. 88.

5. "Forty or Fifty Years Ago," the notation on the title page, places the action between 1835, the year of Twain's birth, and 1845. In chapter 40, Jim's determination to wait out a doctor for Tom even if it takes forty years would project the action ahead into the decade of 1875-1885, when Twain was writing the book.

6. James insisted that the best fiction, as in Zola, Scott, and Balzac, functions as both novel and romance, which are "different sorts and degrees" of the same fictive undertaking, in the New York Edition's preface to *The American* (New York: Charles Scribner's Sons, 1909). See *The Art of the Novel*, ed. Richard P. Blackmur (New York: Charles Scribner's Sons, 1934), p. 31. Hawthorne's statement appears in a letter of November 1850, quoted in James T. Fields, *Yesterdays with Authors* (1871; reprint ed., Boston: Houghton Mifflin, 1900), p. 56.

7. Quotations are from *The Writings of Mark Twain*, Author's National Edition, 25 vols. (Hartford, Conn.: American, 1899-1907), 20:364-70, and 23:161.

8. Comparable instances occur earlier but have no relation to the narrative structure of the book. In chapter 31 the Duke cuts off in midsentence his disclosure of Jim's whereabouts, but Huck already knows it. In chapter 27, during the Wilks affair, Huck keeps quiet about the King's fraudulent sale of the Wilks' slaves on the probably sanguine grounds that the fraud will be exposed and that "the niggers would be back home in a week or two."

EVAN CARTON

Pudd'nhead Wilson
and the Fiction
of Law and Custom

When William Dean Howells, arbiter of civilized American taste, conferred social and literary respectability upon Mark Twain in his *Atlantic
Monthly* endorsement of *Roughing It,* Twain expressed his gratitude in
a simile that, forty years later, Howells would still consider unfit for
print: "I am as uplifted and reassured by [your review]," Twain wrote,
"as a mother who has given birth to a white baby when she was awfully
afraid it was going to be a mulatto."[1] That Twain's image of the relieved
mother would have assaulted public canons of morality and propriety is
plain enough, but Howells, if he brooded on the remark, may have found
it more deeply unsettling. Apprehending its insinuation of a lustful and
secretly degraded maternity, its insistence upon a double intimacy that
must entangle if not confuse the identity of the offspring, its hint of the
mother's cynical willingness to take fortuitous appearances for her vindi-
cation and her veil, Howells may have felt about this remark, as Twain
would feel about the confused, freakish, double-headed story that he
eventually disunited and named *Pudd'nhead Wilson* and *Those Extraordinary Twins,* that its publication "would unseat the reader's reason"
(229–30).[2]

Twain's gratulant quip is most striking, and perhaps most disturbing,
in its suggestion that its compressed drama of biological origination resembles the act of literary authorship. *Pudd'nhead Wilson* bears out this
suggestion; the story of his own sense of authorship that Twain tells in
1893, through a narrative that itself radically involves problems of authorship, identity, and responsibility, is prefigured in the 1872 remark.
Twain's novel issues from a double seed or at least is subject to a double
influence—partly obscure and subversive, partly light and conventional. Its
outcome belies and conceals the former source and affirms the latter, although not without self-punishing irony. As the mimetic evidence of

white skin legitimates the baby, so Mayor David Wilson's climactic identification of the bloody "natal autograph" (217) grants the narrative a resolved and acceptable identity, designates it a novel of crime and detection or of the outcast's social triumph. And Twain, like the relieved mother, is thereby "uplifted" in every sense of the word but the moral and spiritual ones, which, in this instance, are so conspicuously inapplicable.

From its outset, *Pudd'nhead Wilson* meticulously performs the fundamental novelistic act of naming. "The scene of this chronicle," Twain begins, announcing in his choice of the word "chronicle" the narrative's commitment to accuracy and detail, "is the town of Dawson's Landing, on the Missouri side of the Mississippi, half a day's journey, per steamboat, below St. Louis" (55). He proceeds to list the species of flora that adorn the town's whitewashed houses and to note, asleep on each front window ledge, the cat—symbol of completion, contentment, and peace—without which the most perfect home cannot "prove title" (56). The calendar entry that introduces a later chapter will suggest a less sanguine connection between cats and signification, and perhaps between titles and truth: "One of the most striking differences between a cat and a lie is that a cat has only nine lives" (96).

Names in *Pudd'nhead Wilson* are like cats: they "prove title" and, accordingly, are themselves titular in sound and association. "Colonel Cecil Burleigh Essex," "Percy Northumberland Driscoll," and "Pembroke Howard" only incidentally identify particular characters; primarily, they create and fill a place in the social (and the novelistic) order, and help define the community. The bearers of these titles, who represent the town in various official capacities, uphold a code of social conduct whose fundamental precept is clarity of word and deed. Twain himself, who represents the town in language, seems to honor a similar code; it is the language of confident naming, of unambiguous identification, with which he constructs his fictional community: "The chief citizen was York Leicester Driscoll, about forty years old, judge of the county court. . . . He was fine and just and generous. . . . He was respected, esteemed and beloved by all the community. He was well off" (57).

If names inform the social organization of Dawson's Landing, naming is the method by which that organization protects and preserves itself. The second half of chapter 1 exhibits such defensive naming in its account of the community's authorship of Pudd'nhead Wilson. When David Wilson, during his first day in town, declares his wish to own one half of a howling invisible dog and, upon a request for clarification, rejoins, "Because I would kill my half" (59), his "fatal remark" (59) does more than merely imply the interdependency of the parts of any organism; it *evidences* this interdependency by the very structure of the communicative act that it initiates. Wilson's ironic mode obliges his auditors to complete his half-expressed thought and, thus, to complete the execution of the dog as well—a charge that they fulfill repeatedly in their subsequent deliberations on the soundness of Wilson's intellect. By its implication and its example, then, the remark challenges the legalistic distinctions and the proprietary or titular claims that underlie the ordered existence of Dawson's Landing. It rejects the model of community (or of representation) as formal organization, plotted and particularized by discrete bestowals of names and titles, and substitutes a model of community as integrated and dynamic creature of the ongoing enterprise of communication.

The townspeople cannot afford to recognize their intuitive grasp of Wilson's meaning. They agree that the whole dog would die but conclude that Wilson could not have intended this; to conclude otherwise would be to admit his vision of a community in which the individual cannot assume full possession or control of property and events yet must accept full responsibility for them. Wilson's auditors sense this "veiled threat"[3] to their own complacent autonomy and do not unveil it. One citizen—citizen number 2 in the system of parodic particularization that Twain furnishes for this scene—displays an even deeper apprehension of danger when he observes, prophetically, that "if you kill one half of a general dog there ain't any man that can tell whose half it was" (59–60). At this point, the finest proprietary discriminations lapse into impotence and absurdity. If, moreover, the "general dog" implicates a body politic, half of whose members are owned by the other half, then it would follow that the possessors could not dispose of their own possessions without destroying themselves. Either Wilson's remark, then, or the fundamental assumptions of Dawson's Landing must be unintelligible. The townspeople make the choice that will not unseat their reason.

Jonathan Culler, writing of the poetics of the novel, defines readable texts as "those which are intelligible in terms of traditional models."[4] Wilson's text undermines the familiar economic, legal, and ideological models of his public, but there remains an obvious model that might have preempted these more abstract ones and allowed the text to be read. Several critics have contended that the remark would have been perfectly understood as a specimen of frontier humor, an invitation to the kind of jocular hyperbole and friendly verbal complicity with which the locals would have been likely to pass the time.[5] But Wilson withholds the signs that would make this interpretation available; the wink that might disclaim any suspicious depth to his irony, or the smile that might indicate his desire to court rather than unsettle, is absent.[6] "The group searched his face with curiosity, with anxiety even, but found no light there, no expression that they could read. They fell away from him as from something uncanny" (59). The townspeople protect themselves from Wilson's uncanny insight and make him safely readable by bestowing the traditional title "Pudd'nhead," a title that continues to hold Wilson's social identity long after the reasons for its imposition have passed away. But the irony that he introduces and that rebounds to victimize him does not stop here; irony, in this novel, constitutes no simple disjunction between signifier and signified, title and truth—a disjunction that by its stable existence would posit a stable truth. Instead, in what is for Twain a desperate attempt to resist the formal, linguistic, and sociological pressures that his art reflects and even requires, an attempt to make mimesis sustain the creative and moral potential that it necessarily exhausts, irony conflates and implicates facts with fictions, authors with readers, victimizers with victims. Pudd'nhead acquires his name when he is falsely judged to be unaware that you cannot kill half a dog without killing the whole, yet Pudd'nhead—whose own identity and fate cannot remain divorced from the social body to which he belongs[7]—ultimately provides a demonstration of precisely such unawareness. Inevitably, he assumes the identity that the communal fiction authorizes, at which point, of course, he can shed its label.

Living on the fringe of the community, Wilson takes up occupations that reflect and serve its most central institutions and obsessions. He becomes a "land-surveyor and expert accountant" (61) and devotes his leisure time to the collection of what he calls his "records"—fingerprints of all his neighbors, carefully dated and labeled with the identity and age of each subject. Thus, he at once burlesques and epitomizes the community that has stigmatized him—a double role that subtly aligns him with the novel's slaves. For these blacks, the "noble and stately" (64) Roxy and her blue-eyed boy, are white. The four generations of institutionalized miscegenation that have produced Roxy, and the fifth that produces her child, intimately admit her to white society; the institutional judgment that "the one [invisible] sixteenth of her which was black outvoted the other fifteen parts and made her a negro" (64) contravenes the admission and brands her, in the words of her imitation son, an "imitation *white*" (103). Roxy is only black and a slave, Twain writes, "by a fiction of law and custom" (64), a fiction that nonetheless counts as stark fact.

It is her essential imitativeness, however, that most fully measures the irony of Roxy's situation, for imitation at once furnishes power and compels slavishness. Even when turned to subversion, imitation curiously upholds its model; the subversive act that Roxy commits against white society is no less a confirmatory one. This double nature of imitation suggests itself in the two identical infants, who, with their shared birth date, mammy, and "first family" paternity, are born imitations of one another. Even their names, Thomas à Becket and Valet de Chambre, are equivalent in their high-sounding pretentiousness and might easily be reversed by a provincial American on whom the esoteric signification of "valet de chambre" and the irreversible relationship it implies were lost. Paradoxically, Roxy realizes the essential "equality" of the infants as a direct result of her terror that Chambers will be sold down the river. She first recognizes that only superficial trappings—name and clothing— distinguish her child from the other as she prepares him for euthanasia, adorning him in one of Tom's gowns so that the angels will not object that he is dressed too indelicately for heaven. The plan that the twins' resemblance inspires relieves Roxy's need to entrust Chambers to a class-conscious eternity. Yet Roxy, most deeply enslaved in the moment of her liberating act of imagination, requires some authorizing convention in order to carry it out. The one that she hits upon reinforces the paradoxical imitative character of her enterprise: "Tain't no sin—*white* folks has done it! It ain't no sin, glory to goodness it ain't no sin! *Dey's* done it— yes, en dey was de biggest quality in de whole billin', too—kings!" (72). Roxy proceeds to recite a minstrel version of Mark Twain's *The Prince and the Pauper,* which leads her to a crowning rationale—the doctrine of predestination. In remembering that "dey ain't nobody kin save his own self" (72), that an arbitrary God predetermines the circumstances and events of this world, Roxy adopts the slaveholder's traditional defense of slavery and born privilege, an argument that, like her master, she uses to deflect personal responsibility and to naturalize the unnatural. Her attempt to save one twin by dooming the other reiterates the structure and the illusion of the society it challenges. The counter-fiction that Roxy authors, no less than the one it presumes to supplant, is a fiction of law and custom.

Through the workings of habit and convention, Roxy's fiction gradually becomes reality, a somewhat different and more complex reality than she has foreseen. Her reversal of the infants' names and clothing, while leaving the society fundamentally unchanged, yields profound effects that lie beyond her control. Indeed, as the novel's most reflexive passage confides, these effects consummate the self-subversion of her enterprise:

> By the fiction created by herself, he was become her master; the necessity of recognising this relation outwardly and of perfecting herself in the forms required to express the recognition, had moved her to such diligence and faithfulness in practising these forms that this exercise soon concreted itself into habit; it became automatic and unconscious; then a natural result followed: deceptions intended solely for others gradually grew practically into self-deceptions as well; the mock reverence became real reverence, the mock obsequiousness real obsequiousness, the mock homage real homage; the little counterfeit rift of separation between imitation-slave and imitation-master widened and widened, and became an abyss, and a very real one—and on one side of it stood Roxy, the dupe of her own de-

ceptions, and on the other stood her child, no longer a usurper to her, but her accepted and recognized master. He was her darling, her master, and her deity all in one, and in her worship of him she forgot who she was and what he had been. (77)

Under the pressure of the double fiction or double reality that prevails on the Driscoll estate, language itself becomes duplicitous and self-contradictory. Roxy cuffs her ostensible son for "forgitt'n' who his young marster was" (77), and she herself, unguardedly venturing to caress her ostensible master, is warned to "remember who she was" (81). To forget, of course, is to remember; to remember, to forget.

Pudd'nhead Wilson begins with an author's note whose title—"A Whisper to the Reader"—presumes an intimate community, and even suggests complicity, between Twain and his audience. The note's first paragraph offers a wry and desultory assurance that the "two or three legal chapters" in the novel are accurately and realistically rendered. The second paragraph, mimicking the rhetoric of a royal seal, imprints the book's Italian dateline—"Given under my hand this second day of January, 1893, at the Villa Viviani"—and goes on to appropriate a title for Mark Twain:

> And given, too, in the swell room of the house, with the busts of Cerretani senators and other grandees of this line looking approvingly down upon me as they used to look down upon Dante, and mutely asking me to adopt them into my family, which I do with pleasure, for my remotest ancestors are but spring chickens compared with these robed and stately antiques, and it will be a great and satisfying lift for me, that six hundred years will. (53-54)

The interest in legality, title, and ancestral tradition that Twain, however playfully, confesses here aligns him with the citizenry of Dawson's Landing.[8] Both evidence, by such interest, their underlying concern with authority. The immediacy of this concern for Twain is emphasized and elucidated in the account of the genesis of *Pudd'nhead Wilson* that he wrote as an introduction to *Those Extraordinary Twins*. There, he depicts the frustration of his earliest intention by three minor characters—David Wilson, Roxy, and Tom Driscoll—who "got to intruding themselves" and soon "were taking things almost entirely into their own hands and working the tale as a private venture of their own—a tale which they had nothing at all to do with, by rights" (230). Even more disturbing than this usurpation of power and disruption of an authorized novelistic structure was Twain's apprehension that his tale now comprised "not one story, but two stories tangled together; and they obstructed and interrupted each other at every turn and created no end of confusion and annoyance. I could not offer the book for publication, for I was afraid it would unseat the reader's reason" (229–30). Twain capitulates to the pressure of his upstart characters but he reestablishes his own control by severing the double story and disposing of one half. This originative act of violent separation both provides a model for the organization of Dawson's Landing and functions for Twain exactly as its facsimiles do for that society: it underpins a claim to authority, permits readability, and establishes (in this case, between Twain and his readers) "profitable community."

When Roxy switches the social identities of Thomas à Becket Driscoll and Valet de Chambre, she upsets the novel's system of identification as well. A text that allowed the simultaneous operation of two antithetical principles of reference would be dizzyingly chaotic, perhaps unreadable. Thus, Twain must play along with Roxy's fiction, but in announcing his intention to do so he inevitably confers reality and legitimacy upon the fiction that Roxy opposes. "This history," begins chapter 4, "must henceforth accommodate itself to the change which Roxana has consummated, and call the real heir 'Chambers' and the usurping little slave 'Thomas à Becket' (75). The vituperation of Twain's announcement enforces the relation between the threatened social order and the threatened novelistic one. Moreover, it underscores the fact that the very departure from an authorized identity, insofar as it is perceived as a departure, brands that identity deeper still and invests it with even greater (if latent) power. The name "Tom," as Twain agrees to use it, will always resound as "usurper," and ostensibly descriptive epithets like "the false heir" (79) will carry the weight of implacable judgment. Tom will be thoroughly corrupted by the institution to whose fruits his name entitles him, but who will he be when he is called to answer?

The narrative's complicity with the social order, the analogy between its formal demands and the exactions of slavery, is most vividly illustrated in its treatment of Roxy. Percy Driscoll frees her on his deathbed, and she goes off to see the world as a steamboat chambermaid. A few pages later, Twain repossesses her: "It is necessary now," begins chapter 8, "to hunt up Roxy" (100). With a casual brevity that flaunts his plot's gratuitousness, Twain invokes rheumatism, drops the consequently retired Roxy at New Orleans, where, for eight years, she has diligently banked her salary, and declares: "The bank had gone to smash and carried her four hundred dollars with it. She was a pauper, and homeless" (101). Roxy has little choice now but to go back to Dawson's Landing and seek occasional handouts from Tom, to "go and fawn upon him, slave-like" (101). She is, in effect, already sold down the river; Tom only completes the deed, and it ranks with the most devastating of the text's ironies that Roxy's willingness to return to slavery for Tom's sake has often won her, from

Twain's readers, the epithet "noble." Selflessness, and the admiration of it, is a sentimental luxury for white society. In Roxy, who reasons that "Dey aint nothin a white mother won't do for her chile" (174), it merely describes the extent of her enslavement, an enslavement that Twain under-writes in every sentence she utters. "I's a nigger," Roxy pronounces, assuring Tom that lack of proper documentation will not impede her sale, "en nobody ain't gwyne to doubt it dat hears me talk" (174). So she is sold, not just into the deep South but to a plantation managed by a Yankee overseer, a New Englander. "*Dey* knows how to work a nigger to death" (182), she later reports, and we may hear, beneath her voice, the sardonic self-accusation of the ex-Confederate captain turned Connecticut Yankee who had, in a way, been doing that for almost thirty years.

It is no less than poetic justice that, in the end, the man who has sold into the harshest slavery not only a free woman but the woman who gave him life is himself sold down the river. This irony, however, neither privileges nor uplifts; instead, like each viciously cyclical irony in *Pudd'n-head Wilson,* it recoils upon the ironist. For its justice matches slave justice—the justice by which Tom is sold not for any inhuman deed but because he *is* technically inhuman. In chronicling the acts of cruelty that characterize Tom from early boyhood, the novel not merely plots but smooths and even sanctions the horrifying shift from inhumanity as a quality of action to inhumanity as a principle of identity. Twain plays dangerously with the precariousness of such crucial distinctions during Tom's brief period of disorientation when he first learns his true parentage. The play concerns the signification of "nigger":

> If he met a friend, he found that the habit of a lifetime had in some mysterious way vanished—his arm hung limp, instead of involuntarily extending the hand for a shake. It was the 'nigger' in him asserting its humility, and he blushed and was abashed. And the 'nigger' in him was surprised when the white friend put out his hand for a shake with him. . . . The 'nigger' in him went shrinking and skulking here and there and yonder, and fancying it saw suspicion and maybe de-tection in all faces, tones and gestures. (118)

Tom doubtless understands 'nigger' to be a concrete referent to a bio-logical fact. The reader, however, avails himself of the ironic alternative, an alternative that Twain stresses for us by placing 'nigger' between quotation marks. It is not, of course, Tom's genetic make-up that his attitudes suddenly reveal, nor is it a biological identity that 'nigger' sig-nifies. A mere fabrication of pernicious social convention, 'nigger' does not really refer at all: it constitutes only a sign (Twain's enclosing quota-tion marks aptly indicate its self-referentiality) that wields the symbolic

power with which it has been invested, an epithet into which white society has poured its hatreds and fears. This reading, as distinct from
Tom's, must be the right one, yet it will not be able to preserve its discrete
identity, will not be able to keep 'nigger' from referring. Barely a page
beyond the account of Tom's shock and anguish, the novel resumes its
systematic blackening of him. And, shortly afterward, when Tom blithely
betrays the sacred code of honor and adds cowardice to his list of attributes (the judgment stands despite the duel's absurdity), Roxy herself
takes up the condemnatory refrain and, in effect, foretells the novel's
climax. Summoning all the righteous indignation to which her direct
descent from Captain John Smith entitles her, she chillingly pronounces:
"It's de nigger in you, dat's what it is" (157).

Throughout much of *Pudd'nhead Wilson*, the titular character plays a
minor role. Before the climactic investigation and trial, which he dominates, Pudd'nhead makes significant appearances in six out of eighteen
chapters. His assimilation by the community, beyond its abandonment of
hostility toward him in favor of amused toleration, seems minimal. For
the reader, Wilson remains the pariah, the savvy stranger who has himself
read and understood Dawson's Landing and who, by virtue of his superior
insight and sophistication, stands apart from it. This identity is sustained
and reinforced by the aphoristic observations, all bearing the label *Pudd'n-
head Wilson's Calendar,* that head each chapter. In fact, the relation
between the epigraphs and the text re-presents the relation between
Pudd'nhead and the community that the first chapter defines; situated on
the margin of plot, the calendar entries offer whimsical, oblique, and
often inscrutable commentary on it. Only once are they brought directly
into the story, an occasion that Twain uses to reemphasize the distinction
between Wilson and the community and to associate his own narrative
enterprise with Wilson's satirical one. Judge Driscoll, who can afford an
eccentric opinion on the question of Pudd'nhead's intellect, unwisely
attempts to evidence it by showing off a few of its products. Predictab-
ly, this strategy backfires, but the announcement of its failure ("If there
had ever been any doubt that Dave Wilson was a pudd'nhead—which there
hadn't—this revelation removed that doubt for good and all") is immediately followed by a comment whose tone and structure identify it
as a calendar entry: "That is just the way in this world; an enemy can
partly ruin a man, but it takes a good-natured injudicious friend to complete the thing and make it perfect" (86). Wilson and Twain, as this passage and other authorial commentary suggest, take a common approach to
the novel's events; their approach, however, is deceptive, their implied
position untenable. The wry wit and air of superior knowingness that inform both Pudd'nhead's observations and Twain's narration camouflage
the involvement of character with community, of novelist with novel plot,

and belie the very precepts of human interdependency and social responsibility that Wilson's initiatory joke affirms. Epitomized in the epigraphs, they promote the comfortable illusion of "ironic distance," a distance that the reader blithely presumes to share despite its fundamental incompatability with the complex and implicated sense of irony that the novel calls for and repeatedly exemplifies in its action. The epigraphs themselves, however, are deeply involved in the plot, for they fatten a pretense for a denoument that will fell with a single stroke not just one false heir but all the novel's pretenders.

The Pudd'nhead Wilson who stands up in court to present the case for the defense in the murder trial of Luigi and Angelo Capello is a man who has been ostracized, ridiculed, and underestimated in Dawson's Landing for twenty years. Against the accumulated force of this identity, the detail of Wilson's election as mayor, offhandedly introduced several pages earlier, seems barely significant and is easily forgotten. The true culprit, Wilson's most noble tormentor, has time and again demonstrated his reprehensibility. Moreover, he has been called Tom for so long that the reader, although he well knows the secret of Tom's birth, cannot help but think of him as Tom. Wilson unveils his evidence slowly and theatrically, relishing the hour of his revenge on the small-minded citizens whom he has at last indisputably outwitted. Masterfully, he prepares the revelation that will redeem his intelligence (and ours) as it relieves the gathering tension of the well-wrought courtroom scene. An impending climax irresistibly attracts. For all these reasons, the reader enjoys and endorses Pudd'n-head's efforts and eagerly awaits their fruition.

The climax that Wilson finally articulates enforces an association that has already been made. Long before Tom's ultimate exposure, during the period of his violent distress over Roxy's account of his birth and infancy, Judge Driscoll demands of his nephew, "What's the matter with you? You look as meek as a nigger," and the narrative records that "[Tom] felt as secret murderers are said to feel when the accuser says, 'Thou art the man!'" (119). To be identified as a black, for Tom, is to be identified as a murderer; Pudd'nhead merely reverses the terms of the equation when he proclaims: "Valet de Chambre, negro and slave—falsely called Thomas à Becket Driscoll—make upon the window the finger-prints that will hang you!" (222). With these words, the novel attains its formal resolution, Dawson's Landing restores and reaffirms its social order, David Wilson becomes "a made man for good" (224), and the reader, for the first time, clearly and devastatingly perceives the nature of the plot that he has abetted. The judgment implicit in Wilson's identification of the murderer is familiar and irreversible: it is not Thomas à Becket but Valet de Chambre, Negro and slave; it *is*, after all, the 'nigger' in him. Grounded in the principles of personal identity that inform Western civilization and the

novel, the identification of Chambers is inescapably accurate. Yet it is
also technical, partial, illusory. Pudd'nhead kills his half of the man and
expects the other half to live;[9] to the jury's great satisfaction, he promises
that the real Tom, a kitchen slave for twenty years, will "within a quarter
of an hour . . . stand before you white and free!" (222). The method of
identification that has made Pudd'nhead's case suggests no reason why
this should not be true. No sets of fingerprints, not even those of identical twins, duplicate each other. Fingerprints conceal human interdependency. They collapse the distinction between biology and convention, for
they represent biology in the service of convention. Tom's scornful depiction of them as "palace window decorations" does not entirely mistake
their political function.

The concluding pages of *Pudd'nhead Wilson* punishingly elaborate the
implications of the climactic discovery. Percy Driscoll's creditors point
out that, if Tom had been properly inventoried when the estate was sold,
no one ever would have been hurt; "the guilt lay with the erroneous
inventory," they reckon, and Twain adds: "Everybody saw that there
was reason in this" (226). Tom is promptly pardoned and sold down the
river; the other two discordant elements in the society—Roxy and Pudd'n-
head—have already been eliminated, one by exposure and the other by
complete assimilation. Thus, the novel ultimately disables the three characters who, in the early stages of its development, had usurped Twain's
authority and changed its form. The exonerated twins return to Europe.
They are not freaks in this book in order that their relationship might suggest a positive ideal of wholeness, a harmonious interdependency. But
they are minor and insubstantial characters, foreigners, or, as the novel
last describes them, "heroes of romance" (224). The implied claim of this
phrase that Twain's work—with its gimcrackery of bejewelled sheaths and
antitemperance rallies, its aborted subplots and its ramified theme of disguised identity—is something other than romance again points up the
fundamental disunity of *Pudd'nhead Wilson,* its repeated structural imitation of the dividedness that its represented society covets.

"It is often the case that the man who can't tell a lie thinks he is the
best judge of one" (224). Appearing just beneath the word "Conclusion,"
this calendar entry carries Twain's final self-indictment: It takes a liar to
discover a lie. In *Pudd'nhead Wilson,* the very act of discovering a lie at
once constitutes—or reconstitutes—another, because the accepted criteria
of truth are themselves unconvincing. Truths are fictions as well as facts;
lies, facts as well as fictions. The circuit of irony, unbroken and unbreakable, ensures a boundless freedom and imposes an inexorable enslavement.
Twain's novel exemplifies the definition of irony that Kenneth Burke
advances in *A Grammar of Motives.* True irony, Burke writes, is not
"superior" to the enemy: "True irony, humble irony, is based upon a sense

of fundamental kinship with the enemy; as one *needs* him, is *indebted* to him, is not merely outside him as an observer but contains him *within,* being consubstantial with him."[10] Narrative fiction's relation to the world itself exemplifies such irony. As imitation, the novel resides in the convergence of lie and truth and is informed by the tension between its mastery and its slavery. Its author, like Roxy and Pudd'nhead, must in some sense replicate the models and structures that he would transform. But in its complicitous replication, even as it evidences the real and often irresistible power of social organization and ideological convention, the novel does effect a saving transformation. By identifying these models and structures as formal constructs, as fictions, the novel demonstrates their artificiality and, more importantly, reveals our perpetual authorship of them. Represented in art, Hegel contended, the external world is brought into an individual's self-consciousness; its palpable externality is reduced, and one may take unalienated possession of it by rediscovering it in himself. *Pudd'nhead Wilson* offers precisely this opportunity: in illustrating the consubstantiality of its characters with its author and readers (its ultimate mimetic feat), Twain's novel implicates us in its community of disingenuousness and guilt and, by so doing, facilitates our realization of that community (ourselves) and its possible redemption through us. We and Twain, in the end, are neither wholly masters nor wholly slaves; rather, I think, the novel would have us take on a more difficult mediatory position—the assumption of responsibility—as it has done by providing a medium in which responsibility may be recognized and shared.

NOTES

1. Quoted by Justin Kaplan in *Mr. Clemens and Mark Twain* (New York: Simon & Schuster, 1966), p. 149.

2. Quotations from *Pudd'nhead Wilson* are taken from the Penguin English Library Edition of *Pudd'nhead Wilson* and *Those Extraordinary Twins,* ed. Malcolm Bradbury, 1969.

3. James M. Cox, *Mark Twain: The Fate of Humor* (Princeton: Princeton University Press, 1966), p. 234.

4. Jonathan Culler, *Structuralist Poetics* (Ithaca: Cornell University Press, 1975), p. 190.

5. In *Mark Twain: The Fate of Humor,* Cox reiterates this point, first made by Jay B. Hubbell in *The South in American Literature* (Durham, N.C.: Duke University Press, 1954), p. 835.

6. Marvin Fisher and Michael Elliot, in *"Pudd'nhead Wilson:* Half a Dog is Worse than None," *Southern Review* 8, no. 3 (Summer 1972): 533–47, also note the abstraction and expressionlessness that accompany Wilson's remark.

7. Fisher and Elliot, in the article cited above, suggest that "Mark Twain has apparently presented us with two rather separate characters in his portrayal of Pudd'nhead Wilson" (541). It seems more precise, however, to say that Twain allows Wilson's satirical vein (as created and illustrated by his calendar entries) to disguise his gradual

achievement of assimilation and conventionality. The effect of the ending is produced, in part, by the reader's shocked recognition that the sympathy he has extended to an outcast and an ironist is cashed in by Dawson's Landing's mayor and chief apologist.

8. Earl F. Briden, writing on law and legal metaphors in *Pudd'nhead Wilson*, anticipates some of my concerns and suggests Twain's complicity with the Dawson's Landing community when he notes: "In his use of names, the narrator acquiesces in precisely the kind of fiction which is the subject of his story" (178). Briden stops short, however, of considering the roles that the reader and the novelistic structure play in the linguistically constituted social structure. "Idiots First, Then Juries: Legal Metaphors in Mark Twain's *Pudd'nhead Wilson,*" *Texas Studies in Literature and Language* 20 (Summer 1978): 169–79.

9. Slaves and slavery in *Pudd'nhead Wilson* are persistently associated with dogs and with an unsentimental vision of a dog's life. The narrator and various characters refer to Tom, specifically, as a dog, a cur, a hound, and a pup.

10. Kenneth Burke, *A Grammar of Motives* and *A Rhetoric of Motives*, 2 vols. in 1 (New York: Meridian Books, 1962), p. 514.

MARK SELTZER

The Princess Casamassima
REALISM AND THE FANTASY OF SURVEILLANCE

"We do not suffer from the spy mania here," George R. Sims observes in his monograph on the London underworld, *The Mysteries of Modern London:* in this "free land" it is "not our custom to take violent measures" against the secret agents of the nether world. The freedom from violence that Sims celebrates, however, carries a rider that he at once suggests and disavows, and the "spy mania" reappears in a somewhat different guise: "The system of observation is as perfect as can be. . . . every foreign anarchist and terrorist known to the police—and I doubt if there is one in our midst who is not—is shadowed." London's "freedom" is guaranteed by the existence of an unlimited policing and by the dissemination of elaborate methods of police surveillance. An intense watchfulness generalizes the spy mania that Sims has discounted, and for the violence of the law is substituted a more subtle and more extensive mode of power and coercion: a power of observation and surveillance, and a seeing that operates as a more effective means of overseeing. Nor is it merely, in Sims's account, the agents of secret societies and criminals of the underworld who are shadowed by this perfect system of observation. London itself is constituted as a secret society, and everyday life is riddled with suggestions of criminality and encompassed by an incriminating surveillance:

> In the 'buses and the trams and the trains the silent passengers sit side by side, and no man troubles about his neighbour. But the mysteries of modern London are represented in the crowded vehicle and in the packed compartment. The quiet-looking woman sitting opposite you in the omnibus knows the secret that the police have been seeking to discover for months. The man who politely raises his hat because he touches you as he passes from his seat would, if the truth were known, be standing in the dock of the Old Bailey to answer a capital charge.

The melodrama of the secret crime and the secret life passes "side by side with all that is ordinary and humdrum in the monotony of everyday existence." And since there are "no mysteries of modern London more terrible than its unrecorded ones," "silence" can only imply a more nefarious criminality; and not to have been brought to book by the police can only invoke a suspicion of mysteries more insidious and of a criminality more threatening in its apparent innocence and ordinariness.[1]

If Sims's vision of the London streets is marked by a fantastic paranoia, it is also a remarkable piece of police work, an attempt to "book" London's unrecorded mysteries and to supplement the official police record through an unrestricted lay policing. Discovering mysteries everywhere, Sims places all of London under suspicion and under surveillance. Nor is Sims's vision untypical of the manner in which London is seen and recorded in the late nineteenth century. The extensive documentation that accumulates about London from the mid-century on displays an interesting paradox. On the one hand, from George W. M. Reynolds's *The Mysteries of London* (1845-48) to Sims's *The Mysteries of Modern London* (1906), London was reproduced as an impenetrable region of mystery; on the other, as this proliferating literature itself testifies, London was subjected to an unprecedented and elaborate scrutiny and surveillance. The sense of the city as an area of mystery incites an intensive policing, a police work not confined to the institutions of the law (although the expansion of the London police and detective forces was "a landmark in the history of administration")[2] but enacted also through an "unofficial" literature of detection: by the reports of tourists from the "upper world" and by the investigations of an exploratory urban sociology, particularly the work of Henry Mayhew, Charles Booth, and B. Seebohm Rowntree. It is played out also in the "discovery" of the city, and its underworld, by the realist and naturalist novelists.

Henry James's eccentric contribution to the literature of London exploration is *The Princess Casamassima,* his vision of the "sinister anarchic underworld" of London. "Truly, of course," James observes in his preface to the novel, "there are London mysteries (dense categories of dark arcana) for every spectator." *The Princess Casamassima* is a novel about the mysteries of London, about spies and secret societies, and it is also a novel about spectatorship, about seeing and being seen. James offers an obligingly simple account of the novel's origin: "This fiction proceeded quite directly, during the first year of a long residence in London, from the habit and the interest of walking the streets." "The attentive exploration of London," he suggests, " . . . fully explains a large part" of the novel; one walked "with one's eyes greatly open," and this intense observation provoked "a mystic solicitation, the urgent appeal, on the part of everything, to be interpreted."[3] It is the insistent continuity between secrecy and spectatorship, between the "mysteries abysmal" of London and the urgent solicitation to interpretation, that I want to focus on in this study of *The Princess Casamassima*. More precisely, I want to explore two questions that this continuity poses. First, what does it mean to walk the streets of London at this time, and how does this street-walking function as a metonymy for the ways London is seen by James and his contemporaries? Second, how do the content and the techniques of representation in James's novel reproduce the London spy mania and the coercive network of seeing and power that characterize the literature of London mysteries?

Critics of *The Princess Casamassima* have traditionally located its politics in James's representation of London anarchist activities and have largely dismissed the novel's political dimension by pointing to James's lack of knowledge about these activities. The critical impulse has been to rescue the significance of the text by redirecting attention away from its ostensible political subject to its techniques, and these techniques have been seen to be at odds with the novel's political references. Manfred Mackenzie has recently summarized this depoliticization of the text, claiming that James, "because of his prior or primary American association . . . cannot participate in any conventional modes of European social power, only in 'seeing,' or 'knowledge,' or 'consciousness.'"[4] But can "seeing" and "power" be so easily opposed in this literature, and are the politics of *The Princess Casamassima* separable from its techniques, from its ways of knowing? What I hope to demonstrate is that *The Princess Casamassima* is a distinctly political novel but that James's analysis of anarchist politics is less significant than the power play that the narrative technique itself enacts. This is not to say that the politics of the novel are confined to its techniques: the institutions of the law and its auxiliaries, primarily the prison and the police, function as explicit topics in the text. But beyond these explicit and local representations of policing power, there is a more discreet kind of policing that the novel engages, a police work articulated precisely along the novel's line of sight.

If a relation between seeing and power becomes evident in the literature of the London underworld, it asserts itself not because the writer acknowledges the relation but, rather, because he works so carefully to disavow it. Sims, for instance, denies the existence of a "spy mania" on two counts: first, by separating police surveillance from an exercise of power, and second, by attempting to draw a line between his own acts of espionage and those of the police. Sims insists that he does not require a police escort in his wanderings through the London streets: "I have never asked for their assistance in my journeyings into dark places."[5]

Nevertheless, he is uneasily aware of the incriminating cast of his prowling and publication of the London nether world. In his earlier *How the Poor Live* and *Horrible London* (1883), he notes that "it is unpleasant to be mistaken, in underground cellars where the vilest outcasts hide from the light of day, for detectives in search of their prey."[6] Techniques of "disinterested" information gathering are unpleasantly mistaken for exercises of social control.

Additionally, Sims attempts to defend himself from another kind of "mistake," a misreading that would similarly put his motives in question. He introduces his text with a series of disclaimers: "It is not my object in these pages to bring out the sensational features of police romance"; my task "has for its object not the gratifying of a morbid curiosity, but the better understanding of things as they are." But if Sims seeks to tell "only the truth . . . a plain unvarnished tale," his account, again, everywhere takes the form of what he protests against. If he will reveal only the truth, it is because the "truth is stranger than any written tale could ever hope to be"; and he proceeds to detail the underworld of East London as "the romances of the 'Mysterious East.'"[7] His motives and, by implication, the motives of his audience cannot be separated from a morbid curiosity-mongering. Sims's works sensationalize the mysteries beneath the humdrum surface and posit lurid secrets to be detected; they incite and cultivate a fascination with the underworld that converts it into a bizarre species of entertainment. On the one side, putting the underworld into discourse takes the form of a certain detective work, on the other, the purveying of a sensational entertainment. It is between these two poles—policing and entertainment—that Sims wishes to situate his texts, disclaiming both his (mis)identification as a detective and his exploitation of an intrusive voyeurism. Sims tries to open up a narrow space—called "things as they are"—to evade the charge of violating what he sees and reports. But this space is eroded from both sides: watching cannot be freed from an act of violation, from a conversion of the objects of his investigation into, as he expresses it, the "victims of my curiosity."[8]

The double bind in which Sims finds himself, and the alibis he offers to extricate himself, recur frequently in other representations of the London underworld. This literature is always, in effect, playing on the twin senses of "bringing to book," making it difficult to disentangle publication from incrimination, and foregrounding the police work always latent in the retailing of London mysteries. James Greenwood, in his *Low-Life Deeps: An Account of the Strange Fish to be Found There* (1881), feels compelled, like Sims, to offer apologies for his intrusions into the underworld: "The extraordinary endurance of popular interest in the 'Orton imposture' . . . will perhaps be regarded as sufficient justification for here reproducing what was perhaps the most conclusive evidence of the man's guilt at the time, or since brought to light." Greenwood, however, does more than reproduce the evidence and respond, after the fact, to popular demand. His own investigations have in fact produced the confession, and its accompanying popularity. Greenwood has brought Orton to book in the double sense that I have indicated: "I am glad to acknowledge that the confession of 'brother Charles' was obtained by me, the more so when I reflect on the vast amount of patience and perseverance it was found necessary to exercise in order to bring the individual in question to book." The impostor Orton is turned over, in a single gesture, to the reading public and to the police. And what follows Greenwood's self-congratulatory acknowledgment of his agency is Orton's signed confession—the signature juridically reproduced at the close of Greenwood's chapter—serving both as an entertainment in the popular interest and as an instrument of indictment.[9]

Greenwood's gesture toward justification is a momentary confession on his own part of the "power of writing" that he exercises; his documentation of London mysteries, in *Low-Life Deeps* and in his earlier *The Wilds of London* (1874), is also a kind of victimization. More often, however, the victimization is less explicit; the function of supplying an entertainment is more obvious than any overt police action. James, we recall, speaks of "mysteries . . . for every spectator," and it is as a spectacle that the underworld is most frequently represented. Further, James's formulation—"mysteries . . . for every spectator" rather than "spectators for every mystery"—points to the constitutive power that the spectator exerts. The watcher produces, and not merely reproduces, what he sees and puts the underworld on stage as a theatrical entertainment.

The "staging" of the underworld is evident in Daniel Joseph Kirwan's *Palace and Hovel* (1870). Kirwan is an unselfconscious curiosity seeker, and desires simply "to see something interesting." Presenting a series of underworld "scenes," he records, for example, a visit to a thieves' den, and his account is typical in the way it manages to convert a potentially threatening encounter into a moment of theater. His desire to be entertained is immediately gratified: each of the thieves Kirwan interrogates presents himself as an out-of-work entertainer, and each in turn performs for Kirwan's amusement. Crude and prefaced with excuses, the performances are clearly extemporized; the criminals have readily adopted the roles that Kirwan has implicitly assigned, and have cooperated to produce the spectacle he wants to see. The underworld, quite literally, appears as a sort of underground theater. And the play is a power play in another sense as well. Kirwan, like most tourists of the nether regions, is accompanied and protected by a police detective, and the detective has supplied the cue for the performance that results. Before admitting the visitors, the "master of the mansion" has asked whether it is "bizness or pleasure," adding that "hif hits business you must 'elp yourself." "O, pleasure by all means," the detective replies.[10] The displacement of poverty and crime into theater, of business into pleasure, is clearly marked, and the performers are willing to confine themselves to the roles of a beggars' opera in order to escape a more definitive confinement.

The metaphor of the theater also pervades Sims's *The Mysteries of Modern London*. His intent is to take the reader "behind the scenes": "When the interior of a house is set upon the stage, the fourth wall is always down in order that the audience may see what is going on. In real life the dramas within the domestic interior are played with the fourth wall up. . . . care is taken that no passer-by shall have a free entertainment. I am going to take the fourth wall down to-day."[11] Indeed, this is not "free entertainment" but the basis of a literary industry; poverty, conspiracy, criminality are purchasable spectacles, at once opened to the public and reduced and distanced as theater. "'Do show me some cases of unmitigated misery,' is a request said to have been made by a young lady in search of sensation," Mrs. Bernard Bosanquet records in her study of the slums, *Rich and Poor* (1896).[12] The request might easily be that of James's Princess, who "liked seeing queer types and exploring out-of-the-way social corners" (2:234).

But if Sims's fantasy of disclosure—his taking down of the fourth wall—has an immediate theatrical reference, it refers also to another sort of fantasy. The source of Sims's passage might well be the familiar passage in Dickens's *Dombey and Son* in which the author imagines " a good spirit who would take the house-tops off . . . and show a Christian people what dark shapes issue from amidst their homes."[13] There is, however, a more immediate source than this fantasy of a providential supervision, a possible source that makes unmistakable the nexus of policing and entertainment I have been tracing: "If we could fly out of that window hand in hand, hover over this great city, gently remove the roofs, and peep in at the queer things which are going on, the strange coincidences, the plannings, the cross-purposes, the wonderful chain of events . . . it would make all fiction, with its conventionalities and foreseen conclusions, most stale and unprofitable."[14] The speaker is Sherlock Holmes, in A. Conan Doyle's tale "A Case of Identity," precisely the "police romance" that Sims begins by disavowing, and precisely the form that most insistently manifests the twin operations of vision and supervision, of spectatorship and incrimination, that the literature of the underworld engages. The impulse to explore and disclose the underworld in detective fiction becomes indistinguishable from a fantasy of surveillance; and in the figure of the detective, seeing becomes the mode of power par excellence.

In "The Adventure of the Copper Beeches," Watson confesses to an uneasiness about sensationalizing the nether world similar to that found in

Sims and Greenwood. Holmes's alibi is exemplary: "You can hardly be open to a charge of sensationalism," he maintains, "for out of these cases . . . a fair proportion do not treat of crime, in its legal sense, at all." Holmes, as everyone knows, repeatedly acts to mark a separation between his own activities and those of the police detective, and he claims repeatedly that his interest is in those matters "outside the pale of the law."[15] But his investigations appear less to stand "outside" the law than to operate as a more efficient extension of the law. If Holmes's policing is extralegal, it registers an expansion and dissemination of policing techniques and of the apparatus of incrimination: an extension that places even what is avowedly legal within the boundaries of a generalized power of surveillance. Crime, in Holmes's sense, has been redefined to include an expanding range of activities, moving toward the placing of every aspect of everyday life under suspicion and under investigation.

Such a dream of absolute surveillance and supervision is enacted by the literature that the sensational accounts of London mysteries popularize and supplement: the sociological studies of the underworld that began accumulating in the mid-century with the work of the local statistical societies, Thomas Beames's *The Rookeries of London* (1850), and Henry Mayhew's *London Labour and the London Poor* (1851-61) and culminating in Charles Booth's vast *Life and Labour of the People of London* (1889-1903).

The sociologist also represents London as a region of mystery to be deciphered, as a largely unexplored and unknown territory; the intent is to "map" the nether world, to place it within the confines of the "known world." As Asa Briggs suggests, "there was a dominating emphasis on 'exploration.' The 'dark city' and the 'dark continent' were alike mysterious, and it is remarkable how often the exploration of the unknown city was compared with the exploration of Africa and Asia."[16] William Booth's *In Darkest England* (1890), for instance, opens with an extended analogy between the exploration for the sources of the Nile in Africa and the exploration for the sources of poverty and criminality in London. Similarly, Jack London, in his study of the London slums, *The People of the Abyss* (1903), equates investigating London and colonial exploration: "But O Cook, O Thomas Cook & Son, pathfinders and trail-clearers . . . unhesitatingly and instantly, with ease and celerity, could you send me to Darkest Africa or Innermost Thibet, but to the East End of London . . . you know not the way."[17]

As the reference to Cook indicates, exploration of the city appears as a specialized and exotic species of tourism even as it displays a "colonial" attitude toward the underworld. The secretary of a London's Workman's Association, H. J. Pettifer, articulated in 1884 one form that this colonial tourism was taking: the urban sociologists, who in the absence of institutional funding required substantial personal wealth to undertake their studies, "had been talking of the working classes as though they were some newfound race, or extinct animal."[18] Reduced to the status of the colonized primitive or "natural curiosity," the "strange fish" of London's "low-life deeps" are collected as exotic "specimens." Muniment, for instance, in *The Princess Casamassima,* compares Captain Sholto to a "deep-sea fisherman. . . . He throws his nets and hauls in the little fishes—the pretty little shining, wriggling fishes. They are all for [the Princess] ; she swallows 'em down." Hyacinth and Muniment are spoken of as if they were "a sample out of your shop or a little dog you had for sale." "You see you do regard me as a curious animal," Hyacinth complains to the Princess. Sholto and the Princess share a "taste for exploration" and an appetite for queer types; Sholto hunts the slums as he does the imperial territories, bringing back trophies and specimens for the Princess (1:258-59, 229, 292).

There is a more than metaphoric resemblance between this colonial attitude toward the slums and the larger movements of colonization in the period. William Booth, the founder of the Salvation Army, worked to establish "missions" in darkest England, and the larger program he proposed called for the establishment of a series of colonies—"The City Colony, the Farm Colony, and the Over-Sea Colony"—to deal with the social question. And the colonizing of the underworld appears also in a somewhat different, and more comprehensive, form. Booth complains that the "colonies of heathens and savages in the heart of our capital . . . attract so little attention," but in fact they were drawing unprecedented attention. The secret world of London has become, as Booth later admits, an "open secret," and even as the city continues to be spoken of as an impenetrable enigma, the enigma has been systematically penetrated.[19]

The statistical inscription and mapping of the city in the later nineteenth century has been well documented, and is part of what might be called a professionalization of the problem of the city.[20] From the formation of the Statistical Society in 1834 to Charles Booth's *Life and Labour,* London was meticulously explored, documented, and systematized. The intent, as Philip Abrams has observed, was, in part, to put on record "the mode of existence of different families—meals and menus, clothing and furniture, household routines and division of tasks, religious practices and recreation": in short, a scrutiny and recording in detail of the everyday life of the underclasses.[21] There is a preoccupation with statistical and enumerative grids, with the laborious accumulation of detail, with the deployment of a comprehensive system of averages and norms. The investigator constructs an interpretive matrix covering virtually every area and activity in the city, from the average traffic on the London streets and the cubic feet of air circulated in the London tenements to a detailed classification of criminals, delinquents, and other deviants from the specified norm.[22] For the sociologist, as for James's Hoffendahl, "moving ever in a dry statistical and scientific air" "humanity, in his scheme, was classified and subdivided with a truly German thoroughness" (2:137, 55).

In the "amateur" investigations of Sims and in the fictive detective work of Holmes, it is the potential significance of the most trivial detail that instigates a thorough scrutiny and surveillance; in the sociological study, we perceive a more discreet and more comprehensive surveillance, leaving no area of the city uncharted. The professionalization of the city proceeds as a tactful and tactical colonization of the territory, enabling an elaborate regularizing and policing of the city. Crucially, what the sociological discourse establishes is a normative scenario, a system of norms and deviations that effectively "imposes a highly specific grid on the common perception of delinquents."[23] A regulative vision of the city is imposed, "subordinating in its universality all petty irregularities" and holding forth the possibility of that "one glorious principle of universal and undeviating regularity" that the sociologists envisioned.[24] As the British sociologist Frederic J. Mouat observed in 1885, statistics have passed from a merely descriptive stage and become prescriptive: "statistics have become parliamentary . . . and administrative."[25]

The articulation of the sociological discourse of the city is coextensive with, and opens the way for, the emergence and dispersal of agencies of social training and social control: the multiplication of workhouses and reformatories of vocational institutions and of institutions for delinquents, the expansion of the metropolitan police and the penal apparatus.[26] The nominal function of these institutions is to train, to educate, to correct, to reform; but clearly, their effect is to impose a general disciplinary and supervisory authority over areas of urban life that heretofore have evaded scrutiny and control. There is an insistent continuity between the theoretical preoccupation with normative scenarios and the institutionalization of that normative vision. And it is not surprising that when the sociologist proposes a model for urban reform, the model is that of the most highly regulated and supervised institution, the prison and reformatory: "In a well-regulated reformatory may be seen the effect of moral and religious discipline, combined with good sanitary conditions, and a proper union of industrial and intellectual education, upon wayward, ignorant and hardened natures. Such an institution is a type of the great work before us, for there is nothing done in a reformatory which might not, with proper appliances, be effected for society at large."[27] It is the prison, with its routines, timetables, with its all-encompassing control and supervision, that serves as the ideal model for the city. The regulative vision of the city institutionalizes a regulative supervision.

☙

The most evident feature of the discourses of the city that I have been
tracing is an insistent watchfulness, a "spy mania," which appears at once
as a form of entertainment and as a police action. The twin sites of this
obsessive surveillance are the theater and the prison. *The Princess Casamassima* invokes this discursive scenario. James recalled his initial sense of
the novel as a self-implicating network of watchers: "To find [Hyacinth's]
possible adventure interesting I had only to conceive his watching the
same public show, the same innumerable appearances, I had watched myself, and of his watching very much as I had watched" (1:vi). This specular
relation is reproduced throughout the novel, explicitly in the figures of
the police spy and secret agent, whose disguised presence is always suspected, but also in the more ordinary exchanges of sight in the novel. In
The Princess Casamassima, seeing and being seen always implicitly involve
an actual or potential power play. Hyacinth, typically, promises "himself
to watch his playmate [Millicent] as he had never done before. She let him
know, as may well be supposed, that she had her eye on *him,* and it must be
confessed that as regards the exercise of a right of supervision he had felt
himself at a disadvantage ever since the night at the theatre" (2:65). Seeing
makes for a "right of supervision" and a power of coercion; it is the nexus of
seeing and power that I now want to examine in *The Princes Casamassima.*

Hyacinth dates his "disadvantage" from the "night at the theatre," and
it does not take much interpretive pressure to see that a pervasive theatricality runs through the novel. The governing mode of interaction between
characters involves a series of performances: the characters engage in the
"entertainment of watching" (1:307) as they are alternately recruited
"for supplying such entertainment" (1:210). Muniment commandeers
Hyacinth "for Rosy's entertainment" (1:253), as Hyacinth is brought to
Medley by the Princess because his "*naïveté* would entertain her" (2:19).
The Princess especially is repeatedly referred to in theatrical terms, as an
"actress" performing on the "*mise-en-scène* of life" (1:268), and her imitation of a small bourgeoise provides Hyacinth with "the most finished
entertainment she had yet offered him" (2:186).

The insistent theatricality of the novel refers less to any "dramatic
analogy" than to the reciprocal watchfulness that invests every relation in
the novel. What the theater scenes in the novel enact is an indifferent
interchange of audience and play as objects of observation. The theater
is the privileged point of vantage for an "observation of the London
world" (1:189), and if, as Hyacinth notes, "one's own situation seem[ed]
a play within the play" (1:208), it is because one is both spectator and
spectacle. It is in the theater that Hyacinth discovers that he is being
watched, that he has been spotted by Sholto and the Princess, herself

"overshadowed by the curtain of the box, drawn forward with the intention of shielding her from the observation of the house" (1:205). Hyacinth, in the balcony and not in the box, is not shielded from observation, and his vulnerable position indicates that, despite the exchanges of performance between characters, there is a certain asymmetry in this "entertainment of watching." Hyacinth, "lacking all social dimensions was scarcely a perceptible person," and he is gratified that Sholto should "recognise and notice him" in the theater "because even so small a fact as this was an extension of his social existence" (1:192). The underclasses "exist" only when they have become the object of regard of the upper classes. But there is a counterside to this visibility. For if to be seen is to exist, it is also to be objectified, fixed, and imprisoned in the gaze of the other. It is to be reduced to the status of a "favourable specimen" (1:257), to "studies of the people—the lower orders" (1:305). In the largest sense, to be seen is to be encompassed by a right of supervision.

To escape supervision, characters cultivate a style of secrecy, adopt disguises in order to see without being seen; and, indeed, seeing without being seen becomes the measure of power in the novel. Hyacinth insistently promotes the secret life, at times with a certain absurdity: "I don't understand everything you say, but I understand everything you hide," Millicent tells Hyacinth. "Then I shall soon become a mystery to you, for I mean from this time forth to cease to seek safety in concealment. You'll know nothing about me then—for it will be all under your nose" (2:332). If seeing is power, secrecy assumes a paramount value, and if beneath every surface a secret truth is suspected, to allow the "truth" to appear is consummately to disguise it.[28]

The relation between a theatrical secrecy and power is most evident in James's representation of the secret society. Invoking Sims's paranoid vision of London conspiracies, the secret society appears as an almost providential power because it is both pervasively present and invisible: "The forces secretly arrayed against the present social order were pervasive and universal, in the air one breathed, in the ground one trod, in the hand of an acquaintance that one might touch or the eye of a stranger that might rest a moment on one's own. They were above, below, within, without, in every contact and combination of life; and it was no disproof of them to say it was too odd they should lurk in a particular improbable form. To lurk in improbable forms was precisely their strength" (2:275). The spy mania is universal; the secret society, arrayed in improbable disguises, exercises a potentially unlimited surveillance, a potentially unlimited supervision.

There is another species of theater in *The Princess Casamassima* that makes even more explicit the nexus of seeing and power: the scene of the prison. Hyacinth's meeting with his mother in Millbank prison appears as another instance of reciprocal watchfulness: "They had too much the air of having been brought together simply to look at each other" (1:51). Mrs. Bowerbank, the jailer, scripts the encounter, staging a confrontation "scene" and managing the action as an entertainment, expressing "a desire to make the interview more lively" (1:52). She works to direct an occasion "wanting in brilliancy" and finally moves to "abbreviate the scene" (1:53, 56). The prison is a theater of power. Further, the jailer's visit to Pinnie sets the novel in motion; the novel opens under the shadow and gaze of the prison, "in the eye of the law" (1:7) and under "the steady orb of justice" (1:8). And what is most striking about Mrs. Bowerbank is not merely her representation of "the cold light of the penal system" and her "official pessimism" (1:14), but the way in which her unrelenting observation of Pinnie and Hyacinth is experienced as an accusation of guilt and as an arrest by the law. This "emissary of the law" (1:11) imprisons Pinnie in her gaze, and the dressmaker is "unable to rid herself of the impression that it was somehow the arm of the law that was stretched out to touch her" (1:13). When Hyacinth is produced for the jailer's "inspection," he asks: "Do you want to see me only to look at me?" (1:18). But "only" to be seen is already to be inscribed within a coercive power relation, to be placed under surveillance and under arrest. Mrs. Bowerbank's presence transforms the dressmaker's house into a prison house. The jailer appears as an "overruling providence" (1:46); her tone "seemed to refer itself to an iron discipline" (1:14), and Pinnie can only respond "guiltily" (1:8) to her questioning. Pinnie debates taking the "innocent child" to the prison, and "defended herself as earnestly as if her inconsistency had been of a criminal cast" (1:11, 30). Indicted by Mrs. Bowerbank's observation, she attempts to shield herself, imagining the "comfort to escape from observation" (1:40), and distracts herself from the "case" "as a fugitive takes to by-paths" (1:22).

Pinnie, however, is not merely victimized and incriminated by the turnkey's legal eye. The jailer's visit disseminates an array of inquisitorial looks, recriminations, and betrayals, as the law stretches to include each character. But the characters are not merely victims; they in turn become "carriers" of the law. The more discreet and more insidious power of the law that Mrs. Bowerbank represents is the power to reproduce and extend the apparatus of surveillance and incrimination into situations that seem radically remote from crime in the legal sense. The distribution of mechanisms of incrimination works not only to victimize those it stretches out to touch, but more significantly to make its victims also its disseminators.

The opening scene of the novel is a concise instance of this "spreading" of the law, and a summary of the plot of the opening section is a summary of the displacement and extension of the techniques of penality that Mrs.

Bowerbank incarnates. Pinnie, for instance, is not only incriminated by this emissary of the law: she herself becomes Mrs. Bowerbank's emissary. The jailer "would like to see" Hyacinth, and Pinnie undertakes to "look for the little boy," realizing at the same time that to make Hyacinth "visible" is also to bring him to judgment: as she expresses it, "If you could only wait and see the child I'm sure it would help you to judge" (1:3, 15). To produce Hyacinth is to bring him to the law, and Pinnie both undertakes to produce him and proceeds to exercise a disciplinary authority of her own. As she obeys Mrs. Bowerbank's injunction to supply Hyacinth, she displaces the injunction onto his playmate, Millicent. She simultaneously places Millicent under the discipline of her observation—waiting "to see if her injunction would be obeyed"—and links this injunction with an appropriately reduced attribution of guilt—"you naughty little girl" (1:5). Millie, in turn, replies with a "gaze of deliberation" and with a refusal to "betray" Hyacinth to this extended arm of the law: "Law no, Miss Pynsent, I never see him" (1:6, 5). When Hyacinth appears, Pinnie repeats her accusation of Millicent: "Millicent 'Enning's a very bad little girl; she'll come to no good" (1:16). Hyacinth protests and tries to exculpate his friend from a betrayal in which he is implicated; his reply further suggests the displacements of guilt and responsibility that obsessively proliferate in this opening scene: "It came over him," he observes, "that he had too hastily shifted to her shoulders the responsibility of his unseemly appearance, and he wished to make up to her for this betrayal" (1:17).

These shifts and displacements of criminality and incrimination indicate a generalized extension of the power of watching and policing in the novel. In *The Princess Casamassima,* police work is contagious, a contagion that James images as the transmission of a certain "dinginess" from one character to another: Hyacinth "hated people with too few fair interspaces, too many smutches and streaks. Millicent Henning generally had two or three of these at least, which she borrowed from her doll, into whom she was always rubbing her nose and whose dinginess was contagious. It was quite inevitable she should have left her mark under his own nose when she claimed her reward for coming to tell about the lady who wanted him" (1:17). If Hyacinth has shifted onto Millicent the blame for his "unseemly appearance," leading to Pinnie's accusations of her, the shifting of blame and guilt corresponds to the shifting of a mark of "dinginess," the stigma of the slums.

The opening scene plays out, in an anticipatory and understated fashion, the diffusion of penality that traverses *The Princess Casamassima.* It is the prison that provides the model for the contagion. The first principle of the prison is isolation, confinement, but within the novel Millbank prison stands as the central and centering instance of this spread of criminality; the prison

looked very sinister and wicked, to Miss Pynsent's eyes, and she
wondered why a prison should have such an evil air if it was erected
in the interest of justice and order—a builded protest, precisely,
against vice and villainy. This particular penitentiary struck her as
about as bad and wrong as those who were in it; it threw a blight on
the face of day, making the river seem foul and poisonous and the
opposite bank, with a protrusion of long-necked chimneys, unsightly
gasometers and deposits of rubbish, wear the aspect of a region at
whose expense the jail had been populated. (1:42).

Vice and villainy are not confined by the *cordon sanitaire* of the prison;
rather, the prison infects the surrounding area, disperses its "evil air," and
blights the city. The prison spreads what it ostensibly protests against and
is erected to delimit. The atmosphere of the prison extends from the local
site of the prison into every area of the novel, and there is no escape from
the contagion of criminality; as Pinnie notes, every "effort of mitiga-
tion . . . only involved her more deeply" (1:8). "He had not done himself
justice"; "she seemed to plead guilty to having been absurd"; "Hyacinth's
terrible cross-questioning"; "like some flushed young captive under cross-
examination for his life"; "he went bail for my sincerity": one might mul-
tiply these quotations indefinitely, and I abstract them from their local
contexts because it is the multiplication of these references, in the most
banal and "innocent" exchanges in the novel, that establishes a general
context of policing and incrimination in *The Princess Casamassima*. The
very ordinariness of the allusions indicates the extent to which a fantasy
of supervision and police work infiltrates the novel.
    "What do you mean, to watch me?" Hyacinth asks Mr. Vetch, and the
question alludes to more than the fiddler's paternal overseeing of Hyacinth. The possibility that Mr. Vetch is a police spy has earlier been considered; the manner in which the possibility is dismissed extends rather
than limits the spy mania that the novel reproduces: Hyacinth "never suspected Mr. Vetch of being a governmental agent, though Eustache Poupin
had told him that there were a great many who looked a good deal like
that: not of course with any purpose of incriminating the fiddler. . . . The
governmental agent in extraordinary disguises . . . became a very familiar
type to Hyacinth, and though he had never caught one of the infamous
brotherhood in the act there were plenty of persons to whom, on the very
face of the matter, he had no hesitation in attributing the character"
(1:108). The secret agent lurks in improbable forms, and as in Sims's
fantasies of the anarchic underworld, apparent innocence invites a suspicion of concealed criminality. This passage denies suspicion and the purpose of incrimination even as it attributes the character of the police spy
indiscriminately. The attribution attaches, at one time or another, to
virtually every character in the novel. To Captain Sholto, for instance:

"Perhaps you think he's a spy, an *agent provocateur* or something of the sort." But Sholto's form is not improbable enough, a spy "would disguise himself more" (1:214). It attaches also to the Princess, who is suspected of being "an agent on the wrong side."

The Princess, Madame Grandoni tells the Prince, is "much entangled. She has relations with pepole who are watched by the police." "And is *she* watched by the police?" "I can't tell you; it's very possible—except that the police here isn't like that of other countries" (2:310). Indeed, the police here are not like they are elsewhere—they are everywhere. Just prior to this discussion, the Princess and Paul Muniment have left the house at Madeira Crescent on a conspiratorial mission that remains a narrative secret. The spies are themselves spied upon, as the narrative observer comments: "Meanwhile, it should be recorded, they had been followed, at an interval, by a cautious figure, a person who, in Madeira Crescent, when they came out of the house, was stationed on the other side of the street, at a considerable distance. On their appearing he had retreated a little, still however keeping them in sight" (2:301). James initially withholds the identity of the observer who has placed the conspirators under surveillance. His revelation of that identity takes a curious form: "The reader scarce need be informed, nevertheless, that his design was but to satisfy himself as to the kind of person his wife was walking with" (2:301). The disavowal of any need to inform the reader of the figure's identity only points to the reader's initial misidentification. The passage invites a "confusion" of domestic suspicions and police surveillance, and indicates the extent to which all actions in the novel have come to resemble a police action. All characters in the novel are "in danger of playing the spy" (2:348).

There is no space free from the spy mania, from the infection of penality. Medley, the Princess's country-house retreat, provides no escape. The Princess there informs Hyacinth that "I've been watching you. I'm frank enough to tell you that. I want to see more—more—more!" (2:36). And if Hyacinth ceases "to be insignificant from the moment" the Princess sees him, he experiences his accession to significance as a subjection to "cross-examination" (2:35). A dispersed surveillance shadows Hyacinth, both in the Princess's watchfulness and in the supervision of his conduct "under the eye of the butler" (2:41). Medley is, for Hyacinth, the "real country," real nature, but nature itself participates in the general police action: "Never had the old oaks and beeches . . . witnessed such an extraordinary series of confidences since the first pair that sought isolation wandered over the grassy slopes and ferny dells beneath them" (2:46). The witnessing eye of nature and the allusion to the providential supervision of the Garden indicate the thorough "naturalization" of mechanisms of surveillance and policing in *The Princess Casamassima:* nature itself appears to supplement the policing function. Mrs. Bowerbank early comments on Florentine's impending death by asserting that "if she lived a month [she] would violate (as Mrs. Bowerbank might express herself) every established law of nature" (1:14). James's parenthetical interpolation calls attention to the jailer's characteristic mode of expression, her linking of "nature" and the "law," her naturalizing of the penal apparatus. In *The Princess Casamassima,* the power of vision and supervision is not confined to the nominal agencies of the police: it is enforced by the "eyes of the world" (2:401). It is finally impossible to distinguish between the "eye of day and the observation of the police" (2:410).

The spy mania and the incriminating techniques of policing and surveillance are not confined but contagious in *The Princess Casamassima;* the prison and the supervision and discipline it implies reappear at every turn in the novel. I have indicated the proposal of the prison as a model for the city at large in the work of the London sociologists, and I now want to take up the significance of this equation from a somewhat different perspective. Michel Foucault, in his recent history of the rise of disciplinary practices, *Surveiller et punir,* describes the extension of social mechanisms of surveillance and discipline into all areas of modern society. More specifically, he traces the reorganization of Western society around the model of the "punitive city": "Near at hand, sometimes at the very center of cities of the nineteenth century [stands] the monotonous figure, at once material and symbolic, of the power to punish"—the prison. The architectural figure of this social reorganization is Jeremy Bentham's Panopticon, a circular building, divided into cells, surrounding a central observation tower. The Panopticon operates through a controlling network of seeing and being seen: the inmate "is seen but he does not see"; "in the central tower, one sees everything without ever being seen." The inmate is trapped in a "seeing machine," trapped in a state of conscious and constant visibility; as a result, he "inscribes in himself the power of relation" in which he is caught up, and "becomes the principle of his own subjection."[29]

London's Millbank prison was derived from Bentham's panopticon scheme. Convicts were accommodated in six pentagonal ranges that surrounded a central watchtower—the locus of a providential supervision that doubled also, and appropriately, as the prison chapel. James visited Millbank on a December morning in 1884 to collect notes for *The Princess Casamassima.* His description of the prison in the novel emphasizes the power of watching that the Panopticon employs. He records the "circular shafts of cells" ranged about a central observatory, and, further, the "opportunity of looking at captives through grated peepholes," at the women with "fixed eyes" that Pinnie is "afraid to glance at" (1:47); the inmates are dressed in "perfect frights of hoods" (1:46). This last detail recalls the practice at Pentonville, where "all contact with other human beings, except the prison staff, was forbidden, and when convicts left their cells . . . they wore masks with narrow eye-slits in order to prevent identification by their fellows."[30]

The Panopticon effects an exemplary conjunction of seeing and power, the conjunction that extends from the prison throughout *The Princess Casamassima.* "The panoptic schema," Foucault details, " . . . was destined to spread throughout the social body." Foucault discusses the dispersal of this schema in nineteenth-century society, its penetration into the factory, the workhouse, the reformatory, the school, into, in fact, all those institutions that, as we have seen, the urban colonizers deployed and cultivated. And further, the panoptic technique infiltrates "tiny, everyday" social practices, traverses and embraces those "minute social disciplines" apparently remote from the scene of the prison. Confiscating and absorbing "things of every moment," an everyday panopticism is finally universalized: "Police power must bear 'over everything.'"[31]

One final institutionalization of the panoptic technology remains to be considered. It has recently been suggested that Foucault's history might underwrite a radical revision of our sense of the "politics" of the novel, and the problem that I want now to take up, and which has been implicit all along, concerns the relation between these disciplinary techniques and the techniques of the novel, and more particularly of the realist and naturalist novel, which appears on the scene at the same time as the disciplinary society takes power.[32] Foucault suggests that the novel "forms part of that great system of constraint by which the West compelled the everyday to bring itself into discourse."[33] In what way may the realist novel be seen to participate in, and even to promote, a system of constraint?

It has been observed that "excellence of *vision* is the distinguishing mark of realism."[34] "To see" is the dominant verb in the realist text—"la gastronomie de l'oeil" as Balzac expressed it[35]—and realist fiction is preeminently concerned with seeing, with a seeing in detail. The proximity of this realist "seeing" to the overseeing and police work of detection becomes explicitly problematic, and is most evident, of course, in the subgenre of realism that we have already glanced at, the fiction of detection.[36] In detective fiction, the relation between seeing and policing is taken for granted; literally, the range of the detective's vision is the range of his power. That power operates by placing the entire world of the text under scrutiny and under surveillance, and invokes the possibility of an absolute supervision, in which everything may be comprehended and "policed," and in which the most trifling detail becomes potentially incriminating.

Realistic fiction, in a more discreet and, for that reason, more comprehensive manner, deploys a similar tactic of detection; the techniques of surveillance and detection traverse the techniques of the realistic novel. Emerson, instancing Swift, notes "how realistic or materialistic in treatment of his subject" the novelist is: "He describes his fictitious persons as if for the police."[37] Indeed, detective fiction merely literalizes the realist representational scrutiny, its fascination with seeing and with the telling significance of detail, and lays bare the policing of the real that is the realist project. "We novelists," writes Zola, "are the examining magistrates of men and their passions."[38]

The juridical expression of the aims of the realist novelist recurs frequently. There is, for instance, George Eliot's statement in *Adam Bede* (ch. 17) of the novelist's obligation to write "as if I were in the witness-box narrating my experience on oath," and Guy de Maupassant's avowal, in his preface to *Pierre et Jean,* to tell "la vérité, rien que la vérité, et toute la vérité,"[39] The convergence of the literary and the legal recurs also in attacks on the alleged illicitness and "illegality" of the realistic novel; thus W. S. Lilly, writing in 1885, asserts that, in the realist and naturalist novel, "everywhere at the bottom there is filth (*l'ordure*). Those proceedings in the courts of justice which from time to time bring it to the surface—like an abscess—are merely an experimental novel unfolding itself, chapter after chapter, before the public."[40] The realist novel is seen to proceed as a legal action. The realist novelist is the examining magistrate of everyday life.

There is a complementary movement in realistic fiction: toward a documentation of phenomena in precise detail, and toward a supervision of those phenomena. As Zola concisely expresses it, "the goal of the experimental method . . . is to study phenomena in order to control them."[41] The realists share, with other colonizers of the urban scene, a passion to see and document "things as they are," and this passion takes the form of a fantasy of surveillance, a placing of the tiniest details of everyday life under scrutiny. Is it not possible to discover in this fantasy of surveillance a point of intersection between the realist text and a society increasingly dominated by institutions of discipline, regularization, and supervision—by the dispersed networks of the "police"?

There are a number of ways in which the relation between the novel and the law can be explored. There is, for instance, an intriguing resemblance between the realist typologies of character and the typologies proposed by the late nineteenth-century criminologists, chiefly Cesare Lombroso, a resemblance that Conrad exploits in *The Secret Agent,* another novel of the London spy mania.[42] More generally, one might note the encompassing control over character and action which the realist and naturalist doctrine of "determinism" secures. As Leo Bersani has recently suggested, the realist's method works to reduce "the events of fiction to a parade of sameness. For example, it would not be wholly absurd to suggest that a Balzac novel becomes unnecessary as soon as its exposition is over. The entire work is already contained in the presentation of the work, and the characters merely repeat in dialogue and action what has already been established about them in narrative summaries. Their lives mirror the expository portraits made of them at the beginning of the novel."[43] The linear order and progression of the realistic novel enables the novel to "progress" only in a direction always preestablished. Indeed, it is as a "repetition" that Hyacinth experiences his every attempt to break with his origins and "antecedents," to break with his "naturalist" determinants of environment and heredity. His recruitment to assassinate the duke presents itself as "the idea of a *repetition*," as the "horror of the public reappearance, in his person, of the imbrued hands of his mother" (2:419). This "young man in a book" (1:xiv) expresses an interest in the "advanced and consistent realists" (1:315), but this "consistency," a key word in the novel, becomes another name for an entrapment in a (narrative) repetition.

In its fixing of consistent "types," and in its predictive control over narrative possibility, the realistic text gains a thorough mastery over its characters and their actions—a twin mastery of intelligibility and supervision. *The Princess Casamassima* has been regarded as James's primary excursion into the realistic or naturalistic mode.[44] The novel, in its choice of subjects and in its descriptive method, displays an affinity with the consistent realists; and certainly, it everywhere displays that fantasy of surveillance which, I have been suggesting, lies at the heart of the realist project. But we notice that this surveillance becomes in many ways the subject and not merely the mode of the novel, and such a foregrounding of the novel's tactics of supervision indicates, within limits that I will attempt to describe, James's exposure and demystification of the realist mania for surveillance, and his attempt to disown the policing that it implies.

Perhaps the most powerful tactic of supervision achieved by the traditional realist novel inheres in its dominant technique of narration—the style of "omniscient narration," which grants the narrative voice an unlimited authority over the novel's "world," a world thoroughly known and thoroughly mastered by the panoptic "eye" of the narration. The technique of omniscient narration, as is frequently noted, gives to the narrator a providential vision of the characters and action. It is the fantasy of such an absolute panopticism that we have previously traced in Sims's lifting of the fourth wall, and in Dickens's and Doyle's fantasy of "removing the roofs" and viewing the "queer things which are going on." In *The Princess Casamassima,* such omniscient vision is attributed to the master revolutionaries: "They know everything—everything. They're like the great God of the believers: they're searchers of hearts; and not only of hearts, but of all a man's life—his days, his nights, his spoken, his unspoken words. Oh they go deep and they go straight!" (2:383). Hoffendahl's God-like power is also the power of the omniscient narrator, a power of unlimited overseeing.

But if James inscribes in his text an image of comprehensive and providential supervision, the narrative method of the novel departs from this panoptic technique. As a number of critics have shown, and as James asserts in his preface to the novel, *The Princess Casamassima* marks a technical turning point in James's career: a turning away from the style of omniscient narration toward the technique of the "central recording consciousness" or "central intelligence." That technique displaces the authority of the narrative voice and disavows any direct interpretive authority over the action. It can be said that in *The Princess Casamassima,* omniscient authority is held up to scrutiny, and indicted, in being transferred to, or displaced upon, the masters of the revolution.

Can this supervisory power, however, be so easily disowned? In his preface, James imagines his observation of the underworld as a form of espionage: his vision of London is that of "the habitual observer . . . the pedestrian prowler" (1:xxi–xxii). But at the same time, he disclaims any violation or manipulation of the figures he "merely" observes: "I recall pulling no wires, knocking at no closed doors, applying for no 'authentic' information" (1:xxii). It is Hoffendahl, in the novel, who is the arch "wire-puller": "He had in his hand innumerable other threads" (2:55). And it is this puppeteering that James disavows. But having denied such a manipulative power, James proceeds to reclaim what he has dismissed: "To haunt the great city and by this habit to penetrate it, imaginatively, in as many places as possible—*that* was to be informed, *that* was to pull wires, *that* was to open doors" (1:xxii).

James distinguishes his "imaginative" penetration of the city from the manipulative vision and supervision of the conspiratorial plotters. The implication is clear: James would claim that his imaginative wire-pulling is not an act of supervision, that his deep searching of hearts, of spoken and unspoken words, that his seeing and "haunting" of the city can be distinguished from the policing and spy mania that this haunting of the great city so closely resembles. It is just such a separation between "mere" seeing, consciousness, and knowledge and an exercise of power which I have been questioning. James offers the alibi of a "powerless" imagination to extricate himself from the charge of participating in the spy mania that the novel everywhere engages. But James would have no need to insist on the distinction if it were not already jeopardized, already threatened by the compelling resemblance between his haunting and

and perpetual prowling and the surveillance and policing from which he would disengage himself.

It becomes clear that the attempt on the part of the writers we have examined to disown the policing that they exercise can be seen as a "cover" for a more discreet and comprehensive policy of supervision, and it is as such a ruse that I think James's displacing of power and authority works. The recession of narrative supervision in *The Princess Casamassima* appears as one further "shifting of the shame," a displacing of responsibility, culpability, and, in the terms that the novel provides, criminality. The shifting of narrative authority makes reference to an uneasiness concerning the shame of power. If James's novel is systematically the story of a criminal continuity between seeing and power, this continuity is finally disowned. If James works toward a demystifying of the realist policing of the real, this police work is finally remystified, recuperated as the "innocent" work of the imagination.

From one point of view, it is the incompatibility of the novel and the subject of power that is the "message" of *The Princess Casamassima:* it is the incompatibility of aesthetic and political claims that leads to Hyacinth's suicide. Critics of the novel have restated this message, insisting, with approval or disapprobation, that the novel sacrifices its political references to technical preoccupations. In his preface, James himself observes that the underworld of London "lay heavy on one's consciousness" (1:vi). The phrase invites us to read "conscience" for "consciousness," and the substitution registers in miniature what has been seen as James's substitution in *The Princess Casamassima* of the ordeal of consciousness (that is, the work's technique) for matters of social conscience (its political subject). Thus it has been argued that "Hyacinth Robinson's sensitive consciousness is the mirror which controls the shape" of the novel, that James's "ignorance in the face of the reality, the great grey Babylon, which was nearest to him" compelled him to distort that reality by circumscribing it with a "controlling and bizarre consciouness," and that, finally, this technical preoccupation means that *The Princess Casamassima*'s "theme is not political at all."[45] As Leo Bersani points out, "it has been decided by 'politically conscious' Anglo-American critics that James is a nonpolitical novelist."[46] Critics of *The Princess Casamassima,* and of James's work generally, have restated the discontinuity that James himself proposed, enforcing a break between technique and subject, between ways of seeing and the subject of power. It is maintained that "in his quest for a quintessential social reality that was also an alien reality, James must necessarily have found himself recoiling upon the merely psychological and even epistemological, the merely imaginative—upon fantasy."[47] But if James's only "political novel" advertises a radical conflict between politics and the novel, there is, working against this simple polarization, a criminal continuity between the techniques of the novel and those social technologies of power that inhere in these techniques. It is in the rigorous continuity established in James's novels between seeing, knowing, and exercising power that the politics of the Jamesian text appears, and it is this continuity that I have been tracing in *The Princess Casamassima.*

NOTES

1. George R. Sims, *The Mysteries of Modern London* (London: C. Arthur Pearson, 1906), pp. 81, 10, 8.
2. Francis Sheppard, *London 1808-1870: The Infernal Wen* (Berkeley and Los Angeles: University of California Press, 1971), p. 36.
3. Henry James, *The Princess Casamassima* (New York: Charles Scribner's Sons, 1908), 1:xxi, vii, v. Subsequent references to the novel and to the preface are to this edition (vols. 5 and 6 of the New York Edition) and are given in parentheses in the text.
4. Manfred Mackenzie, *Communities of Honor and Love in Henry James* (Cambridge: Harvard University Press, 1976), p. 3. Cf. Lionel Trilling, *The Liberal Imagination* (New York: Viking Books, 1950), p. 92; Irving Howe, *Politics and the Novel* (New York: Meridian Books, 1957), p. 146; John Goode, "The Art of Fiction: Walter Besant and Henry James," in *Tradition and Tolerance in Nineteenth-Century Fiction,* ed. David Howard, John Lucas, and John Goode (London: Routledge & Kegan Paul, 1966), p. 280; and Lyall H. Powers, *Henry James and the Naturalist Movement* (East Lansing: Michigan State University Press, 1971), p. 119.
5. Sims, *Mysteries of Modern London,* p. 12.
6. Cited by Jack Lindsay in his introduction to Jack London's *The People of the Abyss* (1903; reprint of first ed., London: Journeyman Press, 1977), p. 7.
7. Sims, *Mysteries of Modern London,* pp. 9-14.
8. Ibid., p. 12.
9. James Greenwood, *Low-Life Deeps: An Account of the Strange Fish to be Found There* (London: Chatto & Windus, 1881), p. 95.
10. Daniel Joseph Kirwan, *Palace and Hovel; or, Phases of London Life,* ed. A. Allan (1870; reprint ed., London: Abelard-Schuman, 1963), p. 27.
11. Sims, *Mysteries of Modern London,* p. 141.
12. Mrs. Bernard Bosanquet, *Rich and Poor* (London: Macmillan, 1896), p. 5.
13. Charles Dickens, *Dombey and Son,* New Oxford Illustrated Dickens (London: Oxford University Press, 1950), ch. 47.
14. A Conan Doyle, *The Sherlock Holmes Illustrated Omnibus* (New York: Schocken Books, 1976), p. 31.
15. Ibid., pp. 156-57.
16. Asa Briggs, *Victorian Cities* (London: Odhams Books, 1963), p. 60.
17. Jack London, *The People of the Abyss* (London: Arco, 1962), pp. 17-18.
18. H. J. Pettifer, *Transactions,* National Association for the Promotion of Social Science (NAPSS), 1884, as cited by Philip Abrams, *The Origins of British Sociology: 1834-1914* (Chicago: University of Chicago Press, 1968), p. 51.
19. General [William] Booth, *In Darkest England and the Way Out* (London: International Headquarters of the Salvation Army, 1890), pp. 90-93, 16, 91.
20. See, for instance: Briggs, *Victorian Cities,* p. 99; G. M. Young, *Victorian England: Portrait of an Age,* 2nd ed. (London: Oxford University Press, 1953), p. 56;

and Ruth Glass, "Urban Sociology in Great Britain: A Trend Report," *Current Sociology* 4, no. 4 (1955), 5-19.

21. Abrams, *Origins of British Sociology*, p. 61.

22. See, for instance: Henry Mayhew, *London Labour and the London Poor*, 4 vols. (London: Griffin, Bohn, 1861-62); Abrams, *Origins of British Sociology*, pp. 13-30; *Journal of the Statistical Society*, published from 1838, and the *Journal of the Royal Statistical Society*, published from 1887; *Annals of the Royal Statistical Society*, published from 1887; and *Annals of the Royal Statistical Society, 1834-1934* (London: Royal Statistical Society, 1934).

23. Michel Foucault, *Surveiller et punir* (Paris: Editions Gallimard, 1975); my citations are to the English translation by Alan Sheridan, *Discipline and Punish* (New York: Pantheon Books, 1977), p. 286.

24. Herbert Spencer, *Social Statics* (London: J. Chapman, 1851), p. 293; Henry Thomas Buckle, *History of Civilization in England*, 2 vols. (New York: D. Appleton, 1858-61), 2:472. Spencer and Buckle are cited by Alexander Welsh, *The City of Dickens* (Oxford: Clarendon Press, 1971), pp. 49, 50.

25. Frederic J. Mouat, "The History of the Statistical Society of London," *Jubilee Volume of the Statistical Society* (London: Stanford, 1885), p. 52.

26. In addition to the sources already cited, see: T. F. Reddaway, "London in the Nineteenth Century—II: The Origins of the Metropolitan Police," *The Nineteenth Century and After* 147 (February 1950): 104-18; Wilbur R. Miller, *Cops and Bobbies: Police Authority in New York and London, 1830-1870* (Chicago: University of Chicago Press, 1977); and Leon Radzinowicz, *A History of English Criminal Law and its Administration from 1750*, vol. 3 (London: Stevens, 1956).

27. G. W. Hastings, *Transactions*, NAPSS, 1857.

28. Mackenzie discusses the "secret society" in *Communities of Honor and Love*, pp. 8-18.

29. Foucault, *Discipline and Punish*, pp. 116, 200, 202, 207, 202-3.

30. Sheppard, *London, 1808-1870*, pp. 375-77.

31. Foucault, *Discipline and Punish,* pp. 207, 213, et passim. See also Jacques Donzelot, *La Police des familles* (Paris: Editions de Minuit, 1977).

32. I am especially indebted to Leo Bersani, "The Subject of Power," *Diacritics* 7, no. 3 (Fall 1977): 2-21; D. A. Miller, "From *roman-policier* to *roman-police:* Wilkie Collins's *The Moonstone*," *Novel* 13 (Winter 1980): 153-70; and Miller's "The Novel and the Police," *Glyph 8: Johns Hopkins Textual Studies* (Baltimore: Johns Hopkins University Press, 1981). See also Paul Foss, "The Lottery of Life," in *Michel Foucault: Power, Truth, Strategy*, ed. Meaghan Morris and Paul Patton (Sydney: Feral, 1979); Jeffrey Mehlman, *Revolution and Repetition: Marx/Hugo/Balzac* (Berkeley and Los Angeles: University of California Press, 1977), pp. 123-24; and Lennard J. Davis, "Wicked Actions and Feigned Words: Criminals, Criminality, and the Early English Novel," *Yale French Studies* 59 (1980): 106-18.

33. "The Life of Infamous Men," in *Michel Foucault: Power, Truth, Strategy*, p. 91.

34. Mehlman, *Revolution and Repetition*, p. 124.

35. Balzac, cited by Donald Fanger, *Dostoevsky and Romantic Realism* (Cambridge: Harvard University Press, 1965), p. 30.

36. On the detective story, see D. A. Miller, "From *roman-policier* to *roman-police*" and Pierre Macherey, *A Theory of Literary Production*, trans. Geoffrey Wall (London: Routledge & Kegan Paul, 1978), pp. 18-36.

37. *English Traits*, in *The Selected Writings of Ralph Waldo Emerson*, ed. Brooks Atkinson (New York: Modern Library, 1950), p. 647.

38. Emile Zola, "The Experimental Novel," in *Documents of Modern Literary Realism*, ed. George J. Becker (Princeton: Princeton University Press, 1963), p. 168.

39. George Eliot, *Adam Bede*, ed. Stephen Gill (Harmondsworth: Penguin Books, 1980), ch. 17; Guy de Maupassant, *Pierre et Jean* (New York: Charles Scribner's Sons, 1936), p. xxxvi.

40. W. S. Lilly, "The New Naturalism," in *Documents of Modern Literary Realism*, p. 277. Perhaps the most extraordinary indictment of the realist and naturalist novelists occurs in Max Nordau's influential *Degeneration* (New York: D. Appleton, 1895). Nordau classifies these novelists, preeminently Zola, in accordance with the classification of criminal types developed by the criminologist Cesare Lombroso, accuses them of "crime committed with pen and crayon" (558), and calls for the institution of a "critical police" (535) to return them to the law; at the same time, however, Nordau notes the resemblance between the realist text and the "police reports" (489).

41. Zola, "The Experimental Novel," p. 176.

42. On Conrad's use of Lombroso see John E. Saveson, "Conrad, *Blackwood's*, and Lombroso," *Conradiana* 6 (1974): 57–62.

43. Leo Bersani, *Baudelaire and Freud* (Berkeley and Los Angeles: University of California Press, 1977), p. 121.

44. Lyall H. Powers, in *Henry James and the Naturalist Movement*, claims that James had, by the mid-1880s, "made his peace" with the naturalists: "He had by this time come close to sharing fully the aesthetic persuasions of the Realist-Naturalist group" (41). It is, rather, James's attempts to disaffiliate himself from the realist and naturalist "group," and from the politics that their method implies, that I am emphasizing here.

45. The quotations are from, respectively: J. M. Leucke, "*The Princess Casamassima*: Hyacinth's Fallible Consciousness," in *Henry James: Modern Judgements*, ed. Tony Tanner (London: Macmillan, 1969), p. 184; John Goode, "The Art of Fiction: Walter Besant and Henry James," pp. 280, 279; and J. A. Ward, *The Search for Form* (Chapel Hill: University of North Carolina Press, 1967), p. 115.

46. Bersani, "The Subject of Power," p. 10.

47. Mackenzie, *Communities of Honor and Love*, p. 22.

FRED G. SEE

Henry James
and the Art of Possession

The torment of possession is the greatest that man can suffer—
the longest, for the demon never tires; the least understood, for
the cause is invisible; the most dangerous, for it leads to the
irreparable ruin of soul and body.—Leon D'Alexis, *Traicté des
Energumènes, suivy d'un discours sur la possession de Marthe
Brossier, contre les calomnies d'un Médecin de Paris,* 1599

The decade of the 1890s, especially the last five years of the nineteenth
century, was an unusually stressful period for Henry James. Leon Edel
ascribes this to the fiasco of *Guy Domville* in 1895, and Walter Isle to
James's strenuous experiment with dramatic form leading up to that disaster, especially the frustration of seeing his cherished dramatic efforts fail.[1]
Kenneth Graham too attributes this "most troubled decade in James's life
as a writer" to the frustration of his dramatic urge, which represented
deep aesthetic and philosophical objectives.[2] Charles G. Hoffman notes, in
addition to James's obsession with dramatic form, another sign of stress:
"the subtle handling of the theme of evil" begun in the short fiction
written between 1890 and 1894 and intensified in the more mature works
of the middle period.[3] And Edwin Bowden remarks the agitated thematic
concentration (in the long fiction written between 1881 and 1897) that
"found its dramatization in the problem of the moral decision by the individual," a sort of moral decision which is especially vexed, moreover, because it "is seldom a matter only of an ethical choice between right and
wrong, but more often involves a choice between two ways of life, one
offering some opportunity for a greater fulfillment of the human spirit,
and the other offering eventual frustration and aridity."[4]

So there is some agreement that James entered the last years of the nineteenth century in a state of troubled experimental vision, bitterly shaken
by his dramatic failure, resolved to salvage his dramatic form by introducing

119

it into the novel, and concerned to examine an influence that can accurately be termed "evil." The motifs convene; they provide an agenda for the work of that decade: and they are especially clear as they associate in the sensitive young women who fascinate James in texts like *What Maisie Knew, The Awkward Age*, "Maud-Evelyn," "The Turn of the Screw," and *The Spoils of Poynton*. These and other works written during the last years of the century are organized around this complex of intentions which leads James to a major development in the aesthetics of literary realism. Drama, wickedness, selection: these privileged aspects of his art, the relationship of which led James into his major phase, constellate in Fleda Vetch, the heroine of *Poynton* whose struggle reveals a "method at the heart of the madness" of clumsy life's "splendid waste."[5] She is as it were the scene, the dramatic place where his themes and strategies make themselves articulate. One might simplify even more by noting (in her agony, and generally in James) a deepening of the prominent metaphor that James repeatedly used to sum up his vision (and which by the way he shared with his brother William): possession, which for him is sometimes erotic, sometimes materialistic, sometimes demonic, but always the dramatic struggle of one will to circumscribe and use another.[6]

But James's concept of possession emphasizes very particular difficulties. Possession as the thematic manifestation of a particular relationship—in its way ambivalent, contradictory, self-opposed, above all radically bifurcated and yet fundamentally unified: this typically fascinated James (as, at roughly the same time, it did Freud).[7] In a fine insight Martha Banta suggests that the tensions causing this characteristic bifurcation of reality are, for James, "as necessary as those that placed our universe on the rack."[8] I think this is so; and I want to discuss this theme, which generalizes a deeper—even ontological—question of literary language, one that is displayed in a representative text: *The Spoils of Poynton*.

> . . . possessed by what we now no more possessed.
> —Frost, "The Gift Outright"

Never doubt that possession was regarded as real from its beginning. In their time the symptoms of possession were "facts substantiated by evidence irrefragable according to the system of jurisprudence."[9] Possession was an aspect of reality. It implied, among other things, that "man was at all times exposed to the assaults of supernatural enemies, striving to lead him to sin, to torture his body with disease, or to afflict him with material damage"; it meant that "for good or evil, the barriers which divided the material from the spiritual world were slight, and intercourse between them was too frequent to excite incredulity."[10] Indeed this absolute difference explains the fury of possessive spirits. "Spirit lusts toward matter as matter towards spirit. The fallen angels are pure spirit. It is not enough for them. . . . A surge towards matter passes through the hierarchy of the abyss; they rush towards it; they seek the bodies of men and women; they desire to incarnate."[11] Considered in this way, possession clarifies as little else can the extent to which man is the theater of metaphysics.

So one may say of possession what Foucault, writing of the age of reason, says of madness—that it was

> not merely one of the possibilities afforded by the union of soul and body; it was not just one of the consequences of passion. Instituted by the unity of soul and body, [it] turned against that unity and once again put it in question. . . . [It] was one of those unities in which laws were compromised, perverted, distorted—thereby manifesting such unity as evident and established, but also as fragile and already doomed to destruction.[12]

Madness, Foucault goes on, "begins where the relation of man to truth is disturbed and darkened" (91). Precisely: like possession in its periods, madness in the age of reason inflects human consciousness, whose unity is not dissolved but "fissured . . . along lines which do not abolish it, but divide it into arbitrary sectors" (82). Possession is the return of a discredited authority, the reassertion of a violent force which divides consciousness and poses an ambiguous dilemma. It requires the fullest civil and ecclesiastical apparatus to clarify the meaning of the poor wretch whose value is thus both problematic and immense. Like madness, possession brings about the mystification of signs (not only the body, which is the chief sign of possession, but also the universe that surrounds it and whose meaning the possessed body calls into question).

And that space of possession is much more than the body's or even the soul's. It implies all the space that lies within the network of systematic differentiation, everything that man can achieve by the generative and violent exclusion of a ritual victim, that "mechanism which, in a single decisive movement, curtails reciprocal violence and imposes structure on the community."[13] It is the theoretical geography of Culture in other words; and it must also be understood as suddenly having become a space of radical transformation, of a profound reversal of order. It not only represents, it also constitutes a critical condition in which "coherent thinking collapses and rational activities are abandoned"[14] and must be ritually, even sacrificially reasserted. Lévi-Strauss suggests the structurality of this event when he proposes that "the sorcerer-patient dyad incarnates for the group, in vivid and concrete fashion, an antagonism that is inherent in all thought but that normally remains vague and imprecise. . . . The cure inter-relates these opposite poles, facilitating the transition from one to the other, and demonstrates, within a total experience, the coherence of the psychic universe, itself a projection of the social universe."[15] Possession, whether voluntary or involuntary, broaches the barrier between matter and essence, it attacks the capacity of knowledge to distinguish inner from outer, good from evil, even noumena from phenomena. Immiscibles abut here in the possessed and destructured consciousness, which scandalously reverses incarnation and parodies transcendence. Yet even at its most violent this negation indicates something not to be abandoned; even in ruins the subject is valuable; even then it becomes the evidence that value may be stipulated and chosen, that structure may assert itself over chaos. The desperate and equally violent forces of inquisition and exorcism make this clear: they follow possession into a space to contest and reclaim both the details and the totality of discourse; they re-possess structure for the sign.

It may be useful to propose, then, that possession enables us to explore the function of signs (a much more fundamental question, but related in a way to the structure of possession) in the broadest possible manner. To put it less abstractly, James's use of the theme of possession may allow us to infer his intentions in developing a new language for realism. For James, that is, possession served as a means of learning how to represent not only the surface but the structure of reality in an accurate mode. Possession was interesting and important to him because it stressed knowledge in basic ways, and because it illuminated boundaries so clearly. Yvor Winters has spoken of the efforts of James and his characters "to understand ethical problems in a pure state, and to understand them absolutely, to examine the marginal, the semi-obscure, the fine and definitive boundary of experience . . . the moral divorced from all problems of manners and of compulsion, as it appears in the case of Fleda Vetch."[16] Possession demands precisely this inquisitorial understanding of a region which is both frontier and bar-rier for the soul, and James saw the theme into the bargain as a struggle for power that enforced exactly appropriate demands on the literary sign, which, like all signs during an epoch of epistemic inflection, undergoes considerable transformation.[17] It is as if signs themselves experience a similar struggle for possession: as if they become a violent juxtaposition of conflicting references, a conflation in which opposite modes of reality interpenetrate one another, the border separating related opposites be-comes permeable, and reality thus to a certain extent not only appears as, but gradually becomes, a different place. I am in fact arguing that the theme of possession points to such a transformation in the sign, a restruc-turation of significance which is called literary realism (as, earlier, such a restructuring was called Inquisition). I want to suggest, moreover, that possession points to such a transformation in the sign, to a reconstruction of significance; and that possession, for James, is a way of representing the struggle of the sign to transform itself according to the new mode of signifying called realism, which also involved a resistance to romantic models of thinking.

But this is also to say that his theme of possession may dramatize a realignment in the whole process of signification. It is axiomatic that in James (and the other realists) one finds traditional literary language, a fomal and sedimented order, changing as the dimension of concept and belief undergoes its own important change. The balance of the sign shifts; and it is doubtless a measure of the anxiety and uncertainty associated with this profound change (which after all entailed the repudiation of an immense theological system) that the idea of possession should express the relationship. Nothing less than the phenomenal and noumenal orders oppose one another across the frontier that associates and distinguishes them within the tense system of each sign. The incursion of noumena into phenomena, the incarnation of spirit within flesh, the possession of one independent realm by another—with drastic and ramifying realignments of power implied—all these problems are drawn into the discovery of a new literary mode suited to a diminished influence of the signified's province of spiritual or ideal allusion.

The work of the nineties, then, insofar as it is typified in *Poynton,* may be understood to develop the literary sign by exploring possession. Characters are immersed in an atmosphere of evil, which is generally the attempt of corrupting possessive powers to annex a method of knowledge. Whether or not this possession is explicitly demonic its structure is consistent. The "hovering prowling blighted presences," James nominated them in his Preface to "The Turn of the Screw." In the Preface to *What Maisie Knew* his figure is the "infected air" in which Maisie "vibrates." In the Preface to *The Altar of the Dead* it is "some imaged appeal of the lost Dead," a "hauntedness" that threatens "as incessantly as forked lightning may play unheeded about the blind"; in the Notes for *The Sense of the Past* an "ancient brutality," a "liability" which seems "to hover and to menace."[18] Maisie, the Governess, May Bartram, Fleda: each of these haggard free spirits is menaced by some possessive presence seeking to overpower the discrimination and possibility of free utterance they represent.

Unhappily for them, the prospects of possession are always made irresistibly alluring. They consist, for example, of a dazzling collection or beautiful museum shadowed by barren, powerful forces; a brilliant agglomeration of inherited things, or a haunted lovely house or perfect friend whose value is qualified by some immovable obstacle to understanding. Possession is what Fleda first delightedly sees as "a future full of the things she particularly loved."[19] This is the full extent of James's "real": a desperate hazard of art working free of the ornate allure of mystifying attitudes and texts: selection resisting possession . . . is it an obsolete or even romantic order of signs which returns to possess the space from which it has been excluded?[20] One might propose such a reading of "The Turn of the Screw" or of *What Maisie Knew,* or of *Poynton,* in all of which some scandalous claim menaces an independent struggle to understand the fullest scope of reality.

> How slowly, how slowly we learn that witchcraft and ghostcraft, palmistry and magic, and all the other so-called superstitions, which, with so much police, boastful skepticism, and scientific committees, we had finally dismissed to the moon as nonsense, are really no nonsense at all, but subtle and valid influences, always starting up, mowing, muttering in our path, and shading our day.—Emerson, *Journals*, 1842

The plot of *The Spoils of Poynton* is simple. Fleda Vetch, a young woman "whose only treasure was her subtle mind" (13), meets, during a weekend at the vulgar estate Waterbath, the widowed Mrs. Gereth, also a guest, with whom she shares a loathing of the varnish and cheap curios there assaulting their taste. Mrs. Gereth has collected the magnificent antiques assembled at her own estate, Poynton Park; but under the terms of her recently deceased husband's will both estate and collection pass to their son, Owen, a pleasant blockhead whose unfortunate liaison with Mona Brigstock, a daughter of Waterbath, eventually results in marriage. Mrs. Gereth, appalled by the danger of the spoils of Poynton falling into these heavy hands, tries to arrange an attachment of Fleda and Owen, and this interesting possibility develops; but Fleda, though passionately in love with Owen and ravished by the spoils now in his possession (upon first seeing Poynton "her meagre past fell away from her like a garment of the wrong fashion" [11]—she is much like the Governess), insists that Mona should set him free before she herself will hear a promise from him.

Mona, however, like Mrs. Gereth, is an agent of possession rather than freedom. As Professor Banta says, "the cleverly stupid Mona with her monomaniacal will thwarts the fine and vulnerable intelligence of Fleda Vetch" (85), and this is an example of "the possession by the self of what is not the self" (83). Mona insists, naturally, on a full inventory of the objects at Poynton simply because they are legally part of her prospects as the future Mrs. Gereth (she has no feeling for them per se), and she regards Owen, perhaps, as only another such object. In an evil hour she seduces the young man to reaffirm his engagement to her; marries him forthwith, and becomes proprietress of the spoils. These Mrs. Gereth, who is a kind of vampire herself, has first antagonistically carried away to the dower house set aside for her under the will, and then returned prematurely to let Owen understand her willingness to surrender them to such a doyenne as Fleda. Fleda and Mrs. Gereth end by being dispossessed rather than endowed. They lose the spoils, and Owen; upon arriving at Poynton to claim a parting gift from him—a Maltese cross, by all accounts the prize piece of the collection—Fleda finds that the entire estate has been destroyed by fire.

This leaves her, bereft and futureless as she is, the unwilling parasite of Mrs. Gereth, whose companion in nostalgia for the lost signs she has become. She is essentially placeless, like Maisie and the Governess among so many others; she is free of any complicity to set possession against the freedom to choose for oneself, but the price of this is alienation and subservience—at that, preferable to the implied corruption of possession. Most critics have understood Fleda's ethical struggle to be James's chief interest in the novel.[21] Certainly this question may be said to remain ambiguous and important, but it seems to me to stop short of seeing James's text at its most complex or interesting. Clearly *The Spoils of Poynton* concerns itself with her problem of possession, differently no doubt from some of the other possessive tales but also at some level identically. The theme has a structure as well as a context. The contested spoils preside over the text. They determine not only Fleda's passion to claim Owen freely and Mona's to possess him but also Mrs. Gereth's interest in her son's dependence, which shadows Fleda's fine commitment to the independent will. The spoils are the signs onto which the novel's representation of erotic will is displaced; they are the alibi of desire.

Possession of the spoils, and of the claimants who contend for them, therefore focuses meaning in the novel. But long before this they have already come to suggest a loss of significance. This does not mean that they have become meaningless, far from it, but that they represent a radical alteration not only of meaning but of the structure of meaning. Once human will struggled to create them, these "great syllables of colour and form, the tongues of other countries and the hands of rare artists" (22). They even resemble the debris of an original language. But even more they express Mrs. Gereth's "strange, almost maniacal disposition to thrust in everywhere the question of 'things,' to read all behavior in the light of some fancied relation to them" (24)—all behavior including the rituals and counter-rituals of possession that she is driven to face and to pronounce. Each piece carries a dim echo of its own history somewhere within it; Fleda "knew them by the personal name their distinctive sign or story had given them" (73). But that is barely apparent, to us at least. Their original value has given way to the history and even more to the possibility of control or ownership. Mr. Gereth's will has managed, by putting Owen's ownership

above his mother's, to pose the heir this meager possibility of erotic freedom, of an end to maternal possession. This is at the same time a possible
freedom from her mania to collect the signs and icons of a lost and obsolete order—not unlike Huck's freedom from Tom, or Isabel Archer's
from Osmond. It offers some faint hope of recombination. Now the spoils
are the signs of an explosion and a loss of coherence, and of a struggle for
possession which is more interesting than any original meaning. And in
fact that original meaning has already been effaced: "each history of each
find, each circumstance of each capture" inheres in them; still it is scarcely
history that Fleda sees as she and Mrs. Gereth review the rooms at Poynton: "The shimmer of wrought substances spent itself in the brightness;
the old golds and brasses, old ivories and bronzes, the fresh old tapestries
and deep old damasks threw out a radiance in which the poor woman now
saw in solution all her old loves and patiences, all her old tricks and triumphs" (58). They spend themselves, their exhaustion is both sexual and
commercial, and it is Mrs. Gereth whose values and principle of order they
function to display.

These signs are liberated from their first significance, which was doubtless a representation of a spiritual or political order, and even from their
second, which is that of the explosion of those orders; they have become
(this is repeatedly emphasized) the signs of Mrs. Gereth's assembly and
possession, of an order of representation based on the salvage of fragments.
She preserves, by the force of her will, not a lost historical event or epoch
but the priority of her own obstinate possession. But of what? The idea is
scarcely unfamiliar, she is not the only one who has shored fragments
against her ruin. The signs she gathers she revalues, puts back together
under new auspices: arbitrary, narcissistic, an obsession working to deplete
desire.

Collected from all the partitioned empires of Europe, almost entirely
invisible to us as images though relentlessly pressing upon the perceptions
and decisions of the characters—what, in more precise terms, might these
spoils mean? In their places they make "a steady shining light" (231).
Selecting among them is "comparing incomparables" (57); for Mrs.
Gereth, "there wasn't a thing in the house she didn't like best" (50). As
she says to Owen, then to Fleda, "The best things here, as you know, are
the things your father and I collected. . . . there are things in the house
that we almost starved for! They were our religion, they were our life,
they were us! And now they're only me—except that they're also you,
thank God, a little, you dear. . . . they're living things to me" (30-31).
This is of course partly her melodrama, a frenzied offer to share the possessions which attempts to bring Fleda, and through her Owen, and
through him the spoils, back under her control. But even though they
occasion such frenzy they remain vague to us. They are "the glow of a

Venetian lamp . . . a small but splendid tapestry" (70), "the touch of an old velvet brocade, a wondrous texture," a "great Italian cabinet" (71), and the Maltese cross,

> a small but marvellous crucifix of ivory, a masterpiece of delicacy, of expression and of the great Spanish period, the existence and precarious accessibility of which she had heard of at Malta, years before, by an odd and romantic chance—a clue followed through mazes of secrecy till the treasure was at last unearthed. (73-74)

But this is not an objectification of value, and just barely recalls a historical time. James is scarcely precise even in the instance of this best single masterpiece, which for us is at most small and ivory. These objects, all of them, despite their incomparable aesthetic value, have lost their objectivity; they are always on the verge of becoming subjective. However James means, in his treatment of the spoils, to make these signs meaningful, he always ends by showing that a reader can evaluate them only as a question of the relationship between objective and subjective reality.

All along Fleda, on the other hand, has known the objects, and the people she meets as well, neither objectively nor as a connoisseur but "by direct inspiration." Her intelligence is anything but superficial, it is deep and disturbed. "To be clever meant to know the 'marks'" (138); that is, the authentication, superficially inscribed but also concealed, identifying an original value. But Fleda's cleverness is greater yet. She has always had "to look straight at realities and fill out blanks" (140). She can see the spoils as intrinsically rather than referentially valuable, quite unrelated to any conceivable currency. For her, nothing need be possessed. Upon first seeing Poynton she dissolves in tears, "the natural and usual sign of her submissiveness to perfect beauty" (21). It is like a conversion experience. "To give it all up, to die to it—that thought ached in her breast" (23). But, in the event, she finds herself the only hope to keep the vision of Poynton intact. To win Owen from Mona will win Poynton for Mrs. Gereth. It is as simple and as complicated as that. But Owen, being engaged to Mona, is not free to respond to any such opportunity, however delectable it might seem to him: yet for Fleda to be satisfied, Mona must freely give him up so that he may freely choose his new option.

Meanwhile the primary task (Fleda's love remains secret for some time) is that of negotiating possession of the great collection for Mrs. Gereth—ostensibly, to keep it away from the philistine Brigstocks, "from whose composition the principle of taste had been extravagantly omitted. In the arrangement of their home some other principle, remarkably active, but uncanny and obscure, had operated instead" (6). Waterbath is "perversely full of souvenirs of places even more ugly than itself" (7). It reverses

Poynton: it only imitates where Poynton reconstitutes an original wholeness. It is " an aesthetic misery" (9), it is "the presence of the dreadful"—
not taste but "a universal futility" governs its assembly. Waterbath is "an
ugliness fundamental and systematic" (6): "There were advantages enough,"
James points out, which "it clearly didn't possess" (3), and it too means
to seize them, this uncanny and obscure principle, in Poynton. This is very
much like the dreadful structure at Bly, but composed in a different key.

In such grossly empirical custody Poynton must fail of its design, and
this sometimes makes Fleda think, of Mrs. Gereth's intense determination,
that "it was not the crude love of possession; it was the need to be faithful
to a trust and loyal to an idea" (46). But the problem is much more
agonized than this. Fleda finds herself the mediator of a struggle for possession that functions on several levels, each to some extent corrupt, and
all of which work against her own determination to find relationships that
are not possessive at all. Thus her own acceptance of Poynton's values,
which has always been contingent, soon becomes over-determined.[22] No
simple exchange is possible when the status of signs is so vexed, because
no exchange is free from the problem of despoilment. This is exemplified
by the difficulties of erotic relationship in the novel, which are invariably
possessive struggles in one way or another.

Though fascinated by the spoils to be sure—and Owen is doubtless one
of them—Fleda wishes to possess nothing. She is an insufficient agent of
reciprocal freedom, and her dilemma arises in her squalid dependence, a
poverty so helpless that it makes her especially vulnerable to possession.
She is "a young lady without fortune and without talent" (148); she "had
neither a home nor an outlook—nothing in all the wide world but a feeling
of suspense" (145). Fleda, "with her mother dead, hadn't so much as a
home" (14). She is the perfect emblem (like so many of James's young
women) of a zero degree of meaning—inheriting nothing, owning nothing:
her poverty makes her brilliantly free to choose without considering old
allegiances.[23] In this she is also like the heroes of our classic literature. The
condition is ontological; it defines a subjectivity which strives to owe
nothing to the romantic paradigm, that promise of emotional and spiritual
riches, a wealth, a superfluity and an imposition of meaning. In her own
way she struggles as ardently as Phoebe Pyncheon to be free. Fleda attempts
to hold open the possibility that signs, and the whole structure of Culture,
might be freely chosen as well as fully systematic. She wishes to preserve
the replica of the lost perfect structure that the spoils represent; she would
prefer the ideal point of orientation—the "perfect beauty," the "secret
rapture" (260)—to find its custody in perception and in flesh. But Fleda is
a metaphor that fails.

Of course she fails. How could she succeed? The obverse of her freedom
from legacy is her susceptibility to donation. Fleda is easily annexed,

because she has nothing with which to reciprocate. Mrs. Gereth "had made a desert round her, possessing and absorbing her so utterly that other partakers had fallen away" (144)—virtually as if she were the substance of a communion. For others—"her kind little circle at large, who didn't now at all matter"—Fleda's "tendency had begun to define itself as parasitical" (41): "People *were* saying that she fastened like a leech on other people" (60). It must seem like that. But Fleda herself wonders, when Mrs. Gereth requests her company on a long trip abroad, "if this were not practically a demand for penal submission—for a surrender that, in its complete humility, would be a long expiation" (233). The two of them can manage only by admitting the hiatus in their life. Their companionship had "begun to shape itself almost wholly on breaches and omissions" (253), they exist under "the protection of suspended allusions" (257). They will live, one should imagine, a life barren of metaphor, there being no question of a perfect form to which their conversation might refer. Their art will be all displacement and evasion. Even the representation of the spoils is lost now. In dismissing the spoils the novel has also dismissed, as some texts do, "the possibility of restoring or re-constituting, beneath the metaphor which at once conceals and is concealed, what was 'originally represented.'"[24] That original representation is, Mrs. Gereth says to Fleda, "what we don't, you know, by your wish, ever talk about" (256).

One chance does however remain that Fleda's life might be enriched by a sign. Some time after Owen's marriage she receives a letter from him. It seems to her quite beyond interpretation—"it had mysteries for her that she couldn't meet. What did it mean, what did it represent, to what did it correspond in his imagination or his soul? What was behind it, what was before it, what was, in the deepest depth, within it?" (259). Such are the problems of understanding in her condition. But his motive does not seem so obscure. "I want you inexpressibly," he says, "to have as a remembrance something of mine—something of real value. Something from Poynton is what I mean. . . . I want you to take from me, and to choose for yourself . . . the thing in the whole house that's most beautiful and precious. I mean the 'gem of the collection,' don't you know? If it happens to be of such a sort that you can take immediate possession of it—carry it right away with you—so much the better" (258).

Poor gift, poor freedom now to choose! It is a sign of her loss and his that he wishes her to select, though she cannot see that. After her loss Fleda's "obliterated passion" and the spoils are somehow gained "to memory and to love," and she comes to believe that they were "nobody's at all—too proud, unlike base animals and humans, to be reducible by anything so narrow" as the idea of possession (235). But at last, after a long month—it is close to Christmas, that season of the narrative of Bly—she agrees with herself to "go down to Poynton as a pilgrim might go to a shrine" (259). She will "act upon his offer" so as to "have as her own something splendid that he had given her, of which the gift had been his signed desire." In this instance of visiting Poynton, she believes, "she should be able to say to herself that . . . her possession was as complete as that of either of the others whom it had filled only with bitterness" (260).

But as she leaves "it was spoiling for a storm" (261). The "dawn was dolorous," "the green fields were black, the sky was all alive with the wind," and something "had begun to press on her heart" (262). When she arrives, Poynton is in flames. Everywhere her vision is obscure as smoke. In the swimming air she sees "something like the disc of a clock." History —the history once so lucidly recuperated by the spoils—is reduced to this vague flat and circular image. Fleda covers her face with her hands; she "felt herself give everything up." Her options close, her life narrows to the one bitter choice—but it means, no doubt, that she will be possessed herself from now on: "I'll go back," she weakly says (266).

To Mrs. Gereth. And this returns Fleda to the will that first assembled the spoils. They are not merely acquired, they *are* possessed, finally but not only by her. They have been appropriated and re-appropriated and bartered and so on until, like the Malta whose cross epitomizes them, they become the ground not of any inherent meaning of their own but the place of that fundamental question of invasion and possession. To possess these signs—Mona realizes this—is to achieve the custody of power, to re-align significance. For Mona, possession of the spoils turns meaning from one mode to another. It reduces art, history, meaning, whatever the spoils have signified, to a question of personality, a triumph of malice over system. But in this she only seconds Mrs. Gereth.

Or perhaps they first come into Mrs. Gereth's possession through her attempt to recuperate not only beauty but the order of Culture—let us give the benefit of the doubt. Poynton is "all France and Italy with their ages composed to rest," and "England . . . was the wide embrace" (22). But this also makes Poynton a sarcophagus, does it not? The sentence describing the day of the fire is paradoxical in just this way. "The green fields were black, the sky was all alive with the wind"—this language is literal and figurative at the same time without privileging either aspect beyond question; it suggests death, it suggests life; both are present at once; to express a universe through such signs is to be poised, waiting for one or the other to determine what is real. Fleda feels this in losing Owen. Mrs. Gereth must feel something very similar in losing the spoils. They threaten, in passing away from her as they do—into the possession of a rival, a barbarian, a daughter-in-law—an absolute loss of her meaning: "In the event of a surrender the poor woman would never again be able to begin to collect: she was now too old and too moneyless, and times were altered" (47). Not only the age of creation but that of congregation has passed away.

So the collection is, or was, a dimension of power, a monument and a crypt signifying the imperial authority that she chooses to replicate through her possession of its elegant detritus. In a way her possession does preserve the sense of the past. The fragments are remnants of the obsolete imperial gesture she has claimed as her own: she becomes the monarch of the imperial imagination she has appropriated. Mrs. Gereth is like the narcissistic prince of the "ostentatious Baroque tradition" whose palaces are described by Jean Starobinski. For such princes

> the outward show, at least in its older form, was more than mere show: it was a spectacle whose spectators were not to remain distant and objective; their freedom was lost in the captivating magic of the scene; they were systematically bewitched into participation, into a ritual submission, in a magnificent demonstration of the monarch's irresistible will. The ostentation was not simply the sign of sovereignty: it was the expression of power externalized, made perceptible to the senses, able to renew its outward manifestations indefinitely.[25]

Poynton is, for Mrs. Gereth—and for Mona too—what Mark Girouard calls a "power house."[26] Such houses as these were signs of control: displays by those whose possession of political and ideological power followed a clear pattern from medieval times into the nineteenth century. The great house was "an image-maker, which projected an aura of glamour, mystery or success around its owner. It was visible evidence of his wealth. It showed his credentials" (3).

The possession of such a house by the Gereths—or, say, the difficulty it represents as soon as it becomes a legacy—already reveals "a change in the power structure" (9), and a deep shift in the order of Culture. Waterbath puts that change in italics. These houses show that some "economic balance [had begun] to change" (2), to be sure, but the context of the change is complex, and the transformation is broadly ontological as well as social or economic; and clearly the great house is the house of fiction too. All of these signs figure, as they change, a question of power—the power within the sign. "The personal relationship between the monarch and his domains," Starobinski observes, "was visible to the whole world: according to the myth of absolute power, the perception of this expansive glory should immediately transform the observer into a grateful subject, making him an integral element in the circle of royal possession" (14). In the case of a private patron, the owner "may himself determine what function the work shall have" (13); at least, she may struggle toward that end. In the case of Mrs. Gereth, the function is in fact more political than private, it is "the visible demonstration of sovereignty" (14) that represents absolute power. To be sure Poynton is a park, the sort of place in which the wealthy patron "wanted trees and greenery and a garden in which he could relax

and muse freely, away from the petty obligations of official or social functions," but such patrons also needed "elegance, harmony, and a sense of
imposing majesty" (49), for their own power was a representation too, a
metaphor of princely authority:

> the relationship between prince and court was as between possessor
> and possessed; and this constituted the analogical image of the rela-
> tionship the prince desired between himself and the entire world. (14)

The perceived beauty of these objects is wholly subordinated, then, by
the idea of political power (which is threatened in turn by Owen's marriage
to an outsider). Were they ever merely the signs of her nostalgic genius
for assembling fragments? for arranging the scattered aspects of a lost
reality in the walled space which, she is determined, will shut out all possession and all desire but her own? Whether or not, in that space which is
at once so coherent and so divided from any original or even represented
meaning—that is, the space of Poynton Park, which is never more than the
space of possession for us—a new structure is constituted, and an old one
destroyed. Poynton Park, though we see it only inferentially, through the
struggle that transmogrifies objective representation into subjective expression, is the irradiating place of the sign's fission. Here the sign redefines itself; here possession—ideological, erotic, demonic, possession as
enforcement, as a question of law, politics, desire, theology—here all these
senses of possession convene on Poynton, and in the texts of the nineties,
to provide for an exploration of the process by which reality is signified.

> ... only the history of the symbolic function can allow us to
> understand the intellectual condition of man, in which the uni-
> verse is never charged with sufficient meaning and in which the
> mind always has more meanings available than there are objects
> to which to relate them. Torn between these two systems of
> reference—the signifying and the signified—man asks magical
> thinking to provide him with a new system of reference, within
> which the thus-far contradictory elements can be integrated.—
> Lévi-Strauss, "The Sorcerer and His Magic"

All James's tales of possession and haunting focus on that kind of representation which (like the séance in "Maud-Evelyn") depends on "the aid
not only of the few small, cherished relics, but that of the fondest figments
and fictions, ingenious imaginary mementoes and tokens, the unexposed
make-believe of the sorrow that broods and the passion that clings."[27] His
fiction follows the lost order of the signified as it struggles to find a way
back into meaning through such fragments, seeking to possess and re-

possess the scene from which it had been cast out. And his interest in this problem leads to the advance in realist aesthetics which I suggested, at the beginning of my essay, he developed as no one else did. It is a revision of things he means to accomplish, and he works against a trend. His friend Howells, by any account one of the chief arbiters of the realist movement, praised Hamlin Garland for his "fine courage to leave a fact with the reader, ungarnished and unvarnished."[28] Garland, in *Roadside Meetings,* expressed his irritation at "the aloofness of fiction and poetry from the realities of common life and speech."[29] Harold Frederic advised Gertrude Atherton to "listen with a more solicitous, reflective ear—and get the trick of drawing *sound* out of the ink-bottle!"[30] Clemens wrote of *Joan of Arc* that it satisfied by being "mere history—history pure and simple—history stripped naked of flowers, embroideries, colorings, exaggerations, inventions."[31] James complained that though Hawthorne "had a high sense of reality . . . he never attempted to render exactly or closely the actual facts of the society that surrounded him";[32] and Dreiser, though he saw vague "forces" abstractly at work in the universe, concluded "I take no meaning from life other than the picture it presents to the eye—the pleasure and pain it gives to the body."[33]

James expressed himself more generously, perhaps, when five years later, in "The Art of Fiction," he spoke of the way a contemporary writer "converted . . . ideas into a concrete image and produced a reality": "The power to guess the unseen from the seen, to trace the implication of things, to judge the whole piece by the pattern, the condition of feeling life in general so completely that you are well on your way in knowing any particular corner of it—this cluster of gifts may almost be said to constitute experience." Howells too commented at greater length in *Criticism and Fiction,* where he predicted that "when realism becomes false to itself, when it heaps up facts merely, and maps life instead of picturing it, realism will perish."[34]

The problem realism faced was one of restoring to literature what James called (in "The Art of Fiction") "solidity of specification," what Howells (in *Criticism and Fiction*) meant to demand when he said "let fiction cease to lie about life; let it portray men and women as they are, actuated by the motives and passions in the measure we all know" (104). But realism had had to begin by expelling an obsolete tradition of the signified from literary language. It had had to learn how to privilege the brute details that Crane (in "The Open Boat") called "the furniture of the world" as a means of suppressing a tradition of metaphysical allusion. Once that was done it became necessary to rediscover an authentic access to the power of the signified, however, because no language, literary or otherwise, can conceivably function without a coherent noumenal axis, in relationship with which the axis of percepts combines to produce the sign.

James's use of his ghostly themes, especially the theme of possession, addresses exactly this problem. Possession represents the ghost as it were of romanticism, which the realist impulse had excluded from the text and which, as an incoherent order of the signified, is hauntingly searching for readmission to discourse. Possession is the voice of metaphysics excluded by a logic that chooses to emphasize the unvarnished fact as the basis of a literary movement. But the theme of possesssion has an ontological as well as a historical status; it serves the larger question of the structure of the reality that it represents; and from this perspective the motif of possession poses an ominous threat—that noumena might reassume the romantic priority which gave the representation of reality to the custody of the signified. How to find a legitimate basis for the possessive impulse—how to find an accurate metaphor that would restore the order of the signified while neutralizing its theological reference: this was James's dilemma; without a solution, no literary mode could complete itself.

Roland Barthes, speaking of Jules Michelet's *La sorcière,* notes Michelet's definition of the possessed personality as one which is "excluded from the world and necessary to the world"; one who is seeking a "correction of reality."[35] Jamesian possession might be put in precisely these terms. It clarifies an obscure language, one haunted by a force which, though it has lost its mastery, nonetheless means to insist on an irreducible unity of form and meaning—the structure of the sign. That structure had been jeopardized by a romantic crisis of signification and is here inscribing the limit of the realist effort to demystify. This certainly suggests "an anxiety of language," in a phrase of Derrida's, which arises at the point where "the simple significative nature of language appears rather uncertain, partial, or inessential," so that the form of fiction (say) is like "a city no longer inhabited, not simply left behind, but haunted by meaning and culture."[36]

If one prefers historical rather than theoretical argument there is Peter Brooks's fine essay. Brooks develops the idea of a "moral occult"—that "domain of operative spiritual values which is both indicated within and masked by the surface of reality. . . . not a metaphysical system [but] a realm which in quotidian existence may appear closed off from us, but which we . . . must get in touch with since it is the realm of meaning and value."[37] James and Balzac (with whom Brooks links James) reject on the one hand, so Brooks argues, "any metaphysical reduction of real life, and refuse to reduce their metaphysical enterprise to the cold symbolism of allegory." What had James said?—"Hawthorne, in his metaphysical moods, is nothing if not allegorical, and allegory, to my sense, is quite one of the lighter exercises of the imagination."[38] On the other hand, Brooks goes on, James and Balzac "refuse to allow that the world has been drained of transcendence; and they locate that transcendence in the struggle of the children of light with the children of darkness, in the play of ethical mind" (210). It is a struggle taking place within language—the dramatic struggle of meaning with form: of signified and signifier, spirit and matter; language cannot exclude it; language is always haunted, always possessed. Nowhere in literary realism is this struggle of language so fully or so usefully made a problem of meaning as in James's narratives of possession.

NOTES

1. Leon Edel, *Henry James: The Treacherous Years* (Philadelphia: J. B. Lippincott, 1969), pp. 83 ff., 161, 168; Walter Isle, *Experiments in Form: Henry James's Novels, 1896-1901* (Cambridge: Harvard University Press, 1968), pp. 77-119.

2. Kenneth Graham, *Henry James, The Drama of Fulfilment* (Oxford: Clarendon Press, 1975), p. 127.

3. Charles G. Hoffmann, *The Short Novels of Henry James* (New York: Bookman, 1957), p. 52.

4. Edwin Bowden, *The Themes of Henry James: A System of Observation through the Visual Arts* (New Haven: Yale University Press, 1956), p. 53.

5. Henry James, *The Spoils of Poynton*, New York Edition (New York: Charles Scribner's Sons, 1936), 10:vi.

6. See Martha Banta, *Henry James and the Occult: The Great Extension* (Bloomington: Indiana University Press, 1972), pp. 83 ff., 155; see also Gay Wilson Allen, *William James* (New York: Viking Press, 1967), e.g. pp. 281-85; also *The Letters of William James*, ed. Henry James, 2 vols. (Boston: Atlantic Monthly Press, 1920), 2:56-58.

7. See Freud's suggestion in a letter to William Fleiss (17 January 1897) that "the medieval theory of possession, held by the ecclesiastical courts, was identical with our theory of a foreign body and a splitting of consciousness": *The Standard Edition of the Complete Psychological Works of Sigmund Freud*, ed. and trans. James Strachey et al., 24 vols. (London: Hogarth Press, 1953-74), vol. 1, *Pre-Psycho-Analytic Publications and Unpublished Drafts* (1968), p. 242. Later and at greater length Freud treated possession as "an example of the process, with which we are familiar, by which an idea that has a contradictory—an ambivalent—content becomes divided into two sharply contrasted opposites." For Freud this demonological neurosis "contained two sets of emotional impulses that were opposed to each other: it contained not only impulses of an affectionate and submissive nature, but also hostile and defiant ones" (19:86, 85).

8. Banta, *Henry James and the Occult*, p. 85.

9. H. C. Lea, *A History of the Inquisition of the Middle Ages* (New York: Russell & Russell, 1958), p. 505.

10. Ibid., p. 383.

11. Charles Williams, *Witchcraft* (New York: Meridian Books, 1959), p. 128.

12. Michel Foucault, *Madness and Civilization*, trans. Richard Howard (New York: Mentor Books, 1967), p. 80.

13. René Girard, *Violence and the Sacred*, trans. Patrick Gregory (Baltimore: Johns Hopkins University Press, 1977), p. 317.

14. Ibid., p. 51.

15. Claude Lévi-Strauss, "The Sorcerer and His Magic," in *Structural Anthropology*, vol. 1, trans. Claire Jacobson and Brooke Grundfest Schoepf (New York: Doubleday, 1967), p. 177.

16. Yvor Winters, "Maule's Well, or Henry James and the Relation of Morals to Manners," in *In Defense of Reason* (Denver: Swallow Press, n.d.), p. 338.

17. The complex debate on signs is too lengthy to reproduce in this essay, but I am clearly accepting Saussure's development of a theory of signification and his influence

on structuralist and poststructuralist thinkers. For Saussure the sign consists always of two components—signifier and signified—which though wholly different are also indivisible, and which exist only through their relationship to one another: "Whenever only one element is retained, the entity vanishes: instead of a concrete object we are faced with a mere abstraction" or, on the other hand, with a merely empirical fragment. See Ferdinand de Saussure, *Course in General Linguistics,* ed. Charles Bally et al., trans. Wade Baskin (New York: McGraw-Hill, 1966), pp. 102–3. Saussure's signified is conceptual, his signifier perceptual. One claims the authority of ideas or spirit, therefore: the other, matter. Following Jackobson, we may say that the romantic sign is one in which the signified is privileged. Romantic signs tend metaphorically toward the ideal as a means of expressing the particular universe they assume, one in which objective reality is always the basis for a transcendent arc toward the metaphysical. The signified thus romantically predominates to impel understanding toward a noumenal priority, whether certain or questionable; and in romantic language the order of signifiers, the phenomenal real, functions to serve this transcendent aim. Cf. Roman Jakobson, "Two Aspects of Language and Two Types of Aphasic Disturbances," in *Fundamentals of Language,* ed. Jakobson and Morris Halle (The Hague: Mouton, 1956).

But the priority of either aspect, typically negotiated to equilibrium, sometimes becomes problematic. The space of the sign may thus be vexed by a question of possession. Then it becomes helpful to think of the bond between signifier and signified as a theoretical line of difference that demands that each aspect define itself idiosyncratically and to the fullest extent.

Signs are especially vulnerable, and consequently revealing, when they pass out of one custody and into another in this way. Here signification traverses a kind of no-man's land, a region which allows possibilities of restructuring. At this point of crossing, signs may rebuke one definition of what is real in favor of another, since the very structure and tension of the sign allows fundamentally different yet bonded principles of assembly to influence one another. This is a frontier where the sign's identity may change at the core, as proximate but radically different ways of knowing experience assume or concede governance. Or, to say it another way, I am arguing that this change in the sign's deployment of its own capacities becomes apparent in James's consistent use of possession as a means of setting realist language against romantic standards.

18. The New York Edition (New York: Charles Scribner's Sons, 1936): 12:xx; 11:xiv; 17:v, xxiv; 26:312.

19. James, *The Spoils of Poynton,* p. 11.

20. Philip M. Weinstein, in *Henry James and the Requirements of the Imagination* (Cambridge: Harvard University Press, 1971), suggests that as "the outward data of realism became less prominent in James's fictive world," he "shifts his focus to . . . romantic, poetically rendered illusions" (78–79). See also *The Notebooks of Henry James,* ed. F. O. Matthiessen and Kenneth B. Murdock (New York: Oxford University Press, 1961). In the *Notebooks,* and in the midst of composing *The Spoils of Poynton,* James suggests to himself "the little subject there may, somehow, be in the study of a romantic mind" (220). Earlier and at greater length he had considered a larger subject, "the great modern collapse of all the forms and 'superstitions' and respects, good and bad, and restraints and mysteries—a vivid and mere showy general hit at the decadences and vulgarities and confusions and masculinizations and feminizations—the materializations and abdications and intrusions, and Americanizations, the lost sense, the brutalized manner" (196). The senescence of forms whose influence resentfully persists—this theme is much on James's mind in the mid-nineties. One of his working titles for *Poynton* was "The Old Things." Cf. also the *Notebook* entry for 22 January 1879 (p. 9), which sketches a ghost story in which an excluded spiritual presence struggles for readmission to a domestic place.

21. See, for instance, James W. Gargano, "*The Spoils of Poynton:* Action and Responsibility," *Sewanee Review* 69 (October–December 1961): 650. Cf. Alan H. Roper,

"The Moral and Metaphorical Meaning of *The Spoils of Poynton*," *American Literature* 32 (May 1960), esp. 182 n. 3, for a summary of the critical literature on this problem; see also Edmund L. Volpe, "The Spoils of Art," *MLN* 74 (November 1959): 604, 607. Not all the work on this novel deserves commemoration, but in addition to works cited above one might mention John C. Broderick, "Nature, Art, and Imagination in *The Spoils of Poynton*," *Nineteenth-Century Fiction* 12 (March 1959): 295–312. By far the best general discussion of the novel's complex relationship of form and theme is Gary O. Trotter's *The Process of Selection in the Art of Henry James* (Ph.D. diss., SUNY at Buffalo, 1979), esp. chapter 3.

22. See Philip L. Greene, "Point of View in *The Spoils of Poynton*," *Nineteenth-Century Fiction* 21 (1967): "The physical and moral actions of the narrative apparently revolve around the *donnée*, the 'things' at Poynton, but very early in the novel this interest is deflected toward Fleda's secret or concealed love for Owen Gereth" (361).

23. In *Experiments in Form* Isle says that Fleda's "'spiritual' qualities rest in her nonphysical attributes. She exists in idea and ideal, in feeling and in imagination. She ... had the added capacity to interpret" (89).

24. Jacques Derrida, "White Mythology," trans. F.C.T. Moore, *New Literary History* 6 (Autumn 1974): 8.

25. Jean Starobinski, *The Invention of Liberty*, trans. Bernard C. Swift (Geneva: Skira, 1965), p. 14.

26. Mark Girouard, *Life in the English Country House: A Social and Architectural History* (New Haven: Yale University Press, 1978), p. 10.

27. James, "Maud-Evelyn," in *The Complete Tales of Henry James*, ed. Leon Edel, 12 vols. (London: Rupert Hart-Davis, 1964), vol. 11, *1900–1903*, p. 59.

28. In his introduction to the second edition of Garland's *Main-Travelled Roads*. Cited in Harrison T. Meserole et al., *American Literature: Tradition and Innovation*, 4 vols., vol. 4, *Henry Adams to the Present* (Lexington, Mass.: D. C. Heath, 1969), p. 2082.

29. Hamlin Garland, *Roadside Meetings* (New York: Macmillan, 1930), p. 90.

30. From a letter in my possession. It was written by Frederic to Atherton (dated 10 July 1898) and tipped into her copy of Frederic's *Illumination* (the American title of which was *The Damnation of Theron Ware*), published by Heinemann in 1897.

31. In Mark Twain's *Correspondence with Henry Huttleston Rogers, 1893–1909*, ed. Lewis Leary (Berkeley and Los Angeles: University of California Press, 1969), p. 124.

32. Henry James, *Hawthorne* (Ithaca: Cornell University Press, 1956), p. 98.

33. Theodore Dreiser, *Dawn* (New York: Liveright, 1931), p. 588.

34. William Dean Howells, *Criticism and Fiction* (New York: Harper, 1892), pp. 15–16.

35. Roland Barthes, *Critical Essays*, trans. Richard Howard (Evanston: Northwestern University Press, 1972), p. 114.

36. Jacques Derrida, "Force and Signification," in *Writing and Difference*, trans. Alan Bass (Chicago: University of Chicago Press, 1978), pp. 3, 4, 5.

37. Peter Brooks, "The Melodramatic Imagination: The Example of Balzac and James," in *Romanticism: Vistas, Instances, Continuities*, ed. David Thorburn and Geoffrey Hartman (Ithaca: Cornell University Press, 1973), p. 203.

38. James, *Hawthorne*, p. 49.

ALAN TRACHTENBERG

Experiments in Another Country
STEPHEN CRANE'S CITY SKETCHES

In the nineteenth century the big city appeared often in the guise of mystery. To be sure cities always have baffled the stranger with their labyrinths of streets and lanes, moving crowds, noisy markets, obscure carvings on gates: each a unique entity of family and clan and inner places closed to the outsider. Concealment in some measure is inherent in cities. But with new developments in the nineteenth century, particularly in large centers like Paris, London, and New York, mystery deepened beyond initial appearances and developed into a pervasive response. It was deeper too than the middle-class curiosity about the demimonde to which Eugene Sue catered, although the veiled lives of outcasts and criminals contributed a large share to the sense of urban mystery. The pervasive image now shows the city as a perilous and problematic experience for its own citizens as well as strangers, its whole reality hidden within denser crowds, closed off much the way older vistas are now blocked by taller, inexplicable buildings. We find the image on all levels—in guide books and newspapers, in popular Gothicized "mysteries," in serious poetry and fiction: the city as a swarming mass of signals, dense, obscure, undecipherable.

Of course, what was happening in and to nineteenth-century cities was in most ways not mysterious but calculable as the result of new forces of production and distribution pulling in a working class from the countryside, creating on one hand intensely crowded living quarters close to places of work, and on the other new places for display of goods and for shopping. Divisions of space and of styles of life, between production and consumption, were the most visible marks of a new social order imposing itself on older sites. The process was plain and disclosed itself in the growing divisions between rich and poor that beset mid- and late-nineteenth-century urban society. The literary trope of mystery

Reprinted from *The Southern Review* 10 (1974): 265–85, by permission of the editors and the author.

might itself serve as a form of mystification, as Karl Marx showed with exuberant irony in his lengthy analysis of Sue's *Mysteries of Paris* in *The Holy Family:* a device for confirming the social order while seeming to expose its hidden facts. But within the pervasive idea of mystery there does lie an irreducible condition that was fundamental to much urban literature. The physical city had become divided in so many small, insinuating ways that it defied comprehensibility. Its reality had become elusive, always seeming to flee into the shadows of another street. The motto of Edgar Allan Poe's haunting tale of pursuit, "The Man of the Crowd," sums up the essence of the deeper mystery: *Es lässt sich nicht lesen.* The city and its obsessive characters are like a book that does not permit itself to be read. The story of the compulsive wanderer among crowds, and the pursuit of the wanderer to penetrate his mystery, enacts the dilemma of comprehending the incomprehensible in a pristine form. Jean Paul Sartre formulates this paradox that lies at the heart of the city mystery as follows:

> A *city* is a material and social organization which derives its reality from the ubiquity of its absence. It is present in each of its streets *insofar as* it is always elsewhere, and the myth of the capital with its *mysteries* demonstrates well that the opaqueness of direct human relations comes from this fact, that they are always conditioned by all others. *The Mysteries of Paris* stem from the absolute interdependence of spots connected by their radical compartmentalization.

Experienced as an absence, as radically incomplete in any of its moments, the city thus invites pursuit, requires investigation, invasion of other spaces. The image of an impenetrability that provokes quest settled into urban culture, shared in different ways by poets, journalists, and social reformers in Europe and America.

Friedrich Engels describes himself as "a traveler" in London roaming "for hours," submitting himself to the "imposing" impressions of river, docks, houses. "All this is so magnificent," he writes, "that one is lost in admiration." Then leaving the "main streets" and turning into the slums, into an "elsewhere" that enlarges and complicates the picture of London's social reality, the traveler has it "dawn upon him that the inhabitants of modern London have had to sacrifice so much that is best in human nature in order to create those wonders of civilization with which their city teems." The city's physiognomy begins to reveal itself only as the investigator changes his perspective, shifts from one space to another. The problem of point of view, of the appropriate physical stance from which to gauge the social meanings of scenes witnessed, is at the core of investigation, the reformer Charles Booth realized. He writes:

East London lay hidden from view behind a curtain upon which were painted terrible pictures:—Starving children, suffering women, over-worked men; horrors of drunkenness and vice; monsters and demons of inhumanity; giants of disease and despair. Do these pictures truly represent what lay behind, or did they bear to the facts a relation similar to that which the pictures outside a booth at some country fair bear to the performance or show within?

"This curtain," writes Booth about his masterly *Life and Labor of the London Poor,* "we have tried to lift."

The street in particular appeared as the locus of curtained, displaced experience. The idea of mystery came to be particularized as the notion of space fragmented, regularized, specialized. The consciousness of dif-ferentiated space use can be traced in guide books for "strangers" and street directories, themselves perfect expressions of the radical incom-pleteness of any street experience. Often dressed with literary devices and Gothic coloration drawn from the *mysteries,* these verbal maps convey the city as interlocking spaces occupied by functions increasingly unintelligible to each other, in short, as space mystified. Men brought up "in the streets," wrote Frederick Law Olmsted in 1871, develop a particu-lar kind of hardening of the surface of their private spaces: "Every day of their lives they have seen thousands of their fellow-men, have met them face to face, have brushed against them, and yet have had no experience of anything in common with them." He conceived of the city park pre-cisely as an overcoming of the oppressive mystification of the street. "We want a ground," he writes, "to which people may easily go after their day's work is done, and where they may stroll for an hour, seeing, hearing, and feeling nothing of the bustle and jar of the streets. . . . We want the greatest possible contrast with the streets." Olmsted's parks were designed as antitheses to the city, which appeared now as closed and enclosing, as a denial of experience.

By the end of the century spatial barriers appeared threatening and intolerable, and in the rhetoric of reformers the idea of *mystery* itself was the veil that hid the sight of the lower orders and their quarters from the "public," the readers of newspapers and the payers of taxes for whom the slums were par excellence an "elsewhere" shrouded in awe and fear. What Stephen Crane called "the eternal mystery of social condi-tions" begged for solution. Such popular titles in the 1890s as "People We Pass," "The Nether Side of New York," "How the Other Half Lives," confirmed the by then conventional trope of a fragmented urban land-scape; the *mystery* or problem is located entirely in the alarming incom-municability among what Robert Park in the twentieth century described as the "moral regions," the patterns of segregation that make the city "a mosaic of little worlds which touch but do not interpenetrate."

In 1894 Crane published a number of city stories and sketches in the daily press in New York. He thought well enough of these experimental pieces to consider collecting them as "Midnight Sketches." Considering their origins as newspaper sketches, these mainly short, deft impressions of New York street life seem more like apprentice work than finished inventions. One of the reasons for their interest is, however, exactly the fact of their having been produced for the press as newspaper performances. If the stories show the young writer, still in his early twenties, experimenting with language to develop an appropriate style, the newspaper itself must be taken into account as a given of the experimental situation. Crane derived the form itself, the "sketch," from the newspaper, and at a deeper level the form provided a challenge, a barrier to be overcome.

The big city daily, especially as it developed in the 1890s, has its *raison d'être* chiefly in the mystification of urban space, a mystification it claims to dispel as "news" yet simultaneously abets as "sensationalism." The newspaper addresses itself abstractly to a "public" that is the collective identity each isolated urban consciousness is invited to join, a neutral space held in common as the negation of hidden private space. The motive of the metropolitan press, Robert Park writes, is "to reproduce as far as possible, in the city, the conditions of life in the village." In villages "everyone knew everyone else, everyone called everyone by his first name." The tactic of searching out "human interest," of making the commonplace seem picturesque or dramatic, is an attempt to fill the distances inherent in mystified space with formulaic emotion fostering the illusion of distance transcended. In their daily recurrence newspapers express concretely the estrangement of an urban consciousness no longer capable of free intimacy with its own material life. In their form the wish for the commonplace or the demystification of social distance coexists with the wish not to dispel mystery, to retain as surrogate experience the aura of awe, allurement, fear which surrounds street experience.

Crane was not an ordinary reporter on assignment; he wrote as a "literary" observer, a personal reporter of city scenes. His sketches were not "news"; nor were they entirely fiction, though he was capable of "making up" an account of a fire that never occurred and placing it in the New York *Press* as a signed report. The sketches present themselves as personal reports from and on *experience,* frankly colored by a personal style. The convention of such stylized reporting already existed in New York journalism as an expression of the newspapers' need to transform random street experience into *someone's* experience. The convention provided Crane with an opportunity to cultivate an authentic style as a vehicle of personal vision. The danger was that pressure to distinguish his vision, to make his signature recognizable, would lead to stylization.

Choosing themes familiar to newspaper, magazine, and novel readers, Crane developed a distinctive manner, a kind of notation that rendered physical scenes in highlighted color and sound. "When Everyone Is Panic-stricken," his fire report hoax, opens:

> We were walking on one of the shadowy side streets west of Sixth Avenue. The midnight silence and darkness was upon it save where at the point of intersection with the great avenue there was a broad span of yellow light. From there came the steady monotonous jingle of streetcar bells and the weary clatter of hooves on the cobbles. While the houses in this street turned black and mystically silent with the night the avenue continued its eternal movement and life, a great vein that never slept nor paused. The gorgeous orange-hued lamps of the saloon flared plainly and the figures of some loungers could be seen as they stood on the corner. Passing to and fro the tiny black figures of people made an ornamental border on this fabric of yellow light.

The effect is painterly, precise, impressionistic. Crane's eye for detail, his ability to take in a scene and convey its sense, its contours, in a few telling strokes, suggest important correspondence between his visual intentions and those of impressionist painters and photographers. The notation here, and typically in the city sketches, seizes a passing moment and formalizes it as a picture drawn from a precise physical perspective— from the shadowy side street toward the great avenue and its gorgeous yellow light. Within the formalization the scene contains motion, the potential for change, for the appearance of the sudden and the unex-pected. The potency is held in the carefully constructed spatial relation between the black, silent houses in "this street" and the unsleeping, flaring life of the avenue. The relation has, moreover, the potential of an ironic contrast, one that emerges as the "grim midnight reflection upon existence" of the narrator and his companion (identified only as "the stranger"), "in the heavy shadows and in the great stillness" of the street, are disputed by a sudden "muffled cry of a woman" from one of the "dark impassive houses" and the "sound of the splinter and crash of broken glass, falling to the pavement." The pictorial patterns of the open-ing paragraph give way to the frenzy and excitement of a midnight fire. Like the shadowy street itself the stranger suddenly flares into life, clutches the narrator's arm, drags him to the blazing house, himself a mirror of its vehemence. Through his responses Crane registers the effec-tive transformation of the scene from shadow to blaze, from grimness to frenzy: "The stranger's hand tightened convulsively on my arm, his enthusiasm was like the ardor of one who looks upon the pageantry of battles. 'Ah, look at 'em! ain't that great?'" The spatial relations and contrasts of the opening picture contain, in short, visual elements corresponding to the little drama that this fake news story performs.

A similar dramatization of visual detail and spatial relations to deepen and complicate conventional newspaper action appears in many of the sketches. Their interest lies in the fact that Crane used the occasion—the "personal" or "feature" reporter in search of copy—to develop techniques for rendering events on city streets as unique and complex experiences. Defining his literary problem from within such conventions posed certain difficulties; literalism, sensationalism, sentimentality were the ogres of the newspaper story Crane had to slay in his own work. From within the conventions Crane was able to discover a ground for genuine creation. That ground lay chiefly within the spatial structure of the common city story. Crane grasped the element of *mystery* within that structure and made it the basis of his point of view.

The most prominent and sensational of the spatial images in this period was that of the "other half," represented by the maze of streets and alleys and courtyards in lower Manhattan. In his famous exposures of living conditions in the slums, Jacob Riis, reporter for the New York *Sun,* excavated place names like Mulberry Bend, Bottle Alley, and Bandit's Roost. These names joined the "Bowery" as signals of forbidding and exotic territory. Illustrating his stories and books with photographs that explored to the "darkest corner," Riis established a pattern of spatial penetration that provided his readers with vicarious expeditions into mysterious quarters. His technique was that of a guided tour; his aim, to convert the reader from passive ignorance to active awareness and caring. In the sensations of his disclosures lurks some residue of the city *mystery:*

Leaving the Elevated Railroad where it dives under the Brooklyn Bridge at Franklin Square, scarce a dozen steps will take you where we wish to go . . . with its rush and roar echoing yet in our ears we have turned the corner from prosperity to poverty. We stand upon the domain of the tenement . . . . enough of them everywhere. Suppose we look into one? No.—Cherry Street. Be a little careful, please! the hall is dark and you might stumble over the children pitching pennies there. Not that it would hurt them; kicks and cuffs are their daily diet. They have little else. Here where the hall turns and dives into utter darkness is a step and another, another, a flight of stairs. You can feel your way, if you cannot see it. Close? Yes! What would you have? All the fresh air that ever enters these stairs comes from the hall door that is forever slamming and from the windows of dark bedrooms that in turn we see from the stairs the sole supply of the elements God meant to be free, but that man deals out with such niggardly hand.

And so on. The strategy is to place the reader in a moral relation of outrage, indignation, or pity. But it remains a touristic device; the reader is not permitted to cross into the inner world of the slums—into its own point of view—and see the outer world from that perspective. The moral stance that defines the "other half" as "problem" assures distance.

The portrayal of "low life" in much of the popular writing of the period employed analogous devices to preserve distance—devices of picturesque perspective or sentimental plot that protected the reader from the danger of a true exchange of point of view with the "other half." The danger appears as such in an interesting passage in the essay "New York Streets" by William Dean Howells. In his walks through the "wretched quarters," he writes, he permits himself to become "hardened, for the moment, to the deeply underlying fact of human discomfort" by indulging himself in the "picturesqueness" of the scene: "The sidewalks swarm with children and the air rings with clamor as they fly back and forth at play; on the thresholds the mothers sit nursing their babes and the old women gossip together." He remarks then, shrewdly, that "in a picture it would be most pleasingly effective, for then you could be in it and yet have the distance on it which it needs." To be *in it*, however, is "to inhale the stenches of the neglected street and to catch that yet fouler and dreadfuler poverty-smell which breed from the open doorways. It is to see the children quarreling in their games and beating each other in the face and rolling each other in the gutter like the little savage outlaws they are." This reality, if you are a walker in the city, "makes you hasten your pace down to the river" and escape. The passage confesses at once to the denials of the picturesque view and the offensiveness of an unmediated view.

How then was "low life" to be viewed? For Howells, for Riis, and for many concerned writers, a moral posture supplied the necessary screen of protection from an exchange of subjectivities. But the possibility of such an exchange—indeed its necessity if the logic of the convention were to complete itself—is implicit in the spatial pattern. It is precisely this possibility that Crane recognized in his city sketches—a possibility that provides the formal structure of two of the most ambitious of the city stories, the companion pieces "Experiment in Misery" and "Experiment in Luxury," and that illuminates his stylistic intentions throughout the sketches. Already in *Maggie: Girl of the Streets* (1893) and *George's Mother* (presumably composed in 1894, in the same period of the city sketches), Crane had discarded the moral posture of the tourist and had tried to convey physical landscapes equivalent to his perception of the subjective lives of his characters. His materials for *Maggie* seem to have been derived almost entirely from written accounts of the lives of slum people by investigators like Riis and the evangelist T. Dewitt Talmage.

The story is, in effect, a retelling of a familiar plot: Maggie (the name itself was virtually generic), pure blossom of the slums, is driven—by indifference, selfishness, and sexual exploitation—first to streetwalking then to suicide in the East River. For Crane the plot was an occasion to tell a familiar tale with vividness, with exactness of observation, and most of all, with sufficient irony to make it apparent that the characters themselves viewed their world melodramatically, through lenses blurred with the same false emotions they inspired—as "low life"—in the many popular tellers of their tale. Crane aims at accuracy, not compassion. The story is a complicated piece of parody written with a serious regard for the task of rendering a false tale truly. Crane's version of "low life," in *George's Mother* as well as *Maggie,* aims to represent the subjectivities of his characters. Each of the characters in these two novellas lives inwardly in a withdrawn psychic space, possessed by the shadowy feelings and escapist yearnings of the city's popular culture. Each is self-deceived, estranged from all others, occupying an imaginative world of his own.

Crane's recognition of the "mosaic of little worlds" and its demands upon representation is manifest in one of the best-known of the street sketches, "The Men of the Storm." The sketch is of a crowd of homeless men observed on the street during a blizzard as they wait with growing impatience and dangerous discontent for the "doors of charity" to open. Images of the homeless and jobless waiting for charity on the street were common in the writing and graphics of the period. Crane's piece differs from the standard treatment in several crucial ways. It is not a social study; it neither excites compassion for the men nor induces social guilt in the reader for their plight. It is a rendering of a scene, a depiction of a space, as objective as Alfred Stieglitz's street photographs taken with a hand-held camera in the same year. Crane's concern is with the phenomenon before him, and his writing is almost surgical in its sureness of stroke. He writes to achieve an accurate statement of the feeling of the scene and his details are physical correlatives of the men's feelings of pitiless cold, biting wind, and snow that "cut like knives and needles." The men are driven by the storm "like sheep in a winter's gale." Viewed from without, they are also seen as possessing a collective subjectivity. For example, in their fierce condition they still can swear "not like dark assassins, but in a sort of American fashion grimly and desperately it is true but yet with a wondrous under-effect definable and mystic as if there were some kind of humor in this catastrophe, in this situation in a night of snow-laden winds."

A picture of a desperate scene—of men subjected to cold wind, snow, and hunger, alternately clinging to each other for warmth and fighting with each other for shelter—the sketch is also a highly pointed study in the problematics of point of view. Drawn from a detached floating perspective, the sketch contains several limited points of view, each located spatially and each characterized by a feeling linked to its space. The opening paragraphs present a picture of late afternoon busy streets as the blizzard begins to swirl upon pedestrians and drivers of vehicles and horses. The mood is grim at first: people are huddled, drivers are furious, horses slip and strain; "overhead the trains rumbled and roared and the dark structure of the elevated railroad stretching over the avenue dripped little streams and drops of water upon the mud and snow beneath it." But the next paragraph introduces a more hopeful note. The perspective momentarily shifts to an interior, "to one who looked from a window"; the clatter of the streets, softened by snow, "becomes important music, a melody of life made necessary to the ear by the dreariness of the pitiless beat and sweep of the storm." The warmth of the interior in which such musings are likely pervades the paragraph; the shop windows, "aglow with light," are "infintely cheerful," and now "the pace of the people and the vehicles" has a "meaning": "Scores of pedestrians and drivers wretched with cold faces, necks and feet, speeding for scores of unknown doors and entrances, scattering to an infinite variety of shelters, to places which the imagination made warm with the colors of home." The objective scene has been constructed to reveal a subjective mood—the storm is pitiless but the imagination warms itself with images of doors, entrances, home: "There was an absolute expression of hot dinners in the pace of the people." Crane then introduces a conjectural point of view inspired by the scene: "If one dared to speculate upon the destination of those who came trooping, he lost himself in a maze of social calculations. He might fling a handful of sand and attempt to follow the flight of each particular grain." But the entire troop has in common the thought of hot dinners: "It is a matter of tradition; it is from the tales of childhood. It comes forth with every storm." Social calculation might be pleasant, diversionary, but trivial. All classes are reduced to those who speed home in the blizzard warmed with the thoughts of food, and those who do not. At this point Crane performs the sketch's most decisive modulation of perspective: "However, in a certain part of the dark West side street, there was a collection of men to whom these things were as if they were not." The stark negative halts all calculation.

The narrator has subtly worked upon the reader's point of view, freeing it from the hold of customary feeling so that it might receive freely a newly discovered "moral region," the territory of "half darkness" in which occurs another kind of existence. In the description that follows Crane twice again introduces a shift in perspective in order to confirm better the spatial independence of his own. At one point, across the street from the huddled men, the figure of a stout, well-dressed man appears "in the brilliantly lighted space" of the shop window. He observes the crowd, stroking his whiskers: "It seemed that the sight operated inversely, and enabled him to more clearly regard his own environment, delightful relatively." The man's complacency is echoed at the end of the sketch as the narrator notes a change in expression in the features of the men as they near the receiving door of charity: "As they thus stood upon the threshold of their hopes they looked suddenly content and complacent, the fire had passed from their eyes and the snarl had vanished from their lips. The very force of the crowd in the rear which had previously vexed them was regarded from another point of view, for it now made it inevitable that they should go through the little doors into the place that was cheery and warm with light."

By projecting in the contrasted points of view a dialectic of felt values, Crane forces the reader to free his own point of view from any limiting perspective. Crane thus transforms the conventional event of turning corners and crossing thresholds into a demanding event: a change of perspective that as its prerequisite recapitulates a number of limited perspectives. Crane's "Men in the Storm" differs, for example, from a characteristic "literary" treatment of the same theme such as Howells's "The Midnight Platoon" by its achievement of a point of view superior to, yet won through a negation of, perspectives limited by social, moral, or aesthetic standards. Howells's piece concerns a bread line as it is perceived from a carriage by a man who comes to recognize himself as comfortable and privileged. The figure in the story approaches the scene as a "connoisseur of such matters," enjoying the anticipation of "the pleasure of seeing"; he wants to "glut his sensibility in a leisurely study of the scene." The bread line is to him "this representative thing," and he perceives in the crowd of hungry men "a fantastic association of their double files and those of the galley-slaves whom Don Quixote released." His mind wanders in conjecture:

> How early did these files begin to form themselves for the midnight dole of bread? As early as ten, as nine o'clock? If so, did the fact argue habitual destitution, or merely habitual leisure? Did the slaves in the coffle make acquaintance, or remain strangers to one another, though they were closely neighbored night after night by their misery? Perhaps they joked away the weary hours of waiting; they must have their jokes. Which of them were old-comers, and which novices? Did they ever quarrel over questions of precedence? Had they some comity, some etiquette, which a man forced to leave his place could appeal to, and so get it back? Could one say to his next-hand man, "Will you please keep my place?" and would this man say to an interloper, "Excuse me, this place is engaged"? How was it with them, when the coffle worked slowly or swiftly past the door where the bread and coffee were given out, and word passed to

the rear that the supply was exhausted? This must sometimes happen, and what did they do then?

Aware that the men look back at him with equal curiosity, he suddenly recognizes his own "representativity." To them, he realizes, he stands for Society, the Better Classes; the literary picturesque notions dissolve as he feels himself face to face with the social issue. Howells here confronts the social distance, portrays it as filled with middle-class rationalization, and ends with a "problem": what are "we" to do about these men and their suffering?

For Crane, the question is as if it were not. He writes from a curiously asocial perspective—or, at least, a perspective disengaged from that of the typical middle-class viewer; he approximates (though he does not yet achieve) the perspective of the men. That is, what Howells sees as a thoroughly social matter of how the classes view each other, Crane sees as a technical problem: how to represent the scene before him. He is not concerned with converting the reader to social sympathy (perhaps distrustful or weary of the condescension of such a stance), but with converting the sheer data into *experience*. He writes as a phenomenologist of the scene, intent on characterizing the consciousness of the place (which includes its separate points of view) by a rendering of felt detail. Each of Crane's images resonates with significance as a component of the episode's inner structure of feeling; the exactness of the correlation of detail to feeling leads, in fact, to the frequent mistake of describing Crane as a Symbolist. His *realism*, however, in the phenomenological sense, points to the significance, indeed the radicalism, of these sketches. For Crane transforms a street scene, a passing sensation for which a cognitive mold is already prepared in his reader's eye, into a unique experience.

If, following Walter Benjamin, we require that works be "situated in the living social context," then the immediate context is that established by the author with his reader; it is in that relationship that the possibility of each becoming "real" and particular for the other exists. In this case, the relationship is mediated by the sketch's appearance in a newspaper, and at a deeper level, by its formal expression of the newspaper motive: a "human interest" observation on a street. But typically the newspaper does not permit its own formal qualities so intense and exact a realization. Newspapers respond, as I have pointed out, to the increasing mystification, the deepening estrangement of urban space from interpenetration, from exchange of subjectivities. But their response is to deepen the crisis while seeming to allay it. In their typographical form, their typical verbal usage, they serve, Benjamin writes, "to isolate what happens from the realm in which it could affect the experience of the reader." By isolating information from experience, moreover, they deaden the capacity of memory; the lack of connection among the data of the newspaper page reduces all items to the status of "today's events." The newspaper, Benjamin writes, "is the showplace of the unrestrained degradation of the word." In *War is Kind* Crane wrote:

> A newspaper is a collection of half-injustices
> Which, bawled by boys from mile to mile,
> Spreads its curious opinion
> To a million merciful and sneering men,
> While families cuddle the joys of the fireside
> When spurred by tale of dire lone agony.
> A newspaper is a court
> Where every one is kindly and unfairly tried
> By a squalor of honest men.
> A newspaper is a market
> Where wisdom sells its freedom
> And melons are crowned by the crowd.
> A newspaper is a game
> Where his error scores the player victory
> While another's skill wins death.
> A newspaper is a symbol;
> It is fetless life's chronicle,
> A collection of loud tales
> Concentrating eternal stupidities
> That in remote ages lived unhaltered,
> Roaming through a fenceless world.

The poem expresses nicely Crane's recognition of the constricting function of the newspaper as a "market" in which are sold "loud tales" to a world that appears "fenced-in." He has no illusions about the newspaper and the degradation of literature it represents.

Yet, as Benjamin argues, within the logic of the newspaper lies a possible condition for the salvation of the word—in the new relationships it fosters between writer and world, between writer and reader. Crane accepted the condition of newspaper production and produced within it work that, with the complicity of his careful reader, converts the data of street life into memorable experience. He thus transvalues, or as Benjamin would put it, "alienates" the apparatus of production and forces his reader to become an accomplice, that is, to become himself an experimenter in mystified space. The best example among the sketches, an example that reveals Crane's motives almost diagrammatically, is the often misunderstood "Experiment in Misery." In this and in its companion piece, "Experiment in Luxury," published a week apart in the New York *Press*, Crane presents a figure, a "youth," who enters opposite social realms—in

the first a seedy lodging house, in the second the mansion of a millionaire. The report in both cases is of the quality of life, of the awareness
that inhabits each interior. The method in each "Experiment" is to convey the inner feeling by having the youth "try on" the way of life. The
spaces are thus presumably demystified by the youth's assuming the point
of view implicit in the physical structures and the actions of their interiors.
For example, as he lounges with his rich friend, smoking pipes, the youth
feels a sense of liberty unknown on the streets. "It was an amazing comfortable room. It expressed to the visitor that he could do supremely as he
chose, for it said plainly that in it the author did supremely as he chose."
Before long "he began to feel that he was a better man than many—entitled
to a great pride." In each case the narrative point of view projects the
youth's consciousness; he is made into a register of the world-as-it-is-felt
of the particular setting. In this way Crane transmutes social fact into felt
experience.

The stories are not identical in their strategies, however. Both begin
with a frame in which the youth is encouraged by an older friend, in a
conversation on a street, to undertake the experiment. As companion
pieces they together confront the great division that was the popular
mode through which "society" was perceived in the culture of the period:
luxury and misery, rich and poor, high and low, privileged and under-
privileged. Intentionally then, they compose a social statement. In the
"luxury" piece, unlike the other, Crane consciously works from a social
proposition: his "experiment" is an attempt to discover if indeed the
inner life of the very rich justifies the "epigram" "stuffed . . . down the
throat" of the complaining poor by "theologians" that "riches did not
bring happiness." The motive of the "misery" story is less overtly ideological: it is to learn of the "tramp" "how he feels." The narrative technique of the "luxury" story differs from the other in that the youth
carries on his "experiment" along with a simultaneous inner dialogue
based on observation and self-reflection. He learns that the rich do, after
all, live pretty well, if insipidly. He could "not see that they had great
license to be pale and haggard." The story assumes a point of view in
order to shatter a social myth. Being rich makes a difference.

Discursive self-reflection plays no role in the companion sketch. In fact,
to intensify attention on the experience itself, and to indicate that the
social drama of displacing one's normal perspective already is internalized
in the action, Crane discarded the opening and closing frames when he
republished the story in a collection of 1898. In his revision he also added
to the opening paragraphs a number of physical details that reinforce and
particularize the sense of misery. Streetcars, which in the first version
"rumbled softly, as if going on carpet stretched in the aisle made by the
pillars of the elevated road," become a "silent procession . . . moving with

formidable power, calm and irresistible, dangerous and gloomy, breaking silence only by the loud fierce cry of the gong." The elevated train station, now supported by "leg-like pillars," resembles "some monstrous kind of crab squatting over the street." These revisions and others suggest an intention more fully realized: the creation of physical equivalents to the inner experience of a "moral region" of misery.

The first version makes clear that the youth's "experiment" is a conscious disguise in order to search out "experience." "Two men stood regarding a tramp," it opens; the youth "wonders" how he "feels" and is advised by his older friend that such speculations are "idle" (a finely ironic word, as is "regarding") unless he is "in" the tramp's condition. The youth agrees to "try" it: "Perhaps I could discover his point of view or something near it." The frame opens with an awareness, then, of what the older man calls "distance" and establishes "experiment" as a method of overcoming it. So far the situation recalls the wish of Howells's witness of the bread line to penetrate distance, as it does the situation in many similar down-and-out pieces in the period. For example, in *Moody's Lodging House and Other Tenement Sketches* (1895), also a collection of newspaper sketches, Alvan Francis Sanborn writes: "The best way to get at the cheap lodging-house life is to live it,—to get inside the lodging house and stay inside. For this, unless one possesses a mien extraordinarily eloquent of roguery or misery, or both, a disguise is helpful." Crane's youth borrows a disguise from the "studio of an artist friend" (this suggestive detail is dropped in the revised version), and begins his experiment: as Crane puts it with a note of irony, the youth "went forth." The irony is directed at the hint of naïve chivalric adventuresomeness in the youth and prepares for the authentic conversion of his subjective life to follow.

In what follows the youth proceeds downtown in the rain; he is "plastered with yells of 'bum' and 'hobo'" by small boys, he is wet and cold, and "he felt that there no longer could be pleasure in life." In City Hall Park he feels the contrast between himself and the homeward bound "well-dressed Brooklyn people," and he proceeds further "down Park Row," where "in the sudden descent in the style of the dress of the crowd he felt relief, and as if he were at last in his own country" (this last significant detail was added in the revision). The youth begins to inhabit this other country, first by occupying himself with the "pageantry of the street," then "caught by the delectable sign," allowing himself to be "swallowed" by a "voracious"-looking saloon door advertising "free hot soup." His descent deepens. The next step is to find someone with "a knowledge of cheap lodging houses," and he finds his man in a seedy character "in strange garments"; he has a strange guilty look about his eyes, a look that earns him the youth's epithet of "assassin." The youth confesses himself also a "stranger" and follows the lead of his companion

to a "joint" of "dark and secret places" from which assail him "strange
and unspeakable odors." The interior is "black, opaque," and during the
night the youth lies sleepless as the dormitory takes on the grim appearance of a fiendish morgue. Near him lies a man asleep with partly open
eyes, his arm hanging over the cot, his fingers "full length upon the wet
cement floor of the room." The spirit of the place seems contained in this
image. "To the youth it seemed that he and the corpse-like being were
exchanging a prolonged stare and that the other threatened with his eyes."
The "strange effect of the graveyard" is broken suddenly by "long wails"
that "dwindle to final melancholy moans" expressing "a red and grim
tragedy of the unfathomable possibilities of the man's dreams." The
youth feels now that he has penetrated to the deepest recesses of the
tramp's condition.

At this point, however, Crane performs an important act of distancing
the narrative from the point of view of the youth. Fulfilling the earlier
hints of his naïveté, Crane now has the youth interpret the shrieks of the
"vision pierced man" as "protest," as "an impersonal eloquence, with a
strength not from him, giving voice to the wail of a whole section, a class,
a people." An ideological romance settles in his mind, "weaving into the
young man's brain and mingling with his views of these vast and sombre
shadows," and he "lay carving biographies for these men from his meager
experience." With morning and sunlight comes the "rout of the mystic
shadows," however, and the youth sees that "daylight had made the room
comparatively common-place and uninteresting." The men joke and ban-
ter as they dress, and some reveal in their nakedness that they were "men
of brawn" until they put on their "ungainly garments." The normalization
of feeling in this morning scene is crucial. When the youth reaches the
street he "experienced no sudden relief from unholy atmospheres. He had
forgotten all about them, and had been breathing naturally and with no
sensation of discomfort or distress." The respiratory detail confirms the
point; he is now indeed in his own country, where he might feel after
breakfast that "B'Gawd, we've been livin' like kings." In the expansive
moment his companion "brought forth long tales" about himself that
reveal him as a confirmed hobo, always cadging and running from work.
Together they make their way to City Hall Park, the youth now one of
"two wanderers" who "sat down in a little circle of benches sanctified
by traditions of their class." In the normalcy of his behavior he shows
that his experience of misery, since the night before, has become less
meager.

The story closes as the youth on the bench becomes aware of a new
substance in his perceptions. Well-dressed people on the street give him
"no gaze" and he feels "the infinite distance" from "all that he valued.
Social position, comfort, the pleasures of living, were unconquerable

kingdoms." His new world and theirs were separate countries. The separateness is discovered as a difference in perspective, in how the world is seen, felt, and accepted. Now, the tall buildings in the background of the park are "of pitiless hues and sternly high." They stand "to him" as emblems "of a nation forcing its regal head into the clouds, throwing no downward glances." "The roar of the city" is now "to him" a "confusion of strange tongues." Estrangement has become his own experience, no longer a "thought" about the original object of his perception, the tramp. The youth, and through him the reader, has attained an experimental point of view expressed in an act of the eyes in the concluding sentences: "He confessed himself an outcast, and his eyes from under the lowered rim of his hat began to glance guiltily, wearing the criminal expression that comes with certain convictions." The conviction itself, of being excluded by the overarching buildings, accounts for the new perspective.

The two "experiments" conclude that the rich are banal but live well and that the homeless poor are victims whose inner acquiescence is a form of cowardice. More important than such "meanings" are the strategies compressed in the word "experiment." In these strategies lie the specifically urban character of Crane's writings, a character that is his calculated invention out of the materials of the newspaper culture. Crane's "experiments" implicate Zola's but go beyond them. In the misery sketch, "experiment" denotes the subject as well as the method; the sketch is "about" the youth's experiment, an anatomizing of the components of the naturalist's enterprise of investigating human life in its social habitat. But Crane is concerned with the investigator, with the exercise of the logic of investigation upon his subjectivity. The experiment transforms the youth, and it is through that transformation that the life of the city's strangers becomes manifest. The youth is transformed only provisionally, however; he is not converted, not reclassified as a tramp. His experiment is literally a trying-out, a donning of a costume in order to report on its fit and feel. In order to live provisionally as a stranger in another country he must have estranged himself even more deeply to begin with, that is, he must already have disengaged himself from all possible identities, from social identity as such. Crane recognized that the inner form of the newspaper culture was itself "experiment" and to fulfill its logic of disengagement was a prerequisite for recovering "experience" from the flux of the street. Crane's city sketches are "experimental" writing in the sense, finally, that they confront the transformation of literary relations (the writer's relation to his subject and to his reader) implicit in the big city's mystification of social and psychic space; they invent stylistic procedures for re-creating the word as experience.

Crane's direction was a descent to the street and to the constricted visions that lay there as broken images. Out of these he forged a unifying

image of his own, a vision of a city peopled by nameless, desolate creatures, strangers to each other and to their own worlds. "The inhabitant
of the great urban centers," writes Paul Valèry, "reverts to a state of
savagery—that is, of isolation. The feeling of being dependent on others,
which used to be kept alive by need, is gradually blunted in the smooth
functioning of the social mechanism. Any improvement of this mechanism
eliminates certain modes of behavior and emotions." Crane's vision is of a
world already confirmed in its isolation, a world shocking in the absence
of those "certain modes of behavior and emotion" that make subjective
experience possible. The exchange of subjectivity performed by the youth
rarely occurs among the characters of his city fiction; instead, violence
always threatens as the promise of heightened sensation in defiance of the
blunting mechanisms: a wail, a scream, a fire, a clutched arm. Crane's city
people seem always ignitable, verging toward the discharge of feeling in
riot. His own narrative point of view remains cool and aloof, however; his
spatial penetrations end at the edge of sympathetic identification. Unlike
Theodore Dreiser, he was little interested in character, little interested in
exploring the versions of reality his style transcends. The expense of his
expert technicianship was the larger novelistic vision Dreiser achieved.
Dreiser also descended to the popular, to the banal, but the points of view
of his characters were not provisional guises; he took them as self-sufficient
acts of desire. Dreiser's city is a theme as well as a place: a magnet that
attracts. Less than a place, Crane's city lies in the structured passages of
his point of view; it is situated in his technique, in its processes of disengagement and recovery. His sketches are experiments in reading the
"elsewhere" of the street.

DONALD PEASE

Fear, Rage, and the Mistrials of Representation in
The Red Badge of Courage

In the April 1896 issue of *The Dial,* Army General A. C. McClurg, in a critical document interesting less for the general's insight into the novel than the direction of his criticism of it, bitterly denounced *The Red Badge of Courage* as a vicious satire of army life. "The hero of the book, if such he can be called, was an ignorant and stupid country lad without a spark of patriotic feeling or soldierly ambition," the general wrote. "He is throughout an idiot or a maniac and betrays no trace of the reasoning being. No thrill of patriotic devotion to cause or country ever moves his breast, and not even an emotion of manly courage." And after noting the work is that of a young man, and therefore must be a mere work of "diseased imagination," the general concludes, in a catalogue informed with political as well as dramatic principles, that "Soldier Fleming is a coward, a Northerner who fled the field . . . and that is why the British have praised *The Red Badge.*" Suspending for a moment any question of the accuracy in the general's remarks, we cannot fail to register the force in his reaction. Nor can we fail to notice the source of the general's rage: the absence in Private Fleming's account of those virtues usually included in conventional war narratives whenever describing or justifying the excesses of war. Moreover, although the general does not explicitly mention it, his reaction to still another omission proves clear enough from the fury in his final barrage of accusations. That Crane would represent battle conditions frightening enough to produce cowards might perhaps be excusable, but that he would present such conditions in a context devoid of such crucial issues as the slavery question or southern secession, issues bound to inspire in the reader what they failed to evoke from Private Fleming, namely a renewed commitment to the Union cause, must in General McClurg's mind be grounds for the charge of treason.

Clearly Crane inflamed the general's ire by leaving political considerations out of his account altogether. Written at a time when the nation's

155

historian's were characterizing the political and ideological significance of seemingly every battle in the war, Crane's power derived from his decision to reverse the procedure. By stripping the names from the battles he describes, Crane releases the sheer force of the battle incidents unrelieved by their assimilation into a historical narrative frame. And like a naive social historian, General McClurg decided to make good on the debits in Crane's account. In his critical relation to the war novel he restored to the narrative what Crane carefully eliminated from Henry Fleming's confrontation with war: a political and moral frame of reference.

By 1896, many American historians considered the Civil War the decisive moment in the nation's "coming of age." A moment's reflection on the contentions in early documentary accounts of the war should indicate the crucial role it played in providing a young nation with both a historical and a geographical orientation. For many historians viewed this war as a struggle that cross-identified ideological and geographical demarcations and finally granted a name and a sense of place to the United States of America. Given their evaluation of the crucial role the war played in the formation of national character, it was difficult if not impossible to eliminate moral questions from their accounts of the war. While few historians argued that freedom, equality, and union were decisively secured in the aftermath to the war, none denied the ideological power of these abstract principles. Indeed the moral values inherent in these principles not only affected these accounts, in some accounts they replaced battle descriptions altogether.

While Civil War narratives had developed into a flourishing enterprise capable of deflecting all considerations of the experience of the war into an ideological frame of reference intent on justifying it, Crane in registering the effects of the war innocent of the consolations of any coherent ground whatever defied the captains of the war industry. Once we acknowledge the number of reviews and critical studies that have either overlooked or scrupulously read back into *The Red Badge of Courage* what Crane has carefully eliminated, no further evidence of the pervasive hold of the typical Civil War narrative wields over the American imagination need be mentioned. What needs reiteration, however, is the threat not only against the Civil War industry but against America as a nation implicit in Crane's narrative. For if the conventional war narrative used the Civil War as a pretext for an ideological recounting of those principles that gave shape to a nation, Crane, by excluding these principles, was guilty of an assault against the American character. To register the force of this attack, however, we must read Crane through the eyes of a military officer eager to order a young nation to shape up, to conform to the features of stability and confidence delineated and secured by the war. General McClurg in his review, then, did not wish to launch a personal attack on Private

Fleming but to recover those representations Stephen Crane had withheld. As the general's review vividly attests, by 1896 these representations had become ingrained enough in the American character for one of her "representative men" to take their absence as a personal affront.

By mentioning General McClurg's reaction specifically, I do not mean to isolate its eccentricity, but to suggest that in its very force his reaction represents the urgent need to recover that sense of a developing American character Crane's account has taken leave of. Whether commentators attack this lack of character directly as General McClurg does in denouncing Private Fleming as a coward, or denounce it after a manner subtle enough to remain unconscious of it, as do more recent critics, by reading a coherent line of character development into the arbitrary incidents in Henry's life, the wish remains the same in both cases, to recover the sense of exemplary continuity, integrity, and significance for those Civil War events Stephen Crane has forcibly excised from official history. Crane acknowledges the urgency of this need by never failing to drive a wedge between the sheer contingency of Henry's battle experiences and those reflections on them that never account for so much as they displace these incidents with other concerns. What results is an ongoing sense of disorientation, a knowledge of Henry Fleming's involvement in a battle that history will later turn into a monumental event, but whose dimensions never presently convert into anything more than a series of discontinuous incidents, followed by pauses whose emptiness Henry can never fill with sufficient reflections. Without adequate ideological underpinnings these battle scenes flare up as severe emotional and psychic blows without the consolation recognition brings. Instead of absorbing Henry's recollections and the experiences they are meant to describe into the continuities of a narrative, *The Red Badge of Courage* underwrites the absence of continuity in a war that never achieves the epic qualities either Henry or a nation of historians would impose on it.

Indeed the war Henry suffers through seems, in its tendency seemingly to start from the beginning with each encounter, to lack any historical attributes whatever. Unlike the America that found its past confirmed and its geography decisively marked by war, Henry Fleming can discover no frame capable of situating him securely in either time or place. With each explosive battlefield encounter, Henry discovers that the barrier against too much stimulation has been breached, that the recognitions following these encounters and the anticipations meant to prepare him for them are both painfully inadequate. Confronted repeatedly with shocks utterly disrespectful of that lag between recollection and healing forgetfulness when experience has the time to form, Henry witnesses scenes that even when able to leave marks in the memory do so by quite literally leaving him out. In the following scene, for example, Henry records, with a

lucidity heightened through his fears, a series of impressions released from
the control of any fixed reference point:

> It seemed to the youth that he saw everything. Each blade of green
> grass was bold and clear. He thought that he was aware of each
> change in the thin, transparent vapor that floated idly in sheets. The
> brown or gray trunks showed each roughness of their surfaces. And
> the men of the regiment, with their staring eyes and sweating faces
> running madly, or falling as if thrown headlong, to queer, heaped-up
> corpses—all were comprehended. His mind took a mechanical but
> firm impression, so that afterward everything was pictured and ex-
> plained to him save why he himself was there.

In this description, each colorful image surges up as all foreground, with
a suddenness whose intensity is unmediated by a context capable of either
subduing or containing it. Instead of settling into that relationship in
which a figure is clearly contextualized within a stable ground and which a
coherent picture is supposed to guarantee, these "firm impressions" glare
out as if in defiance of an implicit order to move into perspective. Not
only the individual impressions fail to modify one another, however; so do
the sentences in which they appear. These sentences do not describe a
sequence in which new facts are "comprehended" by an overall principle
of coherence. Without any perspective capable of sorting out the relevant
from the irrelevant, everything crowds into Henry's consciousness with all
the force of confusion. Thus the very givenness of this jumble of impressions renders redundant Henry's concluding observation that everything
was explained to him save his own presence in the scene.

In this scene, then, the exclusion of any coherent perspective begins to
function as a perspective, one sufficiently powerful to make audible
Henry's unspoken reaction, his sensed alienation from the scene he observes. In this account, however, Henry Fleming does not assert his alienation as a feeling of separation. If anything he seems utterly absorbed in
the picture he describes. He seems so utterly consumed in a battle scene in
the act of manifesting itself as to be indistinguishable from what he perceives. Because, however, what he perceives are little more than sheer
impressions, unrelieved by any signification whatsoever, it would be more
accurate to say that what Fleming perceives is not a conventional battle
scene but the loss of any framework capable of informing this scene with
significance. In this scene then he becomes absorbed not in a picture but
its loss, the disappearance of what grounds a picture in a significant frame
of reference.

By representing such "private" impressions unverified by either the
accounts of other veterans or historians of the war, Crane depicts a character incompatible enough with the nation's self-portrait to elicit General

McClurg's fear of "foreign" influence. For Henry's chance observations, in the radical incongruity of their sheer givenness, do indeed permit the past to speak in an unfamiliar voice. This voice, in the very strangeness of its inflection, unsettles both the nation's past and the character sanctioned by it. Moreover, when carefully listened to, this voice fabricates a "reality" able to invest the past with an uncanny sense of immediacy, but an immediacy interlaced with an irony unlimited enough to relegate this past to a realm of irretrievable pastness.

It would be a mistake, however, to suggest that this voice dominates the narrative line of *The Red Badge of Courage;* it cannot be accommodated by narrative conventions. Narration, in converting the mere succession of incidents into a meaningful sequence, silences the voice released in the chance encounter. Like a photograph of a battle scene with the captions cut off, this voice counts any explanation capable of guaranteeing a coherent context or selecting out the significant details among the casualties of war. It speaks *through* the impressions surviving Henry's presence at scenes of battles, and by speaking through these incidental details asserts their independence from the war story Henry has to tell. Indeed this voice sustains itself by converting Henry's statements about the war back into pieces of it, so that what gets narrated in *The Red Badge of Courage* never coincides with those incidents that can never be explained but only marked.

If in scenes like the one cited, Henry's impressions denote his awareness of everything except a rationale for his being there, his narration forcibly displaces these impressions by supplying a missing rationale. Thus, the narrative inscribes a discrepancy between the self-image Henry wishes to represent and the incidents that fail to engage any image of the self whatsoever. Given that these marked incidents occupy a different space from those narrated events Henry creates through an act of reflection, the reader must engage this work with a double vision. Once envisioned through this double perspective, however, *The Red Badge of Courage* reveals a conception of the self that is perhaps as much a victim of narrative conventions as the vicissitudes of war. Having begun this discussion with a reflection on the incompatibility between Henry's chance incidents and conventional representations of the Civil War, we are drawn by the very force of this discrepancy to another interpretation, one guided by Henry's struggles to confer a significance on events that would otherwise utterly confound him. Through such an interpretive strategy we feel the pressure first of the merely chance encounter and then the force of Henry's need to recall those incidents in the mold of a meaningful narrative. In many cases the irrational force of the war proves a sufficient rationale to justify Henry's need for a significant narration. But Crane's text is remarkable for its refusal to favor the meaningful narrative. By persistently locating Henry in the space between

unrelieved contingency and imposed narrative, Crane inveigles the arbit-
rariness usually associated with the chance event into the orderly narrative
sequence. More startlingly, however, through this organization of materials, Crane exposes the need to choose Henry's narrative instead of his
experience as still another narrative convention.

Perhaps we cannot acknowledge the force of this recognition until we
ascertain the daring implication of Crane's narrative strategies. In the
arrangement of his plot, Crane did not use the brutality of the war as a
pretext for justifying the humane values implicit in narrative conventions.
Crane's chronology inverts the one we have described. In *The Red Badge
of Courage,* narratives do not follow battles and provide needed explanation; instead they precede and indeed demand battles as elaborations and
justifications of already narrated events.

"Private" Fleming negotiates this "turn of events" in that moment of
reflection he secures for himself in the wake of the excitement following
Jim Conklin's "rumor" that the troops are about to move. In the course
of his reflection Henry does not, as do so many of his fictional and non-
fictional predecessors, envision himself in a project involving the liberation of slaves. The only mention of a Negro in the entire novel appears in
the fourth paragraph, when Jim Conklin's tale creates a state of confusion
that quite literally abandons the Negro's cause. "When he had finished,
the blue-clothed men scattered into small arguing groups between the
rows of squat brown huts. A negro teamster who had been dancing upon
a cracker box with the hilarious encouragement of twoscore soldiers was
deserted. He sat mournfully down." Without any "noble" causes to com-
mandeer his martial emotions, Henry's musings fill this vacuum by turning
to "tales of great movement" as opportunities for personal aggrandizement. These battles, Henry reflected, "might not be distinctly Homeric,
but there seemed to be much glory in them." Having already read of
marches, sieges, conflicts, Henry now "longed to see it all." His busy mind
had drawn for him large pictures "extravagant in color, lurid with breath-
less deeds"; it remained for him to "realize" these narrated pictures with
matching deeds. In the reflections that inevitably follow all of his battle
experiences, then, it is obvious that Henry tries to take possession of himself as the figure he had previously imagined occupying center stage in one
of these extravagant pictures. What may not be obvious, however, is that
Henry's means of taking possession of himself share nothing with his
battlefield ordeals. Battle narratives and conventions from these narratives
provide Henry both with the practice and the position of his acts of self-
reflection. Moreover, these conventions replace the battle condition Henry
survives with previously narrated battle scenes. And these representations
impinge on lived scenes with sufficient pressure for Henry to measure the
adequacy of his response against these representations.

At this juncture, however, Henry's narrative qualifies rather significantly an earlier observation. For in disclosing the distinction between his "narrated self" and actual experiences, Henry does not elide but reveals the rift between the incidents beyond telling and the telltale narrative that displaces them. Even more remarkable, however, is what else Henry implies in his innocent disclosure of his motives for going to war. For if Henry enlisted to appropriate, upon reflection, images of his own aggrandizement, he did not really wish to see action in battle at all. Action in battle was only an alibi for his need to fulfill a preoccupation, gleaned through diligent reading of war narratives, with action at a distance, his ability to take possession of the world through images of an overwhelming effect upon it. As Henry himself indicates in his reflections following the first battle, war exists as a testing ground to prove the power to turn the world into signs of the individual's advance upon it:

So it was all over at last! The supreme trial had been passed. The red, formidable difficulties of war had been vanquished. He went into an ecstasy of self-satisfaction. He had the most delightful sensations of his life. Standing as if apart from himself, he viewed that last scene. He perceived that the man who had fought thus was magnificent. He felt that he was a fine fellow. He saw himself with even those ideals which he had considered as far beyond him.

While it will take a later scene for Henry to acknowledge the distinction between the "image" of "himself" gained after the fact through reflection, and the shocking battle incidents exceeding in their overwhelming immediacy the self's ability either to have experiences or to reflect upon them, it takes no longer than the eve of his first encounter for Henry to delineate the frightening dimensions of the terrible logic at work in war. "From his home his youthful eyes had looked upon war in his own country with distrust. It must be some sort of play affair." The double bind at work in these two starkly phrased sentences lashes out with all the force of a compulsion. Henry must go to war to realize the glories previously only narrated, but once at war he inevitably discovers the need for a narrative to displace actual wartime incidents incompatible with a reality legitimized by and *as* narration. In other words, the "play" war that Henry would "realize" by going into battle upholds no necessary similarity with actual battle conditions; only the conventions of a narration that Henry, through reflection, can read into these insufferable conditions can confer the appearance of "reality" upon these otherwise aberrant circumstances. This is to say that Henry's reflections constitute efforts to reread narratives he had taken to heart prior to taking up the Union colors. When considered in this perspective, however, war does not seem an arbitrary congeries of contingent circumstances. Instead it imparts a sense of the necessary limit to, and indeed the reprieve from, the excesses of already narrated "reality." Crane exploits the contradictions implicit in this perspective when he suggests that Henry's motive for going to war may be nothing more than his wish to coincide with the extravagant deeds, the "*broken*-bladed" exploits attributed to the heroes of traditional war narratives. Consequently not even the "private's" wishes are even truly "his" own but migrate to him from a "generalized" subject of conventional war stories Henry, with all the secret shame of a raw recruit, tries to feel equal to. In *The Red Badge of Courage,* then, Henry Fleming must feel alienated in turn both by those incidents that portend their inaccessibility to significance but also by the very narratives intended to impose significance upon them. Thus from a vantage point quite different from Henry's we begin to understand the urgency of his need to take possession of the war in personal terms. Involved in incidents unable to be retrieved in human terms, Henry must invent a history for himself that would at least guarantee the continuity of his identity, and at best alleviate the pressure of those incidents he merely lives through. In other words, Henry's narrative does not exist as his means of recording events of war but as his principal strategy for taking possession of "his" life.

REPRESENTATIONS AND FEAR

Ironically, however, the only way he can truly possess "his" life in a narrative leads him to assert the independence of his narrative from those literally surrounding him. To prevent "his" absorption in "their" narratives, Henry, on the eve of the first battle, develops a rather perverse tactic. First he acknowledges his debt to already written war narratives by recalling the inspiration he drew from accounts of those soldiers whose extravagant deeds relieved the boredom of his days at home, but then in a curious turn he dramatizes the return to "his" senses by indulging in doubts over his ability to replicate their feats. Surprisingly, these doubts do not lessen Henry's feelings of self-regard but heighten them. Indeed Henry's musings draw a compelling line of connection between fantasies of personal failure and newly discovered personal resources sufficiently different from the conventional to authorize a "private" identity. Positioned between events that alienate him through excessive shock and already narrated events that replace his exploits with those of traditional heroes, Henry charges this space between impossible alternatives by fearing "his" cowardice. Through this fear, Henry makes a virtue of his dispossession by converting this depersonalized separation from both narrated and actual events into a personal act of choice. Without any abstract moral principle to organize and legitimize his behavior, he feels compelled to develop an ethos of fear as his basis for a unique personality. His fear asserts its distinct quality by supplanting the threat to personal integrity usually associated with an object of fear. Instead of a threat Henry discovers hidden reserves strong enough to withstand prospects that would otherwise prove utterly self-destructive.

Consequent to a series of reflections inspired by his fear, Henry feels free to conceive of himself as a figure set apart from the representations of his comrades. A "mental outcast," he must abandon all preconceptions, his own as well as those in the narratives he had earlier consumed so avidly, for "in this crisis the previously learned laws of life proved useless." Instead of a feeling of disgrace, a sense of self-discovery and a challenge to his habitual modes of understanding result from his unparalleled fear. "Whatever he had learned of himself was of no avail. He was an unknown quality. He saw that he would again be obliged to experiment as he had in his earlier youth." Confronted, in other words, with emotions that made him "feel strange in the presence" of the other men, Henry made the most of his estrangement. Refusing to conceive of himself as a fixed object of "their" derision, Henry explores the range of "his" feelings on the subject of his fear, until in the course of these reflections he decides that fear not only sets him apart from the other men but it also situates him above them. On the eve of his first battle experience, Henry invests fear with enough privilege to suggest that "he must break from the ranks and harangue his comrades. . . . The generals were idiots to send them marching into a regular pen. There was but one pair of eyes in the corps." Fear, in other words, enables Henry to enact a drama of his powerlessness reassuring enough in its ancillary benefits to convert his "private" sector into a position of sufficient exemplary power to make his reflections superior to those of the generals. This drama reaches its peak when Henry, in an ecstasy of rejection, imagines the other men reacting derisively not to his fear but to the "refined perceptions" resulting from it. And the advance in rank secured by this imagined humiliation enables Henry to situate himself outside the context of all previously written war narratives, as he assumes "the demeanor of one who knows that he is doomed alone to unwritten responsibilities."

Through fear, Henry discovers the power to shape what he takes to be the "original" style of his powerlessness. Consequently, when he actually takes his part in a battle and does not run away in fear, he experiences this failure to run away not as an influx of courage, the reversal familiar from conventional war narratives, but as a loss of those privileges in rank that fear conferred upon him. So instead of continuing to conceive of himself as set apart from the ranks, in battle Henry "suddenly lost concern for himself . . . became not a man but a member." Surrounded by the din and roar of combat, Henry, working his rifle "like an automatic affair,"

cannot take the time to know fear. Rather, he feels a "brotherhood" with
his comrades, yet a brotherhood that does not result from a shared sense
of purpose. Deprived of a humane cause to motivate them, the members
of this "brotherhood" lose all signs of human purposiveness and seem
less like a group of men and more like a "firework that, ignited, proceeds
superior to circumstances until its blazing vitality fades." Because prepara-
tion for this first battle is secured through the consciousness of a private
who had already made much of his dispossession, what comes as the
greater shock is not Fleming's reduction in stature to the level of a "beast"
or an automaton but his loss of those "private" daydreams that formerly
enabled him to take possession of that alienation. During this incident,
Fleming could not continue to brood over his fear but "lost concern for
himself" and fell into a battle sleep emptied of his dreams and witnessed
all "as one who dozes."

We have already considered Fleming's first reaction to his initiation into
battle. He uses it as an opportunity to appropriate from a distance representations of his ability to measure up to the "red formidable difficulties
of war." As if to underscore the falsity of these representations, however,
Fleming combines them with "ideals which he considered far beyond
him" and which had no influence on his decision to enlist. Following his
first battle, then, Private Fleming fears his apparently courageous battle
actions misrepresent him. When his reflections on the battle turn up a
Henry Fleming who did not feel fear, Henry is jubilant at the discovery
of an ideal representation of himself, but his joy diminishes when he
considers that this ideal is sufficiently at odds with the self-image he has
been manufacturing to constitute a loss of himself.

SHAME

Moreover, when he finally does run away, during the second encounter,
he finds fear a sufficiently generalized response to cease to be "his"
private reaction. We do not realize the significance Henry derives from this
loss, however, until the very end of his narrative, when, upon reflecting on
his victorious encounter, Henry once again feels gratified over his apparently heroic behavior. This time, however, after he spends "delightful
minutes viewing the gilded images of memory," his thoughts return to his
action on the first day, whereupon he fails to recall his initial encounter
altogether. Instead of recollecting the scene in which he actually outlasted
the enemy assault, he can remember only his desertion in the field,
chronologically the second incident, as having happened first: "The ghost
of his flight from the first engagement appeared to him and danced. . . .
For a moment he blushed, and the light of his soul flickered with shame."

This lapse of memory is understandable enough when we recall the trancelike state he continuously falls into when battles actually begin. Another context for understanding this lapse emerges, however, when we recall how effective fear was in enabling Henry to take possession of his alienation. During that first battle Henry effectively forgot his fear, so following the logic sanctioned by his psychic economy, we can infer that this fear, which underwrote Private Fleming's inscription within a coherent narrative, upon returning to consciousness erased Henry's memory of the "first engagement." Yet given Henry's former correlation of his identity with his prolonged dream of fear, this memory lapse was almost an inevitability. Indeed this lapse seems less attributable to Henry's memory than to the loss in this instance of any identity. Without fear, Henry lacks the state of mind capable of conferring the privileges of a continuous identity upon him. Moreover, as a reproduction of those heroic representations familiar from all the narratives he had previously read, Henry's reflections on that first engagement were not "his" any more than they were those of any other member of his regiment. They were postures and actions that belonged to no one precisely because they were the "commonplaces" of war stories. After he finally does run away in fear, Henry does not return to battle intent on recovering the attitude he displaced during that first battle, but to recover that great dream of fear he lost when he fell into battle sleep.

In Henry's eyes, the greatest casualty of war was the loss of those psychic resources he needed to mobilize in order to countermand the anticipated derision and consequent shame he would inevitably experience when others found out about his fear. In the moment that he runs, Henry, like the men he saw retreating from the field before his first battle experience, is not even conscious of the presence of an audience. Like the "proverbial chicken," Henry, cut off from any rationale for his actions, could only save face after the fact by reactivating his earlier daydreams of cowardice and shame. Without an abstract moral principle capable of absorbing his actions into reality, Henry is condemned to "realize" his daydreams. Involved as he is in actions irrelevant to the mastery of any human subject, Henry can only redefine himself as a human subject by willfully conceiving of himself as an object of derision. In short, Henry Fleming who was formerly subject to the delusions of fear, after the second battle engagement releases all the resources of what we might call the subject of fear.

While he runs, Henry replaces his blind fear with fear rationalized, and from this transformed position he recognizes his former deeds. For example, when he runs away from the scene of battle, Henry runs into a scene that reenacts almost precisely the conditions of his first battle engagement. In this quite literal version of a recognition scene, Henry, upon seeing the regiment hold its ground, does not interpret this behavior as a sign of valor but pities the men for being "methodical idiots, machine-like fools." With this recognition, however, Henry does not merely replace the earlier role of hero with the role of deserter, though his ability to play both roles with equal reason does expose the interchangeability of the roles of hero and deserter. In judging as mechanical an earlier version of his activity that might otherwise be interpreted as courageous, he displays the privileges released by desertion. Instead of feeling judged by the men in the field he finds them to be merely elements engaged in strategic maneuvers. By co-opting their accusation, he thereby defuses in advance any judgment these men might level against him. Ironically enough, it is only when Henry is in a position of defensive reaction that he feels in sufficient command of himself to speak with authority.

At this point in the narrative, however, an even deeper irony intervenes. For the only discourse that Henry feels sufficiently powerful as a defense of his desertion is a discourse that has already been spoken. Unable to defend his desertion alone, he must enlist the support of a Nature who "would die if its timid eyes were compelled to see blood." On the eve of the first battle scene, Henry prepared himself for the inadequacy of this attribution of a maternal role to nature. Prior to going to battle he had primed himself for a beautiful scene of departure, one wherein his mother, like the mothers of the Greek epics, was to respond with great pathos to the tragic news of his departure, but not even his mother proved sufficiently maternal to fulfill his superstitions; "she had disappointed him by saying nothing whatever about returning with his shield or on it." We need only recall Henry's earlier "flash of astonishment," the irreconcilability between the apparent indifference of Nature to War and the concern Nature should be demonstrating, to see the wishful thinking in this conception. After all the noise and din of that first battle, Henry looked up at the blue sky and realized that "Nature had gone tranquilly on with her golden process in the midst of so much devilment." Whenever Fleming looks to Nature for signs of grief or solace, Nature responds not with a look of indifference but with the demeanor of one who has already completed the work of mourning for a lost beloved. Instead of functioning as a support system, Nature, like Henry's mother, seems to have subscribed to a series of representations enabling it to explain Henry's death as a commplace occurrence. If anything, this scene only visually reenacts what Henry's mother had said much earlier: "'If so be a time comes when you have to be kilt . . . why, Henry, don't think of anything 'cept what's right, because there's many a woman has to bear up 'ginst sech things these times, and the Lord'll take care of us all.'"

In such scenes as these, Crane takes pains to separate Henry's wish to envision Nature as "a woman with a deep aversion to tragedy" from the

enlistment of Nature to underwrite and hence "naturalize" such totally contradictory sentiments as those expressed by Henry's mother.
Henry dramatizes this need to use Nature as a mode of legitimizing
action when, upon seeing a squirrel "run chattering with fear" from
a pine cone thrown by him, he interprets this behavior as Nature's sign
corroborating his desertion. Then, inspired by this unlooked for support, he intensifies the authority of this sign until it reads like a man-
date. "There was a law, he said. . . . The squirrel, immediately upon
recognizing danger, had taken to his legs without ado." In the very next
paragraph, however, Henry records a sign that fails to reenforce his
argument but seemingly reenacts his feeling of being helplessly trapped.
So when he sees "out at some black water, a small animal pounce in
and emerge directly with a gleaming fish," Henry cannot assimilate
this action to his theme of Nature's sympathy for his plight. Like the
battle incidents before it, then, this scene flashes into consciousness
as an impression closed to reflection, not so much an empty perception as a perception inimical to the categories of representation enlisted to convert perception into cognition.

Henry's desertion is of course no more sanctioned by the "nature" of
things than is the war he flees, but the need to seek this sanction is the
same in both cases. And the moment Henry uses Nature to justify his
desertion marks a turning point in the narrative. In the incidents prior to
his flight, Henry converts his fear into *unrealized* fantasies of desertion
and thereby recovers an identity by making the most of *his* dispossession.
But the moment he wishes to justify his actual desertion he must use the
favorite strategy of the forces mobilized against him: the enlistment of
Nature as a principal agent in a narrative designed to justify a course of
action. In choosing a narrative to justify his actions, however, Henry
abandons his charged position between battle incidents and already related events. For instead of continuing to resist them, he chooses to
appropriate preexistent narratives as signs of the validity of his choice.
Henry's choice of Nature, rather than Slavery or Union or martial heroism,
as the final arbiter for his action proves more telling than any use to which
he might put Nature. By definition the most fundamental because the
least derivative of the narrative discourses at Henry's disposal, Nature and
representation sanctioned by the discourse of Nature promise to be the
most reliable arbiters of action and perception. So when Henry entertains
a "natural" perception, like that of the trapped fish, irrelevant to the discourse of Nature he has been pursuing, he must either register that perception but take no notice of it or force it to cohere with the narrative he
has been elaborating. In view of his efforts to include all of Nature within
a uniform framework of representation, however, a perception unin-
formed with the privileges of that representation must have impinged on

Henry's consciousness like a wound, a mark of what has been cut away from an organized whole.

RAGE

In *The Red Badge of Courage*, Crane focuses less on Henry's attempts to recover coherence by imposing an interpretation than on his failures. For, as we have seen, in these failures Henry repeatedly recovers the force of his character as its inaccessibility to preexistent forms. Whereas Henry formerly elaborated this inaccessibility into compelling dreams supervised by fear, in the course of the desertion that realizes "his" dream, Henry confronts a visionary figure terrifying enough to make even his dream of fear seem ghostly by comparison. Possessed by the need to justify his desertion, Henry happens upon the figure of a dying soldier who should have provided just the occasion Henry needs to give desertion a persuasive rationale. Turned into a ghost of himself by the battle incidents that converted him into just another casualty of war and the war narrative that sacrificed his life to its purposes, this "spectral soldier" effectively marks the point of intersection of the two great forces of alienation Henry equally fears. As the horrible double effect of both battle and battle narratives, Conklin's death should have the power to provide Henry's fear with the justification even Nature failed to supply. When confronted, however, with this horrible justification, Henry does not find still another corroboration for his desertion but a limit to all attempts to justify any activity whatever. Faced with the figure swelled with the redoubled force of alienation, Henry discovers the inadequacy of every attempt at justification. When we recall that it was Conklin, waving his arms in enthusiastic sympathy with the exciting news of troop movement, who awoke Henry's earliest fears, we get a sense of the full extent of their loss. Moreover, when we perceive the spastic arm movements released by his death as after-images of the arm-waving enthusiasm that earlier accompanied Jim's tales of war, we get an uncanny sense of witnessing in this literal correlation of narration and existence not simply the destruction of Jim Conklin but the loss of the power of narration to inform existence. In this scene, Henry mourns both the loss of his friend and the loss of a narration intended to represent this loss. Upon recognizing the identity of the "spectral soldier," Henry comprehends through this terrible recognition the shadowy limitations of his great dream of fear. Conklin's death interrupts Henry's attempt to rationalize his fear at the very moment Henry needs it most urgently, or rather it permanently separates the shock enveloped within his fear from any recognition capable of relieving it. Conklin's death, as the intersection of alienating forces released by battles and narratives, thereby supplants Henry's cowardice in that charged place between actual and narrated events. Henry recovers this space, however, when he turns his urgent need to supply the rationale for his fear into rage over the absence of any rationale whatsoever. This rage expresses itself not through the constraints of discursive narratives but through the breakdown of any attempt to constrain it into meaning:

> The youth turned with sudden, livid rage toward the battlefield. He shook his fist. He seemed about to deliver a philippic.
> "Hell—"
> The red sun was pasted in the sky like a [fierce] wafer.

Instead of being discharged into a "philippic," a convention that socializes rage into a manageable expression of loss, Henry's rage breaks down into a threatening impression, one that glares back at him with all the fury of its inaccessibility to his context. In registering this impression at this moment, Crane does not secretly subscribe to the doctrine of naturalism. As a cultural movement, naturalism only justified man's advance upon nature by reflecting back the force of his encroachment as if it were the course of Nature. Nor does this impression "symbolize" Henry's reaction. Like the color that dominates it, this impression renders visible only a glaring surface. Henry's registration of this perception in place of the philippic marks a transformation in his mode of accommodating himself to events. Formerly, Henry actively ignored events and scenes his representation could not appropriate. After emptying Henry's perception of such vast ideological issues as the liberation of the slaves and the recovery of the Union, Crane investigates perception reduced, as it were, to its least common denominators. In the absence of abstract moral and political principles, fear and shame restore coherence and significance to perception even as they circumscribe its locus. Disrespectful of the seeming irrelevance of Private Fleming's apperception to the events surrounding him, fear and shame intervene and replace Fleming's sense of the sheer contingency of what actually transpires with a conventional drama, proceeding from fear and into desertion but holding out the promise of a triumphant recovery of courage.

By holding out the promise of a recovered mastery, the discourse of fear installs Henry in a position to record and reflect upon his perceptions; thus he can later narrate his adventures. Neither the discourse of fear nor that of shame proves innocent of ideological consideration. By underwriting every other representation they constitute the least common denominators, the constraints of ideological representation. Unlike either fear or shame, rage acts out the loss of what can never be possessed.

Utterly inimical to the claims for coherence and privileged responsibility formerly secured through shame and fear, rage replaces their reflective appropriation of perceptions and actions after the fact with the loss of any fact whatsoever to reflect upon. When enraged, Henry no longer fears being gazed at by another any more than he feels ashamed before the judgment of his projected ego ideals. Instead he becomes so completely absorbed in the loss of any representation capable of doing justice to what he perceives that all of the energy of perception seems to have been redirected. In such scenes as that of the interrupted phillipic, Henry does not speak from the position of one who reflects upon a scene. Unable to begin a philippic on the injustices of war, Henry instead notices that "the red sun was pasted in the sky like a [fierce] wafer." And he seems so utterly identified in this remark with what would otherwise sanction a thoughtful outburst of despair and frustration as to fail in his official duties as a subject. Instead of looking at the red sun, he seems to be looking out from its red surface with all the intensity of a glaring rebuke. Consequently the sentence does not express so much as it restores the rage generating it, nets the loss of what grounds it. Through this impression, Henry acknowledges both the undischargeable force of an event that cannot be assimilated to the Nature of things, and all in Nature that cannot be accommodated to man's need to impose an interpretation. And he accompanies this dual recognition with all the fury of an unmet demand.

In this scene, rage displaces fear and shame as Henry's response to his failure to be assimilated by either actual or narrated events. Through rage, however, Henry does not rest content with a recovery of his sense of dispossession as was the case with the prolonged dream of fear. Rage turns Henry's feelings of impotence into an overwhelming power, for when he is enraged his sense of total loss makes absolute demands on the world. Rage, as the power released through a reaction to power's loss, effectively separates the power of alienation from its cause. When Henry discovers the power released by rage, it is impossible to distinguish the power Henry fights with from the power Henry fights against. This is not to say as was the case with his fear that Henry identifies with either preexistent narrations or battle conditions as his means of justifying his rage. Rage disrupts the line of demarcation between agent and action, system and circumstance, throwing everything into a state of confusion.

When I suggest that Henry replaces cowardice with rage in that charged space between equally alienating alternatives, I do not mean that Henry never fears cowardice again. Earlier Henry's fear that he would fail to measure up released a compensatory belief in the superiority of his perspective. He needed to believe his fear was privileged because "he" felt anonymous, a veritable unknown soldier in the midst of vast actions performed by vast collections of men. Through fear he converts his suspicion that "he" will never be recognized into a discovery of a previously unknown element in his psyche, a cowardice that distinguishes him by setting him apart from his fellows. In the course of events, Henry makes the desertion implicit in this feeling of being apart explicit when he actually runs from the field. When he seeks to render his desertion privileged by articulating its unique rationale, he identifies with all the conventional narratives that justify war by aligning it with the nature of things he earlier found so oppressive. After his confrontation with Jim Conklin, however, he not only recognizes the limitations of this rationale but also fears this limit. In other words, the fear of cowardice that led him to flee the field has become differently valenced. Without any effective rationale to recover the superiority in his former position of "mental outcast," Henry can only identify with a rage that acknowledges total loss and transforms loss into power.

Having experienced the absolute loss of all his former claims, Henry reactivates his fear of being judged a coward not in order to secure the sense of his superior rationale but in order to react with rage against the inadequacy of all rationales. His fear of being judged a coward, in other words, once the sole motivating force for his actions, becomes a pretext for his rage against any viable motivation whatsoever.

After the Conklin incident, Henry no longer feels shame. Shame after all presupposes a prior feeling of belonging to a community capable of making one feel alienated by shame. In his discovery of the limits of his rationale, Henry also discovers the limits of the community justified by it. Through various narrative devices, Crane suggests that the basis for this socializing process is not a shared purpose but a common fear of becoming a figure of public shame. As has been suggested, the ideological power of this process derives from Henry's belief that fear confers a "private" identity upon him. But throughout the narrative, Crane signals the "general" state of this fear by interrupting his "private" fantasy of cowardice with its implicit expressions by others. When every soldier seems engaged in the same "private struggle," this struggle cannot be "his" but must be "theirs" or no one's. After Henry's long reverie of shameful fear prior to that first incident, to offer only the most salient example, the "loud soldier" Wilson indicates his participation in the same "privileged" drama of fear as Henry's when he blurts out a plea that Henry send home, after Wilson's death in the field, packets of letters to his mother. Crane suggests that the very feelings of fear and cowardice capable of releasing the illusion of "privacy" have already been overcoded and directed toward common military aims. And Crane signals this abuse by turning what should be a "private" first-person form into a third-person narrative. For through this narrative strategy Henry's most private thoughts turn out not to be his but "theirs" after all.

After his encounter with Conklin, Henry attempts to regain his shame, but now he knows only "the ghost of shame," the rage he has not been socialized out of. Following the Conklin incident, Henry needs to feel the shame he earlier feared. Shame, after all, would make him feel the inadequacy of some judgment. But Henry always finds the position of shame preoccupied by his rage over its inadequacy. That is why he reacts with such violence when the tattered soldier asks him where he is wounded. A wound would be a justification for leaving the field, and Henry, in discovering the inadequacy of all attempts at justification, has carried his desertion too far. So when he runs back to the field he does not wish to prove himself to the other soldiers—that would only corroborate the adequacy of their categories—but to represent to them the "magnificent pathos" of his rage by dying right in front of them. In short, he wishes to bring "their" judgment up against "his" rage.

Paradoxically, however, Henry's means of reentering the military world is not through a demarcation of his rage but through an apparent identification with that world's ability to judge. A head wound, received when he grabs a deserter and asks for an explanation of his desertion, facilitates this turn of events. The head wound, in its openness to ambiguous interpretation, is what the deserter gives Henry instead of what he asked for, an explanation for desertion. This wound, like the sheer contingency of the battle scenes, is utterly unassimilable to the moral discourse of courage or cowardice. As the record of what gets perceived once privileged representations lose their power to master an event, this wound marks on Henry's body the equivalent to the locus of those losses "the red sun pasted in the sky like a wafer" burned into his consciousness. However much the other men might try to impress this wound to the scale of judgment adjudicated by either courage or cowardice, this wound fails to represent anything but the breakdown of the procedures of judgment. As the mark on his body not of any particular moral code but of his having been *cut off* from these codes, Henry's wound turns every attempt to interpret it as a sign of courage into a vast charade of judgment. Through an identification with this wound, Henry can return to his regiment not as a "member" reincorporated into the "body" of men, but as a wound, a mark of what has already been cut off from the body.

This is not to say that upon returning Henry refuses to engage in judicial exchanges, but that the resultant charade of justice differs significantly from Henry's earlier experience. When in order to forestall Wilson's harsh rebuke of him for fleeing the field, Henry calls Wilson a coward and points to that packet of letters as proof, he performs that same activity of co-optation of judgment enacted earlier in the day. When he delivers this judgment, however, a judgment he himself fears, he does not judge Wilson so much as he converts the feeling of being judged wrongly into a judgment—a judgment whose inadequacy he knows from within the position of the judge. Thus Henry's secret revenge against it disrupts the very judicial system he seems in the service of. To socialize this behavior Henry reactivates that same narrative of the gifted man protected by Nature he used earlier to rationalize his desertion. But neither discourse brings his rage to justice. Each instead leaves a residue, a reaction against his distortions, and recovers for Henry the anger he can only discharge through the fury of his actions in battle.

Upon his return, as a more profound outcast, a figure all the more tellingly "cut off" from his peers than the man who deserted, Henry does not recover his place but reactivates his rage against all that displaces him. Nor does he actually fear the judgments of others, but demands these judgments as excuses for vengeance. When a general curses Henry's regiment for a pack of mule drivers, Henry is grateful for the chance to localize his rage on the general. When he fights on the field he does not fight Confederate soldiers but wages war on the discourses that formerly placed him so securely as a private in the military: he wounds his fear of cowardice with a fury in excess of any judgment and destroys his fear of shame with actions outrageous enough to make all the other soldiers feel ashamed by contrast. Henry, who earlier felt cursed and ashamed by his inability to live up to the heroics demanded by war, displays such extravagant brutality on the field that he becomes a general's means of cursing and shaming other men into battle. But Henry is no longer inspired by heroic representations. His apparent courage derives from the sense that he has already been marked as a casualty of war. Having formerly identified himself with all the representations gleaned from his battle narratives, once he loses those representations Henry fights with all the reckless abandon of one who has already been lost in battle.

Neither cowardly nor courageous, in his elemental fury and rage he arouses the need of those around him to reduce him to this code. Henry has already despaired of a world that the dialectic of courage and cowardice would idealize him back into. In battle he does not discover a personal identity resistant to the mutual dispossession of both actual and narrated events, but revenges himself against the delusions of a private identity and replaces identity with the force of its abandonment. His rage preoccupies every position, whether on the battlefield, in society, or in the narrations that "realize" them all, with a vengeance over the inevitability of their loss. By the end of the novel, then, rage has ceased to be a mere theme and has replaced shame and fear, the principal agents of ideological construction, with the power of its destruction.

When in rage, Henry performs actions that cannot be assimilated by any narrative: they emerge with all the accidental force of battle incidents. Rage replaces duration with immediacy, reflection with "glare," appropriation after the fact with loss as what takes the place of fact. After his final battle scene, when Henry accepts the description of his behavior as courageous, his frame of acceptance does not silence his rage, nor does his memory of the moment of desertion repress his fury. In this moment of acceptance, when fear and shame return with all the force of repressed representation, however, Henry does reveal the opposition between courage and rage, and the narrative that implements it, to be the official means of being absorbed back into the world.

Some of Henry's rage reappears, however, when we recall what Henry does not: that Henry earlier felt alienated by this traditional narrative into which he now willingly reinscribes himself. By way of conclusion, we could begin a list of the many shocks of representation, its inadequacy to the situations it should inform with meaning. We could begin this list, moreover, with shock at our recognition of the completely different social worlds separating the dialect Henry Fleming uses when he actually speaks in the novel from the refined discourse of moral discrimination representing his frame of mind throughout. Whenever we begin such a list, however, we cannot fail to include Henry's decision at the end of the novel apparently to continue to rehearse the discourse that unfailingly misrepresents him throughout. If almost a century of critics have cushioned this shock by subscribing to the conventions of "character development," "fear overcome," "recovered responsibility," and "mature judgment," authorized by Henry's final narrative, we begin to recover some of its force when we recall General McClurg's fierce denunciation. Unlike most commentators, the general does not feel persuaded by Henry's final narrative. Instead of commending him for returning to his duty, the general needs to call Henry a coward, a Northerner who fled from the field, and a British sympathizer. The overreaction implicit in the general's ideological overcoding indicates that he, like Henry Fleming, feels the inadequacy of these terms to account for the experiences of war. Thus, however thoroughly he may repudiate Henry's actions, he finally feels persuaded enough by Henry's rage to use his denunciation of Henry's actions as his means of sharing that rage. Indeed his rage does not emanate from disagreement over Henry's actions in battle but from the failure of his own ideology to do justice to experiences in battle. Moreover, when we reread Henry's decision to use guilt and shame as his own private debriefing ceremony from the general's perspective, another implication of Henry's choice comes into view. Henry always deployed guilt and shame as his means of making moral claims on events utterly beyond the control of any individual. At the end of the novel, however, the guilt Henry feels cannot be ascribed to his failure to measure up to a battle narrative. The source of his shame, the tattered soldier, is not a representative of moral responsibility. Neither a coward nor a hero, the tattered soldier remains etched in Henry's memory as a man who did not desert but was deserted on the field. Haunting the boundary lines of traditional war narratives, this spectral figure delineates the extent of what they failed to include. But if Henry's guilt originates from this shadowy figure, it will not, as General McClurg correctly intuits, facilitate his reentry into a conventional ideological framework. Motivated as it is by the specter of the tattered soldier unrepresented by any narrative convention, Henry's guilt does not reactivate representations guaranteed by shame and fear, but acts out the inability of those representations to reabsorb him into the world.

As we have seen, Crane set out to reduce the Civil War narrative to its barest essentials. He stripped the names from the war battles and emptied out the frame of referents enabling the war to confirm for Americans a sense of their place in the history of nations. By driving a wedge between authorized versions of this war and experiences alien to them, Crane caused a fissure to form in the nation's self-conception, which not even the ideology of union would be sufficient to heal.

JULIA BADER

The Dissolving Vision
REALISM IN JEWETT,
FREEMAN, AND GILMAN

At crucial moments in the works of Sarah Orne Jewett, Mary Wilkins Freeman, Charlotte Perkins Gilman, and other nineteenth-century American women writers, the narrative pauses to suggest that an external reality hitherto objectively perceived and transparently visible can blur and dissolve, that the firm, knowable texture of a familiar world can be shaken and lost. In these works, "real" places or landscapes ordinarily provide stability and rootedness; they can be grasped with fullness and clarity and rendered with reassuring verisimilitude. Yet they stand opposed, in these same writings, to a curious series of phantasmagoric ghost towns, unnaturally vivid bits of flora and fauna, and portentously placed formless shapes, which reflect deracination, loneliness, and fear. The values associated with living in a solid world and the fears associated with tumbling into chaos both take on special force for these writers, who regard them as defining not only the predicaments of many of their female characters, but also their own concerns as women writers. In their hands, the alternation between a confidently realistic shaping of narrative development and a dissolution of this order into grotesque or blurred fragments provides a somber commentary on the process and the hazards of female perception and self-perception.

Usually classified as local colorists, writers like Jewett take for granted the objective existence of an external world; they also tend to assume that this world can be comprehended—that the senses, particularly sight, are capable of perceiving it accurately, and that valid understanding can be based upon sense perception. Their stories, however, regularly display the disruption or collapse of this process. For one or more characters, the external world loses its solidity, sense perception loses its grip on what is "out there," and a gulf opens between the misperceiving, misinterpreting subject and the objects surrounding her. This breakdown, which is often an explicit and central topic of late nineteenth-century stories by American women, is quite different from the superficially similar subversion of realism characteristic of twentieth-century "Modernism." Modernism challenges the ontological and epistemological premises of realism: it casts doubt on the very existence of any reality independent of human perception, and it questions whether individual perception can yield an understanding of the world that has more than subjective validity. But for the nineteenth-century American women writers to be examined here, the source of difficulty is essentially social and psychological. Within a stable, supportive set of sexual, familial, and communal roles, the senses of the women portrayed in (or narrating) these stories are regarded as registering experience vividly and accurately. Their sight—and in some stories their sensitivity of hearing, smelling, or touch—is held to be fully adequate to the tasks of perceiving and interpreting the real world. On the other hand, when the crucially sustaining roles are missing, threatened, or breaking down, the protagonists of these stories are shown to misperceive and misinterpret their surroundings; social, sexual, and psychological dislocations are reflected in a wavering, blurring, and fading of vision. In short, women's relationships with the world at large are represented as fundamentally contingent on their human relationships; the world is sometimes represented as indeterminate for men in these stories, but it is not so for women unless they become subject to pressures or threats from without, usually identified as male in origin and nature.

In *The Country of the Pointed Firs* (1896), for example, the voice of the narrator, the fluctuations of the story line, the movement of emotion, and indeed the very selves being created assume substance and fade back into insubstantiality, for reasons worth exploring in some detail. The causes are numerous, but among the most revealing are the nature of visiting and being visited, and the capacity to propel oneself into another world, sometimes real, sometimes imagined. Mrs. Fosdick, the most artful visitor, is also the most solid. And of course the unnamed narrator of *The Country of the Pointed Firs* is a writer, one of a small band of female artists in women's novels. As she creates her story, she creates the story of her story; that is, the manner in which she was able and unable to "write." This is part of the reality of the world of working and visiting, but it creates a narrative where the palpability of everyday objects and the solidity of homespun emotions must struggle to overcome the mental drift into phantasmagoria and oblivion, the uncreated and the unseen.

In a curious division within *The Country of the Pointed Firs,* the female characters stand for preserving and conserving (not only jams but memories, porcelain, illusions of loved ones), while the male characters suffer from lack of substance, mental derangement, and loss of purpose. The narrator stands in the middle, struggling to join the female community, to become the loved daughter, the member of the reunion. The choices

presented to the narrator encompass the possibilities for women in that
setting: the companion, the recluse, the self created through identification with a more glittery existence, the herb-gathering spinster.

Much has been written about *The Country of the Pointed Firs* as a
pastoral, and it is certainly one of the masterpieces of that genre. But I am
interested in the ways in which the pastoral and the realistic tale are
fused, and imbued with elements of mystery and mental states foreign to
both realism and pastoralism. I would argue that these disparate elements
are necessary in part because the writer and the narrator speak from a
position of femaleness. This femaleness asserts itself in the quiet dignity of
everyday tasks and simple household objects seen as signposts in a fully
lived life, rather than as trivial details that distract from achievement.
Keeping house for oneself, providing food, tending gardens, distilling
perfume, growing potatoes, are presented as conscious acts that reveal
character, allow for meaningful choices, and lead to cathartic resolution.
As in most realist works, what the narrator or characters see largely deter-
mines who they are, or what their possibilities may be. Thus to perceive
through the lens of domesticity is not only to pay respect to the physical
world and the cyles of nature, but also to prize the small individual perspective of mustard greens and willowware, and to exult in the possibility
of deriving meaning and sustenance from private gestures and loved objects.

The realistic setting is made up of objects and landscapes that do not
need to be sublimated or subjugated for the sake of "higher" pursuits. The
female local colorists purposefully develop value systems in the domestic
realm, where the desires and ambitions of women are allowed scope. In
this setting, individual perception takes on the qualities and significance of
some of the basic household objects: humble but aspiring, reassuring in its
mundaneness, revitalizing in its empirical solidity, sometimes threatening
in its repetitiousness. Jewett's and Freeman's women find their salvation,
if at all, in a realistic setting; backed by what is knowable, visible, daily.

Speaking from a position of femaleness often leads these realist authors
to a curious doubleness: the dissolving movement of the narrator's vision
when she imagines the world of men and of impersonal artistic creation,
set against the attempt to center and solidify relationships and feelings.
Through the techniques of realism, its sober accountability, its common-
sensical dailiness, Jewett and Freeman explore the possibilities of meaning
for their female characters. They create worlds where women are neither
rewarded for their obedience to traditional expectations and conventional
roles nor offered romantic love as a mirror for seeing themselves. On the
contrary, the female selves that emerge in these works are given strength
and particularity by the realistic settings that reflect them. They acquire
power and autonomy precisely by controlling some aspect of this setting;
when they lack independence their vision seems distorted, uncentered.

The blind sister of Freeman's "Mistaken Charity" (1887) claims to see "chinks" or apertures through which beloved images break through the darkness: "light streamin' in all of a sudden through some little hole that you hadn't known of before when you set down on the doorstep this mornin', and the wind with the smell of the apple blows in it came in your face, an' when Mis' Simonds brought them hot doughnuts, an' when I thought of the pork an' greens jest now." When she is taken to the old age home she fails to see any chinks, and only regains her "vision" when she escapes from the benevolent dependency in the "home" and returns to her impoverished but solidly rooted cottage. After the dissolution of the familiar world of sounds and smells that had constituted her moments of intense "seeing," the blind woman is again deposited at her old house and exclaims: "Thar's a chink an' I do believe I saw one of them yaller butterflies go past it." Her literal blindness is an extreme representation of the world of helplessness and vulnerability, contrasted with chinks of the accustomed and beloved, which orient and guide her. In fact the story ends with the woman perceiving that her blindness is redeemed by her return to the familiar: "'O Lord, Harriet,' sobbed Charlotte, 'thar is so many chinks that they air all runnin' together.'" As she settles into the stable world where "everything was there just as they had left it," her sense of being "there" widens, and the chinks expand into a fully rounded vision. What we love, these authors suggest, creates in us a sense of completeness and reality, like Jewett's Green Island, "solidly fixed into the still foundations of the world." Memory, joyful association, and a hunger for belonging are often at the base of our pleasure in the familiar, but the longing for "thereness" is presented as an intense need that deprivations and darkness throw into relief.

The Country of the Pointed Firs depicts a place very precisely "seen"; circling around its various locations, we move increasingly into the heart of light, the house and finally the rocking chair of Mrs. Blackett, the wise, accepting mother whose great "unselfconsciousness" is held up as the highest ideal in the tale. Again, the movement is dual: in the quest for meaning the male characters are in constant danger of slipping into the abyss of despair, the widowed ache and emptiness, and the shadowy city of madness, while the female characters strive for and achieve contact, sharing, and comfort.

The topography of The Country of the Pointed Firs is formed before our eyes in the first paragraph, a section titled "The Return":

> There was something about the coast town of Dunnet which made it seem more attractive than other maritime villages of eastern Maine. Perhaps it was the simple fact of acquaintance with that neighborhood which made it so attaching, and gave such interest

to the rocky shore and dark woods, and the few houses which
seemed to be securely wedged and tree-nailed in among the ledges
of the Landing.

The vagueness and tentativeness of the speaking voice is striking in this
first paragraph: the "something" that "perhaps" "seems" the essence of
the town is above all elusive, possibly nothing more than subjective pre-
disposition. As the unnamed speaker arrives at the shore amidst anticipation and excitement, the journey framing her story begins, woven out of
her acquaintance and interest in the region, and we hear the voice take
shape and grope toward a definition of its subject, a center for its attraction. The reverse of this movement takes place in the end, as the visitor is
departing. She sees the characters of her story sweep by in stylized, reduced
proportions—"At such a distance one can feel the large, positive qualities
that control a character." The island at the heart of the narrative, the
town where most of the action has taken place, appears small and vivid,
and then blurs and crumbles into a mass "indistinguishable" from other
places. The vivid, particular, domesticating vision of Mrs. Todd, and the
hazy, visionary "waiting place" of Captain Littlepage are struggling in
the end, with the narrator embodying both kinds of imagination. The
spectre of removal, of becoming alien, haunts this narrative: the speaker
comes as a stranger and strives to become a member (a theme that cul-
minates in the reunion), while she seeks out those who are widowed,
obsessed, separated (she is given Joanna the hermit's pin as a legacy in
the end). Finally, the speaker chooses to leave so as not to become a
stranger to the world she had left for the world of the novel we are
reading: she is moving beyond the region she created for us, and just as
the first paragraph employs the metaphor of windows as eyes, sweeping through the view and constructing it, so the backward look at the
end finds that the region of the tale is "lost to sight."
    The ghost town of Littlepage's tale is in direct contrast to the sunlit,
rocker-centered reality of the women of *The Country of the Pointed
Firs*. The obsession with gloom and insubstantiality in the lives of the
pathetic men is opposed to the expansive, healing, sociable art of Mrs.
Blackett and Mrs. Todd. The narrator and Joanna stand between these
extremes; the narrator is drawn to Joanna's lot as a "place in the heart
of each of us which is remote and islanded," but finally she prefers the art
of "visiting." The drawing together at the great Bowden reunion is an
affirmation of the sustaining power of the social, the familial, and the
solidly real, as contrasted to the lonely, the private, and the eccentric.
It is important that the male, the gloomy captain, is obsessed with the
lofty poetry of Milton, whereas the female characters are conspicuous
nonreaders, spending their time collecting herbs, cooking, and telling

stories. Thus living is opposed to reading, and feeling is opposed to merely "using words" as men (especially ministers) do, in the scheme of *The Country of the Pointed Firs*. (Another widowed captain creates a ghostly homelife, maintaining his house exactly as if his wife were still alive.)

Littlepage's story of the town his friend believed to be in "the next world to this" is a remarkable account of a nightmarish sense of both locale and identity: "They could see the place when they were approaching it by sea pretty near like any town, and thick with habitations; but all at once they lost sight of it altogether, and when they got close inshore they could see the shapes of folks, but they never could get near them,— all blowing gray figures that would pass along alone, or sometimes gathered in companies as if they were watching." The curious thing about this scene is that the shadowy, indeterminate quality of the town and of the inhabitants owes less to a disability in the seafarers' vision than to an intrinsic insubstantiality in the town itself. The nebulous creatures seem "neither living nor dead," and Littlepage concludes that the town "was a kind of waiting-place between this world and the next."

The inhabitants of the ghost town occupy a menacing, silent, disconnected world, which dissolves upon proximity: like leaves in the wind or cobwebs, the "fog-shaped men . . . would make as if they talked together, but there was no sound of voices, and 'they acted as if they didn't see us but only felt us coming towards them.'" And finally the ethereal inhabitants raise a grim and implacable army to drive the earthly men from their shores. Littlepage's story is a wavering, all-male underside of the solid and sociable female village: the inability to communicate, to see and to touch, represents the terror of inhabiting a male consciousness. The female narrator's effort to create the world of Dunnet Landing and to live with the creatures of her imagination connects her with the lonely and terrifying places that are here visualized as the result of men's adventures. In the larger scheme of *The Country of the Pointed Firs* she is described as at first creating and then dissolving the landscape of the story she tells. In an important sense *The Country of the Pointed Firs* sets up the effort to create, to live with one's imagination, against the pleasures of belonging to a solid, tangible world. The narrator continually tries to remove herself from the seductive pleasures offered by the sociable Mrs. Todd and to attempt to write as an onlooker, a hermit. Soon after hearing the captain's tale, the narrator fears that the massive Mrs. Todd will turn into "the cobweb shapes of the arctic town." But instead, all the elements of the visible, realistic setting are affirmed: "Nothing happened but a quiet evening and some delightful plans that were made about going to Green Island, and on the morrow there was the clear sunshine and blue sky of another day." The narrator's fear that Mrs. Todd may turn elusive and ethereal is faced and assuaged: with her herbs and potions Mrs. Todd does partake of the enchanting and mysterious, but she leads the narrator deeper and deeper in a circular movement to the center of a maternally pastoral world. This center is first glimpsed right after Littlepage's shadow town: it is the golden island lit up by the sun in the midst of gloom; it is Green Island, where the mother resides whose small white house is like a "beacon" of light.

As one would expect in a realist narrative, the house on Green Island, along with its garden, is seen more and more clearly as one approaches it: even the crops in the fields are sharply differentiated, as is the waving figure of Mrs. Todd's mother. The realist assumption that you can see—and describe—with increasing precision and authority the closer you get, is demonstrated in the warm, loving "heart" of *The Country of the Pointed Firs,* which is the green paradise of this island. The island is in precise contrast to Littlepage's ghost town, which represents the fear that proximity dissolves emotion, dulls pleasure, and dissipates wholeness. For Jewett both places are timeless and ahistorical, revelations of "the world beyond this one." There is a ghost world of foglike images and of traditional isolation, with Littlepage, who lives for his books, sitting behind closed windows. But alongside this gray world is a golden one, vividly re-creating the childhood happiness and maternal solicitude embodied in homey, everyday objects and simple human emotions. The grotesque and the phantasmagoric issue from fear and dislocation, and attack the ability to shape and to see; the domestic and the realistic result in a heightened and colorful clarity, which delineates detail lovingly and with significance. As psychic traits become allied with genre and style, the writer-narrator occupies a middle ground, drawn in part toward the shifting shadow world of language and created character, yet subject also to the female longing for community and solid bonds expressed through substantial objects and persons.

Related to the question of seeing is the nature of the identity of the self in the solid world. Even when the world itself becomes a shifting one, the integrity of the perceiving mind and eye remains in the foreground; problems of differentiation, uniqueness, and community surface from the physical act of seeing clearly or hazily. Jewett's "Queen's Twin" episode (1899) not only represents the division of the female self into the homely and the grand, the domestic and the worldy; this differentation also registers and accepts these same differences between Mrs. Todd and the narrator, in a subtle doubling that is disguised in the tale. The simple American, Abby Martin, sees herself as Queen Victoria's twin and has fashioned her life to substantiate this fantasy: "Sometimes I've thought 't was left to me to do the plain things [the Queen] don't have time for."

Abby Martin's imagination has provided her with a bond of friendship and meaning that links the everyday acts of her existence with the single reference point of the queen. Mrs. Todd remarks about her friend's obsession: "Such beautiful dreams is the real part of life." Thus to find the other self or the ideal place provides fullness and contentment, and creates something "real" in the most significant sense of feeling rooted. The entire landscape of the story has this effect of "belonging" on the narrator. When she returns to the island in the "William's Wedding" fragment (1910), she reassembles the scenery detail by detail, until the pleasureable emotion produced by the "real" is achieved: "The waiting procession of seaward-bound firs on an island, made me feel solid and definite again, instead of a poor, incoherent being. Life was resumed, and anxious living blew away as if it has not been. I could not breathe deep enough or long enough. It was a return to happiness." In this vision that which is loved and familiar restores the integrity of the self and produces the sensation of reality by creating a solid layer around the easily fragmented human self. The association here between happiness, certitude, and reality is a particular mark of female local colorists. When the eye takes in a beloved scene, and the heart extends into a female community, then dissolution is held at bay, and the world appears real and substantial. "Perhaps it was the simple fact of acquaintance with that neighborhood which made it so attaching," the narrator warns us in the first paragraph of her tale, and the equation of the real with the loved produces a power of perception that is most sharply and domestically applied to familiar objects and landscapes.

The distant and unknown is portrayed as vague and terrifying. This is true not only of the ghost town of Littlepage, but of almost any place where the narrator is *not:* from Joanna's island the mainland lies "dim and dreamlike," and the last section, appropriately titled "The Backward View," chronicles the dissolution of summer, of the Dunnet Landing experience, and finally of the place itself. Indeed, Mrs. Todd and Dunnet Landing are described in terms reminiscent of Littlepage's ghost town: "Close at hand, Mrs. Todd seemed able and warm-hearted and quite absorbed in bustling industries, but her distant figure looked mateless and appealing, with something about it that was strangely self-possessed and mysterious." Just as human beings appear stylized, symbolic, and undecipherable from a distance, so the "attaching" town slowly dissolves in the long view: Dunnet Landing "sank back into the uniformity of the coast, and became indistinguishable from the other towns that looked as if they were crumbled on the furzy-green stoniness of the shore." As both the main human figure and the landscape are "lost to sight," they become unreal; the narrator's gaze, which created them, can no longer sustain the illusion, and as the gaze shifts, realism is wiped away and the indistinct and mysterious takes its place.

In the short stories by Mary Wilkins Freeman, the psychological condition of particular characters is clearly mirrored in the degree of realism of which they are capable. The initial description of the locale is often the most significant clue to the nature of her heroines. In "Gentian" (1887), the first view of nature is surrealistic: "It had been raining hard all night; when the morning dawned clear everything looked vivid and unnatural. The wet leaves on the trees and hedges seemed to emit a real green light of their own; the tree trunks were black and dank, and the spots of moss on them stood out distinctly." The scene is described by a disembodied narrator. The theme of seeing clearly, of the possibility of haziness being washed away, is sounded at the same time that such perception is shown to be glaring and potentially frightening. In the unfolding of the story, the meek Mrs. Tollet tries to cure her tyrannical husband with gentian, and she goes to live with her sister when he finds out about her secret medicinal ministrations. When she decides to return to the imperious old man, she speeds along the same path we saw in the first paragraph:

> There was no moon, but it was clear and starry. The blooming trees stood beside the road like sweet, white, spring angels; there was a whippoorwill calling somewhere across the fields. Lucy Tollet saw neither stars nor blooming trees; she did not hear the whippoorwill. That hard, whimsical old man in the little weather-beaten house ahead towered up like a grand giant between the white trees and this one living old woman; his voice in her ears drowned out all the sweet notes of the spring birds.

As the natural world disappears before the frightened wife, to dissolve into the monstrous shape of her overbearing husband, the narrator nevertheless presents the view of the external world as it is; what is real here appears clearly and calmly to the normal sensitivity, whereas the anxious dependence of the bedraggled wife obliterates that reality. She is unable to see clearly; in her own eyes she is a dwarf and her husband a giant. The clear, rain-washed distinctness of the first image in the story is not for her to experience; it is associated with her spinster sister, who is self-sufficient and independent. In a curious twist, the clear and vivid landscape is termed "unnatural" because all its particular qualities stand out too vividly; by implication, a more dusty, blurred, indistinct greenery would appear "natural." The human equivalent of this hazy sight is the docile wife with no "light of her own" and no unnatural sharpness. Though Freeman suggests that this wifely blurring involves a loss of important faculties of perception, Lucy herself is aware neither of the spring scene nor of her inability to savor it. She is conscious only of the large figure of her husband, not of the beauty he obliterates. Thus the "real" in this story exists beyond its characters; it is spread round them, but used as a foil to their emotional blindness. As often in Freeman, the pressure of personal relationships places the reality of the natural world beyond the reach of constricted characters.

In "Gentian" the distortion and bitterness that arise from Lucy's wifely submission comprise "natural" vision for her, although the narrative voice gives an alternate vision of the "real" scene she cannot see or hear. The extreme clarity of the first paragraph is "unnatural" to her meek personality. As in Jewett, emotional stability and affectionate rootedness are portrayed in terms of realistic, clearly definable and perceivable outlines, whereas loneliness and anxiety are often produced by, and result in, surreal or hazy imagery. In most of these realist works, the signals of the narrator are our most reliable markers for distinguishing what is "real" within a text from what is attributable to extreme emotional states of fancy, frenzy, or fear on the part of characters. Thus when the landscape dissolves for Lucy, it remains solid and pleasurable for the narrator and the reader, just as Jewett's narrator remains unmoved by Littlepage's ghostly vision, telling him to "calm down" and therefore observe more objectively.

When the vision dissolves in a realistic work, it is crucial to note who experiences this, and how permanent it is. Does the thinning of the literary landscape call the "solid" world within the text into question, or does it imply that even our sense of reality beyond the literary experience is illusory? Or, as in "Gentian" and Littlepage's story, is the distortion of the realistic surface a portrayal of the lunacy or diminished capacity of its seer alone? If realism is equated with verisimilitude and truth—an equation basic to most realist texts—then the destruction of wholeness and joy seems to result in the wiping away of the solid world, as the characters stumble into a shifting nightmare.

An essential assumption of realistic works is that the world of its subject can be delineated and perceived. Thus realism presents us with the reassuring impression that the physical world is accessible, unshakeably present. The moments of thinning or dissolution can usually be interpreted as the literary dramatization of the effect of human emotion on landscape: fear and uncertainty somehow destabilize and denude the physical surroundings. These moments then suggest that when the narrator's or characters' powers of observation are functioning properly, their descriptions of settings are solidly referential and densely realistic; when the setting becomes transparent or hazy the characters are proportionately dislocated and anxiety-ridden.

In regional or local color fiction, the sheer emphasis on visualizing the physical setting suggests a belief in the importance of graphic detail as the foundation for situating the reader in a literary work. When apparently realistic details are turned into symbolic signs, the referentiality of the landscape is transmuted and more or less subtly diluted. Freeman's story

"The Selfishness of Amelia Lamkin" (1909) describes the killing house-
work that its self-effacing heroine nearly dies of and finally reassumes as
her inevitable lot. The first paragraph is both a realistic entry into her
physical world and a signal of the effect of her surroundings on her
character:

> It was a morning in late February. The day before there had been a
> storm of unusually damp, clogging snow, which had lodged upon
> everything in strange, shapeless masses. The trees bore big blobs of
> snow, caught here and there in forks or upon extremities. They
> looked as if the northwestern had pelted them with snowballs. Below
> the rise of ground on which the Lamkin house stood there was a low
> growth of trees, and they resembled snowball bushes in full bloom.
> Amelia Lamkin at her breakfast table could see them.

Paradoxically, the narrator records her impressions in an objective, methodical manner and explains the source and cause of the strange, grotesque
shapes, even though the shapes themselves suggest formlessness, objects
out of shape, out of control. The blobs of snow blur and obliterate actual
shapes and seasons, defamiliarizing the landscape of the trees and producing a false bloom for the bushes. These formless, misshapen images
suggest an inanimate equivalent of the exhausted, "fading," "drooping"
heroine, who seems "to balance timidly upon the extreme edge of existence." The strange beauty of the bushes with their snowy bloom represents a recognition of the lure of the other world beyond the oppressively
mundane. Amelia, the housewife, nearly dies into a lovely otherworldy
landscape of a setting without drudgery, and the deciphering of "full
bloom" beneath the apparent strangeness of the blobs of snow suggests a
capacity for seeing more than her downtrodden existence seems to allow.
In a parallel scene toward the end of the story, Amelia lies on her sickbed,
and "as spring advanced she could see, with those patient eyes which
apparently saw nothing, the blue sky crossed with tree branches deepening
in color before they burst into leaf and flower. Amelia saw not only those
branches, but beyond them, as though they were transparent, other
branches, but those branches grew on the trees of God, and were full of
wonderful blooms."
     Unlike Lucy of "Gentian," who sees less than the narrator because of
her wifely timidity, Amelia, an equally meek but less fearful domestic
drudge, sees both her physical surroundings and a symbolic world beyond.
When her vision turns transparent she observes an unfolding of the realistic into the transcendent, which renders the former more comprehensible
and the latter more accessible. Thereby she serves the purposes of a realistic text to make sense and to see clearly, while extending the penetration

of her gaze beyond dissolution into deeper meaning. The ordinary landscape is ordered and parted, disclosing a symbolic intelligence beyond
the merely physical "thereness." And yet in both Jewett and Freeman the
details of landscape are also solidly present for their own sake, to create a
feeling of empirical solidity, of a "real" setting after a rain, or after a
snowstorm, of an "actual" Maine village. Even the transcendental or fearful moments of dissolution show, and describe for us in detail, the coming
apart of a physically assembled setting; the nightmarish world in a realist
text never becomes the norm, as in Kafka, but has to be grasped or shud-
dered at in terms of the accessible everyday world. As the characters
plunge into the disorder of unrealistic settings, they are described making
sense of their otherworldly visions by means of similes and metaphors—
"they resembled snowball bushes"—reassuring linguistic nets that hold
up the outline of the everyday as a model for comprehending the forms
beyond.

The position of the onlooker in a realist work is at the center of Freeman's famous story "A New England Nun" (1891). The spinster who
resists marriage out of fear of upsetting her familiar world is appropriately
glimpsed first seated at her window. The first paragraph of the story
creates a setting of her natural landscape, which she can take in from her
window:

> It was late in the afternoon, and the light was waning. There was
> a difference in the look of the tree shadows out in the yard. Some-
> where in the distance cows were lowing and a little bell was tinkling;
> now and then a farm-wagon tilted by, and the dust flew; some blue-
> shirted laborers with shovels over their shoulders plodded past; little
> swarms of flies were dancing up and down before the people's faces
> in the soft air. There seemed to be a gentle stir arising over every-
> thing for the mere sake of subsidence—a very premonition of rest and
> hush and night.
> The soft diurnal commotion was over Louisa Ellis too.

Louisa Ellis is a woman for whom desire, lust, and vitality have stopped
stirring; only a faint "commotion" reaches her from the outside world,
mostly to reaffirm her choice of calmness and peacefulness. The quiet
surface of the waning light and pastoral restfulness is barely ruffled by
movement and sound, and even such movement is "for the mere sake of
subsidence," to set off the imminent darkness and motionlessness. Louisa's
view takes in the whole scene in all its realistic detail; rooted to her window, she sees the faint stirrings as forerunners of the quiet interior life she
leads. Surrounded by her beloved needlework and garden and view, she
arranges the outside world as a reflection of her own accommodation to
spinsterhood. The flying dust, the swarms of flies, the plodding laborers

are softened and mellowed as they enter her gaze. This view involves a whitewashing or prettification that is analogous to the distortion produced by the unnatural vividness in "Gentian" or the initial formlessness in "Amelia Lamkin."

Louisa Ellis's view is gently distorted because the return of her lover after fourteen years abroad threatens to destroy her reassuring routines and to plunge her into a world of unchained dogs, dusty boots, overturned work baskets. Like the husband in "Gentian," Louisa's lover "seemed to fill up the whole room." As he enters, the fluttering of the terrified caged canary is a measure of Louisa's own fear of the large man who plans to release her from a self-chosen narrowness into a sexualized, alien setting. Louisa is expecting his visit as she looks at the afternoon scene from her window, and the story is structured to show us that her anxiety skews her vision of the scene. "This soft commotion was over Louisa Ellis too," and the phrase "soft commotion" is repeated as a genteel euphemism for sexual activity in the scene in which Louisa overhears her lover declaring himself to another woman: "an exclamation and a soft commotion behind the bushes." Louisa is terrified of losing her own maidenly self. As she overhears Joe and Lily, she sits in a state of "mildly sorrowful reflectiveness" amidst a setting of lush, fragrant vines and bushes, whose wild tangle gives her only a "little clear space."

Threatened by Joe's courtship and demands, Louisa remains "in the shadow," "shut-in" by her fearfulness of the wild abandon and seductive sweetness of the scene. She feels unequal to the requisites of marriage: she worries that her familiar objects will lose their essential solidity: "They would appear in such new guises that they would cease to be themselves." She is vulnerable to the expectations of Joe and the villagers that she should regard marriage to him as desirable, and preferable to her spinster contentment. In the course of the story, she comes to see as mistaken her own prior assumption that she is destined to marry: she releases her lover and consciously chooses the quiet, single life she had been leading all along. The intrinsic properties of her daily life assist in reinforcing the rightness of her choice: her domestic setting takes on new significance when it is threatened by dissolution into a strange household. Her "forebodings of disturbance" about the marriage envelop her in the "soft commotion" of the first scene and produce the distorting haze that is a defense against the stirrings she fears. The events of the story explain the muted, restrained quality of the first scene: the muffled sounds and prettified sights issue from Louisa's position as anxious onlooker. Leashed, caged, and unaware of her terrors, she perceives only what she is able to bear. Having created a new public self by becoming a secular nun by choice, rather than by default, Louisa is again placed before the scene she had initially viewed so narrowly and peculiarly. Her consciousness of her own undisturbed rootedness allows a more full-bodied view of the same spectacle. When she is sewing at her window in the last paragraph, having released her lover to Lily, she peacefully takes stock of the unchanged reality around her: the quiescent dog and canary, her own sedate activities. Yet the scenery outside is now charged with the same pulsing life that she has rejected: "Outside was the fervid summer afternoon; the air was filled with the sounds of the busy harvest of men and birds and bees; there were halloos, metallic clatterings, sweet calls, and long hummings."

We may assume that Louisa is the perceiver of the "fervid afternoon," for the narrator places her at the window contemplating it, rather than shutting her off from it; but in any case, there has been a surprising change in the description of this landscape since its initial appearance in the opening paragraph of the story. Louisa herself seems to have remained the same, yet she has lived through a courtship and a renunciation, she has been threatened by the "disorder" of a new, married unreality and has escaped from it, and she is now able to register the underlying vitality and sexual signals of the scene. This closing tableau confirms her in the appropriateness of her self-chosen lot; her fear of things "ceasing to be themselves" has been averted. Her twilight restfulness lies calmly alongside the fertile, blooming outside world.

The elements of sensuous perception round out the realism of the scene described both in the beginning and the end. The muted landscape of the first paragraph is charged with heat, noise, and activity in the end, as if to affirm the narrator's belief that the scene can be fully experienced, richly grasped. Although Louisa will not directly participate in it, she can view the scene without being touched by the commotion, now that her familiar world is no longer threatened by the looming figure of Joe: "She felt no qualm." Her serenity and lack of anxiety result in the objective, solidly rounded, busy world she is at leisure to observe: the onlooker-character and the realist-narrator can merge in the fully visualized scene, purged of distortion. The outside world has not changed just because Louisa has chosen a cloistered interior life; the realist text asserts its task of making the physical world available and comprehensible to the observing consciousness.

In fiction that represents women as uprooted, manipulated, and constantly threatened by male callousness and tyranny, a gradual and irreversible process of visual distortion often charts the nightmarish psychic experience of the female characters. Freeman's "Old Woman Magoun" (1909) and Charlotte Perkins Gilman's "The Yellow Wallpaper" (1892) detail a progressive dissolution of the physical world around constricted, vulnerable victims. If to see and to describe clearly is to become (or to create) a self, then to fail in sight, or to describe in self-contradictory convolutions (as the speaker of "The Yellow Wallpaper" does) is to be annihilated. These characters are orphans, summer visitors, "strangers" who cannot make the connections with a solidly rooted female world that Jewett's narrator manages. They grasp at objects and patterns of meaning that turn dim or hollow, cannot be centered, cannot be deciphered.

In Freeman's "Old Woman Magoun," the title character is a powerful female figure whose attempt to shield her granddaughter from growing up and being sexually exploited results in a literal dissolution of the girl's physical world. The place the characters inhabit is initially described as a rigid, unmoving one, with the aura of catastrophe hanging over it: "The hamlet of Barry's Ford is situated in a sort of high valley among the mountains. Below it the hills lie in moveless curves like a petrified ocean; above it they rise in green-cresting waves which never break." The valley is poised in arrested motion and development, threatened from all sides, marked by a turbulent river over which Old Woman Magoun has persuaded the decadent males of the hamlet to erect a fragile bridge, a link to civilization. This is a place without hope and without accessibility. Freeman has here reached the extreme edge of realistic description. The anger and vulnerability of the female characters of the story speak to an ageless subordination of female growth and community to male rapacity. The intimate world of the old woman and her granddaughter is hedged on all sides by the force of sexual instincts and the ruthlessness of men. The granddaughter's mother suffered the same fate that awaits her daughter; she was even wronged by the same man. Thus the contours of the external landscape provide an image of an unjust society, and the shape of the female experience at the center of the story is similarly fixed, inevitable, and terrifying.

The child, Lily, has the qualities of "a little mother" and "the making of an artist or poet." Though she seems very passive, and we are not told what she sees, "her retrospective eyes, as clear and blue as blue light itself . . . seemed to see past all that she looked upon." The old woman is described as having an "inconceivably keen" gaze: "She really spoke with her eyes aloft as if addressing something outside of them both," when she sees through the evil, pimping father of Lily. The old woman is entrapped in a dislocated world, and in order to prevent the father from taking Lily away from her, she permits the child to eat deadly berries. The grandmother has affinities with the other powerful distorting figures we have observed in Freeman; she is described as "filling up the doorway with her firm bulk," but in this story her bulk does not simply obstruct vision, but is also a protection against the looming evil of prostitution for Lily. After Lily has eaten the poisonous berries, her eyes dilate and turn black, her vision dims, and she finally goes blind before dying. In a painful and prolonged scene, the grandmother encourages the dying child to "see" a world beyond the one she is leaving, where "it is always light" and "the commonest things shine," where she will be a child forever, protected by her mother in a white room, transmuted into an innocent and sexless angel. Afraid of men's power and of Lily's attraction to them, the old woman has decided to replace Lily's sight with the idealized vision of a heavenly setting. As the physical world dissolves for Lily, the grandmother substitutes for it another unchanging landscape: here, in a beatific version of the petrified landscape from which Lily is being saved, flowers never fade and children never grow up. For Lily there are no chinks of light in the empirical world; she moves inexorably toward darkness. Her blue "retrospective" eyes turn black and dim because she is faced with danger and evil on every side: the slipping away of her physical surroundings is both painful and a kind of salvation. The visual distortion of her deathbed scene brings out the nightmare she is escaping.

Lily's eyes ultimately see what her grandmother wishes her to be: an angel, a protected, doll-like creature. The old woman obliterates the physical world for her granddaughter, and puts in its place a vision—"all the dolls are alive"—that denies growth, sexual maturity, or indeed change of any kind. At the end of the story, the petrified life of the hamlet continues: "Everything went on as usual. Old Woman Magoun continued to live as she had done before." But she has gone mad and now carries Lily's rag doll every time she goes over the bridge, thus substituting it for the dead child whom she has viewed as (and finally turned into) an unchanging, infantilized object. The story thus reflects a deep fear not only of male power as incestuous and rapacious but also of female power as murderous.

Barry's Ford has taken us a long way from Jewett's Dunnet's Landing. The contrast *The Country of the Pointed Firs* maintains between the reassuringly real and the phantasmagorically shifting is collapsed in Freeman's story. Barry's Ford is objectively perceived but its fixity has a terrifying changelessness, not a reassuring rootedness. The beloved solidity of Jewett's Green Island has become a horror of unmoving and fatally poised landscape. In the face of age-old male power, female communities or even small families are not viable. A frightening deadness characterizes both the landscape and the perceptual scope of the characters. The dimming of Lily's vision dissolves into the grandmother's fantasy of heaven. Barry's Ford repels access: its unchanging surface is impenetrable; it is not a realist text. In this setting, vision is extinguished and the mind is "touched" by unreality. Lily's self, like her vision, thins out into the fragments of the other characters' views of her as sexual prey or as innocent angel. Rigidity and terror unhinge the ability to perceive, and the extreme degree of dislocation in "Old Woman Magoun" leads to a snuffing out of both sight and sanity in its female protagonists.

At the emotional base of local-color realism is a promise of association

with simplicity, closeness to nature, intimacy with elemental feelings, all
the physical analogues to the honest heart. In the work of Jewett the
female self seems solid, monumental, and enduring. Women embodying
these qualities provide the touchstone of realism in her works. Freeman's
women are sharply divided into those with strong stable characters and
those with malleable, inchoate ones. The latter types are the most vulnerable to a process of visual dissolution, becoming unreal to themselves as
well as to the reader as their perception shifts and dims. The weight of
visual detail in most local color works implies a confidence in the mean-
ingfulness of the physical surface. The ordering of the landscape creates a
world, even in a stylized text like "Old Woman Magoun," where signals
toward comprehension are flashed by the texture of things seen. This
"thereness" and visual decipherability are called into question in Charlotte
Perkins Gilman's compelling story of a woman's nervous breakdown, "The
Yellow Wallpaper." The narrative voice or the observing eye plays a crucial
role in this first-person, diary-form narrative, where the details seen on the
attic wallpaper of a rented house hold a key to meaning that changes
constantly.

The timid, fluttery voice of the narrator initially locates the story in
a seemingly solid world she is at pains to describe:

> It is very seldom that mere ordinary people like John and myself
> secure ancestral halls for the summer.
> A colonial mansion, a hereditary estate, I would say a haunted
> house, and reach the height of romantic felicity—but that would be
> asking too much of fate!
> Still I will proudly declare that there is something queer about it.
> Else, why should it be let so cheaply? And why have stood so long
> untenanted?

Whether the place is an ancestral hall, a colonial mansion, or a hereditary estate, it will certainly turn into a haunted house, with herself—and
previous inhabitants of the nursery-prison who wore a "smooch" into the
wall by creeping around the room—as the ghosts. The wallpaper of her
barred and infantilizing attic room at first presents her with a mass of life-
like though scary details: "There is a recurrent spot where the pattern lolls
like a broken neck and two bulbous eyes stare at you upside down." The
details are gradually shown to be leading to complete subjectivity: the
wallpaper becomes the woman. She frees her angry, rebellious self by
stripping bare the superimposed bars of patterns. But this act of self-
liberation imprisons her in madness, for she loses her bearings in a world
whose details she sees realistically, but whose meaning she cannot fathom.
Thus "The Yellow Wallpaper" calls into question the decipherability of
the physical world; the house, the garden paths, and especially the

wallpaper continually shift in meaning and even in visual detail. The eyes staring from the wallpaper are a graphic emblem of epistemological disorder: inert external objects acquire the animation, the malice, the power to see and interpret, which is drained from the female character. At times the wallpaper appears to her "like a lot of wallowing seaweed," at other times like "an interminable string of toadstools." She makes the important discovery that there are two layers: an outer pattern whose images vary— she comes to see it as literally "shaken" by the figure behind—and a dim but gradually forming pattern behind it in the shape of a woman.

The hazy, ghostly world of psychic repression surfaces from beneath the realistic pattern; indeed the "ghost town" of this narrative can only be seen when the physical surface is obliterated. The repulsive, funguslike, smelly wallpaper, which "comes off" as a foul yellow color on the clothes of the narrator and her husband, is the gate to a shadowy world where the flamboyant, angry self of the nervous woman rattles the outside pattern.

Parallel with the stifling interior space inhabited and explored by the narrator in the attic is the garden view, which she initially sees objectively, and later increasingly subjectively. At first glance it is a conventional manor-house appendage, "large and shady, full of box-bordered paths, and lined with long grape-covered arbors with seats under them." The narrator is warned against populating the garden with imaginary figures: "I always fancy I see people walking in these numerous paths and arbors, but John has cautioned me not to give way to fancy in the least. He says that with my imaginative power and habit of story-making, a nervous weakness like mine is sure to lead to all manner of excited fancies, and that I ought to use my will and good sense to check the tendency." As her conviction of there being a figure behind the wallpaper grows, however, so does her "seeing" figures on the road, figures who resolve themselves into the same woman or women she discerns behind the wallpaper. Although the imaginary woman mostly skulks and hides, the narrator sometimes sees her as released and free, "away off in the open country, creeping as fast as a cloud shadow in a high wind." On the last day before moving, the unhinged narrator completely merges with the woman behind the wallpaper, but she no longer wants to be outside: "If that woman does get out and tries to get away, I can tie her!" The garden lane is now swarming with "those creeping women," but the speaker is too terrified even to look at them, much less to join them: "But I am securely fastened now by my well-hidden rope—you don't get *me* out in the road there!" Thus her liberation from the confines of the paper is problematic and self-destructive: though anger and aggression and suspicion of her husband are brought into the open, she also becomes a creature self-tied and self-incarcerated, who is still partly motivated by the wish to "astonish" her spouse. And in the end she voluntarily fits her shoulder into "that

long smooch around the wall so I cannot lose my way," having found a
new compelling pattern probably left in the room by previous madwomen
or locked-in children.

The confined female speaker is physically and psychologically destroyed
by the impossibility of attaining a fixed and meaningful structure. As her
room is emptied of furniture before departure, she also strips it bare of
the wallpaper, in order to find some essential self beyond the threatening
chaos of her fury at her husband, her prisoner-status as invalid, her "little
girl," "blessed goose" role as wife, her being mother of a newborn who
makes her "nervous." A hidden self emerges and is perceived as mad by
her surroudings (and by the reader). But there is a kind of lucidity and
sense of accomplishment for the narrator in having pulled off the imprisoning veil of surface decoration. She regards the actual wallpaper as a
false pattern, a set of prison bars leading to the liberated (or liberateable)
woman behind. In the end she tells her astonished husband (to whom,
significantly, she provides the key to her room, fearing his violence in
breaking down the door) that she has "pulled off most of the paper, so
you can't put me back!" That her freedom is purchased at the cost of her
sanity is a chilling statement about the price of tearing off the realistic
surface, even when that surface is neither loved nor reassuring. Even in
this alien, rented setting, the solid detail is a necessary orienting device:
lest she lose her way, the narrator now has to tie herself to the room,
fitting her shoulder into the existing groove.

Curiously, the seemingly docile wife perceives the wallpaper as angry
and violent from the beginning, with its staring eyes trying to read her.
Through her forced, girlish restraint we experience an intensification of
the furious, "loathsome" emotion she attributes to the paper, until she
realizes that the lurking woman is within her, that she has been covered
up by outside patterns and yet comprises both the strangled eyes without
and the shadowy figure within. As her realistic vision of the wallpaper dissolves she sees a more and more direct reflection of her own angry yet
creeping self—just as the blind, dying Lily in "Old Woman Magoun" is
told that she will see a heaven where the brightest creature will wear her
face but be an angel. Here the disheveled creature is a madwoman. But
the thinning of the external pattern points to a psychic identity in both
cases: madwoman or angel, both are revealed as the result of a surface
dissolution caused by despair and anxiety. These emotions are then projected onto the surroundings, but are not amenable to cure within the
world of the stories, except as imaginary heaven or illusory liberation. The
distortions and formlessness, the dimming and stripping away of the
external world become inevitable responses to rootlessness, sexual tyranny,
or social constriction. In the absence of a stable female community, a
realistic surface is no protection against shapelessness and fragmentation.

"The Yellow Wallpaper" is partly a study of the breaking down of realistic perception—although a norm of proper perception is never provided by the first-person narrator except, by implication, through her becoming more disoriented as she is deprived of her writing, her friends, and her autonomy. Woman as imprisoned child and skulking monster is revealed as part of the symbolic landscape of the tale, made visual by the narrator's seeing the creeping women on the garden path. Her common-sensical observations, offered meekly and defeatedly at first, increasingly turn into an obsession with the wallpaper. The dislocation from her realistic world is also measured by the way she populates the wallpaper and the garden with her doubles. In a sense the tale's narrator sees too much and too sharply: the disarray of the wallpaper thrusts itself on her consciousness as an image of the frightening texture of her marital life, and her emotional perception is too compelling for her own continued acquiescence in that life.

Even as an artist-figure, the speaker—who is creating the tale as we read it—destroys the elements of her craft as her vision of a meaningful world dissolves. At first she is writing with excitement and joy, finding an outlet and a confidant in her paper. But as the paper she is writing her objective observations on is replaced by the paper on the wall, which is a projection of her fragmented and shrinking self, she comes to regard her writing as tiring and threatening. Finally she even wants to withhold what she knows from what she writes ("I shan't tell it this time! It does not do to trust people too much"), and this abdication of authorial responsibility is a measure of the loss of accessibility and decipherability she experiences within the tale, and which we as readers feel outside the tale as the first-person narrator's vision becomes more obsessive and solipsistic. The stability and rootedness of the ancestral mansion, the mainstay of an earlier tradition of realistic fiction, has been transformed into whirling images of a gymnasium, a sanatorium, a madhouse, and a jail. Captain Littlepage's phantasmagoric world beyond this one has become the hazy landscape inhabited by deracinated females as well. Curiously, the narrator does not become a furious and flamboyant madwoman who races the wind outside; instead, she remains herself but mad, speaking to her husband "gently and slowly" as she hands him the means of entry to her room, and dragging herself patiently across the time-worn ridges of female imprisonment. She starts with an elaborately detailed wallpaper, but her hungry imagination transforms that inanimate surface into a whirling, indeterminate landscape.

As the narrator's realistic perception breaks down, and as her tactile and olfactory responses are also permeated by the wallpaper, she becomes increasingly isolated from her small community, finally viewing with suspicion even her readers' right to know her story. She retains a pathetic concern not to "lose [her] way," and the way she has chosen—or been forced into by her marital situation—is a tortuously circular one. As she goes round and round the bare room with only its nailed-down bed, she exults in having been liberated from behind the imprisoning wallpaper. The social and moral behavior of the other characters in "The Yellow Wall-paper" is judged with indignant disapproval, as in "Old Woman Magoun." But unlike Freeman's tale, which is narrated and plotted by an omniscient third-person speaker and contained within the powerful will of the old woman, "The Yellow Wallpaper" has a far more blurred and indefinite formal structure, and an appropriately uncertain visual base.

Yet both Gilman's and Freeman's works, though less obviously than *The Country of the Pointed Firs,* play off their shadowy ghostly worlds against a stable, knowable surface, which can be apprehended if the external circumstances and the emotional state of the perceiver allow. Ocular power and ocular vulnerability are crucial issues in realist texts: the need to judge and infer from ordinary objects calls for proper sight, just as the ability to survive and control one's lot depends, both literally and figuratively, on seeing clearly. When Jewett's narrator, sitting in Mrs. Blackett's rocker, looks out the window, she tries to see as the wise matriarch sees; this act is a metaphor for acquiring judgment from a community of women.

I have focussed on episodes of perceptual breakdown in these works, but revealing as they are, such moments tend to be the exception rather than the rule in local-color fiction, which is confident in its assumptions about the regional particularity, the historical solidity, and the empirical palpability of physical detail, and about the way such detail reflects and impinges on character. Most female characters in local-color works discover themselves in relation to the landscape (rather than in their alienation from it, as in modernist works), and this relation is usually a reassuring one. The terrifying realm of visual malfunctioning is glimpsed only sporadically—except in Gilman, where the ocular interference increases and comes to dominate—and the text usually locates the disorder in the private travails of the misperceiving character, rather than in the setting.

The creation of carefully paralleled worlds (such as that of Littlepage in Jewett), the use of initial landscape descriptions embodying the dilemmas the characters will play out (as in Freeman), and the reflection of the speaker's emotional state in external objects (such as the wallpaper of Gilman) all show the realist author at work, plotting meaningful equivalences and explanatory mirrorings. These techniques not only help to carry out the authorial task of making sense of the world, but serve as more or less explicit affirmations of women's and authors' ability to do so. Jewett, Freeman, and Gilman are at once women and authors, and their explanations include an understanding of the bonds that unite communities of women amidst solid landscapes, as well as a portrayal of the plight of the helpless, overworked, isolated women who are driven to misunderstand and misperceive their settings. But even when the characters' vision dissolves, the narrator suggests the sexual, social, or emotional cause of the derangement, and implies that the distorted vision departs from the way things are, from the actual look of trees and sound of birds. Moreover, these narratives are peopled with women who go through processes of change, learn from experience, and are rescued from or imprisoned in their distorted visions according to the more or less optimistic visions of female possibility held by their authors. Along with other techniques and conventions associated with realism, such traits as these help the local colorists to create and sustain an impression of objective existence in a solid world. The moments of dissolution inject brief sensations of formlessness, both in the individual sensibility and in the structure of the narrative, as the empirical order suddenly bifurcates and a shadowy world opens up. Thus formlessness is given weight in realistic fiction by these glimpses of disorder, but the act of describing formlessness is of course already a way of giving it shape and domesticating it. Further reassurance is obtained from the clear implication that dissolution occurs because of the aberrant sensibility of the perceiver. Finally, although it holds the critic's interest, the tale or vision of blurring is usually shown to be less vivid, less rich and compelling than the world it replaces, which by contrast is seen as fluid, various, pulsing with color and light. The narrator comments on Littlepage's narrative of the ghost town: "Weren't they all starving, and wasn't it a mirage or something of that sort?" She suffers him to tell his tale, but the somber story is set off by a swallow, which flies in and quickly escapes, and then by a "late, golden robin, with the most joyful and eager of voices . . . singing close by in a thicket of wild roses." Thus Jewett pits the external world of sensuous pleasure against the dreary cerebration of the deprived captain. The deranged characters whose vision is distorted are not romanticized; they appear crippled, drained, used up. What they see is not only less sharp and clear, but often also less interesting, less poignant than the experience of the normal characters. For the reader, this heightened vividness celebrating a visible world may be the most compelling argument for realism.

The interpretive significance of seemingly trivial objects, the emphasis on surface texture, which exists for its own sake but also reveals deeper meaning, and the sense of a solid world encircling the action are basic elements of realistic fiction. The artist figures within this fiction possess a talent for seeing this deeper meaning beneath the empirical world. For these writers of realistic fiction, the representation of reality is not merely a stylistic illusion but an attempt to reflect a truth about life. An assumption that life has a certain fixed structure that can be seen as it really is produces the recurrent metaphors of local-color writing: the eye as an instrument of knowing, visual distortion as the symptom of emotional devastation. The solid outline of the landscape is presumed to have a special truthfulness; a wavering in this outline suggests a distorted sensibility unable to perceive the truth. The demented, the ghostly, and the overwrought stand apart from the "fact" of things as they are. The blurred and the dissolving can thus contribute to the repertory of realism, through contrast with a normative clarity and steadiness of vision. As I have tried to suggest, the dissolving vision is often presented by Jewett, Freeman, and even Gilman as a sign of weakness and vulnerability on the part of characters, an unfortunate clouding of the basically readable surface. But however sympathetically they may be treated, such characters seem at times to jeopardize rather than foster the realist project of affirming order and significance; for a leaking away of the sharp outline and the decipherable detail can call in question the reliability of vision, the comprehensibility of the world, and the autonomy and very identity of the individual. At certain moments, scenes of dissolving vision intimate the existence of a world beneath or beyond this one, which is *in*comprehensible and *dis*ordered. This parallel world of unmeaning is only a faint ghostly presence in the works of the classic American local-colorists, lurking behind the reassuring assumptions and patternings of the realist mode, but it is there.

WILLIAM E. CAIN

Presence and Power
in *McTeague*

Authors are queer cattle.—Frank Norris

We must stamp out this breed of Norrises!—a contemporary
reviewer on *McTeague*

Life is a search after power.—Emerson

Frank Norris is difficult to write about, and something of an embarrassment as well. Few critics deny the imaginative range and power of his
novels, but even his admirers concede that his style, whatever his skill at
portraying epic effects and action on a grand scale, lurches at times into
the outrageous and laughable. Richard Chase, for example, in his study of
the American romance, notes Norris's kinship with Brockden Brown,
Cooper, Simms, Hawthorne, and Melville, and details his keen interest in
melodrama, sensationalism, and lurid spectacles.[1] Norris surely belongs to
this tradition of the romance, often promoting the genre in his essays and
defining his subject matter—"the unplumbed depths of the human heart,
and the mystery of sex, and the problems of life, and the black, unsearched
penetralia of the soul of man"—in words as darkly exuberant and shocking
as anything we could find in Hawthorne or Melville.[2] But though Chase
argues for Norris's significance, he apologizes for much of the actual writing. Norris, he admits, is too fond of his "theoretical devices," providing
all his characters with "a sort of Darwinian double existence" and hustling
them "up and down the evolutionary ladder, between the animal and the
human levels." His novels are "profound" but clogged, Chase remarks,
with faulty syntax, "bad grammar," and "false rhetoric." "Like Dreiser,"
he concludes, Norris "was unable to tell whether the English he himself
wrote was good or bad."

As often happens when critics discuss Norris, Chase both advances his
case and threatens to subvert it. On the one hand, Norris is said to be
important and influential, because his grotesque entertainments lead us

199

forward to Faulkner, West, and others, Yet all the critics emphasize his stylistic ineptitude and observe that his novels have the effect of "bearing us down and trampling us," in Ernest Marchand's words, "under a rush of brawny adjectives and slashing verbs."[3] Norris is indeed not easy to describe in favorable terms, for when we try to credit his successes and redeem the style, we end up relying on clichés about his epic ambitions, rough-hewn genius, and mythic imagination. Although these seem apt and authentic when applied to Norris, their repetition from one critic to the next is disconcerting—is this the best we can say about Norris? And do these phrases merely soothe our critical conscience for admiring a writer, and highlighting him in our literary histories, who is not even sure whether his English is good or bad? It is doubtless a sense of frustration with the critics as much as with the novelist that leads Warner Berthoff to complain that Norris's "continuing reputation as a serious figure in American literature is hard to understand."[4] In his judgment, Norris's art is so blundering and full of formal deficiencies that it is impossible to accept him as important:

> [Norris] can not write credible dialogue (or dialect, which he unwisely attempts); he can not describe appearances convincingly; the whole tendency of his conveyor-belt sentences, pieced together like exercises in a grammar workbook, is to obscure rather than substantiate the matter at hand. His development of plot and incident is always arbitrary, fantastic without being interesting. Human characters appear to baffle him totally; his own characters, distinguished principally by the presence or absence of "virility," act out the parts assigned to them with comic-strip predictability. All in all, composition in Norris's novels seems to be reckoned exclusively in calculations of decibels and gross tonnage. (225)

At first glance, Berthoff's charges are persuasive; they illuminate as if by spotlight, Norris's dubious handling of dialogue, scene, and character. And in his letters and essays, Norris seemingly plays into Berthoff's hands and indicts himself, attacking "fine writing" and, in one notable outburst, exclaiming "Who cares for fine style! Tell your yarn and let your style go to the devil."[5] Brash and overbearing, Norris appears to value loudness over disciplined craft, declaring to a friend as he prepared for work that "I'm full of ginger and red pepper and am getting ready to stand up on my hind legs and yell big."[6] Though much more sympathetic to Norris's ambitions as a romancer and naturalist, even Chase objects to the "yelling," the straining for grandeur, and wishes that the novelist spent more time polishing his prose.

So we have Chase maintaining that Norris is a major figure despite being a bad writer, and Berthoff protesting that such a horrid writer should not be acclaimed as major in the first place. But Norris is a better, more interesting stylist and strategist than either his backers or foes usually suggest. He is uneven and overblown on many occasions, yet often surprisingly skillful. If he were always a wholly bad and technically incompetent writer, he would not intrigue his critics so; even Berthoff's hammer blows connote a certain fascination. We need to recognize that Norris fails when measured against the Jamesian standards of moral delicacy and formal consistency that still inform our critical judgments, but we should then move beyond this obvious fact. Norris is not a great writer in these terms, but he is an extremely powerful one in his own terms and forceful in his imaginative tactics. The heightened rhetoric, the verbal disorder, the swollen energies of the style, the depiction of characters as if in a funhouse mirror—all intimate a range of novelistic power that makes Norris both compelling and problematical.

What concerns me is the power of Norris's presence in his texts and the forms that it takes. He is a divided writer, aristocratic and high-minded yet aggressively self-advertising as "a man of the people." He labors to rivet his reader's attention on shabby environments, shocking us with the truth about cruelly depressed lives lived in the San Francisco slums. But Norris is not a muckraker or reformer, and he seems more intent on exhibiting and intensifying the scene than decrying it. And his starkest renderings often sit alongside the most "literary" and artificial effects—poetical flights, classical allusions, and so on—as though to remind us of Norris's own detachment from, and superiority to, the spectacles he stages. Norris shows a weird mixture of deep empathy for, and snobbery toward, his characters, and the gaps and overexertions of his style are in part testimony to his self-divisions. He gives the impression of overmastering his material, and remaining in doubt—though anxious not to be—about the forms of power he evokes and works so hard to celebrate. Any complete account of Norris needs to examine his ambivalent attitudes about the place of power in both literature and the world, especially as these are played out in *The Octopus* and *The Pit*. But my more narrow focus in this essay will be on *McTeague*, which Chase, Berthoff, and others agree is Norris's best novel,[7] for it opens up so suggestively the themes of novelistic power and presence that should guide our study of his career.

Understanding Norris's dealings in and with power requires that we first attend to the functions of his style. Early in the novel, McTeague and Trina Sieppe engage in conversation:

> "I was a car boy; all the car boys used to swim in the reservoir by the ditch every Thursday evening. One of them was bit by a

rattlesnake once while he was dressing. He was a Frenchman, named Andrew. He swelled up and began to twitch."

"Oh, how I hate snakes! They're so crawly and graceful—but, just the same, I like to watch them. You know that drug store over in town that has a showcase full of live ones?"

"We killed the rattler with a cart whip."

"How far do you think you could swim? Did you ever try? D'you think you could swim a mile?" (39)[8]

The sentences jump from the informative and essential to the irrelevant, and the words jar against one another ("crawly and graceful"). The dialogue is woeful, but of course it is intended to be so—in all its rather touching craziness and ineptitude. When McTeague and Trina speak to one another, they proceed at cross-purposes. Mentally and linguistically deprived, they cannot respond to the other's words, but can only catch at a term or phrase and pursue a stream of associations. They are attempting a conversation, just as they will attempt a relationship, but it is numbingly restricted, with words being bounced back and forth but not much communication ever taking place.

But while Norris's stylistic "awkwardness" is pointedly used here, it hardly seems intentional on other occasions, as when he describes the romantic yearnings felt by Old Grannis and Miss Baker:

> Was it the first romance in the lives of each? Did old Grannis ever remember a certain face amongst those that he had known when he was young Grannis—the face of some pale-haired girl, such as one sees in the old cathedral towns of England? Did Miss Baker still treasure up in a seldom opened drawer or box some faded daguerrotype, some strange old-fashioned likeness, with its curling hair and high stock? It was impossible to say. (9)

William Dean Howells admired *McTeague,* but regretted the sections dealing with "the silly elders."[9] Top-heavy with adjectives, dependent on simple oppositions ("old" and "young" Grannis), and ungainly in its usages ("treasure up"), this passage seems amply to support Howells's judgment. Norris bathes the characters in sentimentality and alludes to problems of motivation that he does not explore, or cannot handle, or does not care about.

Old Grannis and Miss Baker are verbally confined characters, dwelling in a sentimental world and bound to the conventions of tawdry romance. Miss Baker, for example, tells her friends that Old Grannis is "the younger son of a baronet," cruelly wronged by his stepfather (11). This is, we learn, her "little fiction," created from "some dim memories of the novels of her girlhood." Norris's manner may be silly and sentimental, but this is the way Old Grannis and Miss Baker view one another, as figures from the pages of romantic fiction. "It was impossible to say" is, in fact, less crude than it might seem at first, for knowing exactly how and why these characters act as they do is less important than knowing the maudlin images with which they structure their world.

"It was impossible to say," however, is a curious phrase. Norris was a diligent worker and researcher, priding himself on studying the settings and backgrounds (even reading up on dentistry) for *McTeague*, living among ranchers for months while preparing *The Octopus*, and delving into high finance for *The Pit*. Yet here he implies that despite his fully informed awareness of the Polk Street scene, he cannot "say" the whole story about the characters. For Norris, usually so "immensely willing to comment on the action, to explain the cause of everything that happens,"[10] "it was impossible to say" is oddly withholding. It is not so much, as Berthoff contends, that Norris's characters simply "baffle" him, but rather that he questions his power to reveal their history and see it as accounting for their sentimental responses in the present. There are limits to the novelist's knowledge and authority: from one point of view, Norris is firmly in command of his material and in control of his characters, yet he also appears detached from them, finding their world absorbing but their actions mystifying.

One should not attribute to Norris more modesty and tentativeness about his authority than he deserves. Often he does not press his characters or unravel their motivation because, as he exhibits them, they are too reduced and primitive for such issues to have any meaning. And then his disclaimers about what can or cannot be said reflect more on his characters than on his own capacity to represent them adequately. When McTeague decides to fix Trina's tooth, for instance, he is "puzzled," unable to "say why" he risks his reputation on this tough case. Norris does not cover the process by which McTeague "made up" his mind because, in a word, there is nothing there to see. Later in the novel, McTeague is menaced by Marcus Schouler, his rival for Trina's love, and is again bewildered: "What did it all mean anyway? . . . He was puzzled and harassed by the strangeness of it all. . . . It was inexplicable" (82–83). Experiences strike against McTeague with a thud, and he is dumbfounded by anything that departs from the grooves of his habits and routines. From first to last he learns nothing: he is "stupid" when the novel opens (1) and "stupid" when it ends (249).

Norris's plot does not disclose McTeague's character, but carries it forward from scene to scene. McTeague's fortunes change, but not his mind. He is mentally stunted and brutalized, responding to the "better" life of his first months of marriage only in terms of new creature comforts. But what is so curious about this novel is Norris's interest in, and captivation by, a character who, as he stresses with the force of a pile driver, is grossly "stupid," crude, and lumbering. McTeague fascinates Norris, even as he parodies the character's feelings and mocks his limited life. He does not merely exhibit and lampoon McTeague, but responds himself to the "crude dentist"'s awful displays of power. It is this fascination with power that helps to account for the queer turns, extravagance, and conspicuous unevenness of the style, as when McTeague and Marcus seem reconciled:

> The two stood up and faced each other, gripping hands. It was a great moment; even McTeague felt the drama of it. What a fine thing was this friendship between men! The dentist treats his friend for an ulcerated tooth and refuses payment; the friend reciprocates by giving up his girl. This was nobility. Their mutual affection and esteem suddenly increased enormously. It was Damon and Pythias; it was David and Jonathan; nothing could ever estrange them. Now it was for life or death. (32-33)

Norris appears to be staging melodrama at the characters' expense, showing them caught by their imaginings about friendship. He condescends toward McTeague (even *he* warms to the "drama") and gives an ironic edge to his tone ("what a fine thing") and references to the heroic models.

But Norris is not just making light of McTeague and Marcus, who soon will return to their rivalry and truly fight to the "death." While he pokes fun at this "great moment," he also celebrates it: Norris too feels the "drama" of the act, in all its expansiveness and "enormous" gestures. McTeague and Marcus are, on the one hand, hugely distant from the archetypes of pure and undying friendship. But for all its parodic slant, Norris's style does raise the status of the McTeague-Marcus friendship; for the parody to work, we need momentarily to accept the closeness of the ancient models and the sadly reduced modern exemplars. Though the effects are a bit hard to describe, this passage is more than an ironic spectacle, cast in order to make buffoons of the characters. They are parodied, yet allowed to touch an exalted form of friendship even as they are measured against it. As Norris arranges the scene, it is both noble and bathetic, peculiarly poised between celebration and mockery.

Norris oftens pays tribute to what he parodies and is implicated in the drama that he manages. He presents McTeague for our amusement, deriding him as stupid, gross, and the like, and suggesting that his actions can be readily placed as either absurd or brutal. Yet Norris is drawn to McTeague as a man of crude force, and is involved in, as he designs and shapes, his character's demonstrations of power. Like Norris's other novels, *McTeague* suffers from a great deal of adjectival overinsistence. But here most of what William B. Dillingham calls "the vocabulary of super-adjectives"[11] are specifically deployed to flaunt and celebrate McTeague's terrible strength. Often exaggerated and heightened, Norris's style reveals his obsessions about power and complicity in its violent enactments. Though anxious to distance himself from McTeague, Norris is enthralled by him, and he even conceives of his novelistic projects in terms of power and victimization, as a grim and demanding theater of cruelty.

As Dillingham remarks about Norris, "force was his center, the more vital and dramatic, the more terribly ineffable, the more fascinated he was with it."[12] The rightness of this description becomes especially clear when one examines Norris's essays, notably "Zola as a Romantic Writer," in which he vigorously argues against the "dramas of the reception-room, tragedies of an afternoon call, crises involving cups of tea." Collapsing several terms together, Norris declares that the "real realist," the writer of romances, the naturalist, rejects the "commonplace" and "ordinary," taking

> no note of common people, common in so far as their interests, their lives, and the things that occur in them are common, are ordinary. Terrible things must happen to the characters of the naturalistic tale. They must be twisted from the ordinary, wrenched out from the quiet, uneventful round of everyday life, and flung out into the throes of a vast and terrible drama that works itself out in unleashed passions, in blood, in sudden death.[13]

Stating his objectives with great energy and zest, Norris testifies to his sense of the novelist's power, his ability to disrupt the "common" scene and disfigure his characters. His verbs ("twisting," "wrenching") as muscular as his ideas, Norris insists that the naturalist must play with his characters and act as a coercive presence in his text. Edward W. Said refers to the "molestations" that strike against the novelist's command over his texts and that signify the limits of his power to speak authoritatively.[14] Although these terms can be applied to Norris, they fit him in an opposite way. As he conceives of the naturalist's aims, authority is manifested *in* powerful molestations, in mangling the characters, in lording one's control over them, and in striving to create spectacles "powerful beyond words."[15] To "molest," then, is for Norris the means of bearing witness to authority and of amplifying and broadening the field of the naturalist's power.

It is because Norris's temperament and ideas about fiction are so involved in power that McTeague retains his grip on him. He is entangled in his own plots, caught up in the posturings and performances of his central character, and transfixed by scenes of domination and power. Nowhere is

Norris's own commerce with power more evident than in his treatment of desire and sexuality, which critics have agreed is the novel's major achievement.[16]

Transforming the scene into a monstrous cartoon, Norris depicts McTeague's first stirrings of sexual desire, as he bends over Trina in the operating chair:

> There in that cheap and shabby "Dental Parlor" a dreaded struggle began. It was the old battle, old as the world, wide as the world—the sudden panther leap of the animal, lips drawn, fangs aflash, hideous, monstrous, not to be resisted, and the simultaneous arousing of the other man, the better self that cries, "Down, down," without knowing why; that grips the monster; that fights to strangle it, and thrust it down and back. . . . The struggle was bitter; his teeth ground themselves together with little rasping sounds; the blood sang in his ears; his face flushed scarlet; his hands twisted themselves together like the knotting of cables. The fury in him was as the fury of a young bull in the heat of high summer. (18)

This has all the subtlety of a head-on collision; but perhaps what is most intriguing here is Norris's ability to survive the impact. He outlandishly turns McTeague into a field for the play of sexual desire, making him a composite of vivid metaphors and verbs. In populating the "Dental Parlor" with panthers and monsters, Norris runs shocking risks; yet his writing is too commanding and intensified, and its status as sheer performance too high, to be dismissed as merely absurd. In McTeague a primitive sexual combat is enacted that he is helpless to overrule. He seeks a "refuge" in his work, but fails, at last leaning over and kissing Trina in a sexual violation too frightful to be named—"the thing was done before he knew it" (18).

To condemn Norris's description as "bad writing," as many critics do, is to miss the point. The passage is interesting not for its overblown prose, but rather for Norris's own investment of energy in the scene he represents. To put the matter more precisely: the style is grandly exaggerated and overblown, but revealing of Norris's spectacular presence in his own text. He is as much gripped by sexuality and desire as McTeague, and as obsessed by its violent forms, terrifying dynamics, and unnerving hallucinations. After his kiss, McTeague once more attempts to control desire through concentrating on work. "But for all that," Norris stoutly explains, "the brute was there. Long dormant, it was now at last alive, awake. From now on he would feel it tugging at its chain, watching its opportunity. Ah, the pity of it! Why could he not always love her purely, cleanly? What was this perverse, vicious thing that lived within, knitted to his flesh?" (19). Once sexual desire is felt, it exerts an irresistible force, vicious and brutal in its power to deform the self. McTeague is the victim of "hereditary evil," the "evil of an entire race" (19), and his sexual arousal throws him back to the primitive struggle between caveman and panther.

Norris's writing, we may again feel, has gone careening out of control. He seems to be substituting a horror show for sense and putting on a grotesque drama that he—as well as any discriminating reader—ought to recoil from. But the rhetoric is queerly compelling, as verbally over-charged as the shocks that rack McTeague. Norris asserts that we too are members of the afflicted "race"; he dares us to be outraged and indignant, and this is very much part of his performance. Committed to the tactics of his naturalistic dramas, he wants to wrench and twist his reader, as much as his characters, from "common" routines and attitudes. He aims to shock us out of the "ordinary" and taint the terms by which we might be tempted to gloss over the violent, disruptive power of desire.

Norris's passage is so wound up and aggressive that one can easily miss the most pointedly strategic sentence in it: "Ah, the pity of it!" Norris—student of Shakespeare and the son of an exactress who made her debut playing Emilia in a production of *Othello*—is alluding here to Othello's lament as he weighs Desdemona's betrayal: "But yet the pity of it, Iago. O Iago, the pity of it, Iago" (4. 1. 196-97). Coming from a writer so brazen and imperious, and appearing in a passage so sweeping in its claims, this allusion is surprisingly crafty. Norris, first of all, compliments himself, echoing Shakespeare and thus portraying himself as a fellow-dramatist of anger and destruction in sexual relations. But "Ah, the pity of it" is also an allusive tribute to McTeague. He is a modern member of Othello's line, physically powerful and a figure on a grand scale, however much he is gapingly without Othello's noble language and power of self-fashioning. Like Othello, McTeague's sexual desire and satisfactions end in murderous revenge—Othello's next words are the terrible "I will chop her into messes!" And Norris's allusion thereby helps to forecast the course of McTeague's marriage. It is over as soon as it begins, "undone" (51) right at the start because of the sexual inheritance that enmeshes all men. If anything, McTeague is a greater victim than Othello, because while he does suffer from his antagonist Marcus's treachery, his sexual desire itself is his true enemy—one that he will never "understand." Already containing destructive energies and poisons, McTeague is his own Iago, all the more degenerate because the subversive forces are within and basic to the workings of desire.

When Trina awakes from the ether that McTeague has given her, and hears the dentist's proposal of marriage, she vomits—which is just the first and most explicit form of the horror she feels about her own sexuality. Trina is stunned, and abysmally out of touch with the meaning of her responses. Her desires for McTeague "shouted and clamored" for recognition, but "it was quite beyond her to realize them clearly; she could not know what they meant" (50). But doubting her desire is an essential part of her mixed pain and pleasure. She torments herself and enjoys the sensation, fascinated by the awful power of her longings. Trina feels McTeague's presence as a force in nature—a "cross-current," a "quick, terrifying gust of passion." And in the terms of Norris's sexual economy, she welcomes this keen awareness, like the stab of a knife, of his physical force, his "enormous strength." Before she met McTeague, Norris informs us, she lived "with as little self-consciousness as a tree": "She was frank, straightforward, a healthy, natural human being, without sex as yet. She was almost like a boy. At once there had been a mysterious disturbance. The woman within her suddenly awoke" (50). This is the moment of Trina's sexual differentiation, when she breaks with being boy-ish and responds to the emotional and psychological awakening that McTeague has triggered. In Norris's heady view—one senses his exhilaration at violating our sexual silences and decorums—a woman is a truly "natural" human being only when she is "without sex." "Sex" defines but also deforms her, disturbing the "health" and innocence she once enjoyed.

Like McTeague, Trina is assigned a Shakespearean lineage, and it is tied to her responsiveness to the brute:

> Did she love McTeague? Difficult question. Did she choose him for better or worse, deliberately, of her own free will, or was Trina her-self allowed even a choice in the taking of that step that was to make or mar her life? The Woman is awakened, and, starting from her sleep, catches blindly at what first her newly opened eyes light upon. It is a spell, a witchery, ruled by chance alone, inexplicable—a fairy queen enamored of a clown with ass's ears. (51)

Norris shifts from past to present tense ("is awakened"), suggesting that Trina illustrates the disruptive force of desire always felt by "Woman." Like Titania in *A Midsummer Night's Dream*, Trina responds by "chance" to the brute, captivated by what is revolting and coarse in an inexplicable way. But in Shakespeare's play, Oberon and Puck control Titania, "streak-ing her eyes" with the magic potion and making her "full of hateful fantasies" (2. 2. 257-58). Like Trina, she does not seek the animal form she awakes to find by her side; but rather, as Norris says about Trina, comically transforming the ether McTeague uses, "the spell was laid upon her" (51). But if McTeague's presence is spellbinding and con-trolling, so too is Norris's. For it is not merely "chance" that sets up and activates this drama of Trina's desire. It is Norris, staging the "vast and terrible" acts of his naturalistic theater, who plays with Trina and McTeague, and allows them "no voice" in the matter.

Norris so heightens the theme of sexual desire that it almost assumes the proportions of an imaginative scandal. The scenes of terror and violence demand that we attend to them—again part of Norris's assertive presence and confrontation of the reader; and when we read and recall the novel, we think of little else. But there are exceptions to the pattern of sexual disturbance in *McTeague,* and they count in the novel by way of contrast with its central drama. Old Grannis and Miss Baker, those "silly elders," after years of silently "keeping company together" while remaining in their separate rooms, finally meet. Though embarrassed and ill-at-ease at first, they soon realize their bond of affection:

> The day lapsed slowly into twilight, and the two old people sat there in the grey evening, quietly, quietly, their hands in each other's hands, "keeping company," but now with nothing to separate them. It had come at last. After all these years they were together; they understood each other. They stood at length in a little Elysium of their own creating. They walked hand in hand in a delicious garden where it was always autumn. Far from the world and together they entered upon the long retarded romance of their commonplace and uneventful lives. (185)

Like Howells before him, Donald Pizer complains about these characters, judging their placement in the novel to be "thematically and dramatically weak" and objecting that "their love is asexual."[17] But it is precisely because their love is "asexual" that it has such relevance to the novel's themes. Old Grannis and Miss Baker are intimate, but asexual, living in a static world where it is "always" autumn. Like an elderly version of prelapsarian man and woman, they dwell in a "delicious garden," living innocent and healthy lives—which for Norris means living without the chaos and pain caused by sexual desire. Old Grannis and Miss Baker have "nothing to separate them" in a literal sense, because now they no longer keep to their "separate" rooms. But they are also not "separate" because desire cannot divide them. In Norris's sternly insistent view, desire brings men and women together only to drive them apart, immediately "undoing" them. In the relentless logic of this scheme, a man and woman can therefore be truly bonded only when sexual desire and power disappear. Old Grannis and Miss Baker survive as if in the pages of a sentimental romance, "far from the world," free from sex and time. The reference to Elysium is the surest sign of their difference from others, for in Elysium, those favored by the gods enjoy a full and pleasant life—after death. To escape desire's fateful pressures, a man and woman must be deadened to its force.

Old Grannis and Miss Baker are clearly a special case, however, safe both from sexual desire and from Norris's usual practice of turning

"commonplace" lives into "vast and terrible" enactments. Norris's rendering of their happy life together closes chapter 17, and the next chapter
begins with McTeague and Trina in bed. She is screaming, suffering from
"dreadful nightmares" of savagery and death. "Oh, you and your dreams!"
McTeague says to her. "You go to sleep, or I'll give you a dressing down."
"Sometimes," adds Norris in wicked detail, "he would hit her a great
thwack with his open palm, or catch her hand and bite the tops of her
fingers" (185). Frugal by nature, Trina has become grudging and miserly about money after winning five thousand dollars in a lottery. And
when McTeague loses his job and the couple's fortunes plummet, her
frugality controls and dominates her behavior. She worships money,
acting as a priestess before her piles of gold, kneeling down in front of
them, carefully handling and polishing each piece. "She even," we discover, "put the smaller gold pieces in her mouth, and jingled them there.
She loved her money with an intensity that she could hardly express.
She would plunge her small fingers into the pile with little murmurs of
affection, her long narrow eyes half-closed and shining, her breath coming
in long sighs" (173). Trina loves her affectionate play with the coins. So
taken is she with her money that she attempts to ingest and incorporate
it, her "murmurs" and "sighs" connoting the sexual rhythms of her sensations.

Trina's love for her money is a "passion," a "mania," a "mental disease"
(200), and in her insane overvaluation of the gold, she grows to see it as
far more attractive than her husband. Sexual desire merges with a lust for
capital:

> What had become of her husband Trina did not know. . . . She had
> her money, that was the main thing. Her passion for it excluded
> every other sentiment. There it was in the bottom of her trunk, in
> the canvas sack, the chamois-skin bag, and the little brass match-safe.
> Not a day passed that Trina did not have it out where she could see
> and touch it. One evening she had even spread all the gold pieces be-
> tween the sheets, and had then gone to bed, stripping herself, and
> had slept all night upon the money, taking a strange and ecstatic
> pleasure in the touch of the smooth, flat pieces the length of her
> entire body. (201-2)

This is Norris's most nightmarish exhibition in the novel: Trina's reduction of all the passions to her craving for money, as she luridly fantasizes
that the gold acts as a caressing lover. But the scene is also part of Norris's
extravagant effort to outperform himself and display his own power,
stunning the reader with still greater shocks. Horrifying as Trina's perverse
love-making is, it is mingled for the reader with Norris's own pleasure in
presenting still another installment—as though to allow us to peer into

the privacies of a woman's bedroom "one evening"—in his naturalistic theater.

It is possible to penetrate further into Norris's economics of desire. For Trina, economic gratification is its own reward—no purpose for the money is ever envisaged, except for the perils of the mythical "rainy day." Trina cannot reach an end to her desire, because what she does possess always pales in the light of what she could possess with harder work and more saving. Her passion for money defines and limits her, disfiguring her attachments to others; she regularly cheats McTeague and even refuses to help her struggling parents. In Norris's bold depiction, Trina's character is so twisted and magnified, her sexuality so distorted by her awful drive for money, that she becomes a classic study of the capitalist gone mad. In his essay "The Pathology of the Capitalist Commodity Society," Michael Schneider argues that for the capitalist, "the fetish for money itself assumes the function of the object of lust."[18] "In a certain sense," he observes, the desire for money "fetishizes the entire instinctual structure of man by becoming the dominating content of all his wishes and satisfactions." But while Trina is, to borrow Schneider's terms, portrayed "in the image of the hoarder who . . . is the atavistic prototype of the accumulating capitalist," she also needs to be distinguished from him. Unlike the capitalist that Schneider, following Marx, describes, Trina does not so much deny sexuality as transform it. Her sexual thrill comes through her hoarding, and thus her ecstasies are felt and rendered in erotic terms. Money is Trina's new object of desire, but her "lust" is still sexual. It is not the case, contrary to the terms that Schneider employs, that this money-lust entails the "sacrifice" of sexual desire. In Norris's account, Trina does not give up or "abstain" (as Schneider puts it) from erotic pleasures, for her hoarding is itself sexually charged in its cravings and forms of satisfaction. The grim truth is that whether her object is her husband or the money, her desire is still sexual, and that is why she experiences it with such fascination and power.

Trina's sexuality is, however, even more complicated, and here we encounter one of the most disturbing aspects of Norris's presentation. She feels one kind of sexual bliss as she accumulates funds, but revels in another, more vicious kind: she longs for and enjoys, Norris tells us, the beatings that McTeague administers to her. Having denied her husband in exchange for the gold, she compensates for her act by welcoming his punishments: this is what she deserves for failing to accept him as her object of desire. It might even be claimed that for Trina the pleasure of the beatings exceeds that of her hoarding. Like Maria Macapa, who is also brutalized by her husband, Trina takes a "strange sort of pride" (174) in describing her punishments to others. Seeing herself as a rival to Maria, she declares that McTeague's cruelty is greater, more to be "gloried" in. Thus it is not entirely accurate to say that hoarding becomes Trina's single passion and pleasure. The sexual consummation devoutly to be wished for is to accumulate capital, never achieving full satisfaction, and at the same time to be ruthlessly disciplined. "In some strange, inexplicable way," writes Norris, McTeague's brutality

> made Trina all the more affectionate; aroused in her a morbid, unwholesome love of submission, a strange, unnatural pleasure in yielding, in surrendering herself to the will of an irresistible, virile power. Trina's emotions had narrowed with the narrowing of her daily life. They reduced themselves at last to but two, her passion for her money and her perverted love for her husband when he was brutal. She was a strange woman during these days. (174)

The last sentence is, to say the least, an anticlimax, and leads one to protest against the author—though to respond in this way is to fall prey to Norris's manipulations and ploys to outrage the reader. But there is something askew and wrong here that needs to be pressed. Perhaps Norris is simply unaware of the horror of the psychology that he has exhibited in Trina, and more involved in stating the bare facts of the scene than in grasping their disturbing implications. What grates on the reader is the absence of moral judgment: the vivid scenes are cast and heightened at the expense of any engagement with the ideology they reveal. This is, to be blunt, in part a sign of the limitations of Norris's mind. But it is connected with his strategy of displaying and intensifying his power as author, of flaunting his presence through so much stylistic energy and domination of the characters that he misses the meanings that radiate outward from the spectacles. But while Norris turns away from the significance of his brutal staging of Trina's predicament, and while we may be inclined to do the same, the facts of power he expresses are too important to be bypassed. For its terrible calculus to continue, Trina's desire for money must coexist with guilt and punishment. For capital to accumulate, in other words, domination and victimization must persist. And in the further twist that Norris provides, the brutal forms of domination are seen as pleasurable, justified because the woman seeks its sexual consummations.

McTeague illuminates a network of power and ideology that is all too recognizable to us today. Yet one cannot commend Norris for his achievement in the novel, because he is so vigorously responsive, or on other occasions so inattentive, to the awful facts that he depicts. Norris remains a difficult author to write about, and still an embarrassment. Not, however, as a consequence of his flawed and ungrammatical style, but rather because—and the workings of his style are implicated in this—he embraces and exults in power and in making his presence felt. Norris's strenuous style, surging metaphors, and wrenched syntax reflect his commerce with power with an almost physical immediacy. And in his essays, he contends that the novelist assaults the "commonplace" in order to create scenes of torment and applied force. As Norris conceives of his project, it might even be described as an impulse to overwhelm and conquer—to use the evocative, expansive range of one's writing to control character, and to attain an imaginative preeminence over the scenes and settings. As we read *McTeague,* with its grand enactments of power, we should remember the passages in Norris's other works where he celebrates the triumph of the American empire, rejoicing in "conquest," "subjugation," our "Anglo-Saxon destiny," and powerful impositions of our will on other lands.[19] Norris's formal skills may strike us as uneven, and we may well question the ordering power of his imagination. But he is, more importantly, an unnerving advocate of the imagination of power, and an exhibitor of the stark realities that can be figured in literary texts.

NOTES

1. Richard Chase, *The American Novel and Its Tradition* (1957; reprint ed., Baltimore: Johns Hopkins University Press, 1980), pp. 185-204.

2. Frank Norris, "A Plea for Romantic Fiction," 18 December 1901, reprinted in *The Literary Criticism of Frank Norris,* ed. Donald Pizer (Austin: University of Texas Press, 1964), p. 78.

3. Ernest Marchand, *Frank Norris: A Study* (1942; reprint ed., New York: Octagon Books, 1964), p. 175.

4. Warner Berthoff, *The Ferment of Realism: American Literature, 1884-1919* (New York: The Free Press, 1965), p. 223.

5. Norris to Isaac F. Marcosson, 14 March 1899, in *The Letters of Frank Norris,* ed. Franklin Walker (San Francisco: The Book Club, 1956), p. 31.

6. Norris to Mr. and Mrs. Ernest Peixotto, 7 May 1899, in *Letters,* p. 37.

7. Norris felt the same way. Franklin Walker states in his *Frank Norris: A Biography* (1932; reprint ed., New York: Russell and Russell, 1963) that "Norris looked upon *McTeague,* which he commonly referred to as 'the dentist,' as his best novel" (219).

8. Quotations are taken from the Norton Critical Edition of *McTeague,* ed. Donald Pizer (New York, 1977).

9. See Howells's review in *Literature,* 24 March 1899. It is quoted in Walker's biography, p. 229.

10. W. M. Frohock, *Frank Norris* (Minneapolis: University of Minnesota Press, 1968), p. 14.

11. William B. Dillingham, *Frank Norris: Instinct and Art* (Lincoln: University of Nebraska Press, 1969), p. 104.

12. Ibid., p. 51.

13. Frank Norris, "Zola as a Romantic Writer," 27 June 1896, reprinted in Pizer, ed., *The Literary Criticism of Frank Norris,* pp. 71-72.

14. Edward W. Said, "Molestation and Authority in Narrative Fiction," in *Aspects of Narrative,* ed. J. Hillis Miller (New York: Columbia University Press, 1971), p. 49.

15. Norris, "Zola as a Romantic Writer," p. 72.

16. See, for example, Oscar Cargill, *Intellectual America: Ideas on the March* (New York: Macmillan, 1941), p. 97; Maxwell Geismar, *Rebels and Ancestors: The American*

Novel, 1890-1915 (Boston: Houghton Mifflin, 1953), pp. 15, 20; and Malcolm Bradbury, "'Years of the Modern': The Rise of Realism and Naturalism," in *American Literature to 1900*, ed. M. Cunliffe (London: Barrie & Jenkins, 1973), pp. 377-78. The best essay on the sexual theme in *McTeague* is Joseph H. Gardner's "Dickens, Romance, and *McTeague:* A Study in Mutual Interpretation," *Essays in Literature* 1 (Spring 1974): 69-82. It is reprinted in Pizer's edition, pp. 361-77.

17. Donald Pizer, *The Novels of Frank Norris* (1966; reprint ed., New York: Haskell House, 1973), p. 74.

18. Michael Schneider, *Neurosis and Civilization: A Marxist/Freudian Synthesis*, trans. Michael Roloff (New York: Seabury Press, 1975), p. 132.

19. My quotations are taken from "The Frontier Gone at Last," February 1902, and "A Neglected Epic," December 1902. Both are reprinted in Pizer, ed., *The Literary Criticism of Frank Norris*.

HOWARD HORWITZ

"To Find
the Value of *X*"
THE PIT
AS A RENUNCIATION
OF ROMANCE

The Pit is not a great novel. In making this evaluation, I am concurring with most critics of Frank Norris's last work, who deem it interesting but flawed. It is interesting in that it represents perhaps not the first but the most direct fictional confrontation with the postbellum stock and commodity speculation that by the turn of the century seemed to exercise an increasing and disturbingly fundamental influence over economic values. Its flaws, critics have argued, are twofold. First, Norris's "epic theme" of the wheat, the foundation of his projected trilogy, "lacks force," Donald Pizer writes, because we have no "direct contact with the wheat."[1] Conceptually "the chief actor" in Norris's drama, the wheat is lost in speculation, writes Franklin Walker, since "the manipulation of it upon the board of trade [is] the manipulation of paper representing paper." Thus, the essential "force"—that is, the natural law of supply and demand that the wheat obeys—"must remain an abstraction."[2] There is also a structural flaw: the plot regarding Curtis and Laura's marriage "seems unrelated to" the story of wheat speculation; "there seems to be no common theme in the two," yet not only are they united, but Norris "allowed the love story to gain the upper hand."[3]

There seems no connection between these thematic and structural flaws: the speculation has seemed to enervate the epic subject; and this story for no apparent reason is combined with the love plot. I want to argue the obverse face of the same coin. Speculation, especially according to Norris's conception of "the responsibilities of the novelist," *ought* to violate the epic subject of wheat, and the plots of marriage and speculation should be incompatible. If these elements only remained the disjunctions they seem to be, the novel would be much more powerful. But *The Pit* goes out of its way to exorcize what to many turn-of-the-century Americans was scandalous about speculative activity. Speculation is vanquished and absorbed by natural law, and it is thereby made to suit the wheat theme; as a result, the marriage and speculation plots are harmonized and become versions of each other. Ultimately, the various aspects of the novel, which critics have so well identified but whose rhetorical and polemical principles they have not fully understood, are not disjunctive flaws but are all too harmonious; it is this search for harmony that marks the novel's true failing.

Henry Adams, in his 1869 essay "The New York Gold Conspiracy," provides a most vivid account of the "speculative mania" that captured the nation after the Civil War:

> The Civil War in America, with its enormous issues of paper currency, and its reckless waste of money and credit by the government, created a speculative mania such as the United States, with all its experience in this respect, had never known before. Not only in Broad Street, the centre of New York speculation, but far and wide throughout the Northern States, almost every man who had money at all employed a part of his capital in the purchase of stocks or of gold, of copper, of petroleum, or of domestic produce, in the hope of a rise in prices, or staked money on the expectation of a fall. To use the jargon of the street, every farmer and every shopkeeper in the country seemed to be engaged in "carrying" some favorite security "on a margin."

Before the war, speculative activity—investing money in anticipation of the direction of fluctuation of exchange values—was the province of "regular brokers." Now, "every one speculated," "until the 'outsiders,' as they were called . . . represented nothing less than the entire population of the American Revolution."[4] This last allusion conveys Adams's reproval to his compatriots, for by it he metonymically intimates that America's revolutionary ideals have found their fulfillment merely in speculation.

One might remark that Adams is naïve in his irony, that speculation has always lain close to America's heart. After all, as Charles Beard pointed out in 1913, the Constitution was written with the interests of creditors and land speculators in mind. Michael Paul Rogin has amply demonstrated, with Andrew Jackson as his model, the broad influence of land speculation in the early decades of the republic. And he and Douglass C. North have argued that between 1815 and the early 1840s, a market economy, replacing an economy of household subsistence, became firmly established.[5] Thus the drastic changes that seemed the immediate offspring of the Civil War were in reality the long-nurtured descendants of antebellum developments.

Such an analysis decenters the Civil War's role in economic development, and of course speculation has indeed been important throughout American history. Yet perhaps we can rediscover a fundamental difference between pre- and postwar economic activity by replacing the subsistence and market economy distinction with a threefold distinction. Thorstein Veblen distinguishes among a "natural economy" (premarket, subsistence agriculture), a "money economy" of a "goods market," and a "credit economy" of a "capital market." The money economy is the market economy that Rogin and North identify. Its "characteristic feature" "is the ubiquitous resort to the market as a vent for products and a source of supply of goods." The businessman of this epoch invests in the exchange of goods, owns "industrial equipment," and keeps "an immediate oversight of the mechanical processes"; he sees to "productive efficiency." In a credit economy, the market is no longer an avenue for goods, but is "a vent for accumulated money values and a source of supply of capital." "Traffic," once "in goods," now takes place "in capital," whose definition has changed. Formerly "a stock of material means by which industry is carried on," capital in a credit economy "means a fund of money values" that "bears but a remote and fluctuating relation to the industrial equipment," a "shifting" or "shifty" relation, Veblen often writes. Accordingly, the businessman no longer directs the production of real goods but manipulates "putative" value, or "earning capacity," in "an interminable process of valuation and revaluation." This credit stage of the economic process, Veblen argues, has taken hold since the Civil War, and especially since 1880.[6] Previously, traffic in goods enabled the flow of credit; now credit underlies the exchange of commodities.

With value putative and immaterial, an interminable and shifting process of valuation, the distinction between credit and capital vanishes, and all business activity becomes in some respect "speculative," a matter of inferring distant and future trends and needs.[7] Thus speculation now becomes "one of the chief directive forces in trade and industry," Professor Henry Crosby Emery of Yale writes in 1896. Indeed, "the stock and produce exchanges are the nerve centers of the industrial body . . . in themselves as necessary institutions as the factory and the bank." "By making prices [speculation] directs industry and trade, for men produce and exchange according to comparative prices. Speculation then is vitally connected with the theory of value."[8] But with "real values" a function of, and often indistinguishable from, "speculative values," as a Senator Paddock put it in 1892,[9] America faced a crisis of value. In 1898, Alexander Noyes, financial editor of the *New York Evening Post*, calls speculation (specifically speculation in silver and gold) a "contest over the standard of value." But the violent fluctuations of such contests renders, in Adams's words, "all values unsettled."[10]

This sense of the destabilization of value finds its way into the literary imagination. For example, Henry Blake Fuller's 1895 novel of Chicago, *With the Procession,* opens with the death of "poor old David Marshall," a wealthy grocery merchant "whose sole function was to direct the transmutation of values . . . into the creature comforts demanded" by his family; it is as if a mode of valuation has died. In a more theoretical vein, Henry James writes that "life being all inclusion and confusion, and art being all discrimination and selection, the latter, in search of the hard latent *value* with which alone it is concerned, sniffs round the mass as instinctively and unerringly as a dog suspicious of some buried bone."[11] Norris also views art as a quest for value. The "purpose" of the novel, he writes in one of the essays collected under the title *The Responsibilities of the Novelist,* is "to find the value of *x*." This is the achievement of great writers. "Shakespeare and Marlowe," for example, "found the value of *x* for the life and times in which they lived."[12]

One should note here the temporal limitation of Norris's proposal: the composition of value is not eternal, but can be sought only for a given era. In addition, if Norris believes with James that art is "concerned" with value, the two men also share a conception of value as hidden or "buried." Norris feels that one should not trust to stated prices, value's external trappings, for these can deceive. Ideally, one should penetrate "the clothes of an epoch and [get] the heart of it." Norris thus desires, in the search for value, "not the Realism of mere externals (the copyists have that), but the realism of motives and emotions" (199). "Copyist" Realism "confines itself to the type of normal life" and "notes only the surface of things." In this way, "Realism stultifies itself," for the normal and external do not inspire one to seek the deeper truths. The Realism of Romance, on the other hand, "takes cognizance of variations from the type of normal life," because here, in what is often "the sordid, the unlovely," one can discover the primary motives of behavior, "a complete revelation of my neighbor's secretest life" (280-81). This penetration is achieved by the selection from the confusion of life which James espouses, and one seeks truth, not accuracy. For a "merely accurate description" supplies only the accidental details of a particular circumstance, whereas the "ludicrously inaccurate" may convey the real truth of a circumstance and its effect upon a perceiver (author). "Accuracy is the attainment of small minds"; "To be true is the all-important business" of Romance (284-85), and one succeeds in this enterprise not by settling for surface values but by seeking the flows of the "elemental forces" of business and pecuniary traffic which determine value, the "motives that stir whole nations" (204).

Norris applies this theory of fiction to the business world and draws an analogy between the financier and the great writer: "the genius of the American financier," here "Mr. Carnegie," does not differ "in kind from the genius of" the writer (244). Norris ramifies this comparison: the financier is to the "mere businessman," who simply markets goods, as the poet (or Romancer) is to the mere writer. "You must be . . . something more than just a writer. There must be that nameless sixth sense or sensibility in you. . . ; the thing that does not enter into the work, but that is back of it. . . ; the thing that differentiates the mere business man from the financier (for it is possessed of the financier and poet alike—so only they be big enough)" (201). The mere businessman and mere writer operate at the level of copyist Realism, handling goods and external details, exchanging only stated values. The financier is the extraordinary type inhabiting the credit economy of 1900 America, who, like the true poet, "deals with elemental forces" of valuation that "stir whole nations."

Thus we come to Curtis Jadwin of *The Pit,* who attempts to corner Chicago's wheat market. Chicago is the center of produce speculation because it lies at the crossroads of the transportation lines that convey "Trade—the life blood of nations."[13] As the center of trade and transportation to which the forces of nature are conducted for human use, Chicago seems "civilization in the making, the thing that isn't meant to be seen, as though it were too elemental" (63). Thus the city embodies those unseen elemental forces that lie behind events, the forces that it is the purpose of Romance to reveal. And the wheat pit, the bench-enclosed area on the floor of the board of trade where, so to speak, civilization is transacted, "roars[s] " "in the heart's heart of the affairs of men" (80). The financier's job is "to watch, govern, and control the tremendous forces latent" in his investments, forces that are "reshaping" the nation (280-81); Jadwin is a "successful speculator" because he possesses "that blessed sixth sense" (191) that distinguishes great authors and financiers from copyist writers and mere businessmen.

If speculation and the financier who engages in it embody the epic ideals of Romance, why then, we must ask, does the novel inexorably lead "to the conclusion of Curtis Jadwin's career as speculator" (396)? And by what logic is the end of speculation united with the reestablishment of the Jadwins' marriage? One might think that the novel must conclude speculation because it causes economic hardship to some sectors of society. Ernest Marchand observes, however, that "protest against economic injustice" holds "but a minor" place in *The Pit.*[14] The novel does acknowledge the at times unfortunate results of speculation: Jadwin's manipulation causes various speculative failures; and sometimes farmers receive a low price for their product, or European consumers must pay high prices for bread. Yet these problems receive small attention, because high profits and high costs, or vice versa, are said to balance each other out; and of course failure is precisely what a speculator risks in order to make money.

The real reason *The Pit* must, in Emery's phrase, "suppress speculation"

(194) has to do with the crisis of value I spoke of earlier. Speculative activity violates what Jadwin's friend Charlie Cressler calls "legitimate value." It does so because "Those fellows in the Pit don't own the wheat; never even see it. Wouldn't know what to do with it if they had it. They don't care in the least about the grain" (129). Such an accusation echoes the attitude of many of Norris's contemporaries. An "act of taking advantage of fluctuations in the prices of property," speculation is potentially disturbing because it "deals in invested capital instead of consumable commodities."[15] That is, speculators make money by, in Emery's words, trading on the "fluctuation in price"—called "trading for differences"—and in true credit economy fashion they "are not concerned" with actual commodities or their production.[16] Because of this lack of care or concern for the thing that a security represents, discussions of speculation commonly employ a distinction between "intrinsic," "real," or "actual" value and "fictitious" or "counterfeit" value.[17] "Fictitious value" applies to sales "representing nothing," to cite debate on the Senate floor, sales that in intention do not "contemplate an actual exchange of stocks" or goods, or of "real values."[18] Fictitious sales are most commonly products of "selling short," when men sell what they do not own in anticipation of a fall in prices, at which point they buy actual securities to cover their shorts. Such dealing is the essence of "artificial" or "unnatural" manipulation of prices.[19]

When speculative transactions are entirely fictitious—that is, when men have absolutely no concern with exchanging any actual security and seek to profit only from a chance fluctuation—they are called out-and-out "gambling." Gambling "has no reference to actual trade" and "consists [only] in betting on the course of prices" (Emery, 98). Because it "contemplate[s] no exchange of real values," a gamble in price flucutation "is not a 'transaction' at all." Such gambling "is all risk and no work,"[20] since it in no way pertains to the production or distribution of goods; and it is a risk that usually exceeds the securities one actually owns and can afford to lose. Speculation for price difference on legitimate exchanges seemed precariously like the trading that went on in "bucket shops," which were local (often rural) establishments offering very low margins (3 percent as opposed to the normal 10 percent) to small speculators who often did not know of the legitimate exchanges or that the bucket shops had no official connection with them. Cedric Cowing, in his excellent history of speculation from 1890 through the New Deal, describes their operation: "The shops only pretended to buy and sell in the market; actually they merely booked the transactions and carried the risks of fluctuation themselves. Acting upon the axiom that 'the public is always wrong,' they assumed they could make a steady profit from the hordes of amateur speculators."[21] Clearly, patronage of a bucket shop was sheer gambling.

As much as the legitimate exchanges wanted to distinguish themselves from bucket shops and from the general charge of gambling, even their defenders felt obliged to grant that "there seems to be no clear-cut line between gambling and legitimate business."[22] For fictitious "dealings are in no way different in form from any other dealings. What men are after may be the 'differences,' what they *do* is to buy and sell property" or the rights to property, for this is how contracts read (Emery, 58). Lacking this firm substantial or formal distinction, some men were tempted to ground the necessary differentiation in men's intention either to exchange goods or merely to trade on differences. Yet finally they hesitated "to adopt the somewhat shadowy distinction of 'intent and purpose,' in other words the spirit pervading [contracts]," because these immaterial conditions are determinable only by juridical interpretation (99, 217). "The vast majority" of contracts are resold before any securities are exchanged,[23] and were intention the ground of distinction, most transactions would be judged to be gambling. Therefore, it is generally concluded that stated property obligations in contracts constitute intention and must remain the basis for distinguishing legitimate business from gambling.[24] This method, of course, leaves intact rather than solves the problem.

Commodity speculation, the province of *The Pit,* posed a special version of the ethical dilemma caused by profitable investments with oblique or no reference to actual goods or values, investments "representing nothing." Stock speculation involves, in a phrase I cited earlier, "invested capital instead of consumable commodities"; therefore it already deals with immaterial earning capacity and makes no claim actually to handle objects. Commodity or produce speculation does, however, make the contractual claim to trade not paper securities but bushels, bales, and pounds. Yet, as Cowing points out, "In only 3 per cent of the futures trades was there actual delivery; in fact, to demand delivery was to brand oneself a miscreant and led to ostracism by the brokers."[25] In light of this statistic, given commodity speculation's claim to handle real values, the accusation of fictitiousness seems to apply especially well to such speculation.

Cowing alludes here to "futures," which differ from "options," another kind of contract, in that the former obligates future delivery, whereas the latter signifies no exchange of property but only the "privilege" to buy wheat at a future date, depending on the relation between the future, real price and the present, option price. Not actual transactions, then, options created, needless to say, increased scandal, which precipitated various legislative attempts to curb such practices. The first and most prominent of these, the 1892 Hatch Anti-Option Bill, sought to end options because they were an "unnatural mode of determining prices," as William Hatch, the bill's sponsor, writes in his report to Congress on hearings held in regard to the bill. Remote from labor and production, "the limitless offers of fiat products by the 'short seller,' regardless of the value of or the volume of actual product in existence," constitute not the trading of an "honest market," but assume "the form of swapping contracts."[26] By specifying "that unless the party selling . . . obligates himself to deliver in the future it is a gambling transaction," Hatch's bill was intended to "restore . . . the unfettered operation of the law of supply and demand." Thus, listed value would be determined naturally by the actual value, the existence of the product itself, and no troubling gap between listed and actual value would exist. Yet Hatch, too, realizes that even most legitimate, futures deals, because actual transfer of property is so rarely contemplated, are by his own definition no more than contract swapping, and not, in the term employed in Senate debate on the bill, "legitimate commerce."[27]

We can now appreciate that a well-established tradition lies behind Franklin Walker's discomfort that wheat speculation in *The Pit* is merely "the manipulation of paper representing paper." Norris shares this discomfort, despite his theory that the manipulation of the immaterial forces that generate the value of x comprises both the subject and method of epic Romance. Jadwin at first is "not opposed to speculation" (10). Yet even as he enters modest speculative schemes with his broker, Gretry, Jadwin denies that he is speculating: "this wasn't speculating. . . . It was certainty . . . sure." He compares his first deal to knowing "a certain piece of real estate was going to appreciate in value" (110–11). "I never bet," he will later insist (198).

The distinction between real estate investment and speculation is important. Jadwin has earned his initial fortune in real estate: "He was one of the largest real estate owners in Chicago. But he no longer bought and sold. His property had grown so large that just the management of it alone took up most of his time" (75). The difference between property management and buying and selling to profit from fluctuations in value recalls a distinction Aristotle makes in the *Politics* between chrematistics (wealth-getting or usury), and economy, which in Greek means the management of a household.[28] Aristotle's distinction hinges on one's responsibility to a physical object of value. Economy maintains its object; chrematistics has no direct relation to it. *The Pit,* as well as the debate about commodity contracts, reproduces this distinction about obligations: "legitimate business" (131) manages property, establishes values according to the "Visible Supply," and does not just bet on "rumour" (100). The frenzy of speculation, on the other hand, is "no time to think much about 'obligations'" (328). Indeed, speculation in the novel is said not only to rupture obligations to the grain; finally Jadwin does not even care for the money gained, which would seem the true object of speculation, but cares mainly for the process of manipulation in which he participates: he explains to Laura, "Oh, it's not the money. . . . It's the fun of the thing; the excitement—" (231). Within these terms it is appropriate that when he fails Jadwin should lose both his real estate holdings and the house he bought to commemorate his marriage.

Herein lies the essence of what I am proposing is the novel's real failure, and it is a failure of commitment. Norris theorizes about finding the value of x in the forces of a credit economy; he glorifies the financier as one who possesses the genius of the poet. But he will not seek the value of x according to the mode of valuation to which his theory of Romance has committed him, and *The Pit* stands as a written renunciation of this commitment. The novel repudiates the economics of Romance for what Emery calls an "objective idea of value, that is, the idea that value may be determined by certain physical facts" (113). In a credit economy, we will recall, value is constituted not by physical objects alone but by market forces or attitudes toward these objects. Hence, "the idea of value, which was at the basis of much of the early struggle to control [speculative] prices by law, is entirely inconsistent with the conception of value which gives speculation its sole justification" (193). It is at best contradictory to wish to suppress "gambling" in the same moment that one declares speculative trading legitimate in its facilitation of trade in a complex and widespread society. Both function according to the same notion of value; the form that seems excessive merely exposes the true operation of legitimate exchanges. Value in neither is "intrinsic," inherent in objects; in both it is "putative," in Veblen's term, a matter of conceived earning power, and it is known precisely by the kind and extent of activity surrounding an object (Emery, 150-52). Putative value is no less real than intrinsic value, however, just differently composed; "there is a real increase or decrease in the value of property due to outside causes" like speculative exchange (101). To insist upon a "fetich of delivery" (69), as if actual goods were the exclusive vessels of value, is to wish to inhabit an era or mode of economic behavior that has passed.

With all Norris's emphasis on "forces," not only in this book but in all his work, he tries in *The Pit* (though not, for example, in *McTeague*, which indicts gold fetishism as a mistake that leads to wife-beating and worse) to locate the forces of value in one identifiable, stable object: the wheat. This produces, in the search for value, a naturalization of the forces of supply and demand, and Jadwin believes that his corner is beaten not by market exigencies but by the wheat itself: "The wheat cornered me, not I the wheat" (419); he had been "fighting against the earth itself" (347). "Why the Wheat had grown itself; demand and supply, these were the two great laws the Wheat obeyed" (374). Supply and demand, here, are natural laws, immutable forces of the earth, autonomous of any market; the wheat is a pure embodiment of these laws, which is why it can grow itself.

This naturalization of the forces of supply and demand, the same natural status Congressman Hatch and others attribute to them,[29] is not, perhaps, self-evident and to be taken for granted. "Prices on the exchanges," Emery writes, are certainly "determined by the existing demand and supply. But the existing demand and supply are both speculative, and depend for their strength on the conditions in other markets" (114). The meaning here is twofold. First, a substantial portion of the demand and supply is precisely that of speculators estimating the strength of the market. But moreover, both supply and demand in the arenas of production and consumption always respond to speculative price. In terms of "the production of the raw material," farmers generally decide what quantities of a crop or even what crop to plant according to market price levels.[30] This proposition is well demonstrated in *The Pit*, despite Jadwin's misinterpretation of the situation. His corner is broken by a huge influx of wheat, an influx created precisely by the extraordinarily high price that his corner has induced. To a great extent, Jadwin's corner has grown the wheat, but he insists on thinking it has grown itself.

Since I am accusing Norris of fetishizing the object and naturalizing market forces, it is interesting to note that he chose as a model a corner on wheat—that of Joseph Leiter in 1898—that was as atypical in its operation as it was archetypal in its magnitude. Charles H. Taylor writes, in his *History of the Board of Trade of the City of Chicago,* that Leiter's "was one of the greatest manipulations ever attempted," one that "demanded the attention of the entire civilized world." At the same time, "a new-comer in the field of grain speculation, Mr. Leiter's tactics baffled the old-time traders." He refused to resolve transactions by accepting the "forced settlements" on the difference in price "to which [the 'shorts'] were accustomed." Rather "Mr. Leiter actually bought real grain" and demanded actual delivery of wheat owed him. (We should note Taylor's surprise in the redundant "*actually* bought *real* grain.") Like Jadwin, Leiter claimed that he "for the most part allowed prices to take their own course"; wheat "was very cheap," and the "conditions of supply and demand throughout the world" would force up the price.[31]

Norris, Walker tells us, experienced considerable difficulty grasping the basics of speculative trading; we may therefore assume that Norris was unaware of the anomalies of Leiter's techniques: that Leiter was, in Cowing's term, a "miscreant" with a fetish of delivery who downplayed his manipulation as but a response to the natural flow of supply and demand. Whether consciously or not, Norris was attracted to a manipulation that justified itself as natural because he "had difficulty comprehending how a man could sell a thousand bushels of wheat without owning them."[32] Short selling confused Norris because it violated the intrinsic, substantial, objective determination for the value of x which he sought. And in this desire for substantial determination, the financial plot rejects the values of Romance and shares in the sentimentality that critics have sensed in the love plot.

Before her marriage, Laura—as her sister, Page, observes, and as she herself admits—likes to flirt (68, 132), and she quite naturally contrasts flirting with being in love and, especially, with being married. If this opposition strikes us as normal, it is at the same time part of a rhetorical strategy that is neither ordinary nor necessary. The love and marriage plot incorporates the same terms as the financial plot, and in this conjunction we can see how the novel of speculation can also be the story of what Norris once called in a letter Laura's "career."[33] This conjunction may also lead us to question the naturalization by which marriage and speculation are opposed.

Marriage is conceived as a certain kind of transaction. For example, before their marriage, Jadwin makes a "bargain" with Laura, which he hopes will consummate their relation. He will add a conservatory to their house in exchange for a sudden, surprise kiss, signifying the depth and finality of her love for him. As an exchange, marriage is characterized by the equivalence of goods transferred: a kiss for a conservatory, or, as expressed in this remark by Laura, marriage itself for the pretty gifts that are an index of love—"I would marry a ragamuffin if he gave me all these things . . . because he loved me" (170). If thinking of marriage as a balanced exchange seems somehow vulgar, consider this comment by Sheldon Corthell, the aesthete of the novel, who above all others is spared vulgarity: "When I offer myself to you, I am only bringing back to you the gift you gave me for a little while. I have tried to keep it for you, to keep it bright and sacred and unspotted" (25). This offer of marriage as repayment for the gift of self stands as nothing if not an example of sincere love.

Because love and marriage are imagined to be direct and equivalent exchanges, it is important, in practical terms, to eschew credit and avoid debt once love has been consecrated in marriage: "Dear me, Laura, I hope you pay for everything on the nail, and don't run up any bills" (217). In short, marriage does not "buy on the margin" and always entails an actual exchange of goods. Marriage then is a form of Aristotelian economy, where value is produced by actual and proper handling of objects. To be married means, in the way of acceptable futures contracts, to "be willing to put [one]self under obligations to" one's spouse (140). Obligations are fulfilled, which means that behavior signifying love is exchanged and, in more personal and ethical terms, that one realizes and accepts "certain responsibilities." In this management of marriage, the inner substance of the partner surfaces for cognition: "She began to get acquainted with the real man-within-the-man that she knew now revealed himself only after marriage" (206).

Flirtation, on the other hand, is emotion in the chrematistic mode. Late in the novel Laura explains that her relationship with Landry Court "was all the silliest kind of flirtation," for "he never really cared for me" (376). Speculators "don't care in the least about the grain" (129), and flirts do not care about the objects of their desire, only about the excitement of flirting. Appropriately, Jadwin admits that in his dealings he does not even care for the money earned but only for the "fun" and "excitement" of speculating (231). Nevertheless, like commodity speculation, flirtation pretends commitment to natural objects and not just temporary interest in them. Flirtatious Laura "let[s] every man she meets think that he's the one particular one of the whole earth. It's not good form" (68).

Page's last remark here recalls, in the realm of human relationship, the problem economists encountered when trying to establish definite formal distinctions between legitimate business and gambling. Flirts let their beaus think themselves the sole object of love, the same thing real lovers want their partners to believe. The difference becomes a matter of intention, as exemplified in this exchange, when Laura coyly rejects one of Landry's proposals:

> "As if you really meant that," she said, willing to prolong the little situation. . . .
> "Mean it! Mean it!" he vociferated. "You don't know how much I do mean it. Why, Laura, why—why, I can't think of anything else." (53)

Of course, if intention seems the differentiating factor between love and flirtation, the course of Laura and Jadwin's marriage makes it clear that good intentions alone do not suffice; they must be inferred from the proper behavior or symbolic exchange of love. Jadwin fully intends to fulfill the late "bargain" that Laura demands, in which as a sign of love he will celebrate her birthday alone with her; but although lovers are supposed not to think of anything else but their love, Jadwin forgets the birthday arrangement, so immersed is he in his corner. Laura decides that he does not love her and almost consummates an affair with Corthell; we know that Jadwin "loves" her, but must wonder what kind of love it is that so easily neglects its beloved.

Thus, in dealing with people or obligations in general, flirtation is speculative in form. At the moment Laura becomes disgusted with her flirting, she imagines this activity precisely in gambling terms, with herself as the object of speculation: "No doubt they all compared notes about her." "Now it was time to end the whole business," for "in equivocating, in coquetting with them," Laura "had made herself too cheap," which is not only a colloquial expression for improprietous women but is the actual effect of most speculation, for to be successful short selling must drive prices down. Laura wearies of the "spirit of inconsistency" (127) that motivates her flirtations. When she "[i] sn't definite" (160) and is so "changeable" (165), fluctuating her emotions according to the same "indefinite ... 'sentiment'" that makes stock prices unstable (290), she cannot accept the obligations and responsibilities of marriage, indeed can "love—no one" (127). Marriage promises a "final" stability to an emotional state that otherwise wavers "capriciously" (205).

More than just emotional stability, marriage promises firmer connection to the real world, rather than the mere self-centeredness, the near self-referentiality, of flirtation, where acts are produced by caprices for the sake of excitement, with no true concern for the people with whom one interacts. Jadwin appeals to Laura because he represents the real to her, the "real, actual" drama "in the very heart of the very life in which she moved" (34). Although she seems to understand that the actual consists in the movement or interaction of the forces that lie back of objects, she nevertheless fetishizes these objects, thinking they are the actual itself and not just the phenomenal convergence of these forces; she mistakes the nature of Jadwin's business dealings, thinking, even in the moment he explains that he speculates for neither the wheat nor the money but for the excitement, that he deals not in price differences and speculative trends but in the "wheat—wheat—wheat, wheat—wheat—wheat" (231). She falls in love according to the theory of objective value that Jadwin brings to his speculative ventures: "I only want to be loved for my own sake" (173). If she is loved in this antispeculative manner, she feels, she can be "understood to her heart's heart" (187).

Marriage and speculation cannot coexist in *The Pit,* and for more fundamental reasons than the mere contingency that Jadwin's speculation keeps him away from home. The economy of marriage is radically opposed to that of speculation. In William Dean Howells's *A Hazard of New Fortunes* (1890), Basil March discusses "the enormous risks people take in linking their lives together after not half so much thought as goes to an ordinary horse trade." He hopes that "by-and-by some fellow will wake up and see that a first-class story can be written from the anti-marriage point of view; and he'll begin with an engaged couple, and devote his novel to *dis*engaging them, and rendering them separately happy ever after in the denouement. It will make his everlasting fortune." Basil believes that the "popular demand for the matrimony of others comes from our novel reading."[34] But despite both *The Pit*'s disparagement of "trashy" sentimental novels and Jadwin's "admiration for Bartley Hubbard" (216), whose meanness of spirit devastates marriage in Howells's *A Modern Instance,* the novel insists upon eliminating the "risks" of marriage and all indefiniteness in valuation and human relations. It attempts to suppress risk in its world in a way the real world neither could nor would, and in so doing the novel adopts the very sentimentality that Romance was intended to combat.

Yet I think we must still ask "why," why this insistence upon eliminating risks and upon fixing a stable and objective determination for immaterial forces that are precisely forces of change? And why this insistence when it clearly contradicts Norris's theoretical proclamations? Moreover, as I mentioned earlier, there is nothing natural or necessary about the alignment of marriage and legitimate business against flirtation and speculation, even though the former allies inhabit a rhetoric of the natural by meeting obligations to people and actual objects. Similarly, both Jadwin's success and failure in speculation are justified by a naturalization of economic forces that are clearly market-variable. If this naturalization and the opposition of marriage to speculation are not necessary but polemical, why the polemic? If the exposure of economic injustice is a minor note in the novel, why care so much that flirtation and speculation violate objective value?

The answer, I think, lies in the implications of Norris's theoretical stance. I have argued that Norris, while explicitly casting his lot with the financier, adhered to the "mere" businessman's economy of balanced exchange. In *Looking Backward,* Edward Bellamy supplies the logic that helps us to understand Norris's attraction to the operation of a market or money economy. "Money was a sign of real commodities," Bellamy writes, "but credit was but a sign of a sign." As a "conventional representative of goods," money facilitated their exchange, but once people "accepted promises for money," they "ceased to look at all behind the representative for the thing represented."[35] In a credit economy, the thing represented is lost in representation because people cognitively remain at the level of representation. But there is another reason, suggested by Emery: "The causes influencing prices are too many to permit of tracing the effect of a single cause easily" (119). It is not just that people lazily get stuck in representations, but that when representations are signs of signs, one looks for the signified only to find another sign; one cannot trace the determinants of value to a single cause, but finds only matrices of forces that may always bear further examination and that are always aspects of interpretation.[36]

Norris's discussion of fiction does not center on representation (as do, for example, the realist manifestoes of Howells and Hamlin Garland), yet it has definite repercussions in this area. For Romance to fulfill its aims, it must rupture accurate external representation in search of the hidden forces of value. Indeed, "in fiction, [accuracy] can under certain circumstances be dispensed with altogether" (*Responsibilities,* 285). But if one scorns surface externals as the province of the small-minded, to leave these behind is to enter a world of flux and of Veblen's "shifting" or "shifty" relations, where the rules of perception are never mere givens. Verifiability, tracing causes, is made more strenuous and difficult, open to reinterpretation.

The Pit contains an excellent example of this problem. Page attends the board of trade on the day of Jadwin's failure; ignorant of the proceedings on the exchange, she thoroughly misinterprets the events she witnesses, believing that Jadwin enjoys a great victory. Given these difficulties—even though Norris would firmly deny any desire to be a copyist Realist—the copyist mode, where words signifying external objects unproblematically stand for the things themselves as autonomous entities, and where such accuracy to surface details furnishes the essence of a thing's truth, is far more compatible with Norris's economic ideals than the method of the Romancer.

Still, merely describing this problem does not explain why it makes Norris nervous. For this explanation we must look at two practical consequences of a credit economy. First, speculation and flirtation threaten certain concepts of the self. Ideally, one should be "master of himself" (179), but speculation "seems to absorb some men so" (245); "this trading in wheat gets a hold of you" (232). Self-control is reduced and becomes an aspect or instrument of the forces with which one deals, until it seems as if the forces of wheat execute the trading without the aid or agency of men. Calvin Crookes, the allegorically named leader of the Bear clique that breaks Jadwin's corner, while he, like Jadwin, mistakes the wheat for the forces of exchange, perceives this redistribution of human agency: "They can cheer now, all they want. *They* didn't do it. It was the wheat itself that beat him; no combination of men could have done it" (396).

In her flirtatious mode, Laura lacks the self-control and certainty of self that are absolutely necessary to love and marriage. She cannot marry, she argues, because she is "not sure" of any man's love. "Even if I were sure of [a man], I could not say I was sure of myself." She is sure only that she is not sure enough of herself to love any one. Now of course this uncertainty of the "spirit of consistency" (127) is like the uncertainty of market fluctuation, and if one is changeable by the hour (291), or even is "one girl one minute and another another" (163), the self becomes as putative and insubstantial as the value of commodities. Thus, when Laura says, "I don't know myself these days" (163), she means that her self is unknown. And we can also interpret her remarks, "I love—no one" (127), or "I love nobody," quite literally. She feels she loves no one, not even herself, which is a problematic entity. Or if she is as selfish and self-centered as she keeps accusing herself of being, she still loves no one: she loves herself, who is no one, unknown, not an identity at all in the objective way she requires it to be.

This loss of self-control can develop into insanity. As Jadwin's speculation intensifies, he is overcome by headaches that feel like "an iron clamp on his head" (348). He begins to wonder, "Were his wits leaving him?"

(349), and finally during the "violence" of the collapse of his corner, "something snapped in his brain" (392). Similarly, when Laura is her theatrical, flirtatious self, as opposed to her steady, "sincere" self, she is "moved by an unreasoning caprice" (171). In her loneliness produced by Jadwin's concentration on his deals, she inhabits this self of unreasoning caprice more and more, and her identity begins to seem like "a pit—a pit black and without bottom," which lies at "the end" of the "current" of whimsy that has "seized her" (360). Ultimately, wholly uncertain of her identity and tempted to infidelity with Corthell, "a kind of hysteria animated and directed her impulses, her words, and actions" (401).

If the suggestion that speculation leads to insanity seems melodramatic, it is nevertheless exactly the attitude many of Norris's contemporaries held. Writers often allude to the "speculative manias" or "frenzies" that periodically overcame, as it were, the mental health of the national economy. Adams writes that during the 1869 manipulation of the gold market, "all business was deranged." In "The Ethics of Gambling," one T. L. Eliot speaks of speculation as the activity of an "unbalanced public mind." Speculation is seen to affect the mental health of individuals as well. In congressional debate, Senator Paddock argued that "understanding," "judgment," and "intelligence" are "worse than valueless" in speculation; rather, speculators, in Cowing's paraphrase of Paddock, "like victims of schizophrenia," live in a world of "rumor and secrecy." Eliot complains that the "fascination" and "fever" of speculation cause an "inflamed state of mind" and threaten the "dethronement of reason." The gambler is "intoxicated" to "madness."[37] Charlie Cressler reproduces this scenario: "The Chicago speculator . . . raises or lowers prices out of all reason"; at the individual level, the "fascination" of speculation is "worse than liquor, worse than morphine," and the least taste of it sucks in a man until "finally he is so far in that he can't pull out"; he loses "the very capacity for legitimate business" and "is ruined, body and mind" (129–31).

This effect that speculation has upon one's relation to oneself is paradigmatic of the second effect that disturbs Norris, the attenuation of property relations. As Laura's hysteria builds, she finds that even as she gratifies the many caprices that strike her, "she felt none of the joy of possession; the little personal relation between her and her belongings vanished away" (353). Now ideally one should exercise a kind of final control over the things one owns. Jadwin's corner represents to him this ideal, which is the culmination of the financier's purpose as the novel defines it: to "control the tremendous forces" of valuation. Jadwin imagines a corner as "a master hand, all powerful, all doing," directing the flow of value (259). Indeed, at the climactic moment before his failure, Jadwin's final tactic is to appear on the trading floor for the first time, to daunt "his enemies" by "direct assumption of control." But it is in the nature of the market to "run clear away from everybody." When his corner breaks, Jadwin thinks that "the Wheat had broken from his control," though he "once had held the whole Pit in [his] grip" (389-93).

This goal of direct control was also the aim of Leiter's corner: "to control the price of wheat single-handed against the world."[38] Yet in a time when the manifold currents of value are not finally traceable—and "current" and "flow" are the dominant images in the novel—we may wonder if "the speculative corner" can be any more than "incorporeal" and at best "temporary." For "many of the most active securities represent a capital of such enormous proportions, and so widely distributed, as to make individual control . . . practically impossible. No corner . . . could occur in such securities" (Emery, 174, 182). In a credit economy, where value is not intrinsic or objective, the "property relation" is, Veblen writes, "attenuated"[39] and individual control is abridged. Perhaps, then, Norris from the outset has misconceived the role of the financier; he does not "control" anything but attempts to glimpse and anticipate flows. We might say that Jadwin's true madness lies not in his speculation but in his desire to gain direct possession and control by it. Gretry may well be accurate when, after Jadwin tells him he is going *Into the Pit* to "play my hand alone," he cautions his friend, "J., you're mad, old fellow" (390).

Given his notion of the novelist's responsibilities, it would seem appropriate for Norris not merely to retreat from speculation's dispersal and attenuation of the self and of control of property, but to examine how a credit economy redefines property and the self. A fictional financier who better understands and accepts this redefinition of self and property relations is Frank Cowperwood in Theodore Dreiser's *The Titan*. Toward the end of the novel, Cowperwood seeks a fifty-year extension on his Chicago streetcar franchises so that he might remove himself from financial operations and complete the seduction of young Berenice, the daughter of a former "madame" he has supported in order to win Berenice's admiration. While planning his attack on other Chicago moguls, he surveys his holdings and sees he is "in the control, if not actual ownership" of "tremendous holdings." Ownership is attenuated in his control of securities, but even his concept of control is not simple, like Jadwin's. "The majority of the stock issued was subject to a financial device whereby twenty per cent. controlled eighty per cent., Cowperwood holding that twenty per cent. and borrowing money on it as hypothecated collateral." The interest yielded "on this somewhat fictitious value . . . would leave himself personally worth" approximately "one hundred millions."[40] Control of personal worth, the value of the self, exists under the aspect of hypothecation, the pledging of a debt without actual ownership or transfer of any good or security. If we view the self in terms of its economic mode, Cowperwood is committed to a kind of hypothecated self—as all control is actualized through hypothecation—that always looks elsewhere for its substance and is not controlled or collected in any direct way, as per Jadwin's ideal. Property and the self are not simply the self-sufficient objects or locations in which they are perceived but rather participate in the network of forces, debts, and influx which makes them up. Yet while not simply objective, property and the self are no less real or human, for the matrix of forces is perceived only through the objects and human intentions that convey them.

Marriage is imagined as a condition of direct possession. The bargain for a kiss which Jadwin proposes is intended to certify Laura's love for him so that he will know that she is his "own girl." When Laura is caught in the "insidious drift" of her moods, she cries out for the property relation that is most immediately attenuated by Jadwin's speculation: "I want my husband. I will have him; he is mine, he is mine. There shall nothing take me from him; there shall nothing take him from me" (360). If he thinks only of her, cares only for her—she exhorts him not to "think of anything else but just me, me"—then he is hers and she his (362). In the ideal of marriage,

> all the noisy, clamourous world should be excluded; no faintest rumble of the Pit would intrude. She would have him all to herself. He would, so she determined, forget everything else in his love for her. . . . She would have him at her feet, her own again, as much her own as her very own hands. And before she would let him go he would forever and forever have abjured the Battle of the Street that had so often caught him from her. (402)

In the novel's conclusion, the marriage is restored, which in turn is seen to restore the relations unsettled by redefinition in speculation. Spouses will once again belong to one another, and identity will be stabilized: there will "be only Laura Jadwin—just herself, unaided by theatricals, unadorned by tinsel" (403). These relations are naturally secured, no longer drifting "off the stable earth" (387). Jadwin explains what the restoration has effected: "I understand now old girl, understand as I never did before. I fancy we both have been living according to a wrong notion of things. We started right when we were first married, but I worked away from it somehow and pulled you along with me. But we've both been through a great big change, and we're starting all over again" (417). In this account, their marriage comprises an innocent stage, a fall during which they behave according to a wrong notion of things, and a postlapsarian redemption. If we need any more reminders of *Paradise Lost,* Laura paraphrases its conclusion: "The world is all before us where to choose" (414); and when they approach the carriage that will take them to their new life, they walk hand-in-hand (419), as do Adam and Eve exiting Eden.

I think most of us would agree that Laura and Jadwin live, or want to live, in a dream world, if only by virtue of their misreading of Milton; Adam and Eve are not starting anew and entering upon a time of understanding with a "right" notion of things, but are continuing a process of learning to understand. It is as if the Jadwins feel they are not leaving Eden to learn to manage in the world, but are leaving the pit of hell for an Eden where all has already been cared for. We have seen that Jadwin "abjure[s] the Battle of the Street" just as Norris abjures the speculative economics of Romance for the balanced exchange of the businessman and the copyist Realist; hence we might say that Laura and Jadwin now seek, or believe they enjoy, what Eric Sundquist in a different context has called an "Eden of mimesis," where there is "an emblematic relationship between image and thing";[41] where, in the terms of my discussion, contracts represent an exchange of real and equivalent goods and are not just trading for differences, where obligations to objects and people are necessarily fulfilled, where behavior and words signify what they seem to signify and are subject to none of the loopholes and interpretive ambiguities of futures contracts.

The Jadwins seem to dream of a return to an Edenic money economy. Although I have called this dream Norris's renunciation of his commitment to Romance, *The Pit* still represents an important dramatic grappling with the status of marriage and business in a credit economy; it thoroughly establishes and weaves the terms of the struggle it would like to resolve or escape; that many Americans, as I have tried to show, shared the impulse to escape is suggested in the fact that *The Pit* was for decades Norris's best-selling work.[42] Finally, however, it is not clear that a money economy of contracts for actual goods guarantees the circumvention of the endless representations of credit. Emery notes that once contracts for delivery and not solely actual commodities can be purchased, "full fledged speculation is at length made possible" (39). This possibility leads Bellamy to call money the "original mistake" because it "necessitated endless exchanges." "The confusion of mind which [money] favored, between goods and their representatives, led the way to the credit system and its prodigious illusions."[43] Once money is acceptable, it becomes easy to accept credit promises for money. This, indeed, is the force of Rogin and North's argument that the prewar establishment of a market economy set the stage for postwar credit developments. Once trade constitutes economic organization, credit cannot be far behind. And if one considers credit and speculation, in their effects on property and identity, a pit of hell, as Norris does, then a market economy is no Eden but is precisely the original mistake, the doorway to hell.

Norris attempts to diffuse this troubling fact that trade turns out to be a safe-looking but disguised prelude to speculation. First, that Laura and Jadwin hold hands while walking to their carriage suggests a physical unity that obviates exchange or mediation among different elements—so that nothing stands between them as Jadwin "stood between two sets of circumstances" (419), since the financier functions almost as pure mediation between producer and consumer. That the Jadwins drive to their train "in silence" reinforces this interpretation; their unity requires no exchange of words, no verbal contracts. Second, because radical selfishness, without firm responsibility to others, is the horror of speculation, we may surmise that once there are distinct selves who exchange behavioral and verbal intentions, speculative selfishness is always a possibility, one not effaced by becoming "only" oneself. Norris meets this problem when he resolves Laura's crisis of self by having her recognize not any true self but an "identity ignoring self" (405), as if identity were not known by normal forms of social intercourse; it is known intuitively and immediately or not at all.

The world the Jadwins are entering, then, seems safer even than an Eden of mimesis, of the market exchange that so attracted America. Their carriage seems to take them to a premarket Eden that is prior to exchange and representation, where there is an immediate identity of lovers undistracted by the endless exchanges and currents of the phenomenal world. Such is the experimental condition under which love is tested: "Everything in life, even death itself, must stand aside while love was put to the test" (401). If the test is successful, "all the noisy, clamourous world should be excluded" (402), as lovers "forget everything else" in their love for each other. But if this vision of marriage is intended to end the career of speculation, or to forestall its inception, it nevertheless dwells in the structure of speculation it is intended to avert. In the idyll of love rehearsed in the conclusion, spouses consider and care for each other so intently and exclusively that all worldly obligations are willfully ignored, which is precisely the fear about speculation. There is a limit to this comparison, because of course speculation has more noticeable resonances in the world than does the operation of a marriage. At the same time, however, a marriage has real social, economic, and legal obligations to the world, and one does not sever these for oneself in marriage but alter them. A marriage that forgets the world that makes the marriage contract possible shares in speculation's scandalous insouciance of objects in the world. How redemptive is it, after all, to forget the clamorous world when, by virtue of money won in speculation, one is to board a train for a home further west? If the Jadwins' hermetic love is offered as the best way to escape the difficulties of a credit economy that is but obliquely and shiftily related to the natural world, it is no escape at all.

NOTES

1. Donald Pizer, *The Novels of Frank Norris* (Bloomington: Indiana University Press, 1966), pp. 175–76. My first sentence is a paraphrase of the beginning of Pizer's conclusion. I would like here to express my gratitude to Richard Bridgman, Walter Benn Michaels, and Eric J. Sundquist for conversations about the issues dealt with in this essay.

2. Franklin Walker, *Frank Norris: A Biography* (New York: Doubleday, Doran, 1932), pp. 291–92. In *Frank Norris: A Study* (Stanford: Stanford University Press, 1942), Ernest Marchand emphasizes the "law" of supply and demand (170), whereas Walker stresses the wheat itself as the force.

3. Pizer, *Novels of Frank Norris*, pp. 165, 174; Marchand, *Frank Norris*, p. 86.

4. Henry Adams, "The New York Gold Conspiracy," *Chapters of Erie* (Ithaca: Cornell University Press, 1956), pp. 101–2.

5. Douglass C. North, *The Economic Growth of the United States, 1790–1860* (New York: W. W. Norton, 1966); see esp. pp. v–vii, 1–14, 61–74; Michael Paul Rogin, *Fathers and Sons: Andrew Jackson and the Subjugation of the American Indian* (New York: Vintage-Random, 1975), pp. 251–52: "The primitive accumulation of Indian land initiated a market revolution in America. From 1815 to 1845, . . . America transformed itself from a household economy to a market society. The extension of the market broke down family-based household structures—subsistence agriculture, household manufacture, the master-apprentice system, family welfare. . . . Subsistence farmers produced most of what they consumed, and lacked the surplus to purchase additional goods; farmers producing commodity crops entered the market as buyers."

6. Thorstein Veblen, *The Theory of Business Enterprise* (1904; reprint ed., New York: Charles Scribner's Sons, 1936), pp. 23, 88, 131–33, 135–36, 150–54, 275. Veblen borrows his threefold distinction from economists of the German Historical School.

7. Ibid., p. 165.

8. Henry Crosby Emery, *Speculation on the Stock and Produce Exchanges of the United States*, in *Columbia Studies in History, Economics, and Public Law* (New York, 1896), 7:8, 9, 12.

9. U.S., Congress, Senate, *Congressional Record*, 52nd Cong., 1st sess., 1892, 23, pt. 52:6883. All subsequent references to this volume will be cited in abbreviated form as simply *Congressional Record*.

10. Alexander Dana Noyes, *Thirty Years of American Finance* (New York: Putnam's, 1898), p. 68; Adams, "New York Gold Conspiracy," p. 123.

11. Henry Blake Fuller, *With the Procession* (Chicago: University of Chicago Press, 1965), pp. 3–4; Henry James, preface to *The Spoils of Poynton: The Art of the Novel* (New York: Charles Scribner's Sons, 1934), p. 120.

12. Frank Norris, *The Responsibilities of the Novelist*, in a volume with W. D. Howells's *Criticism and Fiction* (New York: Hill & Wang, 1962), pp. 194, 204.

13. Frank Norris, *The Pit* (Columbus, Ohio: Merrill, 1970), p. 61. This edition is a facsimile of the first Doubleday, Page edition of the novel. In *Speculation*, Emery says that "the greatest speculation in produce which the world has ever seen has grown up in Chicago." (7).

14. Marchand, *Frank Norris*, p. 168.

15. Horace White, "The Hughes Investigation," *Journal of Political Economy* 17 (October 1909): 530–31. This article discusses the findings of a committee established by Governor Hughes of New York after the panic of 1907 to examine the effects of speculation and make recommendations for the stabilization of conditions.

16. In *Speculation*, Emery notes that "the purpose of [speculative] transactions is to secure the difference in price" (7).

17. Ibid., p. 119; Rev. C. H. Hamlin, "Gambling and Speculation: A Symposium," *The Arena* 11 (1895): 413–14; Henry C. Vrooman, ibid., p. 424; *Congressional Record*, pp. 6442, 6881, 6883; Cedric B. Cowing, *Populists, Plungers, and Progressives: A*

Social History of Stock and Commodity Speculation, 1890-1936 (Princeton: Princeton University Press, 1965), pp. 4, 34.

18. *Congressional Record,* p. 6442; Hamlin, "Gambling and Speculation," pp. 413-14.

19. U.S., Congress, House, William Hatch, *Dealing in Fictitious Farm Products,* no. 969, 52 Cong., 1st sess., 1892, p. 3.

20. Hamlin, "Gambling and Speculation," pp. 413-14; T. L. Eliot, *The Ethics of Gambling* (San Francisco: C. A. Murdock, 1886), p. 18; "The risks inseparable from real work, from moving the crops and the manufacture of raw material, are right, but a risk which is all risk and no work is gambling. . . . Necessary hazard is as right as needless hazard is wicked" (Hamlin, 413).

21. Cedric B. Cowing, *Populists, Plungers, and Progressives,* p. 28. I am generally indebted to this book for pointing the way to numerous sources of research.

22. Vrooman, "Gambling and Speculation," p. 416. See also: Ibid., p. 426; Hamlin, "Gambling and Speculation," p. 414; White, *Hughes Investigation,* p. 534.

23. Hatch ("Dealing in Fictitious Farm Products," p. 7) and Emery (*Speculation,* p. 217) employ the same phrase. See also White, *Hughes Investigation,* pp. 534-35: "The greater part of the trading that takes place in the stock, produce, and cotton exchanges is of the speculative kind, and hence has a gambling taint. . . . It is known that 75 per cent of the trades on the stock exchange (some say 90 per cent) are of the gambling type."

24. Emery, *Speculation,* pp. 98-101; White, *Hughes Investigation,* p. 534; Hamlin, "Gambling and Speculation," p. 414; *Congressional Record,* p. 6439.

25. Cowing, *Populists, Plungers, and Progressives,* p. 14.

26. Hatch, "Dealing in Fictitious Farm Products," pp. 1, 3, 6, 7.

27. *Congressional Record,* pp. 6439, 6442; Hatch, "Dealing in Fictitious Farm Products," pp. 6-7.

28. Ernest Barker, trans., *The Politics of Aristotle* (London: Oxford University Press, 1958), 1256A-1258B, pp. 18-29. See Marx's discussion of Aristotle in *Capital* (New York: Modern Library-Random, 1906), 1:68-69. Also see Marc Shell's discussion of this issue in *The Economy of Literature* (Baltimore: Johns Hopkins University Press, 1978), pp. 89-94. In *Walden,* Thoreau makes much of the etymology of "Economy," the title of his first chapter, in trying to establish the kind of economy he seeks by constructing his own house.

29. Hatch, "Dealing in Fictitious Farm Products," pp. 1-3; *Congressional Record,* pp. 6881, 6885.

30. Emery, *Speculation,* p. 148. See also White, "The Hughes Investigation," p. 530.

31. Charles H. Taylor, *History of the Board of Trade of the City of Chicago* (Chicago, 1917), pp. 932, 953, 962. See Charles Kaplan, "Norris's Use of Sources in *The Pit,*" *American Literature* 25 (March 1953): 75-84. Kaplan studies Norris's selection from the many details of Leiter's corner, arguing that he did not change the main pattern of the manipulation.

32. Walker, *Frank Norris,* p. 275.

33. Cited in Pizer, *Novels of Frank Norris,* p. 165.

34. William Dean Howells, *A Hazard of New Fortunes* (Bloomington: Indiana University Press, 1976), p. 479.

35. Edward Bellamy, *Looking Backward* (New York: Signet-New American Library, 1960), p. 161.

36. Many readers will recognize here a strong resemblance between the language Bellamy and Emery employ in discussing credit and speculation and Derrida's notion of the trace. This is not the forum to develop fully the implications of this resemblance for literary theory, but I note it to suggest what I believe to be the economic implications of this Derridean notion.

37. Adams, "New York Gold Conspiracy," p. 123; Eliot, *Ethics of Gambling,* p. 29; *Congressional Record,* pp. 6881-82; Cowing, *Populists, Plungers, and Progressives,* p. 20; Eliot, pp. 18-22.

38. Taylor, *History of the Board of Trade*, p. 948.

39. Veblen, *Theory of Business Enterprise*, p. 146. In *Populists, Plungers, and Progressives*, p. 4, Cowing points out that in real historical terms, during "the antebellum days . . . economic control had been more local and therefore was more personal."

40. Theodore Dreiser, *The Titan* (1914; reprint ed., New York: Apollo-Thomas Y. Crowell, 1974), pp. 473–74.

41. Eric J. Sundquist, *Home as Found: Authority and Genealogy in Nineteenth-Century American Literature* (Baltimore: Johns Hopkins University Press, 1979), p. 131.

42. See Pizer, *Novels of Frank Norris*, p. 166, and esp. Walker, *Frank Norris*, pp. 286, 296, and Marchand, *Frank Norris*, p. 86. By 1932, the date of Walker's work, *The Pit* had outsold *McTeague* and *The Octopus* together, and Marchand reports in 1942 no significant alteration in these proportions. The attractive Edenic impulse to which I am attributing *The Pit*'s popularity is criticized by Henry Nash Smith in *Virgin Land* (Cambridge: Harvard University Press, 1950), p. 259: "Agrarian theory," bound up with "the myth of the garden," "encouraged men to ignore the industrial revolution altogether, or to regard it as an unfortunate and anomalous violation of the natural order of things."

43. Bellamy, *Looking Backward*, pp. 160–61, 211.

JOAN LIDOFF

Another Sleeping Beauty
NARCISSISM IN
THE HOUSE OF MIRTH

Despite the present renewal of interest in *The House of Mirth,* reminiscent of the enthusiasm that greeted its publication in 1905, criticism has not yet explained the single most powerful aspect of the novel, the extraordinary appeal of its heroine, Lily Bart. Lily somehow exceeds the bounds of critical definition as she does the intentions of Edith Wharton's narrative structure. She is one of the most compelling of the female spirits—Emma Bovary, Anna Karenina, Maggie Tulliver, Edna Pontellier—struggling to forge their own destinies, whom, as Diana Trilling points out, literary convention customarily destroys.[1] Critics have recognized the superadded energy of *The House of Mirth*[2] and acknowledged Lily's "mysterious appeal."[3] "Lily Bart is by far the most vivid of Mrs. Wharton's heroines," writes Louis Auchincloss.[4] "Simply as an example of imaginative portraiture," Irving Howe proclaims, she is "one of the triumphs of American writing."[5]

To Edith Wharton, Lily is a victim predestined to sacrifice to a deterministic sense of the inevitability of spiritual destruction by social institutions' collective necessities. Wharton's declared intent was to show, in the only way possible, the tragic possibilities of the idle society of the wealthy by showing what that society destroys.[6] Lily is "a captured dryad subdued to the conventions of the drawing room" (11), conquered by the constant tension between social discipline and the spontaneous feeling of individual impulse. Yet she rises out of the sea foam of this deterministic world with a power of emotional appeal that far exceeds her role as a pawn of hostile social forces. Writes Irving Howe, "before the pathos of her failure, judgment fades into love,"[7] and readers do regularly fall in love with Lily. Lily charms

Copyright 1980, Trustees of the University of Pennsylvania. Reprinted from *American Quarterly* 32, no. 5 (1980): 519–39.

the reader as she does the other characters in the novel (and as she has her creator). We are bewitched by the beauty of her grace and vitality of spirit as well as her appearance. Irrationally, we wish with her for a prince to transport her from her troubled poverty to the paradise of wealth and security she craves; we concur in her yearning to live happily ever after.

These fairy-tale expectations are generated by the emotional infrastructure of the plot; they are thwarted by the same structure. Lily dies at the novel's end, destroyed by the tyranny of social manners; but she is more essentially a victim of the limitations of Wharton's fictive world. Richard Chase has declared that "whenever it turns out to be a brilliant and memorable book, the American novel of manners will also be a romance."[8] *The House of Mirth*, I wish to argue, is primarily a romance of identity. Though it purports to be a novel of social realism (which Gary Lindberg convincingly places in the tradition of the novel of manners), it is controlled by a deeper underlying emotional dynamic. Before the society the novel portrays makes life impossible for Lily, the novel's romance structure forbids the emotional realization the character and plot seek. At the same time, this heroine derives her extraordinary appeal from the nexus of primordial feelings this romance taps.

Traditionally, the romance form makes its external world out of its hero's inner world.[9] It populates a hero's journey of self-discovery with token figures representing aspects of himself he must learn to confront and accept. Reading *The House of Mirth* as a romance, we see the conflicts Lily encounters as, in essence, internal, the other characters as aspects of her own need and feeling structure. Her fate measures the success with which she resolves, or fails to resolve, these developmental conflicts.

The romance form generally permits resolution: an ending in which the hero reclaims the divided aspects of himself in a new personal integration that permits reintegration into society. Women's hero journeys often end in failure because society offers them no adequate forms of active adulthood. When reality thwarts the forward progress of maturation by perpetuating childlike passivity in adult roles, dissonances are felt subtly within the female psyche. Lily is unable to move toward integration; she remains locked in the regressive emotional state of primary narcissism, which in turn mirrors the fictive world in which she lives. This early developmental stage is characterized by a fusion of one's feelings and desires with the outside world. Difficult aspects of the self are projected onto others so that rather than becoming coherent and realistic, the self-concept remains idealized. In this initial mechanism of projection, romance and narcissism are alike; however, while romance allows for recognition and thus reintegration, narcissism prohibits this self-knowledge.

In narcissism, the distinction between fantasy and reality is not clear. Similarly, Wharton's fiction confounds realism with romance. Failing to clarify the difference between the social world and the psychological, her novel does not stay consistently within either framework, but tries to resolve issues from one dimension in terms of the other. What purports in her plot to be a mimetic description of the social world is often unconvincing as material causality. A persistent inability to acknowledge aggressive drives (consistent with cultural images of femininity) results in a confusion within Wharton's narrative framework of the dynamics of moral consequences with the psychic determinism of fantasy. Wharton provides many cues that encourage reading her novel of social realism as a romance. Lily's allegorical progress from house to house down the social scale invites us to read in romance's allegorizing, abstracting mode, as do the symbolically suggestive names: Lily and Rosedale, Bellomont, Stepney. Like the typical romance hero(ine), Lily is an orphan, powerless and alone on her quest for identity. None of the secondary figures are real Others with whom it would be possible for her to have a significant relationship. Silent spaces between characters remain unbridgeable because the characters themselves are the simplistic projections of unintegrated fragments of personality. Paradoxically, while Wharton's fiction operates from a narcissistic fantasy of ecstatic oneness, it creates a world in which communion is impossible and isolation inevitable.

In his introduction to the Gotham Library edition of *The House of Mirth,* R.W.B. Lewis notes that the drama in the human encounters in this novel is unrealized; artfully, he says, suppressed. But the drama of the novel as a whole is inadequately realized. Emotional connections are not made; feelings and events are stopped short of completion. Lily is another Sleeping Beauty, slumbering in a dormant presexual state from which she never awakens.[10] Wharton's narrative not only portrays this state, but itself suffers the same frustrations. A dynamic of repression animates, and deanimates, this fiction. The first book of *The House of Mirth* is consistently powerful; the scenes in book 2 set up to mirror scenes of emotional force in book 1 are, however, frequently inadequate. Lily's charged walk with Selden at Bellomont is reflected structurally by another walk with Rosedale, which lacks all of the color and appeal of the first. Her visit to the working girl Nettie Struther and her infant, and the death scene that concludes the novel, are both stock sentimental pieces substituting for scenes of emotional climax or resolution. Even before the limitations of Lily's character doom her, she is damned to destruction by the constrictive walls of the inhibited psychic world from which Wharton has constructed her novel. This is the real locus of the determinism of Wharton's fiction, in which the consequences of social inhibitions are felt.

Simultaneously, however, Lily derives her potency as a character from the very emotional configuration that dooms her. In her later, more perfectly structured novel, *The Age of Innocence,* Wharton controls in a

more balanced way the feelings she releases with Lily Bart; but no single
character in that novel has quite Lily's appeal. Wharton's language most
clearly reveals the potent emotional sources from which Lily is drawn.
Lily is described by a consistent pattern of imagery built from metaphors
of unrestrained gratification and sensual delight that belong to the universal fantasy of Eden and appeal with the force of lost paradise.

Wharton surrounds Lily with the libidinal imagery of wish fulfillment.
She is presented to us cushioned in pleasure: "Her whole being dilated in
an atmosphere of luxury; it was the background she required, the only
climate she could breathe in" (23). Having a totally sustaining environment, where "everything in her surroundings ministered to feelings of ease
and amenity" (37) is not a luxury for Lily, but a necessity. Her life is
nourished, like an infant's, by an amniotic bath of sensual satisfactions.
Her images are fluid: "She was like a water-plant in the flux of the tides,
and today the whole current of her mood was carrying her toward Lawrence Selden" (51). With Selden, "the horizon expanded, the air grew
stronger, the free spirit quivered for flight," a "sense of buoyancy . . .
seemed to lift and swing her above the sun-suffused world at her feet"
(62). Lily's characteristic motion is the graceful swing of free flight; she
lives not in an earthbound world of gravity, but an unbounded fantasy
world, free from the weight of cause and effect. The verbs that regularly
describe her are: "glow," "throb," "dilate," "dazzle," "kindle," "shine,"
"delight," "quiver," "swing," "soar," "flow," "thrill"—expressions of
quick sensual response, of energy that admits of no channeling. Lily is
"buoyant," "charming," "radiant," "vivid," "intoxicating," "delicious,"
"elegant," "clear," "exhilarating"; this is the aura of her presence. Being
wealthy is another metaphor for this safe and harmonious life of perfect
and effortless pleasure. Marrying money, Lily assumes, would let her "soar
into that empyrean of security [where] she would be free forever from
the shifts, the expedients, the humiliations of the relatively poor" (47). In
this world of wealth, sunlight "caresses" the furniture, rooms afford a
view of "free undulations of a park" (37). In this Eden, one's beauty is
sufficient magic to make all one's desires automatically materialize. And
Lily is beautiful.

Wharton repeatedly uses chiaroscuro lighting to illuminate Lily's beauty
dramatically against the background of drabness (moral and physical) of
the other women around her. Lily feels that "the dinginess of her present
life threw into enchanting relief the existence to which she felt herself
entitled" (32). The first view we have of Lily is through Selden's eyes; he
sees her amongst the throngs at the train station and wonders, "Was it
possible that she belonged to the same race? The dinginess, the crudity of
this average section of womanhood made him feel how highly specialized
she was" (3). (Selden too has features that "gave him the air of belonging

to a more specialized race.") Lily explicitly articulates the perception
that she is "a creature of a different race . . . with all sorts of intuitions,
sensations and perceptions that [others] don't even guess the existence
of" (46).

Lily is persistently characterized with the extreme metaphor of specialness: she sits, stands, and walks apart from others. The special race to
which Wharton makes Lily and Selden belong is that of the fairy-tale
royalty of Freud's family romance, a fantasy generally outgrown, or suppressed, with childhood. Freud describes the typical childhood notion
that one is a changeling, off-spring of royal parents mistakenly placed
among commoners but in truth exalted above them. This fantasy is an
attempt to preserve the narcissistic image of perfection in the face of inevitable disappointments.[11] The dark underside of this glorification is the
instability formed of the child's fears and feelings of powerlessness.

Similarly, beneath the metaphors of beauty and specialness, runs
another strain of Lily language. Holistic and absolute, Lily's moods
swing between the intoxicating rush of triumphant excitement and dull
despair. The brilliance and intensity of her highs is predicated on the
bleak emptiness of her lows. Beneath the free air where her spirit quivers,
expands, and swings buoyantly (62) is a "prison-house of fears" (61).
When things go wrong, she feels not moderate disappointment or frustration, but a deep self-disgust. Never seen as a competent, adult woman,
Lily is regarded as a commodity, a beautiful object of art,[12] but she is
also often imaged as a troubled, helpless child, "longing for shelter, for
escape from . . . humiliating contingencies" (94). Pulling under the imagery of sensual gratification is a second language of intense, ungratifiable
neediness and fear, of a tenacious hunger for comfort and security.

Lily's encounters with Selden elicit from her both extremes of feelings.
In the splendid scene at Bellomont, the luxurious country house where
they are guests, Lily walks through the gardens and woods to sink to a
rustic seat in a set romantic scene. She knows the charm of the spot is
enhanced by the charm of her presence, "but she was not accustomed
to taste the joys of solitude except in company" (58). She wilts: "She
felt a stealing sense of fatigue as she walked; the sparkle had died out of
her, and the taste of life was stale on her lips. She hardly knew what she
had been seeking, or why the failure to find it had so blotted the light
from her sky: she was only aware of a vague sense of failure, of an inner
isolation deeper than the loneliness about her" (58). When Selden appears,
she instantly bubbles back into the luxury of enjoyment and gaiety that
comes with their meetings. The fluid joy of unspoken communication
between them brings a feeling of oceanic oneness; but it is extremely
fragile. With any disagreement, "the flow of comprehension between
them was abruptly stayed." "It was as if the eager current of her being

had been checked by a sudden obstacle which drove it back upon itself. She looked at him helplessly, like a hurt or frightened child: this real self of hers, which he had the faculty of drawing out of the depths, was so little accustomed to go alone" (92).

The fragility of Lily's self-image becomes increasingly apparent. Like a "sea aenemone torn from [its] rock" (295) she is unable to exist alone. The first book ends with a statement that quakes with unintended irony: "It would take the glow of passion to weld together the shattered fragments of her self-esteem" (171). Lily's glow feeds on the absence rather than the abundance of internally animating energies; the intensity of her intoxication manifests her dependence on others for all of her self-esteem. Isolation is terrifying to her: her whole sense of being requires another's presence. Yet she is prohibited by her own emotional structure, and that of the novel she inhabits, from any real possibility of either receiving or giving to others. She appears lovely, a fantasy of perfection. But coexisting with this idealized self is another, a deep void of deficient confidence or stability. As the glowing Edenic imagery of the first book fades, the novel's second book is progressively dominated by language of deprivation, anxiety, resentment, and fear. The persecution and disintegration Lily experiences in the plot are not unrelated to her loveliness, but intrinsic to it. As her charm plays out the graces of narcissistic pleasures, so her fall from social grace, her progressive isolation, and her victimization by vengeful characters who have the power she does not to initiate action, enact the underside of the narcissistic fantasy.

The term *narcissism* is now in vogue in the currency of social criticism.[13] As a psychoanalytic concept, it is undergoing reformulation at the hands of Heinz Kohut and Otto Kernberg.[14] I mean it here neither in the diluted common usage as "self-love" nor in the clinical sense as a specific pathological personality structure. While narcissism is disfunctional as an overall personality defense, Kohut elaborates Freud's formulation to argue that the infant's universally shared primary narcissism can be perpetuated in adults as one in a repertory of responses, a residue we retain from the infant's initial feeling of oneness with the mother. Lily partakes both of its appeals and its disfunctions. Derived from the intense, instinctual level of experience, the narcissistic state is wedded to libidinal energy and sensual pleasure. A striving to return to the elation of this oceanic fusion informs mythologies of Paradise and symbols of Eden's garden. Its sensuality and illusion of oneness exercise continuing appeal in sexuality and in mythologies of romantic love.

The libidinal imagery that defines Lily and her sense of specialness are those of the infant Eden; the fantasy she speaks to of eternal power, wealth, youth, and beauty derives from this paradise free from both work and mortality. Originally, the infant experiences all his needs as being gratified instantaneously and completely by the nurturing mother, whom he perceives as an extension of his own being. Believing his needs and desires to be congruent with the external world, the infant does not feel the necessity of producing effects by generating causes, of earning his own satisfactions. Wishes, not action, motivate his world. The expectation of automatic fulfillment and delight translates into a sense of specialness, of exemption from the laws of causality that govern others' fates.

The characteristic habit of perception of infant narcissism is called *primary process thinking*. For sequential, linear causality, it substitutes symbolism and holistic magic. Monolithic, this world view does not allow the possibility of change or development; everything seems absolute, permanent. All perceptions are rigidly polarized—black or white, on or off, with no tolerance for ambiguity or doubt. The emotional affects of narcissism are either elation or despair, without modulation.

This polarization is absolute because the narcissistic state precedes the development of initiative or assertion; narcissistic thinking cannot aknowledge drives—the wish to act autonomously to attain one's desires, or the capacity to do so. While narcissism presumes magical security and gratification, it in fact entails vulnerable and passive dependence on the generalized environment to provide satisfaction. Its idealized self-image of omnipotence and perfection is preserved only by projecting aggressive feelings onto others, whose helpless, innocent victim the narcissist then becomes. Otto Kernberg explains the need to cling to the narcissistic self-concept: "To accept the breakdown of the illusion of grandiosity means to accept the dangerous lingering awareness of the depreciated self—the hungry, empty, lonely primitive self surrounded by a world of dangerous, sadistically frustrating and revengeful objects."[15] Kernberg's description of narcissistic dynamics summarizes the latter half of *The House of Mirth*.

In Wharton's fiction, as in narcissistic thought, characters and alternative actions frequently are presented as black or white, good or bad. There are no possibilities of compromise or moderate resolution. This fictive world suggests the romance realm of fairy tales, wherein—as Bruno Bettelheim explains—such polarization and externalization of fantasy can be used to work developmental conflicts through to resolution.[16] *The House of Mirth* is sprinkled with fairy-tale allusions. Wharton often uses the language of fairy-tale magic for Lily and gives her magical powers. She has a prince charming in Selden, a frog prince in Gus Trenor, a wicked stepmother in Bertha Dorset and an evil stepsister in Grace Stepney. Lily herself plays Sleeping Beauty, though one who fails at her initiation rites of awakening (as she is failed by those who should help her in those tasks). Wharton appears to be writing an adult version of the stories that, in her childhood, were too frightening for her to face. She writes, in *A Backward Glance*, "I never cared much in my little-childhood for fairytales, or any appeals to my fancy through the fabulous . . . my imagination lay there, coiled and sleeping, a mute hibernating creature." "Fairy tales bored me," she declares.[17] In her new critical biography, Cynthia Griffin Wolff suggests that this boredom was a defense; that as a child, Wharton was "made acutely uncomfortable by their primitive emotional directness." When writing gives Wharton the tools to begin to reexamine feelings that were overwhelming to her when she was young, she is able to return to those emotional depths, and begins to write her own fairy tales—in the form of romance.

Lily's appeal testifies to the success with which Wharton is able to free the rich resonances of early narcissistic longing and the elation of wish fulfillment. At the same time, Wharton maintains some of her earlier ambivalence about acknowledging these emotions, manifest in the novel's unsettled combination of realism and romance. This novel is rather uneasily cast in a satiric mode, a rigid protective style of distancing emotion by rational and verbal artifice. But Wharton's various strategies of narrative control are only partially successful; their fragility is belied by the way feeling repeatedly breaks through. When Lily is pressed by Judy Trenor to participate in the nightly gambling at Bellomont, she is afraid to get involved. Like Pope's "The Rape of the Lock," this card game proceeds on a level of sexual double entendre. Lily fears "the gambling passion" that overtakes her. She "knew she could not afford it" (24). Once caught up in its exhilaration, her spending and repentance are both profligate. Lily has realized that "the luxury of others was not what she wanted." Beginning "to feel herself a mere pensioner on the splendour which had once seemed to belong to her," she is becoming "conscious of having to pay her way" (23). But the ambivalent activity of gambling is the only form of adult responsibility available to Lily. For both Lily and the novel itself, when feeling is released, it does run out of control, because there are no realistic channels to shape it.

Wharton casts this story dominated by emotional issues in social and financial terms. Characters and narrator both persistently confound the language of love and money: love is spoken of in terms of cost, expense, and value, while the stock market is discussed in the language of dependence and independence, betrayal, suffering, and sympathetic affection (p. 117). Wharton's intent in this metaphorical interchange of love and money is sometimes patently satiric, but it is not always clear that she is controlling, rather than controlled by, the substitution. "The underflow of a perpetual need" that tugs at Lily's family is as much a need of emotional security as it is "the need of more money" as Wharton declares. This metaphoric confusion reflects the narrative's inconsistent intermingling of romance with realism.

Wharton's attitude toward her heroine is similarly inconsistent. Although, like Selden, she tries to make Lily a satiric object, Lily's charm exceeds the confinement of that characterization; Wharton's deepest sympathies are aroused by her heroine. At the same time, her punitive assessments of Lily are harsh in the extreme, taking their ultimate form in Lily's death. The judgmental dichotomizing in Wharton's thinking dooms her beautiful child of a heroine as much as do the real constrictions in Lily's social world that forbid her overcoming her childishness.

Polarizing characters and action with the absolutism of primary process fantasy, Wharton establishes impossible alternatives for her heroine; Gerty Farish, especially, is blatantly used "to throw [Lily's] exceptionalness into becoming relief" (86). "Fatally poor and dingy" (86), Gerty provides a background against which Lily glows. They are set up as diametrical opposites. Gerty's "eyes were of a workaday grey and her lips without haunting curves" (86) which are, quintessentially, Lily. Her gown is of a "useful" color, her hat has "subdued lines" (86). Lily finds "something irritating in her assumption that existence yielded no higher pleasures" (86); and indeed, Gerty is as excessive in her expectation of too little pleasure from life as Lily is in hers of too much. When Lily considers whether she should marry Percy Gryce, she sees only two choices for herself: "It was hateful fate—but how escape from it? What choices had she? To be herself, or a Gerty Farish." To be Gerty means to live in an environment "cramped," "cheap," "hideous," "mean," "shabby," "squalid"; while Lily enjoys one of total luxury, beauty, and charm, of softly shaded lights, lace, silk, embroidery, perfume (23).

In her conception of Gerty and Lily, Wharton makes a complete and exclusive dichotomy of pleasure and usefulness: Lily's mode is all pleasure, Gerty's all use. There is no connection, for character or narrator, between material cause and effect, activity and gratification, work and pleasure. Wharton describes Lily's family life as alternating between "grey interludes of economy and brilliant reactions of expense" (26). The passive expectation of swinging between extremes is all that is available to Lily, who is inhibited from action by thinking she has only two rigidly conceived and equally unsatisfactory choices. This all-or-nothing thinking is immature, but within the terms of the novel, it is realistic. Wharton gives Lily only the two radical alternatives (or nonalternatives) she perceives for herself.

The one instrument Wharton allows Lily to initiate action works only by holistic magic. The source of Lily's power to move others is felt to be her beauty, which is conceived as a Platonic ideal, not an expression of adult sexuality. To look on Lily's "loveliness was to see in it a natural force, to recognize that love and power belong to such as Lily" (162). Selden considers Lily's beauty a part of "that eternal harmony" (131), and Lily herself believes it part of "her power, and her general fitness to attract a brilliant destiny" (85). (Her mother trained her to feel that she can give her beauty "a kind of permanence" and use it to win her fortune.) Wharton shares this fantasy of beauty's permanence and power; at the end, she will preserve Lily for us by her death, forever beautiful, forever young.

In one of the novel's key scenes, the *tableau vivante* in which Lily displays herself, literally, as an art object, Wharton shows that Lily does have some of the transforming powers she believes she has. The tableau scene is set to give us "magic glimpses" into "the boundary world between fact and imagination" (130). With Selden we "yield to vision making influences as completely as a child to the spell of a fairytale" (130) and give ourselves to "the desire to luxuriate a moment in the sense of complete surrender" (132). Lily's audience reacts to her beautiful self-presentation with a "unanimous 'Oh'" (131), in an undifferentiated collective spirit whose warm bath makes her joyful. She is pleased to find herself the center of a "general stream of admiring looks" (133). "The individual comments on her success were a delightful prolongation of the collective applause.... Differences of personality were merged in a warm atmosphere of praise, in which her beauty expanded like a flower in sunlight" (133).

Lily evokes from others the response of preautonomous oceanic pleasure in which she thrives. "The completeness of her triumph gave her an intoxicating sense of recovered power" (133). While Lily's elation, the excitement of a successful performer at charming an audience, is credible, her reaction to the responses she evokes is a sugar-high; she mistakes the confection of general admiration for substantial emotional sustenance. Her pleasure stands in ironic and inverse proportion to her real isolation. Loved by everyone in general, she is loved by and loves no one in particular. The autointoxication of this scene is the drunkenness of displaced sexual attraction, but, significantly, its pleasures remain nonspecific and nonsexual. Both her audience's responses and her own are global and diffuse, not active but passive, not other-oriented but incorporative, oral without being genital.

Lily's, and Wharton's, choice of Lawrence Selden as a love object is a primary manifestation of the confusion of passive with active modalities. Wharton suggests that Lily and Selden may be lovers, but like Selden's "Republic of the Spirit," their love has no material base. That both they and Wharton believe it might leads to Lily's destruction. Selden is the one character who elicits Lily's romantic longings. Yet in Lily's relationship with Selden, Wharton dramatizes most concretely Lily's inevitable isolation. When Lily charms Percy Gryce on a train, miraculously making materialize for him a little table of delicacies, and bewitching him into eloquence, Wharton satirizes the fairy-tale scene she sets up, and the

magical powers with which she endows her heroine.[18] But in Lily's scenes
with Selden, Wharton is herself concessive to this romanticism. They meet
in paradisal atmospheres, imbued with the sensual color and protected
security of the Edenic fantasy, but also with its concomitant passivity. On
a hill looking down on Bellomont, "the soft isolation of the falling day
enveloped them: they seemed lifted into a finer air. All the exquisite influences of the hour trembled in their veins, and drew them to each other
as the loosened leaves were drawn to earth" (70). Characteristically, they
"stay silent while something throbbed between them in the wide quiet of
the air"; "neither seemed to speak deliberately . . . an indwelling voice
in each called to the other across unsounded depths of feeling" (69). For
Lily and Selden, silences remain unbreakable; there is never any possibility of completed intercourse—verbal or physical—between them. Invariably, their encounters culminate in frustration, not climax; the novel
itself concludes with a silence made permanent by Lily's death. Scenes
between Lily and Selden operate with the intensity of suppression; they
remain frozen in magical expectations without pragmatic means of realization.

The limitations of this characteristic imagery of hazy softness, miracle,
and magic are immediately apparent in their inappropriateness to practical
financial dealings. While the need for money to sustain life is a social
reality of utmost immediacy, Lily's attitudes toward money manifest her
expectation that the material world should operate as fantasy does. She
thinks about money in the language of magic: she is upset when she cannot "conjure back" a "vanished three hundred dollars" (25). Needing
cash, she goes to Gus Trenor "with the trustfulness of a child." "Through
the general blur her hopes dialated like lamps in a fog. She understood
only that her modest investments were to be mysteriously multiplied
without risk to herself; and the assurance that this miracle would take
place in a short time, that there would be no tedious interval for suspense
and reaction, relieved her" (82).

When Gus Trenor lures Lily to his deserted townhouse, his attempt to
use his financial and physical power to coerce her to sexual relations
makes explicit the real social connections between money, power, and sex
that Lily has purposefully kept from her awareness. But the language and
imagery Wharton uses in this scene show her own confusions, deeper than
the social drama, though undeniably arising from it. Unlike any of the
romantic and always frustrated scenes with Selden, the handsome prince,
this one of attempted rape is the one scene in the novel written in the
rising and completed rhythms of sexual climax.

In contrast to Lily's "freshness and slenderness" (77), Gus Trenor,
sweaty, "red and massive" (77), with a "puffing face" cast in deep crim-
son by a match's glow, is her frog prince. (When a fairy-tale princess

matures beyond her youthful fears of sexuality, she kisses the frog, who is then revealed as a handsome prince; Lily, however, is unable to transcend her early repugnance to unite the two figures.) Lily's scenes with Selden are filled with throbbing and blushing. With Gus, these reactions are intensified, but in fear and anger. His resentful verbal attack makes her feel her "frightened heart throbs." "The words—the words were worse than the touch: Her heart was beating all over her body in her throat, her limbs, her helpless, useless hands" (142). "Trenor's face darkened to rage: her recoil of abhorrence had called out the primitive man." He comes closer "with a hand that grew formidable" (141-42). "She felt suddenly weak and defenseless: there was a throb of self-pity in her throat" (142). When he threatens her verbally "the brutality of the thrust gave her the sense of dizziness that follows on a physical blow" (141). "She flamed with anger and abasement." "Over and over her the sea of humiliation broke—wave crashing on wave" (143). When, at the last minute, Gus withdraws, "the sharp release from her fears restored Lily to immediate lucidity. The collapse of Trenor's will left her in control" (144).

Although this is a scene of verbal confrontation whose explicit emotions are fear and anger, its imagery builds in a pattern of sexual tension and release. Its aftermath for Lily is severe shock. "All the while she shook with inward loathing. On the doorstep, . . . she felt a mad throb of liberation." But once outside and safe, "reaction came, and shuddering darkness closed on her" (144). Lily reacts with terrified dissociation: "She seemed a stranger to herself, or rather there were two selves in her, the one she had always known, and a new abhorrent being to which it found itself chained" (144). "There was a great gulf fixed between today and yesterday. Everything in the past seemed simple, natural, full of daylight—and she was alone in a place of darkness and pollution" (145).

Although Lily is a creature of beauty and sensual charm, sexuality is not an acceptable part of her self-image. Responsibility is transferred to a male character: sexuality becomes Gus Trenor's domain, as hostility will be projected onto Bertha Dorset. The passionate imagery of fulfillment is therefore released from its pressurized control only in the context of brute force and coercion (in short, rape).

The brutality of Lily's encounter with Gus Trenor is complementary to the recurring frustration of her emotionally and physically unconsummated relation with Selden. Inhibited by the same fears that constrain Lily, Wharton has divided her characters in such a way that sexuality is isolated from both loving concern and romantic longing. The only male character who is realistic in his daily behavior and genuinely concerned about Lily is Simon Rosedale, whom she finds wholly unattractive. Structurally, Wharton suggests that Rosedale would be a proper mate for Lily and has named him accordingly. But she is deeply ambivalent toward him.[19] From the start, each encounter between Lily and Rosedale is a negotiation over intimacy, but because Lily is incapable of the closeness he offers, it remains unattractive to her. The first chapter of *The House of Mirth* begins with Lily's tête à tête with Selden and ends with her shunning Rosedale's proffered escort; this is the destructive movement of the novel as a whole.

Whereas Selden, like the narrator, sees Lily through an aesthetic haze and simultaneously passes harsh moral judgments upon her, Rosedale understands her quite plainly and accepts her just as simply. He is the only man who is genuinely kind to Lily and the only one to tell her he loves her. Unlike any of the other voices in the novel, including the narrator's, Rosedale does not confuse the language of love and money, but talks of money when he means money, and love when he means love. Lily and Rosedale engage in honest dialogue and confrontation, as Lily and Selden never do, but neither Lily nor the novel can fruitfully negotiate familiarity and distance because any intimacy is perceived as threatening. Rosedale's advances seem to Lily excessive, "intrusive" (79), "odious"; they freeze her into repugnance[20] (111).

Selden and Rosedale are repeatedly juxtaposed in consecutive or reflecting scenes which should make Rosedale's virtues apparent but instead highlight Selden's appeal. Book 1 ends as Lily awaits Selden in her drawing room; Rosedale comes instead. Selden has deserted her; Rosedale offers marriage, but Lily feels such extreme disappointment over Selden's absence that Rosedale's presence is nothing but an irritation. When in book 2 (247 ff.) Lily walks with Rosedale, Wharton explicitly recalls her earlier golden September walk with Selden which evoked the soaring freedom of flight. In contrast, this November day "outlined the facts with a cold precision unmodified by shade or color, and refracted, as it were, from the blank walls of the surrounding limitations" (247). As she did with Gerty Farish, Wharton makes a life of practical action within accepted limitations seem intolerably harsh.

Considering that she might one day have to marry Rosedale, Lily feels that he stands for "one of the many hated possibilities hovering on the edge of life." Unlike Lily, or Selden, Rosedale operates from a real material base; he "set about with patient industry to form a background for his growing glory." "I generally *have* got what I wanted in life" (172), he tells Lily. It is just the possibilities that make life possible that violate Lily's world of oceanic narcissism. As Gus Trenor was her frog prince, so Rosedale is her Rumpelstiltskin, representing qualities she is unable to integrate within her own personality. An adult figure of autonomous industry, Rosedale shows the initiative and assertion that Lily fears and shuns—as she does him.

In the novel's only congenial scene of domestic "repose and stability" Wharton shows Rosedale with Carrie Fisher's daughter, in a pose of "simple and kindly" "homely goodness" (243). But Lily is unable to decide whether this sight "mitigated her repugnance, or gave it, rather, a more concrete and intimate form" (244). When she considers Rosedale's offer of marriage, she cannot imagine further than her betrothal: "after that everything faded into a haze of material well-being . . . there were . . . certain midnight images that must at any cost be exorcised—and one of these was the image of herself as Rosedale's wife" (242-43).

No image of Lily as wife is possible in the imaginative world of this novel. Dividing essential qualities among disparate male characters, Wharton has not created a hero whom Lily might marry. But marriage is more than a literal solution for Lily and for the plot; it is a symbolic affirmation of maturity. Lily cannot marry because she is incapable of love. Both the ability to love and the capacity for moral responsibility are predicated on the integration of sexual and active impulses. Wharton, however, rejects all assertive drives in symbolically coherent metaphors of pollution. (Anthropologist Mary Douglas has shown how, on a cultural level, pollution taboos similarly disown the chaotic impulses a society is unable to integrate into its symbolic order.) [21] In her Aunt Penniston's house, Lily resents the smell of wax and soap; she "behaved as though she thought a house ought to keep clean of itself, without extraneous assistance." Lily's encounters with the cleaning woman she here resents thread through the novel from beginning to end as moments of moral crisis. When Mrs. Haffen comes to Lily offering her letters with which to blackmail Bertha Dorset and restore her own good name, Lily shuns her offer with disdain, as she has earlier evaded her flood of soapsuds. Wharton suggests that Lily's disgust and sense of contamination are noble, that her refraining is an act of moral courage (102). It is also, however, a refusal to get her hands dirty in taking practical action on her own behalf. Lily obscures the necessity of acting on her own needs or of acknowledging her potent desires for revenge; she maintains the idealized purity of her self-image at the ultimate cost of preserving her life.

The specific metaphor of dirt and cleanliness in which Lily's avoidance of adult responsibility is expressed recalls an oft quoted reminiscence of Wharton herself, one that suggests a specific connection to childhood mothering. In her autobiographical *A Backward Glance* Wharton tells of her first novel, which began: "'Oh, how do you do, Mrs. Brown?' said Mrs. Tompkins. 'If only I had known you were going to call I should have tidied up the drawing-room.' Timourously I submitted this to my mother, and never shall I forget the sudden drop of creative frenzy when she returned it with the icy comment: 'Drawing-rooms are always tidy.'" [22] Cynthia Griffin Wolff's biography demonstrates that this anecdote is not anomalous, but typical of Wharton's impaired relation with her cold and demanding mother.

The array of mother figures in *The House of Mirth* also suggests a pervasive psychic configuration of inadequate maternal nurturance and support. Lily's troubles with sexual love and adult responsibility are symptomatic of a deeper problem. The key to Lily's relation with the male figures of the novel is in her relation to the female figures. The primary motivations that determine the plot of *The House of Mirth* are not actions with or among the men, but feelings of resentment and revenge among the women. Lily has a host of inadequate mother figures, paraded as she sinks from one to another down the social scale. Maternal intimacy suffers the same fate in this novel as sexual intimacy, and is in fact the model for it. The women who are concerned about Lily are made unattractive and powerless. Gerty Farish, truly generous and reliable, is persistently undercut by being made working-class, poor and drab, and a martyr who lacks sufficient sense of emotional preservation. When Carry Fisher is seen with her daughter in a maternal light, Lily finds her affection rather distasteful (as she does Rosedale's paternal pose in the same scene). Judy Trenor, an affectionate and giving friend at the start, is seen ultimately as only a shallow socially contingent creature who "could not sustain life except in a crowd" (38).[23]

While Lily's good mother figures are only ambivalently good and shade toward satiric caricature, the bad mothers are selfishly neglectful or powerfully destructive. Lily's Aunt Penniston, her official guardian whose home Lily finds ugly and impersonal, is caricatured with some of the vicious grotesquerie with which Flannery O'Connor images her powerful and oppressive mother figures (p. 32). In the money for love metaphor of this novel, Mrs. Penniston, the essence of female passivity and repression, gives her niece erratic gifts of money that encourage dependence rather than the trust necessary for autonomy and self-regard (p. 36). Influenced by Lily's poor cousin, Grace Stepney, the wronged and vengeful fairy-tale stepsister, Mrs. Penniston disinherits Lily. In the end, both love and money fail.

The woman whose actions are most immediately responsible for Lily's fate and for the mechanical workings of the novel's plot is Bertha Dorset. Just as Gus Trenor was made the villain of disowned sexuality, so Bertha becomes a malevolent presence so that Lily may be seen as the innocent victim of her manipulations and desires. The only fully enfranchised adult woman in the novel, Bertha is active, sexual, rich, powerful—and ruthlessly evil. She is made as wholly vicious as the wicked stepmother of fairy tales, the singularly cruel being created out of the projected hostility of a child's resentment at wrongs done and love not given, of fears of retaliation for forbidden wishes. Like the feminine figure of projected evil in romances of male development, as long as she cannot be owned and reintegrated, her existence conceptually impedes the heroine's maturation.

While Wharton describes "an unavowed hostility" and a "thirst for retaliation" (116–17) between the two women, she attributes them not to Lily but to Bertha. Bertha first sabotages Lily's designs on Gryce, out of envy of Lily's relation with Selden (who has been Bertha's lover); finally Bertha camouflages a real love affair of her own by implying that Lily is having an affair with her husband. In a brilliant scene in a restaurant, Bertha ruthlessly destroys Lily's reputation by exposing her to public humiliation. The metaphors of Lily's encounters with Bertha are of battles in which words are weapons, weapons that "could flay [their] victims without the shedding of blood," and Bertha is "unscrupulous in fighting for herself" (207).

This triangle with the Dorsets is a variant of the earlier scenario with the Trenors. In both, by a series of thin coincidences of bad luck and bad timing, Lily is observed in what seem sexually compromising situations. Her reputation is polluted; the resulting social ostracism indirectly causes her death. Unconvincing as material causality, these scenes are rather unexamined Oedipal fantasies, which both project responsibility onto the powerful figures of Gus or Bertha, and simultaneously punish Lily for specious guilt. The unresolved Oedipal triangle, however, is a more specific symbol of the pervasive psychic configuration of this novel's world: where inadequate nurturance and support lead to undeveloped self-esteem and a consequent inability to love or to work, the heroine remains fixed in passive dependency and the hungers of the unnurtured childhood state. The mode of primary narcissism remains her dominant emotional style.

The erratic giving and withholding of maternal affection or support is reflected by Lily's male lovers. Selden, especially, is critical and judgmental; he lets her down whenever she needs him most. Yet Lily is compelled to seek in the global fantasies of romantic love that he focuses, a regressive mother-love, of total acceptance and nurturance. The language of dark and hollow craving that surfaces repeatedly in the latter parts of the book reveals the extent to which Lily is controlled by the pervasive childlike neediness that is the underside of her narcissistic ecstasy. With no home, "no heart to lean on" (145) in moments of crisis, craving "the darkness made by enfolding arms" (145), Lily runs to Gerty Farish in "the open misery of a child" (162), and Gerty holds her "as a mother makes a nest for a tossing child" (164).

The scenes in which Wharton attempts to restore Lily to a nurturing relationship do not work. When Lily visits the working girl Nettie Struther and her infant, Wharton tries to use Nettie's good marriage and the baby—who reappears in Lily's fantasies as she drifts into the dream of her ambiguous suicide—to suggest the transcendence of the need for mothering in becoming a mother and experiencing nurturing feelings for a new infant. But the scene is drawn from fiction's stock, not from the novel's deeper sensibilities. The retreat to conventional devices is only a fragile aesthetic response, which cannot match or resolve the resilience, richness, and provocativeness of her earlier evocations of positive narcissistic feelings. (By contrast, in a similar scene in *Jane Eyre*, Brontë recognizes both the anger at deprivation and the need for self-nurture and so is able to conclude her novel in a more realistic, if violent, emotional rhythm.) Wharton's narrative strategy, however, never integrates needs or angers in personality or in plot. Her heroine's hidden anger turns inward against herself in self-destruction, but even this dynamic is unclear for Wharton, whose handling of it is more sentimental than cathartic. Deprivation and anger remain undercurrents pulling beneath the plot; unacknowledged, they undermine the structure in which Wharton tries to confine them.

In *The House of Mirth* Wharton externalizes a personal psychic despair to a pessimistic social determinism, locating in society the forces of inevitable destruction of spirit that proceed from within. Ultimately, of course, there is a reciprocal relation between psyche and society. Like Lily's, the narrative sensibility that creates the social world of this novel is itself shaped by development in society. Wharton shows Lily's destruction by the contradictions and limitations of needing to be independent and adult in a social context that neither equips nor permits her to be. In this, Lily, like many other heroines, acts out a cultural dilemma: when society provides no female adult role of active responsibility and initiative, women are confined to passive and childlike states and cannot mature.

Within the psychic structure of Wharton's fiction, Lily's destruction *is* determined. Her undoing is implicit in the very illumination of her initial descriptions; what attracts us most to her is what dooms her. Reading the novel in this psychological mode is not to deny the destructive effect of social arrangements on women's development, but rather more fully to demonstrate it. The ultimate locus of damage by inadequate social structures is within the individual. The internal arena of the author's sensibility becomes the demonstration ground of the social harms she criticizes; and the flawed structure of her novel, as much as her heroine's death, shows the debilitating limitations of the constrictions on realistic self-assertion. Wharton's statement about the destructiveness of her limited social world is ultimately then strikingly successful, only more indirect than she may have intended.

Cynthia Griffin Wolff's new biography suggests that the unresolved narcissism of the world of *The House of Mirth* parallels Wharton's own delayed emotional maturation. Wharton had not resolved the dilemma of integrating sexuality and assertiveness when she wrote *The House of Mirth*. "Every one of the early fictions," writes Wolff, "had been devoid of genuine adult passion. . . . The terms in which Wharton experienced sexual passion were indelibly colored by the fearful shades of an earlier, more primitive, and more inclusive hunger. . . . a threatening resurgence of that infantile sense of unsatisfied, insatiable oral longing" connected with earlier problems with maternal love.[24] In this context we can understand differently Wharton's determinism. Tied by excessive fears about the destructive powers of assertive passions, Wharton is unable to free herself from believing in the necessary control of the strict code of manners of the society whose rigid constraints on the human spirit she so pointedly criticizes.

Lily has to die because she cannot live. A grown and beautiful woman, she can no longer exist as a child, but neither can she become an adult. We feel the pull of human character in Lily, a growing of sympathy and self-knowledge, but society cannot support her development. All her romance "helpers" fail her. Her evil mother figures have more power to hurt than the good ones do to help. She has only a defective prince charming who has the magical power to change her complacent vision of the world, but is unable to transport her to a kindgom beyond. *The House of Mirth* is both a failed romance of identity and a romance of failed identity. It ends not with wisdom, integrity, and social reintegration, but with regression to infancy and death (like many female *bildungsromane*). Not only does Lily fail in her attempts at growth and self-sufficiency, but Wharton too fails to create a sustained aesthetic structure to legitimate the integrity of her struggle. She is able to make her heroine noble only as a suffering victim; she cannot create a responsible adult of moral dimensions—a tragic heroine. In her ability to image woman's reponsibility for herself, Wharton shares a larger cultural tradition. Lily's stock death acts out the social prohibitions that deny women active maturity (as well as the punitive judgment that blames victims for their victimization). Wharton writes within a central tradition of American thought that manifests itself in literature in the favored use of the polarizing, simplistic form of romance.

Still, something of considerable power is going on in this fiction. In *The House of Mirth,* Wharton is able to tap the well of childhood narcissism and use those resonant feelings to create a brilliantly memorable character. While others of Wharton's novels have a more perfectly balanced structure, Lily's fire appeals directly to those sustained remnants of narcissism in adults. Like a child or a lover, she speaks to our capacity for narcissistic projection; the strength of our response to her derives from the potency of those feelings in us. The historical mythology of romantic love testifies to the intensity of suppressed and withheld passions; thwarted feeling paradoxically heightens emotional and aesthetic effects. As we are charmed by doomed lovers and by dreams of Eden— with all their permanent remoteness in time and place, their nostalgia of impossibility and loss—so we are charmed by Lily Bart. She is able to find in her readers' hearts the place she could never find in her world. In fiction's own magical transformation of constriction to transcendence, the repression of sexual and active energy becomes the potent pressurizing force that forges the lasting power of Lily's appeal.

NOTES

1. Diana Trilling, "The Liberated Heroine," *Times Literary Supplement*, 13 October 1978, pp. 1163–67.

2. In *The Female Imagination* (New York: Knopf, 1975), Patricia Spacks writes, "*The House of Mirth* has the energy of a parable" (p. 241). Gary Lindberg detects in Lily "psychic energies that are unmalleable to social forms." *Edith Wharton and the Novel of Manners* (Charlottesville: University Press of Virginia, 1975), p. 122.

3. R.W.B. Lewis, ed., *The House of Mirth* (New York: New York University Press, 1977), p. vi. This is the text of Wharton's novel used here.

4. Edith Wharton, *The House of Mirth* (New York: New American Library, Signet edition, 1964), "Afterword," p. 343.

5. Irving Howe, ed., *Edith Wharton: A Collection of Critical Essays* (Englewood Cliffs, N. J.: Prentice-Hall, 1962), p. 125.

6. In *A Backward Glance*, p. 207, Wharton writes of *The House of Mirth:* "The problem . . . how to extract from such a subject . . . a society of irresponsible pleasure-seekers . . . any deeper bearing than the people composing such a society could guess? The answer was that a frivolous society can acquire dramatic significance only through what its frivolity destroys. Its tragic implication lies in its power of debasing people and ideals. The answer, in short, was my heroine, Lily Bart." Wharton here establishes a confusion between tragedy and determinism that plagues criticism of the novel in an unresolved debate about Lily's stature as a tragic heroine. All of Wharton's characters live in an essentially deterministic universe. Without a modicum of free will and interior spirit, the moral responsibility necessary for tragedy is hardly possible. Yet the feeling that Lily is a tragic character keeps reemerging. In both Irving Howe's and Edmund Wilson's criticism, the dimensions of tragedy and determinism seem paradoxically to coexist. (See Howe, *Edith Wharton*, and Wilson, "Justice to Edith Wharton" [1941] in *The Wound and the Bow* [New York: Farrar, Straus & Giroux, 1947].) But R.W.B. Lewis states blankly that Lily "is not a tragic heroine" (p. xx) and Wharton's most reliable early critic, Blake Nevius, writes that "we are deceiving ourselves if we try to account for the compelling interest of *The House of Mirth* by the nature or intensity of the moral conflict." (*Edith Wharton: A Study of Her Fiction* [Berkeley and Los Angeles: University of California Press, 1953].) I will argue that the category of tragedy is inappropriate for Lily, because she is conceived as a character and in a fictive world without the capacity for moral responsibility. We must look elsewhere to account for the force of her appeal.

7. Howe, *Edith Wharton*, p. 127.

8. *The American Novel and Its Tradition* (1957; reprint ed., Baltimore: Johns Hopkins University Press, 1980), p. 160.

9. See Joseph Campbell, *The Hero with a Thousand Faces*, Bollingen Series 17 (1949; reprint ed., Princeton: Princeton University Press, 1968), and Northrop Frye, *Anatomy of Criticism* (Princeton: Princeton University Press, 1957).

10. Elizabeth Ammons, in "Fairy-Tale Love and *The Reef*" (*American Literature* 47, no. 4 [January 1975]: 615–28), observes a similar use of fairy-tale motifs to expose female fantasies about love and marriage generated by cultural limitations that encourage economic dependence and sexual repression. I believe that Wharton herself is bewitched by those limitations that shape this novel in ways she is not quite aware, or in control of.

11. See "Family Romances," *The Standard Edition of the Complete Psychological Works of Sigmund Freud*, trans. and ed. James Strachey et al., 24 vols. (London: Hogarth Press, 1953-74), vol. 9, *Jensen's "Gradiva" and Other Works* (1955).

12. Cynthia Griffin Wolff's reading of *The House of Mirth* in "Lily Bart and the Beautiful Death" (*American Literature* 46, no. 1 [March 1974] : 16-40) elaborates this perception of Lily as an object of art. "The death of a beautiful woman as seen through the eyes of her love," was a set piece of American literature. Wharton, however, shows us "what it would be like to be the woman thus exalted and objectified," revealing "the self-alienation that a woman suffers when she accepts the status of idealized object" (39). This reading seems to me not contradictory, but complementary to mine.

13. One of the most influential popular syntheses of the current social applications of narcissism theory is Christopher Lasch's seminal article "The Narcissist Society," *New York Review of Books*, 30 September 1976, and the book into which it is incorporated, *The Culture of Narcissism: American Life in an Age of Diminishing Expectations* (New York: Norton, 1978).

14. Psychiatrists Heinz Kohut and Otto Kernberg also see narcissism as the typical and pervasive twentieth-century malady, replacing the nineteenth century's hysteria. Kohut elaborates Freud's theory of primary narcissism, assuming that narcissism persists as a pervasive tonus in the normal adult personality. Kernberg believes that the clinical narcissistic personality is not only blocked in an earlier state of normative development but also fixated on a self-structure that is not normal but pathological. I follow Kohut, skirting the dispute, and the Freudian emphasis on intrapsychic development, to focus on the interpsychic level of social interaction where the concern is the way in which inner fantasies are confused with appropriate models of dynamic interactions with others. See Heinz Kohut, *The Analysis of Self* (New York: International Universities Press, 1971); "Forms and Transformations of Narcissism," *Journal of the American Psychoanalytic Association*, vol. 14, no. 2 (1966). Otto Kernberg, "Contrasting Viewpoints Regarding the Nature and Psychoanalytic Treatment of Narcissistic Personalities: A Preliminary Communication," *Journal of the American Psychoanalytic Association*, vol. 22, no. 2 (1974). *N.B.* This issue is entirely devoted to discussions of narcissim. See also Marion Michel Oliner, "*Le Narcissisme:* Theoretical Formulations of Bela Brumberger," *The Psychoanalytic Review*, vol. 65, no. 2 (Summer 1978).

15. Otto Kernberg, "Contrasting Viewpoints," pp. 265-66.

16. See Bruno Bettelheim, *The Uses of Enchantment. The Meaning and Importance of Fairy Tales* (New York: Random House, 1977).

17. Edith Wharton, *A Backward Glance* (New York: D. Appleton-Century, 1934), p. 4. Quoted in Cynthia Griffin Wolff, *A Feast of Words: The Triumph of Edith Wharton* (New York: Oxford University Press, 1977).

18. Wharton's language in this scene is explicitly that of fairy tales and narcissistic fantasies: "With the ease that seemed to attend the fulfillment of all her wishes," Lily makes the tea table materialize. Gryce sees this feat as "miraculous"; the tea becomes "nectar," though Lily is reluctant to taste it, still savoring the "flavor" of another prince's kiss. Lily's effect on Gryce is magical: he "grew eloquent," feeling "the confused titillation with which the lower organisms welcome the gratification of their needs, and all his sense floundered in a vague well-being" (18-19).

19. In "Edith Wharton's Secret," his review of Cynthia Griffin Wolff's Wharton biography in *The New York Review of Books*, 23 February 1978, Karl Miller makes this observation in a different context. As a dark, Jewish foreigner, he explains, Rosedale has the ambivalent attraction-repulsion of an outsider. Because his otherness made him socially unacceptable in Wharton's world as a love object, he could become the locus of disowned feelings of sexual attraction.

20. Wharton's language makes Lily's revulsion quite physical and concrete: Lily shrinks "in every nerve from the way in which his look and tone made free of her"

(252). She draws "away instinctively from his touch." When Rosedale's "smile grew increasingly intimate" (111), she withdraws with a "repugnance which kept her in frozen erectness."

21. See Mary Douglas, *Purity and Danger: An Analysis of Concepts of Pollution and Taboo* (New York: Praeger, 1966).

22. Quoted by Wolff, *A Feast of Words*, p. 10, and Wilson, "Justice to Edith Wharton."

23. Wharton accuses one of her characters of "woman like" accusing of the woman (158), and that is her own habit. Blame for the inadequacies of the whole socializing process is placed on the women who teach and enforce social paradigms.

24. Wolff, *A Feast of Words*, pp. 191, 206.

PHILIP FISHER

Acting, Reading, Fortune's Wheel

SISTER CARRIE AND THE LIFE HISTORY OF OBJECTS

Recalling the white mirage of the Chicago World's Fair of 1893 twenty-five years later in his *Autobiography*, Henry Adams wrote, "Chicago was the first expression of American thought as a unity; one must start there."[1] At the Chicago Exposition, which marked that city's coming of age, one of the major attractions was the invention of the engineer George Washington Gale Ferris, a wheel 250 feet in diameter that raised fairgoers in tiny cabins high into the air to let them view the fair as a whole. The Ferris wheel played the part in the Chicago Fair that had been played in the previous Paris World's Fair of 1889 by the famous tower of Dr. Eiffel.[2] This amazing and useless monument, which commemorates only itself and the beauty of structural metal, capped the career of one of the greatest bridge builders of the nineteenth century. The Eiffel Tower is, in effect, a bridge with only one end fastened to the earth, completing the promise that many of the breathtaking nineteenth-century bridges had seemed to offer that someday a bridge would be built that would dispense with the idea of coming down. The Eiffel Tower operates as the bridge builder's dream of linking the earth and the sky as two banks of a great river of air. It is the technological representation of the transition between the bridge and the airplane, which at that moment was the just-about-to-be-born marvel that would extend the bridge's power to leap over space rather than pass through it, turning any two points on the earth into piers of a bridge that is now a small moving metal object.

The Ferris wheel Americanized Eiffel's amazing bridge by bending it into a circle and setting it into motion. It is a bridge that begins and ends at the same point, with the bridge itself now moving rather than the person. It is, therefore, even closer to the airplane and provides for its riders, who leave the earth in a little cabin, rise into the air, and return for a landing, a kind of practice for the as yet nonexistent experience of an airplane

ride. This economical circle that joins the pleasure of rising and the fear of
falling into one repeatable smooth motion became at once a feature of
every carnival and amusement park in America and continues to be the
central identifying symbol—like a cathedral spire seen at a distance mark-
ing a medieval town—of the presence of a carnival or fair.

The mechanization and knowledge of motion that created the assembly
line, the McCormick Reaper, the automobile, and the Ferris wheel, along
with hundreds of other inventions on the same principle in late-nineteenth-
century America has been exhaustively studied in Sigfried Giedion's *Mechanization Takes Command.* Giedion notes that, just as all technological facts
become at some point miniaturized and domesticated as a way of enjoying
what in other contexts might be frightening or oppressive in its novelty,
an increasingly popular American object domesticated and routinized the
steady motion of work, turning it into a lulling relaxation. That object
was the rocking chair.[3] The rocking chair permits one to rest and move at
the same time, canceling motion's effects by allowing it to recur in the
same fixed spot. The rocking chair on a porch—that quintessential American image—permits the rocker to be in motion and yet never to leave the
same place, to be outside the house and yet still in the domestic space, to
participate in street life without leaving family safety, to enter the world
and yet to be protected from it by the porch rail and the inevitable picket
fence at the sidewalk. The state is one of striking in-betweenness, as
though a way had been found to factor out the pleasures of many conditions and fuse them, while discarding all of the inconveniences that generally accompany either rest or motion, domesticity or sociability, family
life or citizenship.

The rocking chair, like the Ferris wheel of which it is a small domestic
arc, displays none of the linear motion of progress and exploration but
rather rising and falling. The world of Dreiser's *Sister Carrie* is composed
of images of motion, of which the most profound are not the horizontal
motions of train rides, carriage excursions, trips to Europe, and walks on
either Broadway or the Bowery, but instead the tragic and vertical motions
of rising and falling: the motion of the rocking chair. The wealth of motion
in the novel insists that the society itself is, by means of its new streetcars,
railway systems, steamships, carriages, and endless places to walk, most itself when in motion. Dreiser's novel begins with Carrie and Drouet flirting
on a train approaching Chicago. Its second half begins with a rhyming
scene that has Hurstwood and Carrie on a train to Canada and then New
York. The novel ends with a train approaching New York carrying the
Hurstwoods to a steamship for Europe. Travels are proportional to wealth.
A trolley ride to work is the shortest trip, impossible for Carrie, whose
four-dollar room and board plus sixty-cent weekly trolley fare exceeds her
four-dollar-and-fifty-cent salary by ten cents. The final trip to Europe is

the longest. Hurstwood, we see, is the only driver, first taking Carrie on a carriage ride in Chicago and later learning to drive a streetcar in New York. Drouet is a traveling salesman on the train routes of the Midwest. Characters walk around all day looking for work, Carrie at the novel's beginning, Hurstwood at its end. Once employed, like Carrie in the chorus line, they march back and forth on the stage to earn a living, or sit, as Carrie also does, punching holes in the shoes that move too rapidly past her on the work line. Entire classes of men have become "tramps" and "drifters," their very names implying constant motion. This society for its pleasure rides out in carriages just to "take a ride," or it promenades on Broadway. Of all these motions—some circular, many fixed by tracks, and almost all forms of living in which one is "Carried" along, as Sister Carrie's name implies—none so dominates Dreiser's novel as that of Carrie again and again rocking in her chair by the window. On her first evening in Chicago and in our final glimpse of her in her suite at the Waldorf, she sits and rocks at the window. The window substitutes for the porch, enabling one to see the street as a spectacle, a performance, without participating in even those controlled ways that a porch makes possible. A window theatricalizes experience both for the one rocking on the inside as well as for the passer-by who glances up and sees the "pretty scene" of a young lady wistfully rocking at her window in the evening light.

Dreiser notes that in Chicago at the time of *Sister Carrie* plate glass windows were for the first time being installed at the street level by businesses of all kinds. These windows turned the work inside into a show designed to play out the operation of the business for the chance spectators who were passing:

> The large plates of window glass, now so common, were then rapidly coming into use, and gave to the ground floor offices a distinguished and prosperous look. The casual wanderer could see as he passed a polished array of office fixtures, much frosted glass, clerks hard at work, and genteel business men in "nobby" suits and clean linen, lounging about or sitting in groups. (16)[4]

The windows turn activities into scenes or photographs but, as Dreiser says at the end of his description, the effect of these windows was to "overawe and abash the common applicant, and to make the gulf between poverty and success both wide and deep" (16). The window creates a polarized world of inside and outside, actor and spectator, rich and poor that would not occur if what were going on inside were simply unknown. All scenes become opportunities for self-classification in that they seem to invite you in and invite you to imagine being in while strongly reminding you that you are out.

The windows that convert reality on both sides to enacted scenes are consciously used by Dreiser to define a state of the self in motion that we might call the self in anticipation. When Drouet first takes Carrie out to eat he "selected a table close by the window, where the busy rout of the street could be seen. He loved the changing panorama of the street—to see and be seen as he dined" (55). The performance of dining in which passers-by become one scene and those they, in turn, glimpse for a moment through the glass another is only the outer shell of an action that repeats itself across the table between the two diners, host and guest:

> Drouet fairly shone in the matter of serving. He appeared to great advantage behind the white napery and silver platters of the table and displaying his arms with a knife and fork. As he cut the meat his rings almost spoke. His new suit creaked as he stretched to reach the plates, break the bread and pour the coffee. He helped Carrie to a rousing plateful and contributed the warmth of his spirit to her body until she was a new girl (56–57).

The performance of serving food that converts objects into setting and props and somehow animates even his rings until they seem to speak, results in transformation of the spectator: Carrie becomes a new girl as his spirit enters her. This meal is the first stage of her seduction and leads to the flight from the Hansons, her taking on of the role of "Mrs. Drouet" (without of course going through the technicality of marriage), and then leads Mrs. Drouet into the role of Carrie Madenda, the stage name that permits her to play the role of Laura in the Elks Club performance. This final role, like the initial dinner, she is able to do only because Drouet comes backstage to almost hypnotize her into confidence. He enters her soul with his gregarious exuberance and, in effect, possesses her from one side in order that she can, from the other side of her being, be possessed by the role and feelings that she must simulate in the drama of Laura.

The windows beside which Carrie rocks or eats with Drouet are also used by Dreiser for his central description of the sources of her vitality. When Hurstwood begins to fall in love with her, Dreiser pauses to describe the inner source of the depth of feeling and spirituality that allures Hurstwood. He finds it in certain scenes: "Her old father in his flour-dusted miller's suit, sometimes returned to her in memory, revived by a face *in a window*. A shoemaker pegging at his last, a blastman seen through *a narrow window* in some basement where iron was being melted, a bench-worker seen high aloft *in some window,* his coat off, his sleeves rolled up" (132, emphasis added). Her connection to these worlds is what gives her a spiritual side that makes her attractive to Hurstwood, "a lily, which had sucked its waxen beauty and perfume from below a depth of waters which he had never penetrated and out of ooze and mould which he could never understand" (132). The waters too deep for Hurstwood are only a slight transformation of what is for Carrie a window, hardened water through which she always sees the other side of toil from which she stems and from which she has only luckily escaped. The windows look back into this world of origins only once. Their normal role is to reveal the future world of anticipation and possibility. On her first night in the shabby little flat of her sister and Hanson, Carrie, after writing a letter to Drouet, "drew the one small rocking chair up to the open window and sat looking out upon the night and streets in silent wonder" (14).

The anticipatory motion of rocking previews and practices the actual later flight from the apartment. Carrie's anticipation resembles the anticipation of Chicago itself. "It was a city of over 500,000 with the ambition, the daring, the activity of a metropolis of a million" (15). The street and trolley lines have already been built out into the prairies in anticipation of houses that will not be built for many years. Streetlights go on and off along these streets where there is not yet either danger or safety. When Hurstwood takes Carrie for their first ride, it is out along the New Boulevard, five miles of "newly made road" with not a single house yet built. The road is *made* in the sense of "made up" because it connects only two parks. It is an anticipatory place for Hurstwood's first anticipations of an affair with Carrie. The vocabulary of speculation—whether economic, civic, romantic, or professional—is so compelling that Drouet's first praise of Carrie's acting ability drives her to her rocking chair by the window, where it "was as if he had put fifty cents in her hand and she had exercized the thoughts of a thousand dollars" (145). The psychological notion of down payments, installment credit, and commodity speculations is here entirely in place in the inner world.

The anticipatory world has as its consequence a state of the self preoccupied with what it is not. Carrie's friend Mrs. Hale has as her pleasure a drive out in the afternoon, "to satisfy her soul with a sight of those mansions and lawns which she could not afford" (106). At one higher level of the same world, Mrs. Hurstwood, who lives in one of those very mansions, cares only about "that little conventional round of society of which she was not—but longed to be—a member" (80). Carrie herself lives with the Hansons while longing for the life represented by Drouet, only to get Drouet and long for the life represented by Hurstwood, and in turn get Hurstwood only to long for the life represented by Ames. Even the Hansons toil and save in their little flat in order to build a house on the two lots on which they have already paid a number of installments.

The anticipatory self has as its emotional substance hope, desire, yearning, and a state of prospective being for which the notion of acting is merely a convenient cultural symbol. Dreiser very carefully differentiates

acting from deception. Carrie acts, Hurstwood deceives. He withholds
from Carrie the fact that he is married, then tricks her into leaving Chicago
with the lie that Drouet is injured and needs her help. He withholds the
fact of his theft, tricks her into a sham marriage, and finally lies to her
about jobs and prospects that he has just around the corner. Acting, in
other words, is not sham, but rather a form of practice. Carrie, while
living with Drouet, practices in her mirror the gestures that she has heard
him praise in other women. She imitates the graces of the railroad treasurer's daughter until she becomes worthy of the role of "Mrs. Drouet,"
and, in time, worthy of Drouet's better, Hurstwood. Acting draws its
moral meaning not from a world of true and false but from a dynamic
society where all are rising or falling. Chicago, as Dreiser first describes it,
is a city of "the hopeful and the hopeless—those who had their fortune
yet to make and those whose fortunes had reached a disastrous climax
elsewhere" (15). This is a world of "might-be" and "has-been." The only
excluded possibility is full present being. Deprived of the present, each is
saturated with either the future or the past. Each is defined by prospective
being and the acting that practices the yearned-for role or by the retrospective being for which Dreiser's image is the newspaper and the compulsive reading that Hurstwood, once fallen, uses to keep track of the things
he has lost. The newspaper is always about yesterday.[5]

A device that marks the self in relation to the future or the past in
selective ways is the mobility of names and epithets in Dreiser's novel.
Carrie is Sister Carrie, Carrie Meeber, Cad, Mrs. Drouet, Carrie Madenda,
Mrs. Murdock, and Mrs. Wheeler, as well as Laura, Katisha the Country
Maid, the frowning Quakeress, and her many other roles. Hurstwood becomes Murdock and then Wheeler, demonstrating the difference between
aliases and stage names. In his final name, Wheeler, he is motion itself, a
wheel broken loose from a carriage that continues to roll only as long as
the path is downhill. He becomes a drifter, a walker of the city, a streetcar driver, a loosened wheel. Opposite him is Carrie, who is also literally
her name, carried on the tides to her fame. Beneath these no longer stable
social names are the many epithets that more accurately describe persons
precisely because they name roles. Carrie is called "Drouet's little shop
girl" or "the little drama student." Drouet is "the drummer" and Hurstwood "the dressy manager" until, after the theft and his flight he begins
to be called, resonantly, "the ex-manager." From then on he can never be
free of this retrospective name that defines him only by what he is no
longer—by his "has-been" status. When he imagines taking a new job, a
humiliating future and a lost past squeeze out the unnamed present:
"Bartender—he the ex-manager!" (311). Or when asked: "What is your
Name?" "'Wheeler,' said Hurstwood" (370). Even when Hurstwood is
learning the new role of streetcar motorman so that he might appropriately

be called "the new motorman" (a future name) or "the scab" (a present name), Dreiser writes: "The *ex-manager* laid hand to the lever and pushed it gently, as he thought" (373). The purchase on either the future or the past is locked in by means of names that aim the self either upward, if it is rising, or downward, once it begins to fall. The names are, in effect, frozen verbs. Manager, actress, driver, drifter, and salesman are nothing but disguised verbs that describe managing, acting, driving, drifting, or selling. In the same way, Carrie and Wheeler are named in only a thinly disguised way for the passive act of rising and the activity of declining.

The force of these epithets arises as one side effect of the use of acting and the theater as central institutional facts in Dreiser's description of the new American world. Proper names are multiplied until they vanish. As the newspaper reports, "the part of Katisha the Country Maid will be hereafter filled by Carrie Madenda" (394). She in turn is only playing the part of Carrie Madenda in the theater. In her neighborhood she is Carrie Wheeler, who has the stage name Carrie Madenda in order to play the role of Katisha. Beneath the layer of the neighborhood, she is unmarried: Carrie Meeber playing Mrs. Wheeler, who has the stage name Carrie Madenda for the role of Katisha. The theatrical language invites us to consider all social life as "parts" and "roles." Wife and salesman, drifter and sister all take on the temporary and fictional aspect of parts that are studied and then performed.

In the half of his novel set in Chicago Dreiser creates a hierarchy of work that rises to more and more directly involve selling the self while at the same time providing a sanctuary for the self within the more clearly acknowledged fictionality of its role. At the bottom of the scale are jobs in which the self is extinguished by toil. Carrie begins by actually making shoes—the poor man's train, carriage, and steamship, his only technology of motion. Her father, whom she pictured covered with the white flour of the mill where he worked, is the perfect illustration for the extinguishing of the self by the toil that produces such goods as flour and shoes. Hanson, who is the image of a lifelong toiler, is a silent man described as "still as a deserted chamber" (48). At the next level above these toilers is the salesman Drouet, connected to objects by selling rather than making them. He handles only "samples" and is not fatigued by the weight of things. What he sells is really himself, his exuberance and pleasure-loving confidence, but as in all sales of this kind a trick occurs at the last moment. The customer who has really bought the salesman finds that he has bought a set of brushes, an encyclopedia, or a vacuum cleaner. The art of sales is the elision of the self and a product throughout the selling process, lending the salesman's personal glow out to the object, then the severing of the connection after the completion of the sale so that the customer is left with only the object.

One step above Drouet is Hurstwood, who, while a salesman, has no object to sell. As manager he, in effect, sells his tone, presence, and air to the nightclub. Standing around, the "dressy manager" rents out his personal approval. Objects have disappeared from the selling process, but the fictionality of social role is increasing. The customers do not *buy* Hurstwood, they purchase the right, by talking to him and being acknowledged by him as worth talking to, to believe that they are his equals. What Hurstwood sells, therefore, is not his personality, as Drouet does, but his air of knowing and making available the entire circle of which the customer would like to imagine himself a member. Drouet's personality and vitality would survive disconnection from the machinery of social life. Unemployed, Drouet would still be a lively and sought-out man. Because Hurstwood sells only his tone and services as an intermediary between figures in a circle, once severed from the social machine he is, as Dreiser says of him in New York, "nothing."

At the peak of the hierarchy of work that Dreiser has constructed is the actress. Her self, her inner emotional being, is what is sold to the ticket buyers. The objects have vanished entirely. The personality and vitality alone remain to sell. Yet, this final identification of self and work is carefully regulated by the fictional shelter of the stage role: Laura, Katisha, the frowning Quakeress. It is only in Drouet that the actual self is naively present and in balance with the objects that it sells and separates from itself in the act of selling. With Hurstwood, self and the fiction of position; with Carrie, self and the more profound split between self and role make more naked the renting out to others of the self, while sheltering the self within a "part." The world of New York is free of shoes, flour, and salesmen with their samples. The economic world is object-free. Transportation and entertainment, moving and acting are all that remain: motorman and actress. In Dreiser's Chicago hierarchy the two poles are paradoxically similar. At the bottom, the self is exhausted, as a result of toil, by the objects that it produces, drained by shoes, covered with flour. At the top, the self is not extinguished but fictionalized and costumed. The flour that covered Carrie's father is replaced by the stage make-up that covers his daughter.

What Dreiser has seized upon in his careful ordering of the world of work and its relation to the self is the privileged role of acting and the theater that had since the beginning of the Romantic Period been seen, on the one hand, as the central institution of the city and, on the other, as the most serious challenge to the romantic theory of the self. In the seventh book of Wordsworth's *The Prelude*, London—a world of performers, orators, ecclesiastical and political actors, and street performers, such as the blind beggar—has as its center the theater and the tumultuous fair. Wordsworth is only one of a group of nineteenth-century writers and artists, including Poe, Baudelaire, Zola, and Manet to name only a few, for whom the theatricalization of life in the city made the theater or that theater of ordinary life—the street—the central spiritual fact about urban life. It is, however, in Rousseau's *Letter to M. D'Alembert on the Theatre* that the most profound analysis of the theater in its relations outward to the community and inward to the self is recorded. Rousseau's *Letter* has been explored by Lionel Trilling in his *Sincerity and Authenticity,* and Trilling's main ideas deserve summary.[6]

Rousseau's concern is to denounce the theater and prove its incompatibility with any acceptable and moral community. He sees three interconnected factors: republican virtue; the position of love in society; and the sharp contradiction between women's social role and their appearance on the stage as actresses. In Trilling's account, a society that is republican, individualistic, and based on citizenship relies on a strong sentiment of self that each person must develop and protect. Each must become himself, know himself, and express himself in his public choices. Each must, to use the political term, *represent* himself. Thus complete self-knowledge and sincerity is of intense civic importance. The essence of acting is, of course, representing what one is not, simulating anger one does not feel, weeping tears at twenty past nine night after night, convincingly representing a miserly landlord one night and a benign and courageous doctor the next. To value and foster the skills of the actor is to reward those able to not be themselves, not feel what they really feel and, therefore, to strike at the heart of a social order based on full individual being and public self-representation.[7]

As Rousseau pointed out, many consequences follow: the conversion of leisure from participatory to spectator experiences; the obsessive centralization of the feelings around the passion of love to the exclusion of more social feelings, such as loyalty, friendship, and familial piety because of the dramatic suitability of sexual love; and, finally, the concentration of the theater on the actress.[8] This final consequence is due to the paradox of female virtue, in its ordinary domestic modesty and retirement, electrifying the theater with the energies of moral reversal.

The intuitive genius that Dreiser brings to his account of the theater and its central position as an image—like the rocking chair or the newspaper—for a description of American society is confirmed by the detailed interconnection of Rousseau's speculations and Dreiser's novel. To note only two characteristics here beyond those that are already obvious will suffice. Carrie's blankness, her lack of attachment or even mood, her easy forgetting of her family, her sister, and Drouet, and her disinterest in ever returning even for a visit, her passivity, and her ability to be almost hypnotized into acting under the gaze of Drouet, even her absence of desires as proved by her realization once she has a great deal of money that there

is nothing she wants to buy: all of these elements of blankness correspond
to Rousseau's assumption that the more successful one is at acting, the
less one has a sentiment of self. Second, the obsessive love interest of all
of the parts played by Carrie, for which the best example is the harem girl
that she plays in New York, goes along with a romantic deadness, a lack
of erotic quality in her relations with men.[9] The audience's obvious fantasy
of being in love with the actress whom they pay to watch display her feelings is the relocated eroticism that has disappeared from their actual lives.
The most intense erotic moment of Dreiser's novel occurs when both
Hurstwood (from his box in the audience) and Drouet (from backstage)
rise to a pitch of desire for Carrie beyond what they have ever felt in reality
as they watch her portray Laura in the Elk's Club play. Similarly, as the
frowning Quakeress in New York Carrie faces an audience whose key can
be found in the aging businessmen rich enough to buy the best tickets.
"The portly gentlemen in the front rows began to feel that she was a
delicious little morsel. It was the kind of frown that they would have loved
to force away with kisses. All the gentlemen yearned towards her" (401).
This erotic pleading, controlled and merchandized, is precisely what
Dreiser had described earlier as Carrie's own relation to the clothes in department stores:

> When she came within earshot of their pleading [that of the clothes]
> desire in her bent a willing ear. The voice of the so-called inanimate!
> Who shall translate for us the language of the stones?
> "My dear," said the lace collar she secured from Partridges, "I fit
> you beautifully, don't give me up."
> "Ah such little feet," said the leather of the soft new shoes, "how
> effectively I cover them. What a pity they should ever want my aid."
> (94)

Merchandise flirts with the shopper just as the actress does with her audience. In both cases, erotic pampering is the covert promise behind the
purchase of tickets and ticketed objects.

The sexualized quality of acting, protected as it is by fantasy and the
barrier of the stage that separates the beloved actress from the numerous
fantacizing suitors in the audience, repeats the paradox mentioned earlier
that, sheltered within the fiction of her role, the actress sells precisely the
vitality of her personality. Intimacy of self-presence and intimacy of sexual
relations are both paradoxically present in the neutralized, stage-lit world
of pretence. One of the first consequences of Carrie's success as an actress
is that she begins to receive a regular stream of marriage proposals from
men who know nothing of her but what they have seen in her performance.

Where Dreiser goes beyond Rousseau is in his refusal to contrast acting
with sincerity, his refusal to oppose the representation of what one is not

to authentic self-representation. Dreiser is the first novelist to base his entire sense of the self on the dramatic possibilities inherent in a dynamic society. Acting involves primarily in Dreiser not deception but practice, not insincerity but installment payments on the world of possibility. In *Sister Carrie* acting is a constant social tactic. As a mockery of sincerity, the words that provide Carrie's break into a speaking part in New York and therefore her rise to stardom are significant ones. To the vizier past whom she is paraded as one of the harem girls, she says, in answer to his idle question, "Well, who are you?" "I am yours, truly." In the very sassy pertness with which she improvises her answer she marks herself as a free and independent woman, while her words (her part) declare her a slave. The final word "truly" caps the elegance of this paradoxical moment. To some extent acting in *Sister Carrie* always serves to preserve a freedom of the self from its appearance, and it is to that degree that it records a higher version of the possible or prospective self in defiance of the momentary "role" or "part" that it is compelled to play and be recognized in. When Carrie first set out to find work in Chicago "she became conscious of being gazed upon and understood for what she was—a wage-seeker. . . . To avoid a certain indefinable shame she felt at being caught spying about for a position, she quickened her steps and assumed an air of indifference supposedly common to one on an errand" (18). She acts the role of one on an errand to avoid the collapse of recognition on the part of others that would freeze her into *no more than* what she happens to be in this momentary role of job seeker. Her acting is a protest on the part of the wider possibilities of her self. Similarly, Hurstwood in decline refuses to go home: "No, he would not go back there this evening. He would stay out and knock around *as a man who* was independent—not broke—well might. He bought a cigar, and went outside on the corner, where other individuals were lounging—brokers, racing people, thespians—his own flesh and blood" (330). It is the cigar that is the costume of this role. The ability to waste money on cigars proves that he is "independent" and not a destitute drifter.

Even when people appear just as they are, they play their appearance as a role. Carrie "looked the well groomed woman of twenty-one" (286). This is exactly what she is. Nevertheless, a small distance occurs so that it is more accurate to say that she looked the part of a "well dressed woman of twenty-one" rather than that she was. The diners at Sherry's restaurant act the part of diners: "All were extremely noticeable." What goes on in the restaurant is an "exhibit of showy wasteful dining." The word "showy" is used many times in the novel to mark the conversion of experience into performance. In Chicago Mrs. Hurstwood wanted to "exhibit" her daughter, Jessica, because it had become time for the part of encouraging suitors. The force of the term "conspicuous" in the phrase "conspicuous consumption," which was invented by the Chicago sociologist and economist Veblen in the early years of Dreiser's career, is here interpreted with great nuance. However, it is not at all consumption that is conspicuous, but anticipatory states of the self.

The importance of clothes in *Sister Carrie* arises from the choice that one can exercise over clothes as a conspicuous performance of prospective being. Drouet seduces Carrie by buying her the clothes that would be the appropriate costume only for the role of his mistress. The clothes are ones that she could not even explain let alone wear were she to stay in her role of working girl at her sister's flat. Similarly, Carrie's first acting jobs in New York translate into the paradoxical ability to buy the clothes for the role of a young actress. On the other side, Hurstwood's shabby clothes *expose* his state, the opposite but equally conspicuous equivalent to the *display* of state that is the normal function of clothes. Because clothes can be changed more rapidly than apartments, they become a more sensitive index to changes of state. Clothes are one's address. Finally, only hotels are places of living sensitive enough to the fluctuations of self to equal clothing as performances of the momentary condition of the self.[10] In New York, after they separate, both Carrie and Hurstwood move through opposite ends of the spectrum of hotels. This hunger for day-by-day accounts of the fluctuation of fortune records the need of a society in which money will be kept in the stock market so that the daily newspaper can show its waverings of value rather than in land or goods, which are, by comparison, subject only to year-long or decade-long readings of change of worth. As the rocking chair is to fortune's wheel, second by second rises and falls, so too are clothes, hotels, and newspapers to the long-term indexes of fortune and value.

In writing *Sister Carrie* Dreiser made two profound structural decisions that are related to the tragic ambitions of his work. *Sister Carrie,* like Dreiser's one other great novel, might have been titled *An American Tragedy,* and in both novels there is special emphasis on the renewed meaning given to tragedy by the dynamics of American life. The essential structural decisions were: first, the division of the novel into two halves, the first taking place in Chicago, the second in New York. The second decision divided the New York half into a balanced and closely modeled double story that compels us to see and comprehend the rise of Carrie by means of the fall of Hurstwood.

In the Chicago portion of the novel we have a familiar nineteeth-century Bildungsroman of the orphan. Arriving in the city, relying only on the intangible energy of her nature, Carrie is the one dynamic, unsettled figure in a world where everyone else represents terminal points, places and levels at which she might arrive and stabilize herself. The Hansons, Drouet, and Hurstwood are the three alternative fixed destinations, each soliciting, in effect, the orphan with the implicit question: "Isn't this enough? Can't you be satisfied to stop here?" They themselves are static (in Chicago); only Carrie is in motion. Society is conceived of as a set of levels with different types and value systems. Chicago is a social comedy of mobility sketched between honest, hard-working immigrant toilers whose lives are decent and respectable, grim and pleasureless, and the upper levels of managers of night clubs large enough to have five bartenders and being a big man at the Elks Club. That is the complete social range. Drouet is the dead center of the scale.

New York is not an extension of this social scale into both higher and lower possibilities. It is an entirely new world, one that is a symbolic simplification into either-or choices. All processes are speeded up, and an inevitable pair of slopes appear: youth and age, not-yet and has-been, celebrity and nobody, female and male, stage lights and total darkness, Broadway and Bowery. The second half of the novel is an absolute world, not a portrayal of a society of layers and alternative values. All that remains are inside and outside, rising and falling, fame and death. In New York not only is Carrie dynamic but she is seen against a social system that has only dynamic possibilities. There is no place as such in this world.

Like all tragic settings, Dreiser's New York is a figuration of time and not of space. It is composed of stages rather than locations. Here the Bildungsroman plot has lost all force; it is a progressive, optimistic plot that is exploratory, comic, and essentially a plot of growth in which the central figure finds a concrete world that by means of marriage, work, home, and social position substantiates the youthful inner possibilities by solidifying them into the facts of a life history. Instead, New York is governed by the decisive contribution of Naturalism to the small stock of curves for human action: the plot of decline. The plot of decline characterizes many of the central novels of the last decades of the nineteenth century. Hardy's *Jude the Obscure,* Zola's *L'Assomoir* and Dreiser's *Sister Carrie* are its masterpieces, and Mann's *Buddenbrooks* is its intergenerational epic. These plots of exhaustion have as their central subject the realm of energy rather than value. They revolve around strength and weakness; not good and evil. Their essential matters are youth and age, freshness and exhaustion. Behind the plot of decline is the Darwinian description of struggle, survival, and extinction. As a theory, Darwinism is characteristically more and more optimistic about larger and larger categories, more and more pessimistic as you reach down to more local or individual events. Species sometimes survive, individuals never, and even species often perish while the total balance of species, adapted to the facts of the environment, improves even at the cost of species, just as species improve even at the cost of individuals. The most acute pessimism arises from a consideration of the individual life cycle as one that rises from the helplessness of infancy to the capacity to ensure individual survival and then declining from that point to death. The primary question for the Naturalist plot is whether the division of life into these two stages (rise and decline) is one of a very long rise that reaches, as it often does in social or financial terms, to the age of sixty, then a short decline. Or is the proportion reversed as it is in the body's strength, a rapid rise peaking at twenty and a long continuous decline that takes up the longest section of personal history? In Darwinian terms, this latter possibility would be a brief rise to the moment of reproduction in the twenties and then a long superfluous decline. The Naturalist plot of decline in Hardy, Zola, and Dreiser bases itself to a large extent on the history of the body and not that of social position. It is therefore a chronicle of subtraction and weakening based on energy, sexuality, and the conversion of freshness to exhaustion.

One of Dreiser's curious emphases is on Hurstwood's age. He is never able to sweep Carrie away emotionally:

> This was due to a lack of power on his part, a lack of that majesty of passion that sweeps the mind from its seat, fuses and melts all arguments and theories into a tangled mass, and destroys for the time being the reasoning power. This majesty of passion is possessed by nearly every man once in his life, but it is usually an attribute of youth and conduces to the first successful mating.
>
> Hurstwood, being an older man, could scarcely be said to retain the fire of youth, though he did possess a passion warm and unreasoning. (199)

This "older man" is thirty-nine, but Dreiser's point is a Darwinian one that refers to mating rather than feeling or passions. The goal of the single youthful urgency is reproduction, not sexual enjoyment as an experience, and Hurstwood's early marriage led to children, as his later affair with Carrie does not.

Only a few years later in New York, "he looked haggard around the eyes and quite old." At age forty-three he is comfortably built and so "walking was not easy" (310). Carrie begins to draw away from him because she begins "to see that he was gloomy and taciturn, not a young strong and buoyant man. He looked a little bit old to her about the eyes and mouth now" (300). His habits are those of a retired, sedentary man of sixty. He reads the newspapers all day, becomes a chair warmer in comfortable hotel lobbies, and parcels out his money like a frugal pensioner who gives up his daily shave so as to have a cigar now and then. What might seem an exaggeration here is a speeding up, a compression of effects much like the rapid rise of Carrie to fame. One component of a tragic rendering of events lies in compressing the inevitable and the incremental into a few shattering or magical events. Thus Hurstwood's theft, which might be viewed as the

cause of his destiny in New York—and so it would be if the order of
Dreiser's world were a moral rather than a Darwinian and economic order
—is only a notation in compressed form of the inevitability in his life of a
balanced moment at which he teeters, unaware that he is no longer rising
but beginning to fall. The theft is a registration of the almost physical
nausea, as on a swing or a Ferris wheel, at that point where effort has
ceased and in an instant gravity takes over to pull one toward the earth.
Dreiser's theory of rise and fall is offered in the best long analytic passage
of his novel, the opening three pages of chapter 33, whose half title is
"The Slope of the Years":

> A man's fortune or material progress is very much the same as his
> bodily growth. Either he is growing stronger, healthier, wiser as the
> youth approaching manhood, or he is growing weaker, older, less in-
> cisive mentally as the man approaching old age. There are no other
> states. Frequently there is a period between the cessation of youthful
> accretion and the setting in, in the case of the middle-aged man, of
> the tendency toward decay when the two processes are almost per-
> fectly balanced and there is little doing in either direction. Given time
> enough, however, the balance becomes a sagging to the grave side.
> (295-96)

Dreiser continues by pointing out that every great fortune, made in youth
and representing the conversion of personal energy into money, would inevitably be depleted and lost by the weakened power of decision as the
owner of the fortune aged, except that such men always conscript younger
minds and energies and buy up their vitality. These words interpret precisely what happens as Hurstwood flees Chicago with the stolen energy,
which is represented both by the stolen money and by the stock of Carrie's
vitality that he has equally stolen from Drouet. Early in the novel Dreiser
refers to money as "honestly stored energy" and it is to that extent the
body's way of spreading out its stock of youthful energy throughout a life
too long for its actual store. Hurstwood's theft is the exact double of his
relationship with Carrie: in each he appropriates the energies of others.
Neither the theft nor the affair is the cause of his fall, because the fall of
which Dreiser is speaking is the inevitable fall of vitality over time. Instead
both the affair and the theft are desperate attempts to stave off, once falling has begun, temporarily and by means of stolen energies, the rapid sinking that converts the hopeful into the hopeless.

Hurstwood's relation to Carrie is only the intimate form of the wider
social fact represented by her relation to her audience: a social group of
aging males whose stored energy in the form of money now disguises the
actual exhaustion of their spirits. What they rent in the theater is her
vitality and youth, and not at all her talent or remarkable beauty. Dreiser

is careful to give Carrie no particular talent, only the traits that are those
of youth itself: freshness, hopefulness, confidence, the imitative skills that
are those of children and the unclouded flexibility of those who have as
yet no concrete world that they would not give up for the chance at something better. She is the "not-yet" to which the only other term is "has-
been." In the theater these two feed off one another as actress and audience
who exchange energy for the honestly stored energy of money.

In Dreiser's novel even sister Carrie's sister, Minnie, at twenty-seven
looks old and used up. The division is that of the body, which reaches its
full height at nineteen or twenty and shrinks from then on to death. This
life history is that of products and objects, which are best when new or
fresh and then become worn out and discarded. The life history of a shirt
is one of continual decline. All goods are used up and replaced. Within
Sister Carrie relationships, houses, cities, and especially living situations
are discarded in the way clothing might be. Hurstwood himself is worn
out rather than captured and submitted to moral or legal defeat. He is
obsolete like a pair of shoes rather than aged like a man. He is a leftover
and a scrap. The Bowery is a collective heap of discarded men. By the end
of the novel he is not so much dead as extinct.

Hurstwood's decline is measured by the shrinking of his space from a
Chicago mansion to a modest apartment to a smaller flat to a room to a
cubicle; it is measured equally by the melting away of his savings, or rather
his stolen savings: $1,300 when he reaches New York, $500 in chapter 33,
$340 in chapter 36, $100 and then $50 in chapter 37. He finally begs for
dimes and beds for a night. An equation is made between the decline of
his health, his eyesight, and the amount of light in his world, and the
shrinking of his money.

Throughout Hurstwood's decline the single act that Dreiser repeats again
and again is his reading of the newspaper. Reading becomes the partner
term to the acting associated with rising, hopeful, prospective being. The
newspaper possesses its reader with lives and events not his own in much
the same way that a role does an actress. The newspaper is a mediating object in New York. Hurstwood's only desire seems to be to go on reading it;
Carrie's highest desire is to be featured in it. Breaking into the theater
seems only a half-way point to breaking into the newspapers. The newspaper is retrospective, defining what happened yesterday. It is literally
about what "has been." As Hurstwood reaches his nadir he is forced to
root around for out-of-date newspapers to see if there is any news about
Carrie.

Dreiser speaks of Hurstwood as "buried in his papers." On a park
bench the newspaper is the blanket of the down-and-out tramp. When
Hurstwood no longer consorts with celebrities, he reads about them in
newspaper stories. Once Carrie has gone she begins to appear in the papers

and he can follow her there. The newspaper becomes a way of not quite dying to a life that he no longer lives. In one of those very lovely inconspicuous scenes that mark Dreiser's work at its best, Hurstwood, so cut off from the world that he would rather not look out the window, reads in the newspapers that a bad storm is due, then in later editions that it has begun, then that it is a record storm, then that it will end soon, and finally, that it has ended. To follow stars and celebrities who are inaccessible is here put in its proper frame of meaning: the newspaper is the essential symbol of decline because it involves a preference for all experience as retrospective rather than lived, even a storm. The disappearance of Carrie from Hurstwood's life is brilliantly done, not by an article in the newspaper, but by the physical object of the paper itself. "He knew that Carrie was not there not only because there was no light showing through the transom, but because the evening papers were stuck between the outside knob and the door" (394).

The resonant final third of Dreiser's novel does not link the stories of Hurstwood and Carrie by way of contrast; that is, only the superficial, social level, of what is a tragic inevitability because Carrie's rise, representing as it does youth itself, and Hurstwood's decline, no more than a compressed account of age itself, are stages that magnify by means of "star" and "tramp" the inevitable small-scale rise and fall that together make up the life history of the self considered as energy. By means of two characters, Dreiser can make simultaneous what is in actual experience consecutive, locating in two persons the prospective and retrospective phases of one life. To achieve this he carefully matches their lives as superficial contrasts connecting deep structural similarities.

Near the end Hurstwood lives at the Broadway Central Hotel. At this point Hurstwood and Carrie each live, as a favor, in a hotel where neither pays. He lives there as a favor to him (a charity) on the part of the kindly manager. She lives there as a favor to the hotel (an advertisement). Carrie's meals are bought for her by men who compete for the privilege. Hurstwood's are free at soup kitchens or as a result of begging from these same prosperous gentlemen. The public buys tickets to see Carrie, and outside the theater they also buy tickets at the solicitation of the exsoldier who harangues them to contribute the price of bed tickets for the hundreds of homeless men, Hurstwood among them, whom he lines up like a chorus line. Hurstwood marches down Broadway in an army of tramps, and Carrie marches back and forth on stage in a harem of chorus girls. Carrie has won for herself a place in the chorus line, and Hurstwood's life is made of calculations of his place in the soup lines, bread lines, shelter lines.

Hurstwood's final job as a strikebreaker is described as a performance. We see him rehearse his role, practicing with the trolley in the yards just as Carrie practices her moves as a chorus girl. The strike-breaking "play" is

performed by running the streetcar with two policemen on board through
a hostile audience of strikers and their families, who jeer and hoot as
though at a bad opera. The streetcar runs are fictional and symbolic; their
purpose is not to carry passengers but to break the strike by demonstrating to the public, via the newspapers, that all of the strikers have lost their
"parts" and have been replaced in their roles by new actors, men simulating drivers. Hurstwood spends a day rehearsing, then goes out to play his
role on the city streets. He is pelted like a bad actor and runs off stage in
midperformance, abandoning his role as motorman or, as the strikers name
his role, "scab." When he became cold on the trolley "he shivered, stamped
his feet, and beat his arms as he had seen other motormen do in the past"
(382). His play is woven by Dreiser directly into Carrie's rehearsals, performances, and breakthroughs. He is pelted off the stage just on the day
when she speaks for the first time and begins her rise to stardom. The
strike is the aging performer's nightmare, just as Carrie's rise is the neo-
phyte's dream. Dreiser's highly conscious repetition of elements in the
two lives derives from his intention that they be seen as stages. Throughout his novel, "Carrie" is only a first name and "Hurstwood" is only a
last. They are first and last names that combine to make one life, first
stage and last stage, rise and fall of fortune's wheel.

NOTES

1. Henry Adams, *The Education of Henry Adams* (Boston: Houghton Mifflin,
1918), p. 340.
2. Giorgio Ciucci, et al., *The American City, from the Civil War to the New Deal*
(Cambridge: MIT Press, 1979), p. 29.
3. Sigfried Giedion, *Mechanization Takes Command* (New York: W. W. Norton,
1948), pp. 396–405.
4. All quotations from the novel are from the Rinehart Edition (New York: Holt,
Rinehart & Winston, 1957).
5. For an analysis of the relations between the spatial structure of newspapers and
urban experience, see Philip Fisher, "City Matters: City Minds," in *The Worlds of
Victorian Fiction*, ed. Jerome H. Buckley (Cambridge: Harvard University Press, 1975).
6. Lionel Trilling, *Sincerity and Authenticity* (Cambridge: Harvard University Press,
1973), pp. 62–67.
7. Rousseau's description clearly distinguishes the actor from the orator or preacher.
"When the orator appears in public, it is to speak or not to show himself off; he represents only himself; he fills only his own role, speaks only in his own name, says, or
ought to say, only what he thinks; the man and the role being the same, he is in his
place; he is in the situation of any citizen who fulfills the functions of his estate. But
an actor on the stage, displaying other sentiments than his own, saying only what he is
made to say, often representing a chimerical being, annihilates himself, as it were, and
is lost in his hero. And in this forgetting of the man, if something remains of him it is
used as the plaything of the spectators. What shall I say of those who seem to be afraid
of having too much merit as they are and who degrade themselves to the point of playing
characters whom they would be quite distressed to resemble." Jean-Jacques Rousseau,

Politics and the Arts: Letter to M. D'Alembert on the Theatre, ed. and trans. Allan Bloom (Ithaca: Cornell University Press, 1960), pp. 80-81.

8. Ibid., pp. 82-92.

9. The role of harem girl exactly represents, in this case, the truth of the actresses' relation to the audience. As we see from the many invitations that Carrie receives, the rich men in the audience who date chorus girls consider them a kind of harem that is literally on display for the audience's choice while being fictionally on display for the vizier's choice.

10. For an analysis of hotels, clothing and sets as components of the self, see Philip Fisher, "Looking Around to See Who I Am: Dreiser's Territory of the Self," *ELH* 44, no. 4 (Winter 1977): 728-48.

WALTER BENN MICHAELS

Dreiser's *Financier*
THE MAN OF BUSINESS
AS A MAN OF LETTERS

Where Nature hath in store
Fowle, Venison and Fish,
And the Fruitfull'st Soyle,
Without your Toyle,
Three Harvests more,
All greater than you wish.

—Michael Drayton, "To the Virginian Voyage"

The difference between a wife and a mistress, according to Dreiser, is the difference between a woman who gives her love in a "sweet bond of agreement and exchange—fair trade in a lovely contest"[1] and a woman who loves without thought of return; "sacrificial, yielding, solicitous," she is motivated only by "the desire to give" (173). In *The Financier,* the wife is Lillian Semple, the mistress Aileen Butler, and the general description of wives and mistresses is, at least to some extent, a report of their respective personalities. Aileen is excessive in everything; her innate love of "lavishness" leads her particularly to admire the "rather exaggerated curtsies" (88) the nuns teach her in convent school. She wears "far too many rings" (137), and her choice of clothes is always "a little too emphatic" (124). Lillian's charm, by contrast, is "phlegmatic"; where Aileen's excesses are the products of a "burning vitality," Lillian's fundamental characteristic is "indifference" (47). These psychological differences between the two women naturally extend to their relations with Cowperwood. The mere thought of losing him causes Aileen to announce with a "passion" that makes him "a little afraid" that if he deserts her, she will "go to hell" (291). Lillian, however, reacts to Cowperwood's actual infidelity with comparative equanimity: "Hers was not a soul that ever loved passionately," Dreiser says, "hence she could not suffer passionately" (243). Having risked little, she has little to lose.

Many critics have questioned the relevance of *The Financier's* love story to its primary subject, the American businessman, complaining, in Donald Pizer's words, about Dreiser's "frequent practice of devoting alternative chapters or parts of chapters exclusively to each of these subjects."[2] Pizer himself thinks that the problem is more than merely formal; "the subjects themselves are incompatible," and Dreiser cannot keep Cowperwood's "two lives, that of the world and that of the spirit,"[3] from contaminating each other. Such a reading presumes, of course, the usual hierarchy between spirit and world, and presumes also, in Richard Lehan's words, a vision of Dreiser as unable to "reconcile the selfish and altruistic motives that fought within himself."[4] Whatever the ultimate merits of this critical contrast between love and money, Dreiser's account of the fair-trading wife and the freely giving mistress should help us begin to see that, in his view anyway, Cowperwood's sentimental relations are hardly incompatible with his financial ones. In fact, the sentimental for Dreiser is already financial. Hence I would like to begin this essay by exploring some of the ways in which wife and mistress provide paradigms for the major competing accounts of value in *The Financier's* general economy.

Cowperwood's courtship of Lillian Semple, for example, takes place in an atmosphere marked by extraordinary financial turbulence, the panic of 1857, which, as Cochran and Miller have written, put an end to a "decade . . . of unprecedented prosperity in the United States."[5] During this decade, Frank Cowperwood had established himself as a successful stockbroker, but the panic and subsequent slide into depression dramatize for him "what an uncertain thing the brokerage business was." He begins to think about getting out of "stock-gambling" and into "bill-brokering, a business which he had observed to be very profitable and which involved no risk as long as one had capital" (48). At the same time, he finds himself attracted by marriage in general—the "home idea" seems to him society's "cornerstone" (62)—and in particular by Lillian, whose "lethargic manner" and "indifference" convey to him a sexually charged sense of "absolute security" (64).

Marriage to Lillian is thus represented as a kind of emotional bill-brokering, where "you were dealing in securities, behind which there was a tangible value not subject to aimless fluctuations and stock-jobbing tricks."[6] This equation of security and securities with "tangible value" enforces a parallel between the "home idea" and the idea of production. Children, obviously, play a role in this parallel (Cowperwood thinks of having babies as if it were a form of capital accumulation—"he liked it, the idea of self-duplication. It was almost acquisitive" [61]), but much more important is the stability guaranteed by what Dreiser calls the primacy of "fact." The "fact" of marriage allows "no possibility of mental alteration or change" (65), whereas the problem with the stock market is that it is "all alteration" because "buying and selling must be, and always was, incidental to the actual fact—the mine, the railroad, the wheat crop, the flour mill" (43). Cowperwood imagines himself a producer and imagines in production a refuge from risk; the vision of value that emerges here might almost be called agrarian, an economy shielded from fluctuation by the joint facts of marriage and of commodities themselves.[7]

Yet the appeal of Aileen, as we have already begun to see, involves values very different from those represented by Lillian. Dreiser himself insists on the financial implications of this contrast by juxtaposing Cowperwood's growing attraction to Aileen's "vitality and vivacity" (90) with his almost unconscious return to "an atmosphere of erratic and [as it initially seems] unsatisfactory speculation" (94). Entering into an agreement with the Philadelphia city treasurer, George Stener, Cowperwood undertakes to drive a large issue of city loan certificate to par essentially by creating a false demand, buying initially from the city for the city, and thus misleading investors as to the strength of the market. The real attraction of the plan, however, one that makes Cowperwood forget all his reservations, is that as long as the city will "ultimately get par for all its issues," he and Stener can make an extra profit for themselves by speculating in the certificates: "Having the new and reserve issue entirely in his hands, Cowperwood could throw such amounts as he wished into the market at such times as he wished to buy, and consequently depress the market. Then he could buy, and, later, up would go the price" (104). The point here is that the instability Cowperwood fears when thinking of himself as a potential producer of commodities is the phenomenon that makes his success as a speculator possible. "Speculation," as one financial writer defined it in 1909, "is the act of taking advantage of fluctuations in the price of property."[8] Cowperwood, however, not only takes advantage of these fluctuations, he goes one step further; he creates them—they *are* his commodities, the source of his profit. Instead of wheat or steel, the financier produces "fluctuations," "manufactured" by "manipulative tricks" (104).

To speak of Cowperwood as manufacturing fluctuations is, of course, to translate production into an unsettlingly abstract vocabulary, but Dreiser makes it clear that this love of abstraction is central to the financier's career. Cowperwood's first job is in the commission business, brokering flour and grain, but he decides early on that "there was no real money in it," which turns out to mean not simply or even primarily that trading commodities does not provide sufficient opportunity to make big profits. The trouble with commodities, he thinks, is that they are not "mental enough." He has no interest in flour or grain: "Money was the thing—plain money, discounted, loaned, cornered, represented by stocks and bonds—that interested him."[9] The financier's dislike of stability thus emerges even more explicitly as a distaste for commodities, and the opposition between the phlegmatic wife and the passionate mistress, between stability and alteration, finds itself reinscribed in the difference between values that are "tangible" and those that are "mental."

Put in these terms, the conflict between wife and mistress can now be understood as a version of the more general conflict over how, exactly, the value of things will be determined. Is value a function of production or of speculation? In America, in the late nineteenth and early twentieth centuries, this question was dramatized most spectacularly in the rapid development of the commodities exchanges after the Civil War and in the subsequent battles (in many respects not yet resolved) over whether and how they were to be regulated. Some economic historians have represented the commodities exchanges simply as "technological advances" in marketing, "bringing buyers and sellers into immediate contact, standardizing quality, codifying trade practices and developing systems of business ethics that speeded all transactions."[10] But it was always clear both to producers (especially farmers) and to speculators that the primary technological advance, the futures contract, could be used for radically different purposes. The mechanism of the futures contract was simple: it allowed the producer of a commodity to sell the commodity on an exchange for future delivery; it allowed him, in other words, to sell a product that he did not yet have, and allowed the consumer of a commodity (for example, a flour miller or a cotton manufacturer) to buy a product before he actually took possession of it. In theory, then, the futures contract permitted the producer to insure himself against a sudden drop in the price of his product before (or when) it actually went to market and to spread his sales out over the year, while permitting the consumer to insure himself against a sudden rise in the price of the product and to distribute his purchases over the year.

In practice, however, the futures market, in the eyes of producers and consumers both, seemed mainly to provide a source of profit for a whole new class of middlemen who neither produced nor consumed commodities but speculated in them. Thus agrarian interests seeking to reform the exchanges characteristically distinguished between two "classes" of future contracts. One, which they approved, involved situations in which (as one witness before the House Agriculture Committee put it) "you do have the grain and you do expect and intend to sell grain. You may not have it at this instant in your possession. It may not be raised yet . . . [but you] expect and intend to deliver the grain."[11] The other class, of which they disapproved, involved the sale of a contract "by a party who does not have the grain and does not expect to have it and does not want to have it, selling to a party who does not want the grain, does not expect to get it, and does not intend to get it, and in fact, does not get it."[12] Contracts of this kind were denounced as nothing more than bets on the price of grain, placed in the same spirit as bets on cock fights or horse races.

Such "fictitious dealings" thus aroused the ire not only of agrarian interests but of many who were disinterestedly concerned with the protection of American morality. The producers were infuriated by the ability of speculators to manipulate prices for their own ends, offering large quantities of, say, "non-existent" wheat and so temporarily depressing the market "in order to buy cheap from the farmer and later sell dear to the miller." Moralists in general were concerned about the difficulty of distinguishing between hedging (as a form of insurance), legitimate speculating, and outright gambling. The difference between the desire to insure oneself against "uncertainties" and the desire "to get rich without labor" was startlingly difficult to define.[13]

The source of this difficulty was, of course, the futures contract itself, which, for better or worse, institutionalized and facilitated the selling of property that one did not own. One of the more immediate and (to the producers) dumbfounding consequences of this practice was that, as Cedric Cowing notes, the "number of bushels and bales traded on the exchanges exceeded the annual production from 1872 on and in several years toward the end of the century amounted to sevenfold the annual crop."[14] The farmer could only grow so much wheat, but speculators, selling short, seemed able to bypass the physical conditions of production and even the fundamental laws of identity. What Cowing calls "the physiocratic bias against those who produced no primary products" and in favor of what Dreiser called "tangible value" was at its most intense when confronted with the tricks made possible by the abstract nature of money. And it is these tricks which constituted, in Dreiser's words, the "arts of finance" as practiced by innovators like Cowperwood, who knew

> instinctively what could be done with a given sum of money—how as cash it could be deposited in one place, and yet as credit and the basis of moving checks, used in not one but many other places at the same time. When properly watched and followed this manipulation gave him the purchasing power of ten and a dozen times as much as his original sum might have represented. (109–10)

The art of finance is the production of money by "pyramiding" and "kiting" instead of investing. The financier recognizes in money a quirk of identity that makes it possible to transcend the limitations of any "actual fact." Money can be in two, three, even four places at one time. Seeing this quirk of identity as a principle of productivity, the financier makes ten or twelve times what he has to start with. From the standpoint of the producer (the *real* producer) of wheat, oil, or whatever, money's ability to reproduce itself seems to mark its scandalous difference from the material commodity. Money may be cash and credit both, but a bushel of wheat is no more or less than a bushel of wheat. And yet what is truly terrifying about money and the financier's use of it is not finally its difference from real commodities but its similarity to them. For the scandal of the futures market and of the fictitious dealing it makes possible is that, sold as futures, bushels of wheat, like dollars, can be in more than one place at a time. Indeed, as we have just seen, it was precisely this principle of excess (seven times more wheat bought and sold than was actually produced) that infuriated the agrarian interests.

"Money was the thing." Conceived by the producers of primary products as a convenient symbol of the value of those products, it seemed (to producers and speculators both) to take on a life of its own. More "mental" than wheat or oil, it was able to flout ordinary conceptions of identity, producing its own harvests and determining the value of products whose worth it was intended only to symbolize. But at the same time that it was insufficiently material, it was too material, "mental" but a mental "thing." Hence the development of a national money market and of money exchanges, as if money were "real," a commodity to be marketed like any other. Shocking by its immateriality and its materiality both, money seems finally to point to something problematic in the very notion of a commodity and thus to question the opposition between producer and financier with which we began. For if the financier, creating money, is a kind of producer, is not the producer, exchanging his product in trade, a kind of financier?

The force of collapsing these two terms into one another may become clearer if we recognize that, despite the rhetorically strident opposition between producer and speculator that dominates so much of the financial dialogue of the period (and that, as we have seen, has its place in Dreiser's *Financier*), some of its most crucial economic battles were fought on rather different terms. We have only to remember that, as important as the futures market was, certainly the greatest advance in finance technology in the nineteenth century was the development of the trust; the overwhelming fact of American economic life at the turn of the century was the monopoly. In certain respects, of course, the controversies over the trusts repeat some of the central features of the disputes over the commodities exchanges. The heroes of Ida M. Tarbell's *History of the Standard Oil Company,* for example, have a distinctly agrarian cast. The affection of these oil producers and independent refiners for their "oil farms" and refineries is like that of a man for his children, the "fruits of his life": "The thing which a man has begun, cared for, led to a healthy life, from which he has begun to gather fruit, which he knows he can make greater and richer, he loves as he does his life."[15] And the career of

the independents' great enemy, John D. Rockefeller, was marked from
the very start by the financier's distaste for production. Allan Nevins, his
biographer, tells of the thirteen-year-old Rockefeller lending $50 at 7 per-
cent interest and digging potatoes for 37½¢ a day; when the borrower paid
him his interest, "John was impressed by the fact that capital earned
money more easily than muscle did."[16] More important, Rockefeller decided early on that the production of oil was the one aspect of the business
with which he would never have anything to do.

It would, however, be a mistake to see the struggle between the oil producers and the Standard as a version of the conflict between producers
and speculators and, in particular, to see Rockefeller in any simple way as
a version of Cowperwood. Indeed, one might say instead that Rockefeller
and Cowperwood actually embody two very different models of the
accumulation of wealth. Psychologically, they are almost complete inver-
sions of one another. Rockefeller was raised in what Nevins describes as
"an atmosphere of hazard and dubiety." His father, "Big Bill" Rockefeller,
was a brilliant but erratic man, a moneylender, a pitch man selling patent
medicines (mainly oil!), an accused horse thief. The impact of his example, Nevins thinks, was to produce in John "a profound desire for
certainty and dependability; for a stable home, stable earnings, stable
resources, a stable place in society."[17] Dreiser represents Frank Cowperwood's father very differently; the "soul of caution" (2), he was "content
to be what he was" and so destined to be only "moderately successful"
(10). Along the same lines, Rockefeller was particularly proud of his self-
control ("I never had a craving for tobacco, or tea and coffee. I never had
a craving for anything")[18] and his ability to accumulate capital by saving,
whereas Cowperwood never saves a dime; "it was not his idea that he
could get rich by saving," Dreiser writes, "from the first he had the notion
that liberal spending was better, and that somehow he would get along"
(19).

Given this portrait of Rockefeller, it may seem anomalous that he, like
the speculators in grain futures and like Cowperwood himself in his battle
against the eponymous iron-manufacturer Skelton C. Wheat, should have
found himself opposing the oil farmers. If Rockefeller embodied the
wifely virtues of production, how was it that his bitterest enemies were
the producers? The answer to this question is that in Rockefeller's astute
judgment, oil production was not a source of "tangible value" but was
instead a form of speculation. The "curse" of the oil business, he thought,
was the "terrific unpredictable fluctuations in prices, the alternations of
glut and shortage."[19] And the cause of these fluctuations was the producers' inability to control production, to regulate the flow of oil and so
stabilize the market. This failure made the producers speculators against
their will, and the establishment of oil exchanges turned both shortage

(due to the normal perils of oil-drilling—fires, dry wells, etc.) and glut (due to what Rockefeller denounced as "unlimited competition") into opportunities for the speculator. Echoing the agrarians, Nevins writes that the oil industry had become nothing but "a new form of gambling." Production and speculation were thus seen by Rockefeller as two variations on the same theme, and the job of the refiner (as monopolist) was to regulate the market, controlling the producer and eliminating the speculator. Hence the Standard Oil Trust.

What the example of the oil industry demonstrates, however, is not only that production could be seen as a form of speculation but that the producers were their own worst enemies. For the greatest threat to oil prices was, just as Rockefeller said, unlimited competition resulting in tremendous overproduction, which in turn resulted (as even the producers acknowledged) in depression for the entire oil industry. In a situation like this, production, especially from the standpoint of the producer, takes on a rather equivocal status. It is, of course, the means of his livelihood, the source of his wealth, but it is a source that requires always a vigilant control, because production carried too far produces not wealth but poverty. One might even say that in a certain sense the competition that gave rise to the trusts was imagined not only as competition between producers but as competition between the producer and his product, or between the producer and what Tarbell called "nature."

"Nature," Tarbell writes, "has been in the oil game."[20] In this scenario, the goal of the producer is actually to regulate nature, to keep her from knocking the bottom out of the market with a glut of oil, wheat, whatever. The temptation is to moralize this process as nature's revenge on business and profit. Thus, describing one of the periodic failures of the oil producers to control their output, Tarbell writes that "it seemed as if Nature, outraged that her generosity should be so manipulated as to benefit a few, had opened her veins to flood the earth with oil."[21] Production here lashes out against the economy that has produced it. The oppositions internal to business—between producer and regulator, regulator and speculator—are absorbed by the great opposition between business and nature herself. Producing commodities—making them, mining them, even growing them—ceases now to guarantee economic virtue and becomes instead the primary form of economic exploitation. In Tarbell's text, this is a particularly dramatic moment, since her own affection for the producers is based largely on their structural proximity to nature, a proximity that nature herself repudiates in the moment of overproduction, exposing *all* businessmen (speculators, manufacturers, farmers) as manipulators.

This very literal naturalization of production is by no means unique to Tarbell. Nature, in the form of the wheat harvest, plays an almost identical role in Frank Norris's *The Pit,* where Curtis Jadwin's bravura attempt to corner the wheat market is broken not by opposing "brokers, traders, and speculators" but by the "wheat itself" and the "very earth herself": "The new harvest was coming in; the new harvest of wheat, huge beyond possibility of control; so vast that no money could buy it, so swift that no strategy could turn it."[22] The effect of Jadwin's failure is, of course, disastrous, not only for Jadwin but for the wheat farmers and for all the investors who had their money in the rising market. But the final victory of Jadwin's enemies in *The Pit* also makes clear a fact that Tarbell's account of the oil industry never really confronts—nature's uncontrollable bounty does *not* punish every businessman, indeed it positively favors a few. For the crash in prices caused by nature's cornucopian excess punishes producers and monopoly-inclined regulators (Rockefeller, Jadwin) while paradoxically rewarding those whom Nevins calls "speculators in depression," the short-selling bears.

There were, of course, two kinds of speculators, bulls and bears; bulls bet on a rise in prices, bears bet on a fall. Jadwin, the "Great Bull," is trying to buy the entire wheat crop; owning it all, he will be able to drive prices as high as he wants. The bears, selling all they have and almost invariably more than they have, want to drive prices down; they count on being able to buy (or buy back) what they sold at prices much lower than the ones at which they sold. The general public, as virtually every commentator on the subject has noted, is always overwhelmingly bullish, investing for a rise and regarding the great bull traders as, in Cowing's words, "builders" and "doers" with "great dreams of the future." The bears, on the other hand, were "the manipulators whom the public feared and resented." Cowing represents this distaste primarily as a consequence of their "dour personalities," but naturally there were also more substantive reasons.[23] Foremost among these was, no doubt, the profit that the bears made from everyone else's financial distress. A small ring of speculators profits from Jadwin's failure, but the collapse of his corner also starts off a "long train of disasters," sweeping away hundreds of "little fortunes" and culminating eventually in a return of "hard times."[24] By the same token, Cowperwood's "great hour" is one of "widespread panic and disaster" (492); "selling as high as he could and buying as low as he could on a constantly sinking scale" (498), he makes a fortune in the panic of 1873, which ushered in the longest depression (six years) of the nineteenth century.

But more sinister even than this vision of the bear as vulture, profiting from the misfortune of others, is the vision of a bear presiding over the uncanny juxtaposition of material plenty with financial distress. Hard times are seen here as a function not of scarcity but of overproduction, and so what gives the bear his particularly awful character is that he marks the inversion of traditional economic values. The historian Daniel Rodgers has pointed out how many businessmen in the late nineteenth century began to "worry that there were too many factories for the economy to absorb." "Production," Rodgers notes, "had long been the chief of the economic virtues. . . . But if the industrial cornucopia could easily spill out far more goods than the nation was able to buy, what then was the place of work?"[25] The bear here, emblemizing the simultaneity of increased productivity and hard times, is a figure for the irrelevance or even counter-productivity of work; not only does he profit from the labor of others, he succeeds in turning their labor against them, in converting it into the agent of their misfortune.

Yet even this analysis does not quite succeed in accounting for the fearsomeness of the bear. For not only does he profit from the misfortune of others, not only does he wizard their own hard work into the *cause* of their misfortune, he does all this in conjunction with nature! What the bear reveals is that nature at her most productive and the unproductive speculator (neither growing nor making anything, not even, when he sells short, *owning* anything) are collaborators. The bear's world is a nightmare version of the American dream in which the promise ("Three Harvests more") of unprecedented plenty has turned into the threat ("All greater than you Wish") of overproduction. The land so bountiful no one need work becomes a land whose bounty succeeds somehow in starving instead of feeding its inhabitants. The bear now emblemizes an economy in which the source of production is so uncontrollable, so indifferent to human interests, that labor consists only in betting on what nature will do. The bear puts his money on nature's generosity.

Such an alliance between speculation and production helps explain what would otherwise seem some peculiar inconsistencies in *The Financier*. We have, for example, already noted Dreiser's identification of marriage with an agrarian commitment to production and "tangible value" while noting at the same time his identification of the mistress with the speculator's "mental" manipulations. But when, in more general terms, he attacks marriage and defends the philanderer, he seems to invert the argument, representing the mistress as a physiocrat and the wife as a manipulator of artificial "conventions": "One life, one love, is the Christian idea, and into this sluice or mold it has been endeavoring to compress the whole world. Pagan thought held no such belief . . . and in the primeval world nature apparently holds no scheme for the unity of two beyond the temporary care of the young" (146). Cowperwood's finances may be as divorced as possible from the physiocratic, but Dreiser still relies on nature to justify his sexual practices. Hence when the "sweet bond" of marital "exchange" becomes "the grasping legality of established matrimony" (197), it is contrasted not only to the love between man and mistress but to the single most powerful paradigm of natural affection, the love of a parent for his or her child, "broad, generous, sad, contemplative giving without thought of return" (211).

But what the example of the bear makes clear is that this juxtaposition of Cowperwood as speculator, profiting from utterly artificial stock fluctuations, with Cowperwood as pagan lover, flaunting nature in the face of Christian law, is not a simple contradiction. For the mistress and the parent are conucopian lovers; disdaining "exchange," "giving without thought of return," they produce affection with the disruptive and inhuman power of nature making commodities. And if what unites the speculator with nature is precisely the attraction of the cornucopia, what unites the wife and the producer is the fear of unlimited production—of wheat, oil, or love. The hostility of wife to mistress thus turns out to be a version of the producers' mistrust of nature. The mistress, a figure for unproductive manipulation, is also (by nature's illogic of excess) a figure for infinite productivity.

In a certain sense, of course, this naturalization of the "industrial cornucopia" is as dramatic an example of economic mystification as one can imagine. Rockefeller drew attention to the sentimentality of this myth when, responding to Tarbell's vision of "Nature" outraged by the profiteering of the Standard and avenging herself with an oil glut, he remarked that "nature would not have opened her veins if the producers had not compelled her to do so."[26] But the sense of nature as producer does not serve simply or even primarily to disguise the role of the real producers and to relieve them of responsibility for their actions. Rather, as we have seen, it testifies first to their frustration at seeing agrarian virtues become the instruments of speculative vice, and second to their general sense that the economy was completely out of control. What is most natural about production is ultimately its refusal to respond to human intentions. Nature here comes to represent capitalism itself, not, however, as an immutable and exploitative social order but as the principle of mutability, the omnipresence and irreducibility of risk.

The Financier nicely illustrates the double-edged character of this naturalization of the economy. Nothing about Dreiser is better known than his susceptibility to Spencerian "physico-chemical" explanations of human behavior. And nothing in Dreiser's work provides a better example of this susceptibility than the allegory of the lobster and the squid that opens *The Financier* and, from an intellectual standpoint, clears "things up considerably" for the young Frank Cowperwood. The "heavily armed" lobster gradually devours the weaponless squid, and answers in the process a question that had long troubled Frank: "How is life organized?" (5). "Things lived on each other—that was it." The moral of this story, as Cowperwood and Dreiser come to see it, is the irrelevance of anything but strength in a world "organized" so that the strong feed on the weak. Such a moral is, of course, congruent with the Spencerians' Social Darwinist tendency to find in natural law a justification for the robber-baron practices of the most predatory American businessmen. But it is curiously inapplicable to the events of *The Financier* itself, which persistently exhibit nature not primarily as an organizing force dedicated to the survival of the fittest, but as the ultimate measure of life's instability, the "mystic chemistry" that embodies the "insecurity and uncertainty of life" (211).

Along these lines, Dreiser presents both the Chicago fire of 1871, which temporarily ruins Cowperwood, and the panic of 1873, which restores his fortunes, as inexplicable and unpredictable *lusūs naturae*. Events like the fire, "unheralded storms out of clear skies—financial, social, anything you choose," make wise men "doubt the existence of a kindly, overruling Providence" (226). Part of his point is that nature can be cruel, bringing "ruin and disaster to so many," but more important is what we might think of as nature's ability (and propensity) to be unnatural. Thus Dreiser's language here anticipates the headlines proclaiming Jay Cooke's failure (Cowperwood's great opportunity) in 1873: "A financial thunderclap in a clear sky," "No one could have been more surprised . . . if snow had fallen amid the sunshine of a summer noon" (491). Nature, in *The Financier,* is most herself when she is least like what she usually has been; hence the business crisis, understood by Dreiser as an essentially natural phenomenon, cannot be mastered or even predicted by any system of thought, any account of life's 'organization'—theological, scientific, even economic. "It was useless, as Frank soon found out, to try to figure out exactly why stocks rose and fell" (40). The financier is a gambler "pure and simple."

The financier's inability either to master or confidently predict events in the economic world around him turns out to have more general implications in the drama of judgment that dominates the last few hundred pages of the novel. The emotional and, as it turns out, legal question raised by these pages is one of what Dreiser calls "control," the relation between intentions and consequences. Charged by Aileen's father with having ruined her life, and urged by him to make her do what is right, Cowperwood proclaims his impotence. If "you know anything above love," he tells Mr. Butler, "you know that it doesn't always mean control" (383). His "intentions" toward Aileen were "perfectly good"; "if this panic hadn't come along," he had planned to divorce his wife and marry her. His legal defense against the charge of having stolen sixty thousand dollars from the city is identical; his "intentions were of the best" (385), but the unexpected severity of the panic prevented him from restoring the money to the city treasury before he failed.

Neither Butler nor the State Supreme Court buys this defense, arguing in effect that the consequences of Cowperwood's act constitute the best evidence of the "fact" of his intent. Only the dissenting Judge Rafalsky is convinced, and his agreement is articulated in such a way that its force, like that of the natural economy, is double-edged. The effect of upholding Cowperwood's conviction, Rafalsky writes, is to extend "the crime of constructive larceny to such limits that any businessman who engages in extensive and perfectly legitimate stock transactions may, before he knows it, by a sudden panic in the market or a fire, as in this instance, become a felon" (397). There is, in other words, no necessary relation between intention and consequence, and the court, in convicting Cowperwood, is punishing him for something he never meant to do, making him responsible for events that he did not, in his own words, "create": "I did not create this panic. I did not set Chicago on fire" (264). But to put the argument in this way is, in Dreiser's terms, to expose its weakness. For what does the financier create? What Dreiser calls his "harvest" (199) depends not on hard work, not even finally on his "subtlety," but on his happening to be in the right place when a crisis comes. If the financier has neither "earned" nor "deserved" (271) his success, then the fact that he has not created the conditions of his failure ceases to count as a mitigating circumstance. Rafalsky is right. The court's decision reduces the difference between the businessman and the thief to a matter of "accident"; judicially determining guilt and innocence is only "glorifying *chance.*" But, of course, Cowperwood's whole career is a glorification of chance, and the constant lesson of *The Financier* is that accidents will happen.

In an economy where nature has taken the place of work, financial success can no longer be understood as payment for goods or services. It becomes, instead, a gift, and for Dreiser this economy of the gift functions at every level. We have already seen how it characterizes the love of a parent or mistress and how it also characterizes the winning and losing of speculative fortunes: "Who is it that can do anything it was not given him to do? All good things are gifts."[27] The literal force that Dreiser attaches to this claim cannot, I think, be overestimated. Love and money are gifts, personal identity ("Who by taking thought can add one cubit to his stature? Who can make his brain better."[28]) is a gift, even art, although explicitly dissociated from the making of money, participates in the general economy of the gift.

Of course, there are no artists in *The Financier,* a fact consistent perhaps with the absence of producers in general. But there is a good deal of art, procured for Cowperwood by an art dealer whose "fiery love of the beautiful" does duty for a less commercial version of the artistic temperament and awakens in the financier a desire "to make a splendid, authentic collection of something."[29] He begins with furniture, buying, "after the Georgian theory," "a combination of Chippendale, Sheraton, and Hepplewhite modified by the Italian Renaissance and the French Louis."[30] The inventory of brand names is appropriate here: Dreiser lists the objects without describing them; what interests him is accumulation. Cowperwood's "passion" for art takes the exclusive form of a desire "to possess" it, and his way of developing an understanding of it is "by actual purchase."[31] Dreiser calls this, astonishingly enough, the love of "art, for art's sake,"[32] by which he means that Cowperwood has no desire to make money from the art "business." For him, the simple accumulation of the objects themselves is "distinction" enough. Art for art's sake and accumulation for the sake of accumulation thus come to the same thing.

This identification is, however, by no means a simple one. For in almost the same context that Dreiser equates art with the principle of accumulation, he equates it also with what would seem its opposite, the principle of philanthropy. "Great art," he says, is the only appropriate "background" for the "great beauty" (162) of Cowperwood's mistress, Aileen. But the relation between Aileen and great art is closer than that of foreground to background, for the particular quality of Aileen as mistress, her "sacrificial, yielding, solicitious attitude" toward Cowperwood, is "related to that last word in art, that largeness of spirit which is the first characteristic of the great picture, the great building, the great sculpture, the great decoration—namely, a giving, freely and without stint, of itself, of beauty" (173). Linking acquisition with expenditure, Dreiser defines the love of "art for art's sake" as the love of giving or receiving but never exchanging. Another way of putting this might be to say that art, like mistresses and speculators, has no sympathy for the principles of fair trade, which animate wives, farmers, perhaps even artists. The financier loves a glut. He makes his living on the disruptions produced by excess, and he understands philanthropy and accumulation both as a form of excess. Beauty, given "freely," "without stint," "without thought of return," reinscribes excess as the principle of cornucopian generosity.[33]

Dreiser was not alone in believing that art should be free. He himself once described William Dean Howells as the "great literary philanthropist,"[34] and a few years before the interview that provoked this description, Howells had written that there was "something profane, something impious in taking money for a picture, or a poem, or a statue." But the essay in which Howells makes this claim, "The Man of Letters as a Man of Business,"[35] turns out to have a notion of philanthropy very different from Dreiser's. To begin with, Howells thinks of art's generosity as a characteristic that would ideally mark its exemption from the economic condition of a "huckstering civilization" (3). Hence he starts by asserting a radical distinction between business and literature: "Every man ought to work for his living," Howells writes, but no man "ought to live by an art" (1). Art, in other words, should never be conceived as work but only as a "privilege" for which no one should pay or be paid. Because there is "something false and vulgar" in taking money for, even in setting a price on, culture, the "results" of art "should be free to all." But then, having begun by emphasizing art's independence of economic relations, Howells goes on to end the essay, surprisingly enough, by chiding artists for imagining a difference between themselves and the "working-man" (33). Artists are "the same as mechanics, farmers, day-laborers" (34); their "glory," he writes (in words that immediately evoke the agrarian hostility to finance), is that they "produce something."

These accounts of art, first as the "exercise" of a "privilege" and second as the product of "work," are obviously in some sense contradictory. But it would be a mistake to conclude from this contradiction that they are fundamentally incompatible. When Howells describes art as radically different from business, he suggests that business has no way of valuing art's "absolute" and "invariable significance" (2); "work which cannot be truly priced in money cannot be truly paid in money" (1). The strategy here is to preserve art's "absolute" value by divorcing it from all economic activity, a strategy that clearly breaks down when he goes on to conceive of the artist as a kind of day laborer. But although the strategy is altered, the end it serves remains the same. For Howells describes the artist-laborer as one of those "who live by doing or making a thing" in contrast to those who live by "marketing a thing" (33), and hence conceives of the work of art as a commodity whose value is determined by the labor invested in it and not by the fluctuations of the marketplace. Business remains "the opprobrium of Literature" (2) not because literature and work are opposed but because they are the same, both opposed to "marketing." Indeed, one might now say that the whole point of Howell's essay has been to keep "making" and "marketing" apart and to insist that value, both literary and economic, is a function always of making and never of marketing.

This attempt to save literature by understanding it as a form of labor turns out to have consequences very different from those intended. For, thinking about literature as a commodity, Howells quickly notes its somewhat problematic relation to other commodities. The writer's product, unlike, say, "meat, raiment, and shelter" (32), has no "objective value." Food and shelter, Howells writes, are a "positive and obvious necessity," and this necessity confers upon them their "objective" status. Literature, however, is "subjective"; "precious to one mood of the reader, and worthless to another mood of the same reader" (31), its value is "from month to month wholly uncertain" (32-33).

The cause of this instability is obvious—the value of literature depends on what Howells here calls "acceptance," and the acceptance (or lack thereof) achieved by novels can never be as stable as the acceptance of necessities. We might thus conclude that the attempt to preserve literature's "invariable significance" in an economic form has failed because the analogy between the work of art and the commodity just is not sufficiently persuasive. But the truth, in Howellsian terms, is more disturbing than this; the analogy between the work of art and the commodity has turned out to be *too* persuasive. For in distinguishing between literature and the necessities, Howells has almost nonchalantly introduced as a common criterion the very determinant of value he has been concerned to deny—the market. The difference between the necessity and the work of art, he writes, is that one has a stable market value and the other does not. But the whole point of conceiving of literature as a commodity in the first place was to identify it as a form of "making" and to deny the relevance of "marketing" in the determination of its value. Admitting the market at this stage in the argument thus amounts not only to confessing literature's instability but to proclaiming that art, which Howells wants to think of as too pure even to have a market value, has come to emblemize its own contradiction, the impossibility of ever eliminating the market. The attempt to save the absolute value of literature by thinking of art as a commodity has not only failed to save literature but has wound up jeopardizing the value of the commodity itself.

By contrast, Dreiser's conception of art as philanthropy is based neither on an attempt to contrast art with business nor on an attempt to bring them together under the rubric of a labor theory of value. If for Cowperwood, "wealth and beauty and material art forms" are "indissolubly linked,"[36] what links them is the primacy of the free gift. Howells's failure is Dreiser's success: art in *The Financier* offers no refuge from the instability of the market; it embodies that instability and generalizes the principles that identify nature and the market economy. "All good things are gifts." Speculation is nature's way.

Rockefeller, as we have seen, mocked Ida Tarbell's notion of nature avenging herself on all those who sought to profit from her by spontaneously producing a market-breaking glut of oil. Refusing to think of production as ultimately a human activity, she was able first to absolve her beloved oil farmers of any responsibility for the overproduction that ruined them and then to depict all businessmen as speculating middlemen, exploiting nature as the commodity traders exploited the commodity producers. In Rockefeller's view, this sentimental naturalization of production obscured the man-made, and hence controllable, character of all economic institutions. Dreiser's economic morality, at least as I have described it, was very different from Tarbell's but surely, from the standpoint of someone like Rockefeller, no less sentimental. Nature in *The Financier* is the speculator's ally, not his enemy, but she is for Dreiser as implacably uncontrollable as she was for Tarbell. And she is even more powerful. For Dreiser not only thinks of capitalist production as natural, he goes on to think of nature in all her manifestations as capitalistic; art and sex are as speculative as the stock exchange. Thus the "new world" (500)—Chicago and the west—toward which Cowperwood lights out at the end of *The Financier* seduces by its promise of a "vast manipulative life," sexual, aesthetic, economic. And if Tarbell's sentimentalism (like Howells's) proclaims her hatred for what the almighty dollar had wrought in America, Dreiser's proclaims his attraction to an even more powerful vision of the new world—"Earth's onely Paradise"[37] of finance capitalism.

NOTES

1. Theodore Dreiser, *The Financier*, with an introduction by Philip Gerber (New York: Crowell, 1974), p. 211. All subsequent references to this edition are cited in parentheses in the text. Reference will occasionally be made, however, to the original 1912 text; these occasions will be footnoted. I have chosen whenever possible to cite Gerber's reprint of the 1927 revision not for aesthetic reasons but because it is currently the only edition available to most readers. And, while I am on the subject, I would like to thank Jane Tompkins for finding a copy of the 1912 original for me and for commenting along with Howard Horwitz on some of the problems raised by my readings of Dreiser in this essay and in "*Sister Carrie's* Popular Economy," *Critical Inquiry*, vol. 7, no. 2 (Winter 1980): 373–90.

2. Donald Pizer, *The Novels of Theodore Dreiser* (Minneapolis: University of Minnesota Press, 1976), p. 170.

3. Ibid.

4. Richard Lehan, *Theodore Dreiser: His World and His Novels* (Carbondale, Ill.: Southern Illinois University Press, 1969), p. 100. Other useful discussions of *The Financier* include: Robert H. Elias, *Theodore Dreiser: Apostle of Nature* (Ithaca: Cornell University Press, 1970), pp. 152–76; F. O. Matthiessen, *Theodore Dreiser* (New York: William Sloane, 1951), pp. 127–58; Henry Nash Smith, "The Search for a Capitalist Hero," in *The Business Establishment*, ed. Earl F. Cheit (New York: John Wiley & Sons, 1964), pp. 77–112; and Wayne Westbook, *Wall Street in the American Novel* (New York: New York University Press, 1980), pp. 155–58 and passim.

5. Thomas C. Cochran and William Miller, *A Social History of Industrial America* (1942; rev. ed., New York: Harper, 1961), p. 90.

6. Theodore Dreiser, *The Financier* (New York: Harper, 1912), pp. 88–89.

7. Cedric B. Cowing (following Hofstadter) uses the term *agrarian* to designate not only farmers but all those "who, for various reasons, endorsed the pre-industrial, pro-agriculture rhetoric." *Populists, Plungers, and Progressives: A Social History of Stock and Commodity Speculation, 1890–1936* (Princeton: Princeton University Press, 1965), p. 4. I will use the term in a similar fashion but with an even more extended application, because part of my point is that the ideological hostility toward speculation and an economy of fluctuation was as central to many industrialists and indeed to many artists as it was to the staple crop growers and their political champions.

8. Horace White, "The Hughes Investigation," *Journal of Political Economy* (October 1909): 530.

9. Dreiser, *The Financier*, p. 55.

10. Cochran and Miller, *A Social History of Industrial America*, p. 151.

11. Clifford Thorne in U.S., Congress, Committee on Agriculture, *Future Trading*, 66th Cong., 3d sess., 1921, p. 993.

12. Ibid., p. 992.

13. White, "The Hughes Investigation," 533. There is a particularly illuminating exchange on this subject between Thorne and Congressman Edward Voigt of Wisconsin

in which Voigt maintains that "there can not be hedging without there being gambling" and Thorne disagrees but is unable finally to give any reasons for his disagreement. *Future Trading*, p. 997.

14. Cowing, *Populists, Plungers, and Progressives*, p. 5.

15. Ida M. Tarbell, *The History of the Standard Oil Company*, 2 vols. (New York: Macmillan, 1904), 1:155.

16. Allan Nevins, *John D. Rockefeller: The Heroic Age of American Enterprise*, 2 vols. (New York: Scribner's, 1940), 1:68. In addition to being an extraordinarily informative and readable biography of Rockefeller, this is an invaluable text for the study of American social history.

17. Ibid., 1:90.

18. Ibid., 1:111.

19. Ibid., 1:177. The potential profits of speculation in oil were almost as spectacular then as now. Nevins tells the story of "Uncle Russell Sage," who held oil certificates for fifty thousand barrels at 60¢ and then sold them near the end of the oil boom of 1895 at $1.30. Not near enough the end, however. Had he waited just another week, he could have sold them at $2.70, increasing his profit by another 250 percent. When prices broke, the Standard intervened, "sustaining the market during some tense days in which an excessively rapid drop would have ruined many producers and refiners" (2:326).

20. Tarbell, *History of the Standard Oil Company*, 2:157.

21. Ibid., 1:125.

22. Frank Norris, *The Pit* (New York: Doubleday, 1903), p. 374. There is an even more lurid example of nature's opposition to regulation in Norris's *The Octopus*, where the railroad agent S. Behrman is murdered at a climactic moment by some hostile wheat.

23. Cowing, *Populists, Plungers, and Progressives*, pp. 36–37.

24. Norris, *The Pit*, p. 419.

25. Daniel T. Rodgers, *The Work Ethic in Industrial America 1850–1920* (Chicago: University of Chicago Press, 1978), pp. 27–28.

26. Nevins, *John D. Rockefeller*, p. 429.

27. Dreiser, *The Financier*, p. 479.

28. Ibid.

29. Ibid., p. 285.

30. Ibid., p. 281.

31. Ibid., p. 283.

32. Ibid., p. 287.

33. It is worth reiterating that Dreiser depicts this generosity as a source of great strength, particularly in sexual relations. We have already seen how even Cowperwood is a little afraid of Aileen's capacity for "self-sacrifice," and in *The Genius* (written just before the Cowperwood novels and revised just after them), Angela almost loses Eugene by trying "to save herself" and Christine wins him by giving "of herself fully." Theodore Dreiser, *The Genius* (1915; reprint ed., New York, 1946), pp. 167–68, 164. By the same token, as Beth Ruby has pointed out to me, George Stener's failure to give Cowperwood the additional city money he needs to ride out the 1871 panic marks the treasurer as a "jelly-like" weakling, incapable of Aileen's passion.

34. Theodore Dreiser, *A Selection of Uncollected Prose*, ed. Donald Pizer (Detroit: Wayne State University Press, 1977), p. 144.

35. All subsequent references to this essay are to William Dean Howells, *Literature and Life* (1902; reprint ed., New York: Kennikat, 1968).

36. Dreiser, *The Financier* (New York, 1912), p. 181.

37. Michael Drayton, "To the Virginian Voyage" in *Poems*, ed. with an intro. by John Buston (Cambridge: Cambridge University Press, 1953), p. 123.

NOTES ON CONTRIBUTORS

Julia Bader is associate professor of English at the University of California at Berkeley. She is the author of *Crystal Land: Patterns of Artifice in Vladimir Nabokov's English Novels* (1972) and is currently writing a study of literary representations of female experience in nineteenth- and twentieth-century American literature.

Richard H. Brodhead teaches English and American literature at Yale University. The author of *Hawthorne, Melville, and the Novel* (1976) and a number of essays on American fiction, he is now at work on a book about tradition-formation in American literature.

William E. Cain is associate professor of English at Wellesley College. His essays on modern criticism and literary theory have appeared in *Novel, College English, Georgia Review, Virginia Quarterly Review,* and other journals.

Evan Carton has published essays on Chaucer, Dickinson, and Hawthorne and is working on a philosophical and rhetorical reading of American romance entitled *Parodies of Possibility: The Language of American Romance.* He teaches English at the University of Texas at Austin.

Eric Cheyfitz, who teaches English at Georgetown University, is the author of *The Trans-Parent: Sexual Politics in the Language of Emerson* (Johns Hopkins, 1981). His poetry has appeared in *Esquire, Times Literary Supplement,* the *New Review,* and other magazines.

Philip Fisher teaches English at Brandeis University and is the author of *Making Up Society* (1981). His essays on the city and art in a civilization of museums and mass production have appeared in a variety of journals and collections.

Laurence B. Holland was, at the time of his death in 1980, professor of English and chairman of the Department of English at The Johns Hopkins University. His books include *The Expense of Vision: Essays on the Craft of Henry James* (1964; Johns Hopkins Paperbacks edition, 1982) and, as editor, *Who Designs America?* (1966) and *The Norton Anthology of American Literature* (1979).

Howard Horwitz is a graduate student in English at the University of California at Berkeley, where he is writing a dissertation entitled "Hazardous Compositions," a study of American literature and economic theory in the age of realism.

297

Joan Lidoff teaches English at the University of Texas at Austin. She is the author of *Christina Stead* (1982) and is currently completing a study of the relationship between women's literary style and female psychology entitled "Fluid Boundaries."

Walter Benn Michaels is associate professor of English at the University of California at Berkeley and the author of essays on American literature and literary theory that have appeared in *Critical Inquiry, Georgia Review, MLN,* and other journals.

Donald Pease has published essays on Blake, Whitman, Poe, Emerson, Milton, Williams, and Hart Crane, and has completed a book entitled *The Legitimation Crisis in American Literature.* He received the outstanding teaching award for 1981 at Dartmouth College, where he teaches in the English Department.

Fred G. See teaches English at the State University of New York at Buffalo. He has published essays on Melville, Howells, and Dreiser, and is now working on a book about desire in nineteenth-century American fiction.

Mark Seltzer teaches English at Cornell University. His work on Charles Brockden Brown has appeared in *Early American Literature,* and he is currently completing a book on the politics of Henry James's later writings.

Eric J. Sundquist teaches American literature at the University of California at Berkeley. He is the author of *Home as Found: Authority and Genealogy in Nineteenth-Century American Literature* (Johns Hopkins, 1979) and "Faulkner: The House Divided" (Johns Hopkins, forthcoming).

Alan Trachtenberg is professor of American Studies and English and chairman of the Department of American Studies at Yale University. His books include *Brooklyn Bridge: Fact and Symbol* (1965) and *The Incorporation of America: Culture and Society in the Gilded Age* (1982).

The Johns Hopkins University Press

American Realism: New Essays

This book was composed in Baskerville text and display type
by Horne Associates, Inc., from a design by Alan Carter.
It was printed on S. D. Warren's 50-lb. Sebago Eggshell
paper and bound by Universal Lithographers.
The manuscript was edited by Jane Warth.